GENDER AND DIFFERENCE

IN THE MIDDLE AGES

MEDIEVAL
CULTURES

SERIES EDITORS

RITA COPELAND
BARBARA A. HANAWALT
DAVID WALLACE

*Sponsored by the Center for Medieval Studies
at the University of Minnesota*

Volumes in the series study the diversity of medieval
cultural histories and practices, including such inter-
related issues as gender, class, and social hierarchies;
race and ethnicity; geographical relations; definitions
of political space; discourses of authority and dissent;
educational institutions; canonical and noncanonical
literatures; and technologies of textual and visual
literacies.

For more books in the series, see pages 355–57.

GENDER AND
DIFFERENCE IN
THE MIDDLE AGES

SHARON FARMER AND
CAROL BRAUN PASTERNACK, EDITORS

Medieval Cultures, Volume 32
University of Minnesota Press
Minneapolis
London

Published by the University of Minnesota Press
111 Third Avenue South, Suite 290
Minneapolis, MN 55401-2520
http://www.upress.umn.edu

Library of Congress Cataloging-in-Publication Data

Gender and difference in the Middle Ages / Sharon Farmer and
        Carol Braun Pasternack, editors.
        p.   cm. — (Medieval cultures ; no. 32)
    ISBN 0-8166-3893-4 (HC : alk. paper) — ISBN 0-8166-3894-2
(PB : alk. paper)
        1. Women—History—Middle Ages, 500–1500.   2. Sex role—History—
To 1500.   3. Sex differences—Philosophy—History.   4. Social
history—Medieval, 500–1500.   5. Civilization, Medieval.
I. Farmer, Sharon A.   II. Pasternack, Carol Braun.   III. Series.
HQ1143.G44   2001
305.3'09'02—dc21   2002011020

Printed in the United States of America on acid-free paper

The University of Minnesota is an equal-opportunity educator and employer.

12 11 10 09 08 07 06 05 04 03   10 9 8 7 6 5 4 3 2 1

Contents

PART III. INDIVIDUAL CHOICES, STRATEGIES OF RESISTANCE

ACKNOWLEDGMENTS

The editors would like to thank the Interdisciplinary Humanities Center at the University of California, Santa Barbara, for providing funds for research and editorial support. We are also grateful for the excellent research and editorial work of Kathy Lavezzo and Tanya Stabler.

Introduction

Sharon Farmer

The essays in this volume take seriously the variety of recent theoretical stances that have compelled feminists to consider not only the fluidity and multiplicity of gendered identities but also the ways in which gendered constructs interact with other categories of difference. Most salient to our project are the insights of multiracial and postcolonial feminists, who have pointed out that genders are constructed in historically specific and changing ways within a range of interlocking inequalities—a "matrix of domination," as Patricia Hills Collins has called it. In the twentieth-century United States, prominent components of that matrix include class, race, sexual orientation, and gender.[1] Postcolonial feminists remind us, moreover, that matrices of domination function differently in different contexts: in order to understand the contingency of our own culture's matrix of domination and the gendered constructs that emerge within that matrix, we must look beyond the borders of our own society; in order to understand the implications of colonialisms, both premodern and modern, we must look at the multiply mixed identities that emerge in colonial contexts and on the borderlands between societies.[2]

Looking at medieval societies provides us with one opportunity for crossing borders, and, indeed, a number of medievalists have paved the way for this project. Since the early 1980s, Caroline Walker Bynum has brilliantly highlighted the permeable and elastic nature of gender categories in western medieval Christian culture and the multiple positions that men and women could assume within the dominant constructs. Thus, for instance, the salvific, embodied God-man—Jesus—was often imagined in a feminized form, and male clerics often imagined themselves as brides to his bridegroom or as mothers to their own flocks. Moreover, the concepts of incarnation, bodily resurrection, and transubstantiation placed the holy, salvific, and often feminized body at the center of medieval Christian theology, thus subverting apparent binaries that might seem to devalue bodiliness and the feminine.[3]

More recently, medievalists have examined the ways in which other categories of difference complicated gendered constructs. Steven Kruger and Louise Mirrer have highlighted a tendency for western Christian polemicists and vernacular authors to portray Jewish and Muslim men as effeminate, even going so far as to imagine that Jewish men menstruated.[4] Robert Bartlett and David Rollo have discussed how, in their attempts to portray the Irish as barbarous, the colonizers of Ireland emphasized bestial sex and the production of "perverse" genders, such as women with beards and hermaphrodites.[5] Jeffrey Jerome Cohen has drawn on Gloria Anzaldúa's concept of "mestiza" consciousness in order to elucidate, in the writings of Gerald of Wales, "that middle formed by the overlap among a multitude of genders, sexualities, spiritualities, ethnicities, races, cultures, languages."[6] Kathryn Gravdal has analyzed the ways in which masculine and aristocratic privilege worked together in stories about knights who raped peasant women.[7] Paul Freedman has discussed how elites portrayed peasant men as cowardly and inept at love, and thus less masculine than aristocratic men.[8] Elizabeth Castelli has argued that late antique religious women achieved a form of maleness by remaining virgins, and Jo Ann McNamara has discussed the reasons why this formulation of virile womanhood was acceptable in the early Middle Ages but not in the High and late Middle Ages.[9] Ruth Mazo Karras, David Lorenzo Boyd, and Michael Rocke have argued that in late medieval England and Florence men who took the passive role in sexual couplings with other men were portrayed as acting "as a woman," thus becoming something other than fully male.[10] Carolyn Dinshaw has emphasized that the ambiguities and inconsistencies in such portrayals point to the malleability and performativity of gender.[11]

Drawing on and engaging with multiracial and postcolonial feminisms, medievalists have broadened our understanding of the medieval past, and they have made important contributions to theoretical discussions among those who focus their attention on more recent epochs. Nevertheless, medieval feminist scholarship continues to exhibit at least two limitations. First, despite an emphasis on the multiplicity, malleability, and fluidity of gendered categories, most medieval feminist scholars continue to fall back into old binaries, even as we attempt to highlight examples that stretched the boundaries of those binaries. A reading of recent scholarship on the gendering of medieval Jews, heretics, monsters, and men who engaged in non-normative sex, for instance, can lead to the conclusion that, although elite male Christians included a broad variety of persons possessing male bodies within the category of "the feminine," a single set of fixed binary oppositions nevertheless worked to construct a masculine/feminine binary.[12] The second limitation has to do with scholarly focus: despite recent attention to "the postcolonial Middle Ages," most of the scholarship that looks at the Middle Ages through the perspectives of feminist and postcolonial theories has been generated by literary scholars studying a narrow range of texts that were produced by Christians (most of them male) in northwestern Europe.[13]

This volume attempts to address these limitations by bringing together scholars in a variety of fields—history, literature, Arabic and Islamic studies, Near Eastern studies, religious studies—who have asked questions about constructions of gendered hierarchies in four different medieval cultures: western Christian, Jewish, Byzantine, and Islamic. Moreover, in an effort to push the volume toward an emphasis on "matrices of domination" rather than gendered binaries, the editors asked each of the contributors to engage with the intersections of gendered categories with at least one of three other categories of difference—social status, religion, and sexualities. The resulting essays work together to call attention to the multiplicity of gendered possibilities in medieval hierarchical constructions and the contingency of western constructions. Several of the essays, moreover, explicitly describe multiple gendered categories within a given social imaginary.

MEDIEVAL CATEGORIES OF DIFFERENCE: RELIGION/ETHNICITY, SOCIAL STATUS, SEXUALITIES

Since part of the project of looking historically at social categories and structures of domination is to expose their fluidity and contingency, we need to approach past societies with precision, taking care not to assume a priori that we know what the categories of domination were and how they worked. For that reason, contributors to this volume have tended to avoid terms like "race" and "class," which might cause the reader to conflate medieval and modern categories of difference.

While there is ample evidence that medieval people were aware of variations in skin color, and that they often assigned hierarchical values to those variations, medieval perceptions of such differences did not necessarily correspond to modern constructions of biologically inherited racial characteristics.[14] Drawing on texts that were produced over several centuries, Steven Kruger argues that western European Christian culture constructions of race, religion, and sexuality included both a moral element, suggesting "choices that might be changed," and a biological element, which sometimes seemed to disappear upon conversion but sometimes pointed to a more intractable "nature."[15] Robert Bartlett and David Nirenberg, by contrast, have placed greater emphasis on chronological development over the course of the Middle Ages. Bartlett argues that up until the fourteenth century most western Christian representations of ethnic differences focused not on biology but on malleable characteristics such as customs, language, and, most especially, religion.[16] Along similar lines, Nirenberg has suggested that until the end of the fourteenth century the semen of a Muslim or Jew might be considered both corrupt and corrupting for Christians who came into contact with it, but those corrupting effects were thought to disappear once the man converted to Christianity, and a child who resulted from the semen of a Jew or Muslim could be raised as a Christian even if the father did not convert.[17]

Bartlett and Nirenberg suggest that around the fourteenth century the boundaries between ethnic groups in Europe began to harden, and there was a shift from attitudes stressing malleable characteristics to attitudes stressing biological descent. Bartlett observes that in German towns guilds began to pass statutes limiting membership to those of German descent and prohibiting ethnic intermarriage.[18] Similarly, Nirenberg suggests that after the forced conversion of large numbers of Spanish Jews in 1391, Spaniards who competed with the *conversos* for social and economic position began to assert that, despite their apparent Christian affiliations, *conversos* and their descendants retained a corrupt "Jewish" nature. Nirenberg reminds us, however, that it took time for the new attitudes to take hold, because "far from being obvious or natural, the ideological work involved in grafting culture onto blood was monumental."[19]

Like the term "race," "social class" has specific modern resonances. The now classic formulation of modern class formation is that of E. P.

Thompson, who argued that the self-consciousness of the modern working class arose not automatically, as a result of the common position
that workers held vis-à-vis modern industrial capitalism, but as a result
of the workers' conscious agency:

> Class happens when some men, as a result of common experi-
> ences (inherited or shared), feel and articulate the identity of their
> interests as between themselves, and as against other men whose
> interests are different from (and usually opposed to) theirs.[20]

Central to Thompson's formulation is the idea that "class" cannot happen until a group becomes conscious of itself. Implicit to his formulation is the understanding that nineteenth-century laborers experienced
their work relations in ways that were fundamentally different from the
ways in which pre-nineteenth-century workers experienced such relations.

To be sure, groups of individuals were also marked in the Middle
Ages by their common relationships to the means of production. There
were sharp divisions, for instance, among those who did not have to
work because they lived on landed incomes, those who traded in goods
that others made, and those who labored with their own hands; and there
were important differences between those who depended upon rural
sources of income and those who depended upon urban sources of income. Moreover, some of the people whose positions were marked off
by those divisions developed group identities: genealogical and courtly
literatures certainly point to a group consciousness among the landed
aristocracy in twelfth-century France.[21] We even catch occasional glimpses
of self-conscious group identity among those who lacked power, wealth,
and prestige: in fifteenth-century Catalonia, for instance, peasants based
their claims to freedom from servitude on their common descent from
mythical Muslim ancestors who had converted to Christianity.[22] Still,
the fault lines of economic and political power were different in the
Middle Ages, multiple group identities (competing craft guilds, for instance) often worked to undermine the collective identities of those with
similar economic positions, and the divisions between those who
"owned" the means of production and those who added value to raw materials by working them with their hands were not as clear as they were
in the classic era of industrial capitalism. For these reasons contributors

to this volume have employed the expression "social status" rather than "class."

In approaching the question of medieval sexualities, many medievalists have drawn on queer and performance theorists, arguing that despite illusions of fixed and stable sexual identities, as constructed either by modern or by premodern dominant fictions, sexual behaviors and identities are, and were, fluid and unstable.[23] Concerning the question of dominant fictions, however, medievalists have disagreed on the degree to which modern dominant fictions—like the heterosexual/homosexual binary—differ from the dominant fictions of the Middle Ages. Social constructionists have urged us to view the heterosexual/homosexual binary as a peculiarly modern western fiction. Before the nineteenth century, they argue, people engaged in sexual "acts" that were more or less condoned, but performing sexual acts did not result in either internally or externally constructed sexual identities: performing "sodomy" (which was itself an unstable signifier) did not make one a "sodomite."[24]

Michael Rocke's research into the prosecution of sodomy in fifteenth-century Florence largely supports the constructionist position that the homosexual/heterosexual binary is a modern invention: criminal court records suggest that while the Florentine state officially condemned sexual contact between men, the majority of males in Florentine society went through a life stage when they engaged in sexual acts with other males. The most important behavioral boundary entailed not sexual object choice, but performing in a manner that was appropriate to one's age: adult males (who usually coupled with boys or with women) were expected to engage in sex in a "masculine" way—as the active partners. By focusing on court records, which he views as windows onto the actual behavior of Florentine men, Rocke is able to conclude that there was no heterosexual/homosexual binary in fifteenth-century Florence, and that individuals did not have fixed sexual identities.

However, if we shift our gaze from documents of practice to the dominant fiction—as constructed in the Florentine legal codes—we might come to somewhat different conclusions. After all, the state did draw boundaries between acceptable and unacceptable behavior, and all sexual contact between people of the same sex was included in the unacceptable category. Moreover, the classification of sexual behaviors into those that were acceptable and those that were unacceptable constituted something of a binary, even if that binary was not made up of "homo-sexuals" and "heterosexuals."[25] In his analysis of the dominant fiction in twelfth-century France—as constructed in the vernacular literature of aristocratic elites—Simon Gaunt concludes that that fiction did indeed construct a heterosexual/homosexual binary. He argues, moreover, that the category of the despised homosexual served, much as it does in modern times, to create a dominant heterosexual (and, we might add, aristocratic) culture.[26] In this volume, Mathew Kuefler analyzes the so-cial and political reasons for this "sodomitical panic" in twelfth-century French literature and its importance for the multiplication of gendered categories.

Even in the literature of twelfth-century France, however, sodomites and heterosexuals operated within a sexual framework that differed from our own. Karma Lochrie has suggested that a much more pervasive bi-nary than that contrasting homosexual and heterosexual acts was that which opposed "natural" and "unnatural" sex. In the constructions of clerical elites, she points out, "natural" sex was limited to a narrow range of possible options: "sex in the proper vessels with the proper instruments in the proper positions with the appropriate procreative intentions in or-derly ways and during times that are not otherwise excluded."[27] Another working binary, which was closely related to the construction of a narrow range of "natural," and therefore acceptable, sex acts, was that which divided the abstainers—virgins, ascetics, and clerics, who gained reli-gious prestige by not engaging in sexual acts—from nonabstainers.[28] As Ulrike Wiethaus, Simon Gaunt, and Amy Hollywood have argued, many of those who abstained from bodily sex for religious reasons transposed their sexuality—in fluid and often "queer" ways—to the religious realm.[29] In this volume, Ulrike Wiethaus explores some of the ways in which as-cetic identities and "queer" mysticism complicated gender categories.

Continuing debates among medievalists about the contours and char-acteristics of medieval categories of difference highlight both the need to read the sources with as much precision as possible, and the important role that such categories of difference played in medieval polities. This volume takes the next step by examining the intersections of gender cat-egories with other categories of difference, thereby revealing the multi-plicity of possible matrices of domination. Several of the essays also con-sider strategies of resistance to the discourses of domination.

GENDERS AND OTHER IDENTITIES IN THE FIRST MILLENNIUM: DIFFERING CULTURES, DIFFERING POSSIBILITIES

The first four essays in this volume examine gendered constructs in four cultures—rabbinic, Muslim, Byzantine, and Germanic. Each of these cultures both inherited and transformed aspects of the cultures of the Hebrew Bible, the Hellenistic world, and the empires of ancient Rome and Persia. Sharp differences among these four cultures highlight both the contingency of each set of constructs and the malleability of preexisting paradigms.

Daniel Boyarin discusses two fundamentally different formations for sexuality and gender: that of western platonism, which ultimately shaped the dominant forms of late antique and medieval Christianity in the West, and that of rabbinic Judaism. Through a discussion of the late-twentieth-century psychoanalytic theory of Lacan, Boyarin highlights the ways in which the platonic formulation has continued to influence western thought. Boyarin argues that Lacan's association of the Phallus with reason—the "Logos"—and his argument that its representational function is to separate masculinity from the embodied male can be traced back to the platonizing Judaisms of Philo and Pauline Christianity. We can detect this dissociation of masculinity from embodiment, Boyarin argues, in Philo's reading of the two creation stories in Genesis 1 and 2: Genesis 1, according to Philo, concerns the creation of a "spiritual Adam" who was different from the physical Adam of Genesis 2 from whom Eve was created. In this reading, Boyarin emphasizes, "Bodily gender—structurally dependent, of course, on there being two—is thus twice displaced from the origins of 'Man.'"

Boyarin highlights at least two problems in the way that Lacanian theory implicitly draws on this platonizing tradition. First, it vacillates in its presentations of the Phallus, sometimes suggesting that it is a historically specific, yet dominant, western fiction, sometimes implying that it is a human universal. Further, Lacan's very choice of "Phallus" as the symbol of disembodied reason unavoidably links disembodied reason to masculinity and to men, thereby perpetrating the very gender system that Lacan's theory could serve to subvert. Boyarin suggests that the counterexample of late antique rabbinic thought exposes the historically contingent nature of the Phallus. We can read this difference, he suggests, in rabbinic interpretations of Genesis 1, according to which the first human being was a physical hermaphrodite who was cut in half in order to create the man and woman of Genesis 2. In this formulation there never was a "spiritual man": men and women were associated equally with originary embodiment. Boyarin thus suggests that rabbinic thought differed from ancient and medieval hellenistic and Christian dualisms, which often associated masculinity with disembodied reason and femininity with embodiment. He goes on to argue, however, that the rabbinic system placed its own oppressive limitations on women. Boyarin's reading of rabbinic culture thus reveals the culturally contingent nature of Lacan's Phallus, and the multiplicity of symbolic systems that could give rise to gender oppression.

Everett K. Rowson takes us to the Abbasid court of Baghdad, to show us a radically different intersection of gendered identities with sexualities and social positions, and a radically different set of valuations for sexual and gendered behaviors. From the mid-eighth century on, sexual relations among men were widely accepted, if not officially licit, at the Abbasid court. As was the case in fifteenth-century Florence, "masculinity" in sexual relations was attributed to the individual who took the active sexual role. However, the privileged men of the court of Baghdad had a broader range of "not-males" to choose from than did the men of fifteenth-century Florence: adolescent boys, eunuchs, male entertainers who dressed as women, slave women who cross-dressed to look like adolescent boys, and women who dressed as women. Rowson discusses the parallels and differences between two categories of cross-dressers: *ghulāmīyāt,* slave girls who cross-dressed as adolescent boys in order to enhance their alluring qualities for aristocratic men with homoerotic tastes, and *mukhannathūn,* male transvestite entertainers. Eventually, both of these categories of cross-dressers became sexual object choices for aristocratic men. However, the *mukhannathūn* were not, at first, automatically assumed to engage in sex with other men. Thus, Rowson argues, cross-dressing and sexual object choice were not necessarily linked, and while the two *were* linked in the case of the *ghulāmīyāt,* the cross-dressing of these women was a function of the sexual object choice of the aristocratic men whose households the women served, not of the women themselves. Rowson also points out that for those who engaged in cross-dressing, the acceptability of their gendered behaviors depended, to a great deal, on their social status. Through his analysis, Rowson enhances our understanding of the distinctions between dressing in the manner of a given gender (as a woman, for instance), being identified as behaving in the manner of a given gender ("effeminately," for instance), and taking a given role (the passive, for instance) in sexual acts. Rowson portrays a secular society that, despite the norms that were promulgated by its religious authorities, accepted a variety of sexual behaviors and constructed a variety of genders and gendered behaviors.

Like Daniel Boyarin and Everett Rowson, Kathryn M. Ringrose examines a gender system—that of Christian Byzantium—that was strikingly different from those of the Christian West. Ringrose reminds us that Byzantine society institutionalized a third bodily sex through its dependence on sexually altered males, or eunuchs, for the maintenance of its bureaucracies. She argues, however, that the gendering of this third sex was by no means automatic. In the late antique period eunuchs, who tended to come from lower-status backgrounds, were gendered half male, half female. By the tenth century, however, when they often came from more elite backgrounds, they were gendered as a special category of males. By the later period, as well, eunuchs had attained greater status as religious ascetics, and it is even possible that the tenth century constructed two genders for eunuchs: one for court eunuchs and another for church eunuchs. Ringrose offers a variety of explanations for the changes over time, and she highlights the changing status of both court and church eunuchs by analyzing changing Byzantine interpretations of the biblical story about the prophet Daniel. Ringrose's analysis reminds us of the malleability and contingency of cultural inheritances: while Byzantine writers saw signs of eunuchry in the Daniel story, western writers saw none. Moreover, Byzantine readings of those signs of eunuchry changed over time, as the status and gendering of eunuchs evolved within Byzantine society.

Like Daniel Boyarin, Carol Braun Pasternack points to the differences between a cultural system that valued reproductive sexuality and constructed its genders in relationship to that sexuality, and late antique/ early medieval Christianity, which devalued the reproductive body and attempted to shape gendered identities by dissociating them from reproduction. Her focus is Anglo-Saxon England, where Christian leaders introduced very different notions of gendered subjectivities from those of pagan Germanic culture. The result of the meeting of these two gender systems was not a uniform dominant discourse, but diverse discourses that handled various cultural formations in significantly different ways. Through an examination of a seventh-century law code and a seventh-century penitential, Pasternack reads the tensions between the old system of aristocratic gendering, in which elite men gained prestige through polygynous marital associations and the resulting progeny and women were constructed as part of a man's property, and the new system, which elevated virginity, devalued marriage and procreation, and circumscribed both polygyny and (ultimately) divorce. Her discussion highlights the fluidity and multiplicity of gendered identities in a culture that was undergoing a prolonged process of conversion and conflict. Pasternack suggests, moreover, that rather than erasing pagan paradigms, Christian documentary culture merely dominated them.

GENDERS AND OTHER IDENTITIES IN WESTERN CHRISTIAN EUROPE, 1100–1500

The essays in the second and third parts of the book broaden our view of western Christian Europe, a culture with many local permutations that was only beginning to take shape in the period examined by Pasternack, and that continued to evolve in the first half of the second millennium. Our original intention was to subdivide these essays into three sections: one on intersections of genders and social status, a second on intersections of genders and religious difference, and a third on intersections of genders and sexualities. In reading the final essays, however, the editors encountered a dilemma, one that indicated how successful the volume has been in achieving its goals: most of the essays analyze at least two categories of difference that intersected with and complicated gendered categories. We have decided, therefore, to divide the essays into two groups: those that focus on discourses of domination, and those that consider, in addition to discourses of domination, individual choices and strategies of resistance.

DISCOURSES OF DOMINATION

Mathew S. Kuefler's essay argues that in twelfth-century France a new discourse about gender, sexuality, and aristocratic identity developed as part of an attempt to constrain behaviors and to undermine solidarities.

He argues that as part of an effort to challenge and undermine elite male solidarities, allegations of sodomitical practices were combined with a new claim that men who engaged in sex with other men were less than masculine. Kuefler suggests that the homosocial bonds that were being called into question had once served to create cohesion within military culture. Kuefler's analysis suggests that there were both social and political forces behind this "sodomitical panic." He does not go so far as to maintain that the "sodomitical panic" resulted in the formation of a new gender within the aristocracy, but he suggests that the gendered identities of aristocratic men who had strong bonds with other men were certainly threatened by the new dominant fiction.

Martha G. Newman focuses on a different set of twelfth-century texts that served to mold individual behaviors and identities. Focusing on late-twelfth-century Cistercian saints' lives from the low countries, she argues that the authors of those lives presented their male and female membership with two models of spiritual behavior, which differed according to the social status, rather than the gender, of the individual monk or nun. On the one hand, choir monks and nuns were presented with role models of saintly individuals who expressed their religiosity by becoming spiritual brides of Christ. On the other hand, lower-status male members of the order were presented with models of saintly individuals who expressed their faith in bodily terms. Only these *conversi*—the manual laborers of the order—were associated with extreme forms of bodily asceticism. In the early thirteenth century, however, Cistercian authors fell under the influence of the saints' lives that were generated by a new order of religious men, the Order of Saint Dominic. As a result, the Cistercians constructed a new gender system, in which all religious women were associated with the body and bodily asceticism, while monks alone were represented in disembodied terms as brides of Christ. The specific spiritual possibilities that earlier Cistercians had constructed for *conversi* disappeared in this new, more restrictive, formulation.

Newman's essay depicts a more complicated gendered universe than that of Caroline Bynum's work on medieval women's spirituality. Bynum argued, in *Holy Feast and Holy Fast: The Religious Significance of Food to Medieval Women,* that in the High and late Middle Ages women's spirituality was expressed in bodily terms because women were associated with the body while men were associated with reason and spirit. Newman's essay suggests that at certain times and in certain places, social status functioned more powerfully than gender as the boundary line between the realm of the spirit and the realm of the body.

Ruth Mazo Karras's essay shows how definitions of women as essentially sexual and the valuation of sex as essentially sinful could be used to regulate the behavior of all women, but that such regulation affected women of different social statuses to different degrees. She argues that in late medieval England the regulation of prostitution applied "one standard of behavior to women generally," thereby threatening "any sexually deviant woman with classification as a whore." She goes on to argue, however, that the dominant culture constructed different expectations for women of different social statuses, and that poorer women bore the brunt of both urban regulations concerning prostitution and male sexual aggression. Her discussion indicates that the classification of a woman as sexually deviant profoundly affected her social status.

Michael Uebel's essay highlights the uses of gendered and sexual categories in attempts to constrain and control social and economic relationships that crossed political and religious borders. Focusing his attention on two fourteenth-century texts, but drawing as well on earlier material, he discusses western Christian polemicists who attempted to map the differences between the Christian West and the Muslim Orient by contrasting apparent gender and sexual binaries. He suggests, however, that those mappings served to undo the very differences that they attempted to construct. Uebel argues that western crusader polemicists contrasted a dangerously aggressive homoerotic Muslim male with an ascetic, heterosexual, and Christian western male. Such polemics were meant to awaken western Christians to the dangers of their own practices—in selling slaves to Egypt, one polemicist argued, Christians fed not only the sexual appetites of Muslims but also the armies by which they themselves were defeated. The paradox, however, was that in the very process of describing the sexual appetites of Muslim males, and the succulent boy slaves with which they fed their appetites, Christian polemicists stimulated their own awareness of the possibilities of homoerotic pleasures, thus undoing the very gender identities that they wished to create for themselves. Uebel's analysis calls attention to the operations of desire, enjoyment, and fantasy in the construction of gender categories.

INDIVIDUAL CHOICES, STRATEGIES
OF RESISTANCE

Like all of the other essays in this book, the three essays in this final section highlight the intersections of gender categories with other categories
of difference. The three essays stand apart, however, in their attempts to
call attention to ways in which individuals either resisted or transformed
dominant discourses.

Like Martha Newman, Sharon Farmer argues that the body/soul binary could sometimes be drawn along the lines of social status rather
than those of masculinity and femininity. Farmer reads in the Genesis
account of the punishments of Adam and Eve gendered definitions that
distinguished feminine from masculine not through a body/soul binary
but through the association of men with productive activity—manual
labor—and women with reproductive activity. She then unpacks a single thirteenth-century narrative concerning a married, poor, disabled
woman, arguing that several categories of difference complicated the
association of men and women with each of the two gendered activities.
First, in clerical representations of necessary labors, men's productive
realm remained separate from women's reproductive realm, but differences of social status contributed to the construction of intellectual versions of manual and reproductive labors for elite men and women and
of physical versions of manual and reproductive labors for lower-status
men and women. Second, differences between necessary and penitential labor affected the degree to which clerical elites dissociated women
from manual labor: when the manual labor was necessary, clerics dissociated women from it; when it was performed for religious purposes, as
a form of penance, they associated women with it. Finally, Farmer suggests that the behavior and words of lower-status men and women indicate that their actions and choices were only sometimes shaped by clerical formulations.

Ulrike Wiethaus goes even further in her investigations of forms of
resistance to dominant discourses. Examining the "hidden transcripts"
of homoerotic resistance that religious women inscribed in texts that
were destined primarily for the eyes of other religious women, her essay
highlights the intersections of sexual desire and spiritual desire with
gendered identities and the resulting fluidity and multiplicity of those

identities. Wiethaus argues that in her religious poetry, the thirteenth-century Beguine Hadewijch constructed a variety of erotic and gendered relationships to represent her own desires for Christ, Minne (Love), and her fellow Beguines. Throughout her writings she endowed both herself and her love objects with shifting genders. Thus, sometimes she was bride to Christ's bridegroom, sometimes she took a male position vis-à-vis Christ. In her devotional writings addressed to Minne, who was neither feminine nor masculine "yet both," Hadewijch was sometimes male and sometimes female. Through these unstable gender and erotic positions, Wiethaus argues, Hadewijch constructed a discourse in which she could safely express her subversive erotic desires, despite the constraints of the dominant discourse outside of her community. Wiethaus's stress on instability and multiplicity, her examinations of intersections of genders, religious desires, and sexualities, and her interest in the subversive possibilities of Hadewijch's texts aptly highlight several themes in this volume.

Elizabeth Robertson's essay also stresses strategies of resistance in the work of a single author, Geoffrey Chaucer. In contrast to Hadewijch, however, Chaucer wrote for a broader, public, audience, which was comprised of both bourgeois and aristocratic readers. Robertson's reading of Chaucer's Man of Law's Tale differs sharply from earlier feminist readings, which have interpreted both Chaucer and his portrayal of the heroine of the tale, Constance, as reinscribing a medieval gender hierarchy that presented women as submissive and powerless. Robertson suggests, by contrast, that Chaucer brought together categories of female aristocratic gender and religious difference to create in Constance a figure of uncanny power, and to use her to propose an alternative to violent, imperialistic Christianity. She argues that through this interweaving of gender, social status, and religious difference, The Man of Law's Tale undermined dominant essentialisms, transcending "the restrictive category of feminine identity." Moreover, she posits that in this story about an aristocratic Christian woman who becomes an object of male desire both in the Islamic East and in pagan England, it is the Christian woman Constance—and not Islamic or pagan individuals—who embodies "radical otherness." Constance's radical otherness, Robertson argues, is that of apostolic Christianity, a form of Christianity that Chaucer identified with characteristics often viewed as feminine and that he deliberately contrasted with more masculine, imperialistic, and violent forms of religion—both non-Christian and Christian.

Robertson's discussion points to a central theme of this volume: that genders are always intersecting with other categories of difference, and that categories of difference are always in service to something else. Because each text, each situation, discussed in this volume was shaped by different political, religious, and social contingencies, no single essay does the work of the volume as a whole. Only by reading the essays together can the reader begin to understand the diversity of gendered hierarchies and constructs in medieval cultures, and multiple ways in which those constructs were employed and transformed. Other categories of difference—social status, sexualities, religious difference—were, and are, always in the process of reconfiguring gender, and those other categories are themselves always in flux. And yet, in the end, differences always seem to reinscribe hierarchies, and gender, however fluid and malleable, always seems to matter. Gender is and was one of the fundamental categories of difference affecting hierarchies of power. But because, in historic time at least, there have always been other categories of difference, there have never been just two genders.

NOTES

I thank Carol Pasternack and Jeffrey Jerome Cohen for helping me to rethink earlier versions of this introduction.

1. Patricia Hill Collins, *Black Feminist Thought: Knowledge, Consciousness, and the Politics of Empowerment* (Reprint ed.: New York, 1991), 225–30. See also *This Bridge Called My Back: Writings by Radical Women of Color*, ed. Cherríe Moraga and Gloria Anzaldúa; foreword, Toni Cade Bambara (Watertown, MA, 1981); Maxine Baca Zinn and Bonnie Thornton Dill, "Theorizing Difference From Multiracial Feminism," *Feminist Studies* 22 (1996): 321–31; Chela Sandoval, "U.S. Third World Feminism: The Theory and Method of Oppositional Consciousness in the Postmodern World," *Genders* 10 (Spring 1991): 4; bell hooks, *Feminist Theory: From Margin to Center* (Boston, 1984); Norma Alarcón, "The Theoretical Subject(s) of *This Bridge Called My Back*," in *Making Face, Making Soul/Haciendo Caras: Creative and Critical Perspectives by Feminists of Color*, ed. Gloria Anzaldúa (San Francisco, 1990), 356–69; Nalini Persram, "Politicizing the *Féminine*, Globalizing the Feminist," *Alternatives* 19 (1994): 275–313; Elizabeth Spelman, *Inessential Woman: Problems of Exclusion in Feminist Thought* (Boston, 1988), esp. chap. 7.

2. Persram, "Politicizing the *Féminine*"; Homi Bhabha, *The Location of Culture* (New York, 1994); Gloria Anzaldúa, *Borderlands/La Frontera: The New Mestiza* (San Francisco,

1987); Jeffrey Jerome Cohen, "Hybrids, Monsters, Borderlands: The Bodies of Gerald of Wales," in *The Postcolonial Middle Ages*, ed. Jeffrey Jerome Cohen (New York, 2000), 85–104; James F. Brooks, *Captives and Cousins: Slavery, Kinship, and Community in the Southwest Borderlands* (Chapel Hill, 2002).

3. Caroline Walker Bynum, *Jesus as Mother: Studies in the Spirituality of the High Middle Ages* (Berkeley, 1982), 110–69; Bynum, *Holy Feast and Holy Fast: The Religious Significance of Food to Medieval Women* (Berkeley, 1987); Bynum, *Fragmentation and Redemption: Essays on Gender and the Human Body in Medieval Religion* (New York, 1991); Bynum, *The Resurrection of the Body in Western Christianity, 200–1336* (New York, 1995).

4. Steven Kruger, "Becoming Christian, Becoming Male?" in *Becoming Male in the Middle Ages*, ed. Jeffrey Jerome Cohen and Bonnie Wheeler (New York, 1997), 21–41; Kruger, "Racial/Religious and Sexual Queerness in the Middle Ages," *Medieval Feminist Newsletter* no. 16 (Fall 1993), 32–36; Louise Mirrer, *Women, Jews, and Muslims in the Texts of Reconquest Castile* (Ann Arbor, MI, 1996). See also Diane Owen Hughes's discussion of stereotypes of both Jewish men and Jewish women as hypersensuous: Hughes, "Distinguishing Signs: Ear-Rings, Jews, and Franciscan Rhetoric in the Italian Renaissance City," *Past and Present* no. 112 (1986): 3–59. For a discussion of the blurring of the lines, in Christian representations, between Muslim homoeroticism and Christian heteronormativity, see Gregory S. Hutcheson, "The Sodomitic Moor: Queerness in the Narrative of *Reconquista*," in *Queering the Middle Ages*, ed. Glenn Burger and Steven F. Kruger (Minneapolis, 2001), 99–122.

5. Robert Bartlett, *Gerald of Wales* (Oxford, 1982), chap. 6; David Rollo, "Gerald of Wales' *Topographia Hibernica*: Sex and the Irish Nation," *The Romanic Review* 86 (1995): 169–89. Rollo argues that Gerald of Wales's portrayal of the "perversions" of the Irish was directed more against Angevin rulership than against the Irish per se, but that Gerald's text was employed by later generations to vilify the Irish. See John Gillingham, "Conquering the Barbarians: War and Chivalry in Twelfth-Century Britain," *The Haskins Society Journal: Studies in Medieval History* 4 (1992): 67–84, for a compelling attempt to understand why the Irish, Welsh, and Scots were portrayed and treated as barbarous others from the twelfth century on.

6. Cohen, "Hybrids, Monsters, Borderlands," 86.

7. Kathryn Gravdal, *Ravishing Maidens: Writing Rape in Medieval French Literature and Law* (Philadelphia, 1991), chap. 4.

8. Paul Freedman, "Cowardice, Heroism, and the Legendary Origins of Catalonia," *Past and Present* no. 121 (November 1988): 3–28; Freedman, *Images of the Medieval Peasant* (Stanford, CA, 1999), chaps. 5 and 7.

9. Elizabeth A. Castelli, "'I Will Make Mary Male': Pieties of the Body and Gender Transformation of Christian Women in Late Antiquity," in *Body Guards: The Cultural Politics of Gender Ambiguity*, ed. Julia Epstein and Kristina Straub (New York, 1991), 29–49; Jo Ann McNamara, "The *Herrenfrage*: The Restructuring of the Gender System, 1050–1150," in *Medieval Masculinities: Regarding Men in the Middle Ages*, ed. Clare A. Lees (Minneapolis, 1994), 3–30.

10. Ruth Mazo Karras and David Lorenzo Boyd, "'Ut cum muliere': A Male Transvestite Prostitute in Fourteenth-Century London," in *Premodern Sexualities*, ed. Louise Fradenburg and Carla Freccero (New York, 1995), 101–16; Michael Rocke, *Forbidden Friendships:*

Homosexuality and Male Culture in Renaissance Florence (New York, 1996). See also Francesca
Canadé Sautman's nuanced discussion of the trial of Arnaud de Verniolle in the inquisitorial register of Jacques Fournier, "'Just Like a Woman': Queer History, Womanizing the
Body, and the Boys in Arnaud's Band," in *Queering the Middle Ages*, ed. Burger and Kruger,
175–86.

   11. Carolyn Dinshaw, *Getting Medieval: Sexualities and Communities, Pre- and Postmodern* (Durham, NC, 1999), 111.

   12. On Jews, see above, note 4. On heretics, see Sara Lipton, "'Tanquam effemina-
tum': Pedro II of Aragon and the Gendering of Heresy in the Albigensian Crusade," in
Queer Iberia: Sexualities, Cultures, and Crossings from the Middle Ages to the Renaissance, ed.
Josiah Blackmore and Gregory S. Hutcheson (Durham, NC, 1999), 107–29. On monsters,
see Jeffrey Jerome Cohen, *Of Giants: Sex, Monsters, and the Middle Ages* (Minneapolis,
1999), 52. On men engaging in non-normative sex, see Karras and Boyd, "'Ut cum
muliere,'" and Karma Lochrie, *Covert Operations: The Medieval Uses of Secrecy* (Philadelphia, 1999), chap. 5. In her discussion of Wycliffite claims that Catholic clerics engaged in
sodomy, Carolyn Dinshaw points to multiple masculinities rather than gender binaries:
Getting Medieval, chap. 1.

   13. Thus, for instance, all of the essays in *The Postcolonial Middle Ages* and in *Queer
Iberia* concern texts authored by western European Christians; twelve of the fourteen essays in *The Postcolonial Middle Ages* were written by specialists in medieval English literature, one other by a specialist in medieval French literature. In a recent issue of *The Journal of Medieval and Early Modern Studies* entitled *Race and Ethnicity in the Middle Ages*,
William Chester Jordan was the only contributor who looked beyond the Catholic Christian perspective, examining both Jewish and Arabic texts: "Why 'Race'?," *Race and Ethnicity in the Middle Ages*, ed. Thomas Hahn, special issue of *The Journal of Medieval and Early
Modern Studies* 31 (2001): 165–73.

   14. Jean Devisse and Michel Mollat, *The Image of the Black in Western Art* (New York,
1979); Geraldine Heng, "The Romance of England: *Richard Coer de Lyon*, Saracens, Jews,
and the Politics of Race and Nation," in *The Postcolonial Middle Ages*, ed. Cohen, 135–72.
For examples of positive medieval representations of persons with dark skin, see Maghan
Keita, "Deconstruction and Reconstruction: Africa and Medieval and Renaissance History," *Medieval Feminist Newsletter* no. 16 (Fall 1993), 11.

   15. Steven Kruger, "Conversion and Medieval Sexual, Religious, and Racial Categories,"
in *Constructing Medieval Sexuality*, ed. Karma Lochrie, Peggy McCracken, and James A.
Schultz (Minneapolis, 1997), 164; see also pp. 165 ff.

   16. Robert Bartlett, *The Making of Europe: Conquest, Colonization, and Cultural Change,
950–1350* (Princeton, NJ, 1993), chap. 8.

   17. David Nirenberg, *Communities of Violence: Persecution of Minorities in the Middle
Ages* (Princeton, NJ, 1996), 150.

   18. Bartlett, *The Making of Europe*, 236 ff.

   19. David Nirenberg, "Miscegenation: Spain and Latin America in the Multicultural
Imagination of the United States" (paper delivered at New York University and University
of California, Santa Barbara, April 1997). Sally McKee has argued for a similar late medieval
hardening of the lines between ethnic groups in the Venetian colony of Crete: "'Passing'

before Race: Taken for Somebody's Other in a Late Medieval Colonial Town," paper delivered to the seventy-seventh annual meeting of the Medieval Academy of America, New York, 4–6 April 2002.

20. E. P. Thompson, *The Making of the English Working Class* (London, 1963), 9–10. See also William H. Sewell Jr.'s discussion of the impact of Thompson's approach to class formation and some of the problems with that approach: "How Classes Are Made: Critical Reflections on E. P. Thompson's Theory of Working Class Formation," in *E. P. Thompson: Critical Perspectives*, ed. Harvey J. Kaye and Keith McClelland (Philadelphia, 1990), 50–77.

21. Georges Duby, *The Chivalrous Society*, trans. Cynthia Postan (Berkeley, 1977), chaps. 10, 13.

22. Freedman, "Cowardice, Heroism, and the Legendary Origins." The implication of the peasants' argument was that Christianity and freedom went hand in hand.

23. See especially Judith Butler, *Gender Trouble: Feminism and the Subversion of Identity* (New York, 1990), and Butler, *Bodies That Matter: On the Discursive Limits of Sex* (New York, 1993); Eve Kosofsky Sedgwick, *Between Men: English Literature and Male Homosocial Desire* (New York, 1985). Important contributions by medievalists to these discussions include Dinshaw, *Getting Medieval*; and Allen J. Frantzen, "Between the Lines: Queer Theory, the History of Homosexuality, and Anglo-Saxon Penitentials," *Journal of Medieval and Early Modern Studies* 26, no. 2 (Spring 1996): 255–96.

24. See, for instance, David Halperin, *One Hundred Years of Homosexuality and Other Essays on Greek Love* (New York, 1990), 26; and Mark D. Jordan, *The Invention of Sodomy in Christian Theology* (Chicago, 1997). On "sodomy" as an unstable signifier see, in addition to Jordan, Rocke, *Forbidden Friendships*, 11–12; and Bruce Holsinger, "Sodomy and Resurrection: The Homoerotic Subject of the *Divine Comedy*," in *Premodern Sexualities*, ed. Fradenburg and Freccero, 245.

25. Rocke, *Forbidden Friendships*, 4–5, 13–15.

26. Simon Gaunt, "Straight Minds/'Queer' Wishes in Old French Hagiography," in *Premodern Sexualities*, ed. Fradenburg and Freccero, 155–73.

27. Lochrie, *Covert Operations*, 199.

28. Kruger argues along these lines, "Conversion and Medieval Sexual, Religious, and Racial Categories," 165; and Gaunt comes close to making this point, "Straight Minds/ 'Queer' Wishes."

29. Gaunt, "Straight Minds/'Queer' Wishes"; Amy M. Hollywood, *The Soul as Virgin Wife: Mechtild of Magdeburg, Marguerite Porete, and Meister Eckhart* (Notre Dame, 1995); Ulrike Wiethaus, "Sexuality, Gender, and the Body in Late Medieval Spirituality: Cases from Germany and the Netherlands," *Journal of Feminist Studies in Religion* 7, no. 1 (Spring 1991): 35–52.

PART I

DIFFERING CULTURES,
DIFFERING POSSIBILITIES

1

ON THE HISTORY OF THE
EARLY PHALLUS

DANIEL BOYARIN

For Dina Stein

PART THE FIRST: HOW THE PHALLUS
HID ITS PENIS: A JUST-SO STORY

The Phallus-that-is-not-the-penis owes its historical origins to an extremely powerful and extraordinary move that much western thought makes at its origins: the inscription of the body as female.[1] As Judith Butler has remarked of the very founding text of a certain strain of modern feminism:

> Although Beauvoir is often understood to be calling for the right of women, in effect, to become existential subjects and hence, for inclusion within the terms of an abstract universality, her position also implies a fundamental critique of the very disembodiment of the abstract masculine epistemological subject. That subject is abstract to the extent that it disavows its socially marked embodiment and, further, projects that disavowed and disparaged embodiment on to the feminine sphere, effectively renaming the body as female.... Beauvoir's analysis implicitly poses the question: Through what act of negation and disavowal

does the masculine pose as a disembodied universality and the feminine get constructed as a disavowed corporeality?[2]

Through what act indeed? Let us begin, then, at a Beginning.

One of the foundational thinkers for the version of Judaism that was to become Christianity was Philo, a Jew of Alexandria, and a slightly older contemporary of Paul of Tarsus. Philo was preoccupied with sexual difference. In accordance with one of the characteristic features of his discourse, he articulated his concern as part of a commentary on Genesis, on the dual accounts of the creation of humanity and sexual difference that we find in the first two chapters of the Bible:[3]

Genesis 1:27–28

[27] And God created the earth-creature in His image; in the image of God, He created him; male and female He created them. [28] And God blessed them, and God said to them: Reproduce and fill the earth.

Genesis 5:1–2

This is the book of the Generations of Adam, on the day that God created Adam in the image of God He made him. [2] Male and female He created them, and He blessed them, *and called their name Adam,* on the day He created them.

Genesis 2:7 ff.

[7] And God formed the earth-creature of dust from the earth and breathed in its nostrils the breath of life, and the earth-creature became a living being. . . . [20] And the earth-creature gave names to all of the animals and the fowls of the air and all of the animals of the fields, but the earth-creature could not find any helper fitting for it. [21] And God caused a deep sleep to fall on the earth-creature, and it slept, and He took one of its ribs and closed the flesh beneath it. [22] And the Lord God constructed the rib that He had taken from the earth-creature into a woman and brought her to the earth-man. [23] And the earth-man said, this time is bone of my bone and flesh of my flesh. She shall be called wo-man, for from man was she taken.

In the first story it seems clear that the original creation of the species humanity included both sexes, while the second one is seemingly a narrative of an original male creature for whom a female was created out of his flesh. The contradiction of the two accounts accordingly presents a classical hermeneutic problem.

In the interpretation of Philo, the Adam of the first account is an entirely spiritual being, of whose noncorporeal existence it can be said that he is male and female, while the second account first introduces a carnal Adam who is male and then from whom the female is constructed. Bodily gender—structurally dependent, of course, on there being two— is thus twice displaced from the origins of "Man":

> "It is not good that *any* man should be alone," For there are *two* races of men, the one made after the (Divine) Image, and the one molded out of the earth. . . . With the second man a helper is associated. To begin with, the helper is a created one, for it says "Let us make a helper for him": and in the next place, is subsequent to him who is to be helped, for He had formed the mind before and is about to form its helper.[4]

Philo here regards the two stories as referring to two entirely different creative acts on the part of God and accordingly to the production of two different races of "Man." Thus, both myths are comprised in his discourse: a primal androgyne of no sex and a primal male/secondary female. Since the two accounts, that is the one in Genesis 1 and the one in Genesis 2, refer to two entirely different species, he can claim that only the first one is called "in the image of God," that is, only the singular, unbodied Adam-creature is referred to as being in God's likeness and his male-and-femaleness must be understood spiritually. That is to say that the designation of *this* creature as both male and female means really neither male nor female. This creature is, however, Adam, or at any rate, the Idea of Adam, and therefore while neither male nor female, he is also somehow male. This transcendent androgyne, like Adam himself even before there was an Eve, only seems to be both male and female, but "actually" is singularly male.

However, there is more to be said here. The "helper" in the Bible is, of course, the woman. For Philo, however, this helper is the body, and what has "been formed before" is the mind. For Philo as perhaps for many Greek-speaking Jews, the oneness of pure spirit is ontologically privileged in the constitution of humanity. Putting this into more secular terms, I could argue that for Philo and thence for those who follow in his wake,[5] the essence of the human subject precedes its accidental division into sexes. The "true self"—we would say the "subject"—exists before being assigned a gender. Genderlessness, however, seems always to be conflated with maleness. Thus spirit becomes written as male, and body, what is divided into gender, becomes written as female. This is an example of the mechanism within which gender itself comes to be female. The transcendent androgyne is male.

We notice here, however, another crucial element in the Platonic thinking of this Jewish arch-Platonist, Philo. If indeed, in the "second" creation story, the division is between mind (male) and body (female), in the first creation story, it is only an Idea of Man that is created at all. It is here, then, that Philo locates a point of origin for his Platonism altogether: The first human, the ungendered, male androgyne, is Idea, while the second human, the gendered one, is material, even though it is, itself, composed of both a male principle (mind) and a female one (body).

Ultimately, as Karen King suggests, the two myths of gender "are quite compatible in that both imagine the ideal to be a unitary self, whether male or androgynous, whose nature is grounded in an ontology of transcendence and an epistemology of origins" (oral communication)—and thus, I would add, always masculine in its configuration.

As we have learned from the work of several feminist historians of Christianity, the paradigmatic literature of early Christianity (and pre-rabbinic Judaism) frequently projects the "utopia of the neutral sex," that is, the possibility and promise of a transcendence of sexual difference and sexual domination.[6] For Philo, there were two types of anatomical females: virgins and women.[7] Elizabeth Castelli has described the situation with regard to one of the earliest and most explicit Christian texts, *The Gospel of Thomas:*

> The double insistence attributed to Jesus in the *Gospel of Thomas* saying—that Mary should remain among the disciples at the same time as she must be made male—points to the paradoxical ideological conditions that helped to shape the lives of early Christian women. At once they are to have access to holiness,

while they also can do so only through the manipulation of conventional gender categories.[8]

We notice, however, immediately that "the manipulation of conventional
gender categories" issues in a female becoming male.[9] One of the most
striking and powerful narrative representations of this "paradoxical ideological condition" is the story of Paul and Thekla from the Apocryphal
Acts of the Apostles. In this account, the young woman refuses the marriage bed, cuts her hair, dresses like a boy, and becomes Paul's close
companion in his travels and apostleship.[10]

In another text of the same genre, we find a strikingly similar moment of neutralization of gender via celibacy. In *The Acts of Andrew*, the
apocryphal apostle begs Maximilla to remain steadfast in her decision to
cease having sexual intercourse with her husband in the following terms:
"Therefore, I beg you *wise man [sic]*[11] that your clearsighted mind stand
firm. I beg you, mind unseen, that you may be protected. I entreat you,
love Jesus. Do not be overcome by the inferior. You whom I entreat as a
man, assist me in my becoming perfect."[12] Here it is absolutely and explicitly clear that the goal of gender neutralization for both women and
men is to become a man. Celibacy removes the anatomical female from
the status of woman and makes her a man, because her male invisible
mind is now dominant over her female body. Her husband, in his devotion to the carnal, is now "the inferior," the woman. Andrew himself
needs her help in becoming perfect as well, in becoming male. As Maud
Gleason has pointed out, "Masculinity in the ancient world was an
achieved state, radically underdetermined by anatomical sex."[13] One of
the revolutionary innovations of Christianity was that anatomical women
could also achieve masculinity, but anatomical men somehow always
seem to have an easier time of it.[14]

In early Christianity, just as in Philo's Judaism, virgins were not
women but androgynes, a representation, in the appearance of flesh, of
the purely spiritual non-gendered, presocial essence of human being.
For these forms of Judaism (and early Christianity is, of course, also a
form of Judaism), this dualism is the base of the anthropology: equality
in the spirit, hierarchy in the flesh. As Clement of Alexandria, a second
century Christian Platonist, expressed it, "As then there is sameness [with
men and women] with respect to the soul, she will attain to the same

virtue; but as there is difference with respect to the peculiar construction of the body, she is destined for child-bearing and house-keeping."[15] As this quotation suggests and Christian practice enacts, this version of primal androgyny provided two elements in the gender politics of the early church. On the one hand, it provided an image or vision of a spiritual equality for all women—which did not, however, have social consequences for the married; on the other hand, it provided for real autonomy and social parity for celibate women, for those who rejected "the peculiar construction of the body," together with its pleasures and satisfactions. As Clement avers in another place, "For souls themselves by themselves are equal. Souls are neither male nor female when they no longer marry nor are given in marriage."[16] We find similar and equally trenchant representations of this virtual commonplace in late-fourth-century Fathers as well. In these writers, however, the maleness of this androgyny is open and stipulated. Thus we find in Jerome, for instance: "As long as woman is for birth and children, she is different from man as body is from soul. But if she wishes to serve Christ more than the world, then she will cease to be a woman and will be called man."[17] And again in Ambrose: "She who does not believe is a woman and should be designated by the name of her bodily sex, whereas she who believes progresses to complete manhood, to the measure of the adulthood of Christ. She then does without wordly name, gender of body, youthful seductiveness, and garrulousness of old age."[18]

This is a mythic representation by certain Judaisms and Christianities of their understanding that the metaphysics of substance that subtends the notion of transcendence is itself a masculinist inscription of the abstract (spirit) over the concrete (body). These texts are mythic or ritual enactments of the "myth of the primal androgyne,"[19] and, as such, don't really disturb gender categories; they instate the split between Universal Mind and Disavowed Body. This then constitutes a reinstatement, even a reinforcement, of masculinism: The androgyne in question always turns out somehow to be a male androgyne. Mary is made male, Thekla becomes a virtual boy, and the celibate Maximilla is a "wise man." Jean-Joseph Goux, following Irigaray, has called this a "metamorphosis into the masculine-neutral," a neutrality or universality that in its very drive toward that neutrality, already is masculine. Early Christians understood this well and remarked it explicitly,[20] and therefore, I would claim,

Goux is quite mistaken in seeing this as a modern phenomenon, indeed as "the immanent logic of modernity."[21]

To put this structuration of sexual difference in Lacanian terms—with which it is strikingly similar, and for which, I claim, it is a point of origin—the Phallus is indeed not the penis here, since neither women nor men have it, and both have to strive to achieve being male. Just as in Philo we have seen that the first Adam is not a male body but rather the male androgyne represented as pure Mind and as an Idea of the male, so also, the Phallus is not the penis, but it is a disembodied idealization of the penis, a Platonic Idea of the penis.

The Philonic and Christian texts that we have visited provide us with several closely related examples of the representation of a primary androgyny, a masculine neutral sex, ontologically first in the constitution of the human being. They do not, however, represent this male-androgyny as the Phallus. For this icon it seems, we have to look for non-Jewish-Christian sources. In a remarkable essay, Jean-Joseph Goux provides a narrative of the origins of the Phallus in western culture. Goux begins by tracing the origins of the cultural phenomenon back to the myth of Osiris and Isis, just as did, as we shall see, the Neoplatonic authors who were most crucial in the invention of the Phallus. In this myth, it will be remembered, the body of Osiris, Isis's brother and husband both, was dismembered after his killing by Typhon and the pieces of the corpse were scattered widely. Isis carefully gathers fourteen parts of his body in order to reconstruct the body and bring it back to life. The only part that she cannot find is his penis, for which she constructs a simulacrum, eternally erect, and ordains the worship of this simulacrum. According to various late ancient texts, this myth gave rise to rites that were the direct ancestors of the Eleusinian Mysteries, which are perhaps only Mysterious Allusions.[22] This ancient Phallus, however, is a direct, conscious, explicit representation of the penis. As such, it is typologically related to the Lingam of Shiva in Indian culture as well. Is this the Phallus of which psychoanalysis speaks, however? Were it so, it would be very hard to imagine how Lacan or anyone else could ever conceive of the Phallus not being the penis, as Lacan's famous—perhaps most famous—formula would have it. Also, quite impossible to imagine how anyone could speak of the Phallus as that which both men and women equally lack, or as the very signifier of a universal lack.

Goux has asked this question too, in rather different language, however. He asks: "Why and how did the undeniable phallophorism of antiquity (rites of Osiris, figures of Hermes, of Dionysius) give way to an
apparent amnesia of this central function, an amnesia which can only
be lifted via oblique paths of an experience no longer collective and ritu-
alized [to wit, psychoanalysis]? Something had to change in the mode of
consciousness, in the relationship to images, in the trajectory covered in
the formation of the subject. This would allow the new (unconscious)
system of rapport with the phallus to be established."[23] Following the
work of Virginia Burrus, I would suggest that it is the "veiling" of the
Phallus, its hiding from explicit representation, from sometime in the
fourth century and on, that has most enabled it to do its cultural work,
while remaining itself immune, as it were, to further "history."[24] More
had to have happened, however, before this final step in the story of how
the Phallus lost its penis could be taken, as it were.

The crucial step in the Phallus losing its penis is the third-century
Neoplatonism of Plotinus.[25] Building on the Platonic/Aristotelian notion that "conception" consists of the father planting an Idea in the womb
of the mother, "Any engendering is the result of the union of two different
principles, a male principle which is intelligible reason (ideas, model,
father) and a female principle which is matter,"[26] from here it was quite
an easy step for Plotinus to conclude that

> Only the form, the idea, the *logos* are fruitful. That is the meaning
> of the perpetual erection of god the inventor. Matter is only the
> receptacle and a wet-nurse: it is sterile and receives without giv-
> ing. The only true principle of generation, including perceptible
> things, is in the *logos*. It was for this reason, I think, that the an-
> cient sages, speaking in riddles secretly and in the mystery rites,
> make the ancient Hermes always have the organ of generation
> ready for its work, revealing that the intelligible formative prin-
> ciple *[ton noeton logon]* is the generator of the things in the sense-
> world, but revealing too.[27]

Lacan's association between the Phallus and the Logos is thus not an ar-
bitrary, "wild," aleatory representation within western culture, but a precise interpretation of its foundations, for there can be little doubt but
that Plotinus's Neoplatonism has found its way deeply into those very

foundations, primarily by way of the crucial patristic thinkers who were so influenced by him.[28]

This idea is not only the province of such an elite and recondite thinker as Plotinus but also already active and pervasive in such a "popular" writer as the middle-Platonist Plutarch. For Plutarch, the father (and thus the Phallus) is not a physical, corporeal entity but a purely spiritual one. Thus, for example, Plutarch asks why Plato describes God as both maker and father of the universe. His answer is striking and characteristic. After considering various other possibilities, Plutarch finally concludes that "There are two constituent parts of the universe, body and soul. The former god did not beget; but matter having submitted itself to him, he formed and fitted it together. . . . The soul, however, when it has partaken of intelligence and reason and concord, is not merely a work but also a part of god and has come to be not by his agency but both from him as source and out of his substance."[29] As a recent commentator has paraphrased him: "God is the *maker* of the universe in so far as he has fashioned it out of pre-existent matter after the manner of an artist or a carpenter. But he is the *father* of the universe in so far as he has imbued the universe with rational life."[30]

Even more graphically, Plutarch writes:

> And that is the reason why they make the older Hermae without hands, or feet, but with their private parts stiff, indicating figuratively that there is no need whatsoever of old men who are active by their body's use, if they keep their mind [or their power of reason, *logos energon*], as it should be, active and fertile.[31]

For Plutarch, as for Plotinus, it was so obvious that the stiff private parts of the Herm were not related to the "body's use" that he didn't even have to argue the point; he could assume that his readers would understand it implicitly. The stiff Phallus of the Herm simply *is* the Logos. Here we see *Nous* and *Logos* together and both clearly equated with the Phallus. If we combine Philo's "mind," Νοῦς, which is the male, created before the female bodily helper, and the stiff Phallus of the Herm, which, for Plotinus, is simply identical to both *Nous* and *Logos*, then Lacan is exactly right to see in his phallic signifier this very ancient (but historically and culturally specific) structure. "The function of the [phallic][32] signifier here touches on its most profound relation: by way of which the

Ancients embodied in it both the Νους [*Nous*, sense] and the Λογὸς
[*Logos*, reason]."[33] No wonder then that both *Nous* and *Logos* are arche-
typically male attributes.[34] The Phallus, then, as a representation, consists
precisely of the separation of masculinity from the embodied male body.
It is the separation of the Phallus from the penis, the veiling of the penis,
that enables the production of the very "magical relations of reciprocity"
of which Butler speaks. I shall refer to this phallic structure of gender—
using Kaja Silverman's brilliant coinage—as the "dominant fiction."

PART THE SECOND: THE DOMINANT
FICTION REVISITED

Kaja Silverman's book *Male Subjectivity at the Margins* theorizes a version of masculinity that she refers to as the "dominant fiction."[35] This is
an extremely useful term, because it allows for the possibility of discontinuities, strains, breaks, resistant genderings, and sexualities that terms
like "western culture" foreclose. This dominant fiction that she theorizes is, however, constituted by the myth of *the equation of the penis to
the Phallus,* that is, by a narrative that ascribes to maleness, indeed defines maleness through ascribing to the male, an "unimpaired bodily
'envelope' . . . —fiercely protective of its coherence."[36] The penis > Phallus becomes then the very symbol of power and privilege, as well as of
completeness, coherence, univocity. And thus Silverman concludes, "Conventional masculinity can best be understood as the denial of castration,
and hence as a refusal to acknowledge the defining limits of subjectivity.
The category of 'femininity' is to a very large degree the result" (46).
The reading of the binary opposition of the genitals as signifying male
unity, singularity, and plenitude and female difference, multiplicity, and
lack has had enormous cultural consequences. This construction seems
to be attestable very far back in western culture,[37] and it is this that ultimately gives rise to such patternings as

man is to woman as
substance: accident
form: matter
univocity: division and difference
soul: body

meaning: language
signified: signifier
natural: artificial
essential: ornamental.[38]

Silverman refers to this constellation as "the dominant fiction." Her very use of the term "fiction"—something that is made—and its association as well with the political power implied by "dominant" suggest strongly a particular historical, cultural construct. This would also pose the possibility of other cultures having other dominant fictions, other narratives of how male is related to female symbolically. However, at many points in Silverman's discourse she seems rather to accept than contest a certain version of psychoanalysis that would read this narrative not as the dominant fiction of a particularly cultural formation but rather as the normal, structuring organization of the human psyche, always and everywhere, except when (temporarily) ruptured by particular "historical" circumstances. Thus at one point she describes such a rupture as when "a historical event...brings a large group of male subjects into such an intimate relation with lack that they are at least for the moment unable to sustain an imaginary relation with the phallus."[39]

In other words the default situation is one in which male subjects are so out of touch with lack, so protected against their own "castration" that they can imagine that the penis is identical to the Phallus and thus project all lack onto female subjects. This ordinary situation, however, by being contrasted to history is itself projected as being beyond history or above and outside of history. Elsewhere Silverman uses the telling phrase "the history of the normative male subject,"[40] a phrase which does *not* mean the historical conditions or matrix within which the normative male subject of a singular, particular cultural formation arises, but rather the historical vicissitudes to which the normative male subject, always and everywhere the same, is subject and prey. This normative maleness, imagined precisely as anatomical wholeness, is always the same, always threatened by the same trauma of castration, always "a bound and armored ego,"[41] always determined through an anatomical lack that is projected onto the female body owing to the symbolism—always the same—of her genitalia as absence. Note that this transhistoricality, paradoxically, is qualified, within this very passage, by the modifier "ideologically," suggesting the possibility of other ideologies.

In addition to war, Silverman describes certain Christian formations of masculinity as being also marginal to male subjectivity, as putting maleness as masculinity into question through some or another
sort of extreme corporeal behavior like martyrdom or extreme ascetic
practice.[42] She also recognizes a category of disempowered males whose
phallic identification is at risk: "Oppression experienced in relation to
class, race, ethnicity, age, and other ideologically determined 'handicaps'
may also pose major obstacles in the way of a phallic identification, or
may expose masculinity as a masquerade."[43] The very language chosen
here, however, in spite of the scare quotes, indicates the position taken.
These male subjectivities, as well as the male subjects of war and gay
men, are inscribed by Silverman as marginal to the ordinary, the timeless, the normal form of male subjectivity, in spite of the explicit challenge
to that kind of male subjectivity that Silverman wishes to urge. Although
it is clear that the pull of Silverman's work is towards the historicist
pole, we need a more trenchant historicization of the psychoanalytic account of male subjectivity and the Phallus. Another way of describing
this project would be to suggest that psychoanalysis has been almost
entirely oriented toward describing the formation of subjectivity within
one culture, from Oedipus to Hamlet to the Wolfman, and vigorously
denying, I will claim, another cultural formation that subsisted, as it
were, within itself, a cultural formation that I will refer to here as "the
subdominant fiction."[44]

In order to be able to historicize the dominant fiction, however, we
first have to be able to see it for what it is/was. The dominant fiction of
gender (and thence of so much else) in western culture, I would claim,
is not of an *equation* of the penis with the Phallus but of a *split* between
them. Going back to the foundational texts with which I began this
study, we can see that they all work hard to dissociate the physical male
body and its organs from both the Phallus and from masculinity itself.
Returning as well to the list of oppositions symbolized via the primary
opposition of male and female, we can also see that they are much more
easily described via a split between the male body and masculinity, or
between the penis and the Phallus, than by their equation. The "dominant fiction," then, has its origins deep in the founding moments of
western culture, in the impact that Plato and the developments that follow in "his" wake have had on the combinations of Platonism and ancient

Israelite religion that we call Judaism and Christianity.[45] It is thus, I suggest, through the separation of Phallus from penis, that which Lacan calls the "veiling of the Phallus," that the male is successfully produced, in an ideology that seems so natural as to be almost unquestioned before modernity, to be simply equatable with the human. The relation of history to the dominant fiction is thus not one in which historical trauma disrupts the always-already existent dominant fiction, but rather a story of the production of the dominant fiction in historical time and space. It is precisely, then, the production of the Phallus, *via its historical separation from the penis,* the notion that maleness can be abstracted from the particularities of bodies with penises and thus projected as the universal human (even as the ideal universal human that no one successfully embodies and thus as an absence, an illusion, or a lack), that constitutes the dominant fiction of western masculinity.

THE FRAUDIAN PHALLUS

"[The Phallus] is even less the organ, penis or clitoris, which it symbolizes."[46] This section of my text will consist of an extended gloss on this highly ambiguous and crucial Lacanian dictum. As we have observed above in Silverman, according to feminist Lacanians it is only the equation of the Phallus with the penis that leads to an unproblematic assertion of male privilege. This approach is dependent, however, on the assumption that the Phallus is a real entity, psychic or ontological, independent of the penis, not produced by language or culture, and thus confusable with the penis. Thus, while Elizabeth Grosz calls the Phallus "a signifier," as distinct from "the penis, an organ," she also writes about "the misappropriation of the penis by the phallus," indicating that the Phallus is an already existing entity. In her explanation, it is through "the misappropriation of the penis" that the Phallus becomes effective in causing women to be regarded as "castrated."[47]

Lacan refers to "the subject as in the form that is, strictly speaking, the imaged embodiment of the minus-phi $[-\varphi)]$[48] of castration, which for us, centers the whole organization of the desires through the framework of the fundamental drives."[49] On passages such as this, Jacqueline Rose comments:

> When Lacan is reproached with phallocentrism at the level of
> his theory, what is most often missed is that the subject's entry
> into the symbolic order is equally an exposure of the value of
> the Phallus itself. The subject has to recognize that there is de-
> sire, or lack in the place of the Other, that there is no ultimate
> certainty or truth, and that the status of the Phallus is a fraud
> (this is, for Lacan, the meaning of castration). The Phallus can
> only take up its place by indicating the precariousness of any
> identity assumed by the subject on the basis of its token.[50]

According to Rose as well, then, the possession of the Phallus is an illusion occasioned by confusion of the penis with the Phallus, thus producing a hallucination of proprietorship (phallucination). If we were to
recognize, as we need to, our universal castration, then phallocentrism
would not be identical anymore to androcentrism.[51] But the utterance
that the Phallus is not the penis does not interrupt the equation of maleness with having the Phallus. In fact, it shores it up. Such an equation is
always necessarily and paradoxically implied by the very separation/ide-
alization of the Phallus that European culture—including some "Lacan"
seemingly—promotes.[52] It is the transcendent immateriality of the Phallus, and thus its separation from the penis, that constitutes its ability to
project masculinity as the universal—as the Logos—and by doing so
significantly enables male projects of domination, including especially
"the terror of abstract universality" that is Empire.[53] Precisely because
the Phallus is *not* the penis but signifies the penis, any theory of subjectivity that bases itself on the Phallus and castration will always be an instrument in the service of the dominant fiction. The Phallus is not the
penis and neither men nor women have it, but as Rose herself acknowledges, "There seems to be a constant tendency to literalise the terms of
Lacan's account and it is when this happens that the definitions most
easily recognized as reactionary tend to appear."[54] We shall see, however,
why this literalization *must* happen, why indeed it is not a mistake engendered by the errors of those very (presumably gifted or even more)
analysts trained by Lacan *but a necessary* consequence of his use of the
Phallus—and even more, of "castration"; indeed that it reproduces a
necessary tension in Lacan's text also, and not only the tendentious error of epigones.[55] *Psychanalytique discourse, even as it resists this natural-*

izing move, at the same time reifies it, suggesting a psychic association be-tween masculinity and human perfection.

Lacan's definition of the Phallus and its significance amounts to an argument that the one constant of human symbol systems is the Phallus as the signifier from which all other signifiers flow—the seminal signi-fier. It is this movement from the male organ, via a sublation, to the transcendental signifier of language that subtends the writing of male as transcendence in accord with the dominant fiction. As the privileged signifier, the phallus is equivalent, in another way of speaking, to the Lo-gos, the Word, the ideal and abstract origin of all other words. Once again, a key sentence: "The function of the [phallic][56] signifier here touches on its most profound relation: by way of which the Ancients embodied in it both the Νους [*Nous,* sense] and the Λογὸς [*Logos,* reason]."[57] We find here, however, in this Lacanian formula an ambiguity that I shall seek to widen through this text: Is Lacan claiming that the Phallus was discovered by the Ancients, and therefore provides evidence for the time-lessness and ahistoricity of the phallogocentric psyche; or, is Lacan's point that the Ancients produced the Phallus as a historically specific representation?

In either case, the cultural system "embodied" by the Ancients is lit-erally phallogocentric, because the Phallus is not a male organ but an abstract signifier. As Kaja Silverman has summed up the point, "Elevat-ing *[Aufhebung]* the phallus to the level of a signifier does not apparently diminish its virility."[58] Since signifiers are not paired ontologically to their signifieds, there *could* conceivably be a natural language in which this signifying relation had changed. Moreover, at a theoretical level, the argument against any privileged pairing of signifier and signified, even synchronically, is also convincing. But, nevertheless, in ordinary, every-day *parole,* in Lacan's natural language, as in Freud's, as in ours, the sig-nifier "phallus" certainly calls up, refers to, the signified "penis," and then, arguably, the referent, penis. Lacan has seemingly (sometimes) el-evated this ordinary language to the status of an ontological (or, at least psychological) given.

Let me elaborate. Language is a *system* of signifiers, that is, abstract symbols that have meaning insofar as they are distinct from other such symbols. (Male) animals who do not speak have only penises.[59] Humans symbolize and can signify the Phallus. The Phallus is an element in a language of symbols, in a symbolic system, and as such must be abstract. An organ cannot be a signifier.[60] "[The Phallus] is even less the organ, penis or clitoris, which it symbolizes."[61] Signifiers, however, signify only as functions of the system, and if the system changes, so do they. "Green" would mean something quite different if we had no "blue" in our language. Following such a notion (essentially the Saussurean account of language),[62] one would expect that the Phallus as a signifier would be prey to precisely the same plays of difference as any other signifier in a symbolic system, indeed, that there would be languages in which there is no "Phallus" at all. There is no a priori reason to assume that human beings everywhere and everywhen would have settled on the penis as the symbol of completeness and the fulfillment of desire.[63] Lacan, however, refers to this Phallus as "privileged"—one might be tempted to say transcendental—and as the signifier that anchors the whole system, as if to say that while everything else in the system moves, the Phallus remains stationary.

Indeed, every signifying system needs at least one positive term to establish a field of differences. In order to understand this better, let us imagine for a moment a minimal signifying system, a binary one with only two terms—like the signifying systems that make computers work. This system will need, in fact, only one positive term, because the absence of that term will provide the other. You don't need two switches to make a computer work, only one that can be turned on and off. The Phallus is the "on" position, its absence is the "off" position, and this pure system of presence and absence, of the "typographical" "one" and "zero" is what generates symbolic systems in humans. But why precisely should the Phallus play this role?[64]

I suggest that Lacan is himself entrapped (as we all are) by his own culture's language, by the weight of the language's history. Slavoj Žižek writes, "[e]very element of a given ideological field is part of a series of equivalences: its metaphorical surplus, through which it is connected with all other elements, determines retroactively its very identity. . . . But this enchainment is possible only on condition that a certain signifier— the Lacanian 'One'—'quilts' the whole field and, by embodying it, effectuates its identity."[65] The use of "the One" already reveals the Neoplatonic father-land of these ideas. In the language of our western culture, the Phallus has been long (at least since Plotinus and probably much longer) identified with "the One." Lacan is thus not only the "most radical contemporary version of the Enlightenment,"[66] but also the most radical contemporary version of Neoplatonism as well.

The "Phallus" thus functions in two ways in Lacan's system, and it is impossible to keep them apart. On the one hand, the Phallus is the privileged signifier, what allows signification to take place, the minimal plus sign that goes with the minimal minus sign (the absence of the Phallus) that produces signification itself. No one has that Phallus. À la Lacan, we are all castrated, and this "castration" makes no sexual difference. As Lacan has written, "It is in as much as, at the heart of the experience of the unconscious, we are dealing with that organ—determined in the subject by the inadequacy organized in the castration complex."[67] This is the Symbolic Phallus, as opposed to the Imaginary one, but as I will argue, or at any rate, assert, in terms of the political effects of the use of language, this makes no difference.[68] But, at the same time, the Phallus and even "Phallus" are signifiers in another sense. They are elements in a signifying system, a real natural language.[69] In that real natural language, if the plus sign is Phallus, the minus sign is the symbolic (not in the Lacanian sense of symbolic) female organs. The very abstraction of the Phallus as the mark of signification as such is precisely then what gives the female as the signifier of materiality and lack, and from there to a transfer onto the actual realm of penis and vagina [sic!], male and female people, is almost inevitable. Grosz argues: "If the penis assumes the function of the phallus this is because female sexuality is considered a mutilation or castration,"[70] neatly, I would suggest, putting the cart before the horse. I would argue: If wholeness is spoken of in a human language, including the language of therapy, as "the Phallus," then female sexuality will always necessarily be considered a mutilation or castration, and insisting that the penis is not the Phallus will only enhance this phallic potency.

Since the Phallus has so successfully been separated from the penis in western thought for hundreds if not thousands of years, one can easily forget that this separation is itself a mystification. One thus comes to imagine that one can speak of the Phallus without instantiating male privilege.

The insistence on separation of the Phallus and the penis, therefore, which is correctly apprehended as foundational to the Freudian system, not only is no answer to feminist criticism but only demonstrates even further the complicity between the Phallus and male domination, because it is that very abstraction away from the body that has enabled this mastery.[71] The Phallus is not the penis, but it is a disembodied idealization of the penis, a Platonic Idea of the penis, just as Adam, for Philo, is not a man but a Platonic Idea of man. It is this idealization, this sublation (= repudiation of femininity!) of the penis, and not the possession of a physical penis, that is the bedrock of misogyny.

In a sense, what I am doing here is to reverse a generally held position. In Silverman's work, for instance, the thesis is that the Phallus (a real theoretical entity) is not the penis, but historically the dominant fiction (the European myth of gender domination) is founded upon conflating them. Similarly, Jane Gallop argues that the inability to keep Phallus and penis separate is a "symptom of the impossibility, at this moment in our history, to think a masculine that is not phallic, a masculine that can couple with a feminine," and further that "this double-bind combination of necessity and impossibility produces the endless repetition of failed efforts to clearly distinguish Phallus and penis."[72] My argument is the exact opposite. I suggest that, theoretically, the penis is the Phallus, or rather that there is no Phallus at all. Theoretically, the Phallus is the product of the Imaginary of a given cultural formation. Historically, however, the Phallus is not the penis; that is, it is the ideological separation of Phallus from penis, produced in history, but forgotten *as* history, that enables the Phallus to do its work, that founds the dominant fiction.[73]

Historicizing "the Phallus" thus becomes crucial to a political retrieval of the entire psychoanalytic project, that is, a retrieval that is generated by a perspective that enables it to be "theoretically correct" and thus therapeutically useful.[74] Lacan's own text, however, more often seems to be moving in the opposite direction, in the direction of an unchanging and ahistorical (structural) conception of the Phallus:[75]

> The Phallus is the privileged signifier of that mark where the share of the logos is wedded to the advent of desire. One might say that this signifier is chosen as what stands out as most easily seized upon in the real of sexual copulation, and also as the most symbolic in the literal (typographical) sense of the term, since it is the equivalent in that relation of the (logical) copula. One might also say that by virtue of its turgidity, it is the image of the vital flow as it is transmitted in generation.[76]

In reading this passage we detect two themes, the privilege of the Phallus as signifier and the derivation of that privilege from a constant, unchanging, ahistorical function of the penis, its status in the "real of sexual copulation," its turgidity. This passage of Lacan's text assumes and insists implicitly that there could be no other privileged signifier at any time and in any language or culture; the Phallus is naturalized and dehistoricized as the privileged signifier.[77] Lacan's claim, then, following Freud, amounts to an argument that the one constant of human symbol systems is the Phallus as the signifier from which all other signifiers flow—the seminal signifier: "One might also say that by virtue of its turgidity, it is the image of the vital flow as it is transmitted in generation." Lacan, following Freud here, has understood the very task of psychoanalysis as discovering "the Phallus" as a psychic universal, "common to all men,"[78] and consequently reinstating all of its phallocratic charge.

Accordingly, Lacan's text frequently fails as a critique of the phallocentrism indigenous within western thought and threatens (at least) to become an instantiation of it. The abstraction of the Phallus, then, its separation from the penis and concomitant idealization, is that which anchors indeed a whole symbolic system in which male becomes the privileged signifier of the Symbolic itself and female the unsignifying, insignifiant, body, in short the dominant fiction.[79]

The insistence that the Phallus is not part of the male body is, I repeat, what consummates this motive. This is, after all, the same paradox of western culture that renders the male body itself as always already female precisely because it is body. Lacan himself does not escape it, as the entire European tradition of thought has never been able to escape it, because there is no escape.

The Phallus is pretending not to be the penis; this is indeed one of the most potent sources of its strength. It is hardly surprising then that even the most capable and faithful of Lacanians—and sometimes Lacan himself—keep removing the Phallus from linguistic, that is, historical contingency. Thus maleness gets to be the non gender, the universal, while femaleness absorbs all gender, all embodiment, all difference. The Phallus-that-is-not-the-penis is thus foundational for the dominant fiction of European gender ideology, and Lacan seems merely to be reproducing this dominant fiction.

It is here, then, that we find Lacan's sublation (*"Aufhebung"*) that produces the Phallus from the penis as both a synchronic and a diachronic structure, or perhaps, ambiguously one or the other, but this is a crucial ambiguity, as we shall yet see. If the Phallus is unhistoricized, then, in whatever way it is understood—whether the "Phallus" is a presence or an absence,[80] whether we speak of Φ or of $-\varphi$, or of universal, unisex "castration," whether we speak of the Imaginary or the Symbolic phallus—the weight of the language will always inscribe male precedence. As Luce Irigaray has already argued, if psychoanalytic theory sees itself as "whole, absolute, and without any historical foundations," then analysts "become the defenders [willy-nilly] of an *existing order*, the agents or servants of repression and censorship ensuring that this order subsists as though it were the only possible order."[81]

LACAN HISTORICIST

The force of the critique of Lacan disappears, however, if Lacan himself is historicizing, describing the historical condition of his/our culture. Then he would be diagnosing and (implicitly) criticizing the situation of western patriarchy and arguing that its sexual representations, male socialization, child-rearing arrangements, etc. produce the confusion of Phallus with the cause of desire.[82] Then Lacan would be demystifying, precisely bringing to consciousness that which is in the historical unconscious of western culture, unveiling the veiled Phallus. There are textual nodes in which it seems that this is what Lacan is about. Here is a crucial text:

> For the Phallus is a signifier, a signifier whose function, in the intra-subjective economy of the analysis lifts the veil perhaps from the function it performed in the mysteries.[83]

> Car le phallus est un signifiant, un signifiant dont la fonction, dans l'économie intrasubjective de l'analyse, soulève peut-être le voile de celle qu'il tenait dans les mystères.[84]

I would like to suggest that this is what he is saying: The Phallus became the Phallus, that is, became separated from the penis, by being veiled in the Mysteries of the Greco-Roman period, those very same Mysteries in which "there was no male and female," and the maleness of the androgyne became mystified, those same Mysteries, moreover, that both Neoplatonists, Plutarch and Plotinus, appealed to in almost the same way and the same terms that Lacan does.[85] The function of the "Phallus," that is, the function of talk about the Phallus, in the dyadic relation of the psychoanalytic encounter is to lift this veil, to demystify the Phallus and return it, like the genie back into the bottle, to the fleshly penis, the unsignifying penis. Lacan's psychoanalysis, on this account, would be the foundation of a powerful feminist theory and praxis.

No one, according to Lacan, has the Phallus, neither men nor women, and therapy consists of learning this. Had Lacan figured this unveiling as learning that there is no Phallus in the Psyche but only in the language, that is, that "the Phallus" is only a social and historical construct—as the force of his reading of the Mysteries suggests, and as his trenchant delineation of the Oedipus complex as a historically and culturally specific product would ratify[86]—perhaps we would have been less confused by him, and he too would have been less mysterious. It seems unfortunate, then, that Lacan chose to refer to this therapy, this lifting of the veil, as "castration," rather than as recognition that the Phallus is only a misrecognized penis. Unfortunate that in Lacanian language, "castration" is the recognition of universal lack, the lack on which human desire is founded, for at the very moment of demystification, of unveiling, the use of the term "castration" produces precisely another veiling, another hypostasis of the Phallus.[87]

There are, we could say, two "Lacans": There is a Lacan that insists that the Phallus is not the penis and thus facilitates the confusion of the Phallus with the cause of desire endemic to western engendering.[88] There is, however, another that insists that it is an error to separate the Phallus from the penis; the Phallus is a mystification of the penis (one that came into being in a particular historical cultural product, in the Mysteries), and lifting the veil of this mystification, revealing the penis underneath the veil, revealing that the Phallus is only a penis, is the goal of analysis and thus the subversion of the dominant fiction of "the West." It is not "Lacan" the author who is being interrogated here but a set of discursive practices that his texts enact and set in motion. My reading has produced two "Lacans." The "second" Lacan has brilliantly written, "[t]he human being has always to learn from scratch from the Other what he has to do, as man or as woman. I referred to the old woman in the story of Daphnis and Chloe, which shows us that there is an ultimate field, the field of sexual fulfillment, in which, in the last resort, the innocent does not know the way."[89] According to this Lacan, whatever it is that is constant and natural in the human psyche, it is not the lineaments of sexual object choice or of sexual roles. It is the second of these "Lacans," Lacan historicist, who makes possible psychoanalysis as a feminist discourse and diagnosis of the dominant fiction.

SUBDOMINANT FICTIONS

> Scientific storytelling is a consequential political practice. A queer reading of evolution might interrupt the highly consequential scientific discourses of heterosexual manhood.[90]

I am not claiming that we have any resources other than those generated as side-effects and at the margins of hegemonic discourse.[91] The point is not, surely, to claim that we can simply be liberated from the "dominant fiction" and arrive at a feminist utopia. For one thing, the Phallus, as a concept, as a conceptual formation from Philo through Lacan, provides for the possibility of radically non-teleological thinking of the nexus between sex, gender, and desire. It is, after all, this very dualism between Phallus and penis that enables us to drive a conceptual wedge between the physical and the symbolic bodies. For all the problematic that "making Mary male" provokes,[92] it nevertheless enables a de-essentialization of both gender and desire. It enables the phenomenally important distinction between sexual "instinct" and "drive," as that which is "intrinsically bound to representation."[93] For another thing, any other version or fiction or account of sexual difference that we can locate historically seems equally as problematic. Focusing on the homologies between ancient and modern debates about sex and gender will help to clarify this point.

According to one strand of the Lacanian text, the Phallus is absence, a hole in being, and not a presence which has an absence—castration—as its binary opposite. At this level of conceptualization, sexual difference itself has been relegated to the Imaginary, as a product of the Ego, just as for Philo sexual difference is a product of a secondary and inferior formation. Both this version of Lacan and Philo himself can be strikingly compared to one strain of modern feminism, namely the critique of ontologically grounded sexual difference of de Beauvoir and her even more radical epigone, Monique Wittig. The parallels between the mode of thinking gender that we find in these prerabbinic Jewish and early Christian texts and that of the feminist thought of Monique Wittig are stunning. Wittig takes Simone de Beauvoir's notion that "one is not born a woman" to its logical extreme. Like Philo and Paul and the traditions that they represent, she considers sexual intercourse that which produces women. Wittig, realizing this connection, explicitly connects lesbians and nuns: "One might consider that every woman, married or not, has a period of forced sexual service.... Some lesbians and nuns escape."[94] She calls for a "destruction of sex" as the necessary condition for liberation of the class of people called "women."

Butler demonstrates clearly how dependent Wittig's "destruction of sex" is on the very same metaphysics that generated Philo's destruction of sex "in the beginning," and is thus finally also predicated on the same masculinist ideologies of transcendence:

> Hence, Wittig calls for the destruction of "sex" so that women can assume the status of a universal subject.... As a subject who can realize concrete universality through freedom, Wittig's lesbian confirms rather than contests the normative promise of humanist ideals premised on the metaphysics of substance.... Where it seems that Wittig has subscribed to a radical project of lesbian emancipation and enforced a distinction between "lesbian" and "woman," she does this through the defense of the pregendered "person," characterized as freedom. This move not only confirms the presocial status of human freedom, but subscribes to that metaphysics of substance that is responsible for the production and naturalization of the category of sex itself.[95]

According to Butler's incisive analysis, Wittig's position reflects the Philonic/patristic ideology of freedom as pregendered and non-gender as male. Wittig's "lesbian" is another version of the woman of Hellenistic Judaism or early Christianity made male and thus free through celibacy, although to be sure with the enormous difference that sexual pleasure is not denied Wittig's lesbian. Metaphysically speaking, nothing has changed. Thekla and Philo's "virgins" are not women, and Wittig's lesbian is not a woman.[96]

Philo, not surprisingly, also envisions a radical destruction of sex as an ideal. In his *On the Contemplative Life,* Philo describes a Jewish sect, the Therapeutae, living in his time on the shores of Lake Mareotis near Alexandria.[97] It is clear from the tone of his entire depiction of this sect and its practice that he considers it an ideal religious community. The fellowship consisted of celibate men and women who lived in individual cells and spent their lives in prayer and contemplative study of allegorical interpretations of Scripture such as the ones that Philo produced. Once in seven weeks the community came together for a remarkable ritual celebration. Following a simple meal and a discourse, all of the members began to sing hymns together. Initially, however, the men and the women remained separate from each other in two choruses. The extraordinary element is that as the celebration became more ecstatic, the men and the women would join to form one chorus, "the treble of the women blending with the bass of the men." I suggest that this model of an ecstatic joining of the male and the female in a mystical ritual re-creates in social practice the image of the purely spiritual masculo-feminine first human of which Philo speaks in his commentary, indeed, that this ritual of the Therapeutae is a return to the originary Adam.[98] Although, obviously, the singing and dancing are performed by the body, the state of ecstasy (as its etymology implies) involves a symbolical and psychological condition of being disembodied and thus similar to the primal androgyne. This sect, very closely related to the Mysteries of which Lacan speaks, thus provides a synecdoche, a miniature and minor example of the discourse that was a historical source or point of origin for the Phallus.

The society and religious culture depicted by Philo *does* permit parity between men and women and religious, cultural creativity for women as for men as long as women renounce what makes them specifically female.[99] Autonomy and creativity in the spiritual sphere are predicated on renunciation of both sexuality and maternity.[100]

In sharp contrast to Philo's interpretation of the ratio between Genesis 1 and 2 stands the interpretation of another group of ancient Jews, the Rabbis (the authorities of Palestinian and Babylonian Judaism of late antiquity). The dominant rabbinic interpretation insisted on the first male-and-female human as a physical hermaphrodite. It resists the abstraction of the male body and the veiling of the penis that produces the Phallus, and forms, accordingly, a subdominant fiction within the cultural space of the dominant fiction. We will see, however, that this subdominant fiction is no less problematic in the end than is the dominant.

According to the midrashic interpretation of the early Rabbis, the primordial Adam was a dual-sexed creature in one body. The story in the second chapter of Genesis is the story of the splitting off of the two equal halves of an originary body:

> And God said let us make a human etc.... R. Samuel the son of Naḥman said: When the Holiness (Be it blessed) created the first human, He made it two-faced, then He sawed it and made a back for this one and a back for that one. They objected to him: but it says, "He took one of his ribs (ṣelaʿ)." He answered [it means], "one of his sides," similarly to that which is written, "And the side (ṣelaʿ) of the tabernacle" [Exodus 26:20].[101]

The first Adam, the one of whom it is said that "male and female He created them," had genitals of both sexes, and the act of creation described in Genesis 2 merely separated out the two sexes from each other and reconstructed them into two human bodies.[102] Far from gender (and woman) being a secondary creation, we have in the second creation of humanity an Aristophanic separation of an androgynous pair of joined twins, physically sexed from the very beginning. In the rabbinic culture represented by this text and its parallels, the human race is thus marked from the very beginning by corporeality, difference, and heterogeneity. For these Rabbis, the body and its sexual difference belongs to the original created (and not fallen) state of humanity. As is well known, however, together with the body and sexual difference, rabbinic culture seems to inscribe and enforce an inescapable social structure of male domination and nearly total female constriction. The female is not wiped out, rendered insignificant in absorption into a masculine or universal male. The male is not written as spirit (the Phallus) nor the female as body. The female in the rabbinic formation has indeed been "restored to her place and identity"—but with a vengeance! Women, in that formation, can never escape their anatomically destined and single role.

Rabbinic discourse on sex/gender refuses this narrative of one-ness fallen into two-ness, insisting on a two-ness of humanity in the flesh from the very beginning, from the conception by God, as it were. Two sexes exist from the beginning and sexual joining does also. Heteronormativity is thus ontologically grounded within the rabbinic tradition.

In their refusal to read sexual difference as secondary and fallen, the Rabbis anticipate, I suggest, the same refusal on the part of the feminist thinker who typifies the tradition in opposition to the (masculinist) metaphysics of substance, Luce Irigaray. "The human species is divided into *two genders [sic]* which ensure its production and reproduction. To wish to get rid of sexual difference is to call for a genocide more radical than any form of destruction there has even been in History."[103] What does Irigaray mean by this surprising statement? Can she really mean that the suppression of sexual difference through the achievement of even a masculine-neutral androgyny will lead to an end to physical reproduction? Even disaggregated bodies can get pregnant, even the body of the radical constructivist theorist who claims that "she" "has" no vagina could presumably give birth. The radical decentering of desires/pleasures that Wittig calls for does not preclude desires and pleasures that would result in human births in sufficient numbers to forestall genocide. This, then, can't be what Irigaray means. I suggest, therefore, that the "genocide" to which Irigaray refers is not the end of humanity, but the end of women, a gynecocide via the disappearance of sexual difference into the "masculine-neutral" that would be the ultimate triumph of the masculinist economy, the fulfillment of a masculinist dream of a world without women, and thus the ultimate triumph of the Phallus.

Goux reads this apocalyptic formulation as effectively providing a near mythic statement of Irigaray's philosophy of gender that he, with his usual clarity, reduces to two strong statements of conviction:

1. To overthrow patriarchal and phallocentric power does not mean denying the difference between the sexes but living the relation between them differently.
2. To assert the difference between the sexes is *not* at all the same thing as positing an essential femininity (or masculinity)....It is sexuation that is "essential," not the content of dogmas fixing once and for all, in an exhaustive and closed definition, what for eternity belongs to the masculine and what belongs to the feminine.[104]

Another way of saying this would be that while there is no fixed essential nature to either woman or man (indeed, there is no woman per se, no man per se), there are material differences between being-a-man and being-a-woman which are productive of different (but not fixed or essen-

tial) subjectivities and relations to language and sexuality: "Woman's being is acquired, won, determined, invented, produced, created. Not by
totally denying its biological preconditions (which would be both absurd
and dangerous—not to say unjustified in its complicity with an ancient
patriarchal ideology that has devalued in advance this natural substra-
tum), but through an elaboration of the sexuate."[105] Different attitudes
of the body in sexual intercourse (one enclosing, the other being enclosed),
the capacity to menstruate, gestate, and lactate, all of these form a sort of
material base for a subjectivity that is different from that of men *but do
not prescript of what that subjectivity will consist or how it will be lived.* As a
final way of conceptualizing this, I would propose the following formulation: There is nothing in the being of a male or female body that pre-
scribes a particular way of conceiving of the world, a particular relation
to language, but the use of the male genital (the sex that is *one*—already
a heavily ideologized construct in its eclipse of the testicles) as primary
symbol of language and thought has produced, of course, the masculinist economy of the same. As Irigaray herself has put it, she invokes not
anatomy (as destiny) but the "morphology of the female sex"[106] as organizing metaphor. Imagining a symbolic organized around female genitals ("this sex which is not One") could lead to a different subjectivity
and thus to a different politics of desire and of the social organization of
the life of sexual difference (including "love").[107] It should be clear by
now—indeed, I imagine that it is commonplace—that among the meanings of Irigaray's "One" is the Neoplatonic One. Irigaray's project of the
installation of a female alternative to the Phallus and the Logos has been
read as a classically Derridean move. By reversing the polarity of the
valued and devalued terms of a binary opposition, the very terms of that
opposition are set into oscillation and destabilized. In other words,
Irigaray's insistence on the irreducibility of sexual difference while at
the same time reimagining a symbolic (not an imaginary) of fluids, lips,
and concrete language to displace the symbolic of the column, the unit,
the abstract and transcendent phallogos is not an essentialism but a deconstruction.[108] Rabbinic Judaism, it can plausibly be claimed, operates
without the notions of Logos and Phallus that inscribe the male genital
as the anchor of the symbolic system. Thus Goux's Beauvoirian/Witti-
gian ultramodern masculine neutral that is resisted by an Irigarayan
postmodern is revealed as the logic of an ancient Philonic-Christian
drive for the Universal that is resisted by rabbinic Judaism.

Rabbinic Judaism did, however, implacably and oppressively prescript women's roles even as it avoided and resisted the essentialist dualism that in the West almost always constructed the spirit as masculine (even in a woman) the body as feminine (even in a man).[109] Owing to its iron-clad insistence on universal marriage (for men and for women), it differentiated gender roles more sharply certainly than Christianity, perhaps even than many cultures have done. When compared with much of historical Christianity we find that within historical Judaism women have been much more powerfully constrained to occupy one and only one position entirely, namely that of wife and mother.[110] Even if any theory of transcendence was already appropriated by the male, there was somehow in the Christian world an opportunity for women to achieve it.[111] Not so in Judaism. There are virtually no Jewish equivalents of Thekla, Hildegard, Claire, or even Heloise. While the theory of dualism was lacking, the practice nevertheless confined women exclusively within bodily realms, while men were afforded the realms of the body (sexuality, parentage), the intellect (study of Torah), and the spiritual (full religious lives). There was no pregendered, postgendered, androgynous, or even male space for a woman to escape to. A story like the famous one of Yentl (by Bashevis Singer and Streisand) who dressed as a boy in order to study is exemplary of the frustrations and pain felt by many women occupying this society as late as the nineteenth century.[112] Women were trapped within the category of gender precisely because it was understood as ontologically primary, as definitional for what it is to be a human being.

The distinction between the rabbinic and a typical (if extreme) Christian discourse as the signs of two different configurations of androcentrism can be delineated sharply in the contrast between the Rabbis and Tertullian on clothing and cosmetics.[113] In Tertullian, as in Jerome and many others in the patristic tradition, "Woman" is identified with all that is artificial and merely decorative and thus counter to the purpose of God:[114]

That which He Himself has not produced is not pleasing to God, unless He was unable to order sheep to be born with purple and sky-blue fleeces! If He was able, then plainly He was unwilling: what God willed not, of course, ought not to be fashioned. Those things, then, are not the best by nature which are not from God, the Author of nature. Thus they are understood

to be from the devil, from the corrupter of nature: for there is
no other whose they can be, if they are not God's; because what
are not God's must necessarily be His rival's.[115]

Familiar by now is the association of women's decorations with the devil.
For Tertullian, indeed, the evil of women's adornment lies precisely in
that it is inappropriate to the "ignominy of the first sin," that is for her
who is after all "the devil's gateway."[116] This virulent antifeminism paradoxically gives rise to a discourse of female liberation. Thus Tertullian
states, "Nay, rather banish quite away from your free head all this slavery
of ornamentation." Similarly Clement of Alexandria refers to jewelry as
"fetters and chains."[117] Indeed, some of the Fathers go further and speak
of the unadorned female as the Image of God which is spoiled by artificial additions. For all of these writers, pregnancy and lactation are signs
of female bondage also, and only renunciation of sexuality can free women
from these chains: "At the first sound of the angels trumpet, the widows
will leap forth lightly, easily able to endure any distress or persecution
with none of the heaving baggage of marriage in their wombs or at their
breasts."[118] The discourse of disparagement of female sexuality can accordingly become a discourse of female liberation,[119] as in general in
early (and later) Christianity sexual renunciation is at least as often imagined as the road to freedom as it is a reaction of contempt for the body.[120]
Once again, for these early Christian writers, as not for the Rabbis, the
human person can be separated from "his" gender via celibacy.

In contrast to this categorical denunciation of feminine adornment,
that is, female sexuality, in the rabbinic culture, ornamentation, attractive
dress, and cosmetics are considered entirely appropriate to the woman
in her ordained role of sexual partner. Thus a bride even in mourning is
permitted/required to use makeup, for otherwise she might become unattractive to her husband. The language of the Hebrew text hides this
productive ambiguity by using the participle, which would be roughly
translated into English as a present tense, "Mourning women *put on*
makeup, in order not to become repulsive to their husbands." That
Hebrew participle incorporates a "permission" that constitutes a fiat. The
valorization of the female body and female sexuality is thus precisely the
vehicle for the production of "forced sexual service." Women are similarly permitted/required also to put on makeup on holidays, although
painting and drawing are forbidden, because the use of cosmetics is

considered a pleasure for them and not work (Babylonian Talmud *Moed Katan* 9b). In the view of Rabbi Akiva, even a menstruant may/must wear her makeup and jewelry in order that she not become unattractive to her husband. That is to say, her sexuality and the external signs of her sexual allure are not suppressed even when menstruating. This is a discourse that in the guise of a valorization of the female body and of female sexuality subordinates women almost entirely to the needs of men.

A rather concise example of how the rabbinic valorization of sexual difference oppresses women can be found, not surprisingly, in their discourse on desire and speech.[121] Discursive practices related to female desire that appear in Talmud and Midrash constitute a structure that functions as an equivalent to the "conjugal right" of European legal discourse in terms of the ordering of sexual relations between the genders. The hegemonic rabbinic discourse provides for male sex-right paradoxically through a mystifying construction of women as being needy for sex and of men as being primarily service providers to their wives. The married man was considered by talmudic law under a legal-contractual obligation to sleep with his wife regularly for her pleasure and benefit. This obligation was derived by the Rabbis from the verse of the Torah that, speaking of the taking of a second wife, says that he must not "reduce the flesh, covering, or seasons" [Exodus 21:10] of the first wife. This philologically puzzling list was variously interpreted in the midrash, but the hegemonic opinion is that "flesh" means food, "covering" refers to clothing, and "seasons" to regularity of sexual intercourse. This obligation was also made contractual in the standard rabbinically approved marriage contract, which reads, "I will feed you, clothe you, and have intercourse with you, in accordance with the customs of Jewish husbands." In this context, the Mishna discusses the exact definition of "regularity," that is, what constitutes fulfillment of the husband's sexual debt to his wife.

The Mishna reads:

> If one takes a vow not to sleep with his wife; Bet Shammai say two weeks, and Bet Hillel one week.[122] The students may go away from their homes for study of Torah without permission for thirty days and laborers for one week. The "season" [required frequency of intercourse] which is mentioned in the Torah: for the *ṭayyalin*,[123] it is every day; for laborers twice a week; for donkey drivers, once a week; for camel drivers once in thirty days;

for sailors once in six months; these are the words of Rabbi Eliezer. (Ketubboth 61b)

What is arresting about this discourse is the total mystification that it enacts of male sexual desire and male sexual need. It thus masks almost entirely its own oppressiveness of women, and the way that men are securing their own sexual needs here.[124]

The Babylonian Talmud on Eruvin 100b includes the following discussion:

Rami bar Ḥama said in the name of Rav Assi: a man may not force his wife to have sex with him.[125]

Rabbi Shmuel the son of Naḥmani said in the name of Rabbi Yoḥanan: Any woman who requests sex from her husband will have children such as were not seen even in the generation of Moses.[126]

It is not accidental that the prohibition on wife-rape and the endorsement of the open expression of female desire are juxtaposed so closely in the Talmud, because the second fulfills a cultural function rendered unfulfilled by the prohibition on wife-rape that the first encodes so unambiguously, namely the securing of male access to female bodies. In other words, the furnishing of a strong religious, cultural incentive (the provision of children of a certain preferred type) for women to desire sex, and, according to this view, to express their desire, obviates the need for *patria potestas*. This argument is supported by the continuation of the text that proposes, in contradistinction to the cited view of Rabbi Yoḥanan, that it was the curse of Eve to desire her husband when he is about to go on a journey but to express her desire only through signs of various types and not to openly request sex. This is, moreover, to the best of my knowledge, the only interpretation of the verse "To your husband will be your desire, and he will rule over you" (Genesis 3:16) within classical rabbinic texts. A verse that is taken in other, non-rabbinic, Jewish traditions (and much Christian writing as well) to endorse wife-rape is understood by the Rabbis to enjoin on husbands a particular "attentiveness" to their wives' sexual needs, as a sort of noblesse oblige. Thus although the wife has the right in principle to refuse sex on any occasion, her consent can be understood through silence and necessarily ambiguous signs.[127]

As feminists (including especially for the Jewish context, Laura Levitt) have pointed out, any consent through silence works seriously to reduce its significance as real power and autonomy for women. Moreover, the Talmud has already informed the husband that under certain circumstances, for instance when he is about to depart for a journey, that his wife needs him to have sex with her. In other words, through the construction of sexuality as a form of the husband taking care of the wife's needs and through the construction of her needs as both compelling and in part inexpressible, male sex-right, forced sexual service for women, is achieved absolutely and without *sanctioned* violence. If, on the one hand, rabbinic legal discourse never construed marriage as an abandonment on the part of the wife of her right to say "no," on the other, all women, without exception, were expected to be wives.

Difference, the very opposition to the universal same, it seems, potentially (perhaps always) portends enormous dangers for women as well, the dangers, precisely, of essentialism,[128] while universalism seems to threaten an end to woman entirely.

The modern dilemmas of feminist discourse on the Phallus seem thus to closely reproduce the terms of a very ancient dilemma of our culture with respect to gender, a dilemma that I have figured as a drama of the conflict of fictions, one dominant, one subdominant. Insistence on the value and ontological primacy of sexual dimorphism, with its recognition of both male and female desire, of the value of the female body in reproduction, indeed of reproduction itself, seems fated always to imprison women within a "biological" role, while transcendence, liberation of the female, seems always to be predicated on a denigration of the body and the achievement of a male-modeled androgyny, a masculine-neutral, the Phallus. The former seems as implacable as the latter, and yet our project must be to find a way past the impossible terms of this Hobson's choice.

NOTES

I wish to thank Gil Anidjar, Chris Bracken, Jonathan Boyarin, Sergei Dogopolsky, Charlotte Fonrobert, Galit Hasan-Rokem, Kenneth Reinhard, and Ruth Stein for their generous critiques of an earlier version of this paper. I am grateful to Virginia Burrus beyond words for many exciting and fertile conversations during which the ideas herein delivered were conceived. She also read several versions of this text and helped me, once again, to realize that historicism is not historiography. Shuli Barzilai has suffered with me through several revisions of this text with grace and patience, and to great avail. An extraordinarily generous and highly critical reading by Judith Butler of what I had thought a "final" version of this text resulted in a complete revision. None of these friends are responsible for my opinions or especially my errors. The paper is a very much expanded version of an argument presented in condensed form as Daniel Boyarin, "Gender," in *Critical Terms for the Study of Religion*, ed. Mark C. Taylor (Chicago, 1998), 117–35.

1. It may have once been thought that such a notion was a virtual universal, as was posed by Sherry B. Ortner, "Is Female to Male as Nature is to Culture?" in *Women, Culture & Society*, ed. Michelle Zimbalist Rosaldo and Louise Lamphere (Stanford, CA, 1974), 67–87, but that is hardly the case any more. One of the offices of my present project is to join to the chorus of those who see historical specificity in this structure, where once a certain inevitability was perceived. The possibility of perceiving such specificity is the sign that the ideology of the Phallus is passing, i.e., that "the need for whatever already exists has partially exhausted itself."

2. Judith Butler, *Gender Trouble: Feminism and the Subversion of Identity*, Thinking Gender (London, 1990), 12.

3. My own translation from the Hebrew.

4. Philo, "Allegorical Interpretation of Genesis II," paragraph 4, trans. F. H. Colson and G. H. Whitaker, *Philo in Ten Volumes*, vol. 1, Loeb Classical Library (Cambridge, MA, 1929), 227.

5. Philo himself is almost certainly on the nearly accidental remnant of what must have been a much wider tendency of thought, a form of thought that we know of as Middle Platonism: Thomas H. Tobin, S.J., *The Creation of Man: Philo and the History of Interpretation*, The Catholic Biblical Quarterly Monograph Series 14 (Washington, DC, 1983); John Dillon, *The Middle Platonists: 80 B.C. to A.D. 220* (Ithaca, NY, 1977); David Winston, *Logos and Mystical Theology in Philo of Alexandria* (Cincinnati, OH, 1985).

6. Daniel Boyarin, "Paul and the Genealogy of Gender," *Representations* no. 41 (Winter 1993): 1–33.

7. Dorothy Sly, *Philo's Perception of Women*, Brown Judaica Series (Atlanta, 1990), 71–90.

8. Elizabeth A. Castelli, "'I Will Make Mary Male': Pieties of the Body and Gender Transformation of Christian Women in Late Antiquity," in *Body Guards: The Cultural Politics of Gender Ambiguity*, ed. Julia Epstein and Kristina Straub (New York, 1991), 33.

9. To be sure, there are representations in late antique Christianity of males "becoming female" as well. See Virginia Burrus, "The Male Ascetic in Female Space: Alienated Strategies of Self-Definition in the Writings of Sulpicius Severus" (paper presented at SBL/AAR [1992]), and Verna E. F. Harrison, "A Gender Reversal in Gregory of Nyssa's First Homily on the Song of Songs," *Studia Patristica* 27 (1993): 34–38.

10. Virginia Burrus, *Chastity as Autonomy: Women in the Stories of the Apocryphal Acts*, Studies in Women and Religion (New York, 1987).

11. The *"sic"* is in the translation I am citing.

12. J. K. Elliott, ed., *The Apocryphal New Testament: A Collection of Apocryphal Christian Literature in an English Translation Based on M. R. James* (Oxford, 1993), 257 (emphasis added).

13. Maud Gleason, "The Semiotics of Gender," in *Before Sexuality: The Construction of Erotic Experience in the Ancient Greek World*, ed. David M. Halperin, John Winkler, and Froma Zeitlin (Princeton, NJ, 1990), 391.

14. Elizabeth A. Clark, "Ascetic Renunciation and Feminine Advancement: A Paradox of Late Ancient Christianity," in *Ascetic Piety and Women's Faith: Essays in Late Ancient Christianity* (New York, 1986), 175–208. I am inclined to argue that this version of gender is already adumbrated in Plato's *Symposium* itself, i.e., that Diotima *was* indeed a woman, and the whole point of the argument is that given Plato's reconfiguration of sexuality, women could also be men. The Christian paradox then would go back to Plato himself. See now also Virginia Burrus, *Begotten, Not Made: Conceiving Manhood in Late Antiquity*, Figurae (Stanford, CA, 2000), but this is an argument for another day.

15. Clement of Alexandria, "The Instructor," ed. Alexander Roberts and James Donaldson, in *The Fathers of the Second Century*, The Ante-Nicene Fathers II (Grand Rapids, MI, 1989), 20.

16. Clement of Alexandria, "The Stromata, or Miscellanies," ed. Alexander Roberts and James Donaldson, *Fathers of the Second Century*, 100.

17. Jerome, *Commentary on the Letter to the Ephesians*, Patrologia cursus completus, series latina (hereafter *PL*), ed. J.-P. Migne (Paris, 1841–66), 26:533; translation from Vern Bullough, "Medieval Medical and Scientific Views of Women," *Viator* 4 (1973): 499. For Jerome on gender, see esp. Elizabeth A. Clark, *Jerome, Chrysostom, and Friends: Essays and Translations*, Studies in Women and Religion 2 (New York, 1979).

18. Ambrose, "Exposition of the Gospel of Luke," in *PL* 15:1844. See also Bullough, "Medieval Medical and Scientific Views of Women," 499, who provides the translation.

19. Wayne A. Meeks, "The Image of the Androgyne: Some Uses of a Symbol in Earliest Christianity," *Journal of the History of Religions* 13, no. 1 (1973): 165–208; Dennis Ronald Macdonald, "Corinthian Veils and Gnostic Androgynes," in *Images of the Feminine in Gnosticism*, ed. Karen L. King (Philadelphia, 1988), 276–92.

20. Cf. Goux himself in another context: "Far from belonging to the order of symptoms or deliriums, far from translating a psychic disorder, the myth is a form of knowledge about deliriums and symptoms" (Jean-Joseph Goux, *Oedipus Philosopher*, trans. Catherine Porter, Meridian: Crossing Aesthetics [Stanford, CA, 1993], 22). In short, I am claiming here that Christianity is "on the side of the clinician, not the patient."

21. Jean-Joseph Goux, "Luce Irigaray Versus the Utopia of the Neutral Sex," in *Engaging with Irigaray: Feminist Philosophy and Modern European Thought*, ed. Carolyn Burke, Naomi Schor, and Margaret Whitford, Gender and Culture (New York, 1994), 178. John Whittaker has observed that "in ancient Greek, and in particular in the Greek of Plutarch's period, the transition back and forth from neuter to masculine is easily achieved. And indeed it would be not exaggeration to regard this grammatical phenomenon as one of the most important components in the theologies of the Roman empire" ("Plutarch, Platonism and Christianity," in *Neoplatonism and Early Christian Thought: Essays in Honour of A. H. Armstrong*, ed. H. J. Blumenthal and R. A. Markus [London, 1981], 54), and then,

specifically, "And as one would expect, God is *one* masculine when considered as a person, but *one* neuter—in fact *the One*—when considered as a metaphysical principle" (ibid., 56 [emphases original]).

22. Jonathan Z. Smith, *Drudgery Divine: On the Comparison of Early Christianities and the Religions of Late Antiquity,* Chicago Studies in the History of Judaism (Chicago, 1990).

23. Jean-Joseph Goux, "The Phallus: Masculine Identity and the 'Exchange of Women,'" trans. Maria Amuchastegui, Caroline Benforado, Amy Hendrix, and Eleanor Kaufman, *Differences* 4, no. 1 (Spring 1992): 45.

24. Burrus, *Begotten.* See also her "Reading Agnes: The Rhetoric of Gender in Ambrose and Prudentius," *Journal of Early Christian Studies* 3, no. 1 (Spring 1995): 25–46, and esp. "'Equipped for Victory': Ambrose and the Gendering of Orthodoxy," *Journal of Early Christian Studies* 4, no. 4 (Winter 1996): 461–75.

25. "The figure of Plotinus, greatest of Platonists in Antiquity, constitutes a new source, a beginning of new lines of development within Platonism itself, and in its interaction with Christianity": H. J. Blumenthal and R. A. Markus, "Preface," in *Neoplatonism and Early Christian Thought,* ed. Blumenthal and Markus, ix.

26. Goux, "The Phallus," 46.

27. Goux, "The Phallus," 47, quoting Plotinus, *Enneads,* trans. A. H. Armstrong, Loeb Classical Library 287 (Cambridge, MA, 1987), vol. 5.

28. For a very useful collection of studies documenting this influence in its various forms, see Blumenthal and Markus, eds., *Neoplatonism and Early Christian Thought.*

29. Plutarch, "Platonic Questions," in *Moralia XIII,* trans. Harold Cherniss (Cambridge, MA, 1976), 29.

30. Whittaker, "Plutarch, Platonism and Christianity," 52. For Plutarch's very important influence on what was to become orthodox Christianity, see H. Dörrie, "*Formula Analogiae:* An Exploration of a Theme in Hellenistic and Imperial Platonism," in *Neoplatonism and Early Christian Thought,* ed. Blumenthal and Markus, 49. "In particular many of Plutarch's conceptions lie close to, and have in fact exercised influence upon, Christian Platonism, a fact which was noted at an early date by Christians themselves and helps in part to explain the popularity of Plutarch's works": Whittaker, "Plutarch, Platonism and Christianity," 61. See also Hans Dieter Betz, *Plutarch's Theological Writings and Early Christian Literature* (Leiden, 1975).

31. Plutarch, *Moralia X,* trans. Harold North Fowler (Cambridge, MA, 1936), 10:153 = *Moralia* 797F. See also Goux, "The Phallus," 49.

32. The word "phallic" is present in the version of the text printed in Lacan (*Écrits: A Selection,* trans. Alan Sheridan [London, 1977], 291) but absent in the Mitchell-Rose text (see next note).

33. Jacques Lacan, "The Meaning of the Phallus," in *Feminine Sexuality: Jacques Lacan and the École Freudienne,* ed. Juliet Mitchell, ed. and trans. Jacqueline Rose (New York, 1985), 85.

34. Goux, "The Phallus," 46–49.

35. Kaja Silverman, *Male Subjectivity at the Margins* (New York, 1992).

36. Silverman, *Subjectivity,* 61.

37. That is to say, that it forms one very dominant, if not to say hegemonic, strain within the culture of Europe, beginning, at least, in the crucial fifth-century Athens, B.C., the so-called Greek miracle.

38. Genevieve Lloyd, *The Man of Reason: "Male" and "Female" in Western Philosophy*, 2nd ed. (Minneapolis, 1993), 3.

39. Silverman, *Subjectivity*, 55.

40. Silverman, *Subjectivity*, 62.

41. Ibid.

42. Silverman, *Subjectivity*, 192.

43. Silverman, *Subjectivity*, 47.

44. Once more, the advantages of this term are palpable in my opinion. By referring to rabbinic Jewish culture here as the "subdominant fiction," I immediately disarm any reading of my work—finally, after much internal and external struggle—that would interpret the presentation of rabbinic gender "theory" as more "true" or less mystified than that of the dominant fiction. Also, by using the term subdominant fiction, as I do here, I clearly indicate that rabbinic Jewish culture is not separate from the cultures of which it is a part but forms a complexly related subculture, at the same time avoiding as well the romanticism and claims for privilege that a term like subaltern (which I have used previously) would levy. Finally, the relation of the term subdominant fiction to the primary term from which it is derived allows as well for that culture to be riven by conflict, local variation and shift, and resistance, as well as resistant individual subjects within itself.

45. "From the second to the fourth centuries, we can follow the birth, out of the traditional faith of Israel, of not one but at least two religions. Rabbinic Judaism, which emerged at Yavneh before the end of the first century, grew into a full-fledged religion with the development of Talmudic culture, during the same centuries in which Christianity developed into a new religion with a structure and an identity that were quite different from those of its genitor": Guy Stroumsa, "From Anti-Judaism to Antisemitism in Early Christianity?" in *Contra Iudaeos: Ancient and Medieval Polemics between Christians and Jews*, ed. Ora Limor and Guy G. Stroumsa, Texts and Studies in Medieval and Early Modern Judaism 10 (Tübingen, 1996), 10. In *Border Lines: "Heresy" and the Emergence of Christianity and Judaism*, Contraversions: Jews and Other Differences (Stanford, CA, 2004), I am pursuing some of the textual traces of this double-birth.

46. Lacan, "Meaning," 79.

47. Elizabeth Grosz, *Jacques Lacan: A Feminist Introduction* (New York, 1990), 116.

48. *Phi* is the algebraic symbol for the Phallus.

49. Jacques Lacan, *The Four Fundamental Concepts of Psychoanalysis*, ed. Jacques-Alain Miller, trans. Alan Sheridan (Harmondsworth, 1979), 88–89.

50. Jacqueline Rose, "Introduction II," in *Feminine Sexuality*, ed. Mitchell and Rose, 40.

51. Jane Gallop, "Phallus/Penis: Same Difference," in *Thinking Through the Body*, ed. Jane Gallop (New York, 1988), 126; Elizabeth Abel, "Race, Class, and Psychoanalysis?: Opening Questions," in *Conflicts in Feminism*, ed. Marianne Hirsch and Evelyn Fox Keller (New York, 1990), 184–204.

52. Cf. an analogous point in Tania Modleski, *Feminism Without Women: Culture and Criticism in a "Postfeminist" Age* (New York, 1991), 95. By placing "Lacan" in quotation marks here, I hope to be indicating clearly that it is not the author (who?, what?) Lacan, that is in question but certain texts that are circulated with his name on them as author, not even the entire corpus of such texts but texts that have power nevertheless. One of my strategies in this text is going to be a stipulation that a persistent source of "misunderstanding" (scare quotes) of "Lacan" is the product of an unthematized fissure in his use of terminology, such as "the Phallus." See also Judith Butler, "The Lesbian Phallus and the Morphological Imaginary," *Differences* 4, no. 1 (Spring 1992): 147–48.

53. Jean-Joseph Goux, *Symbolic Economies: After Marx and Freud*, trans. Jennifer Curtis Cage (Ithaca, NY, 1990), 207, and see his fascinating explication there of the custom of eating "pearl salad" in the later Roman Empire.

54. Rose, "Introduction II," 45.

55. Lacan wrote ambiguously: "It is very difficult for us to imagine that the whole of this psychology isn't eternal" (*The Ego in Freud's Theory and the Technique of Psychoanalysis, 1954–55*, in *The Seminar of Jacques Lacan: Book II*, ed. Sylvana Tomaselli, notes by John Forrester [New York, 1988], 6), and see Dylan Evans, "Historicism and Lacanian Theory," *Radical Philosophy* 79 (Sept./Oct. 1996): 40, n. 17, where it is made clear that Lacan "is criticizing the tendency of some of his followers to read his own writings ahistorically," but, also, I think, pointing to his own difficulty in avoiding such readings of himself by himself. I am suggesting that Lacan's text is already and necessarily divided against itself. This is not a critique of Lacan but a restatement of the impossibility, as Spivak has put it, of "saying an 'impossible "no" to a structure, which one critiques, yet inhabits intimately'" (quoted in Gyan Prakash, "Postcolonial Criticism and Indian Historiography," *Social Text* 31/32 (1992): 8–19 on 11).

56. See above, note 32.

57. Lacan, "Meaning," 85.

58. Kaja Silverman, "The Lacanian Phallus," *Differences* 4, no. 1 (Spring 1992): 89. Irigaray's joke is even subtler: "If the earth turned and more especially turned upon herself, the erection of the subject might thereby be disconcerted and risk losing its elevation and penetration" (*Speculum of the Other Woman*, trans. Gillian C. Gill [Ithaca, NY, 1985], 133). I think that there are important ways in which my argument in this paper parallels that of Silverman's although with some significant differences of emphasis.

59. Similarly: "The father comes into being not by sowing his seeds, but with the logos: for only humans have a father, though animals are often begotten like humans. A father is a figure that, within the strategies of the logos, acquires a set of meanings and functions—source of the son's legitimacy, provider of livelihood and cares, holder of authority. Thus the father is a fountainhead of goods, an inspiration for the moral life of the son. In a word, he may be equated to a sort of transcendental signified" (Pietro Pucci, *Oedipus and the Fabrication of the Father: "Oedipus Tyrannus" in Modern Criticism and Philosophy* [Baltimore, MD, 1992], 3).

60. Malcolm Bowie, *Lacan* (Cambridge, 1991), 123.

61. Lacan, "Meaning," 79.

62. See Joan Copjec, "Sex and the Euthanasia of Reason," in *Supposing the Subject*, ed. Joan Copjec, S 1 (London, 1994), 20, for an important, concise critique of Saussure.

63. Bruce Fink, *The Lacanian Subject: Between Language and Jouissance* (Princeton, NJ, 1995), 102.

64. Another way of saying this would be to grant that any signifying system or signifying practice needs some still "quilting point," in Lacan's evocative term, but why on earth should it be the Phallus? Some Lacanians go so far as to say that whatever it is—God, the class struggle—it is always the Phallus. See Slavoj Žižek, *The Sublime Object of Ideology*, Phronesis (London, 1989), who, following page after page of resistance, finally collapses and refers to the "quilting point" as "this 'phallic', erected Guarantee of Meaning": 100. See also Fink, *The Lacanian Subject*, 74, who nominates the "name-of-the-Father" as performing this role.

65. Žižek, *Sublime Object*, 88.

66. Žižek, *Sublime Object*, 7.

67. Lacan, *Four Fundamental Concepts*, 102.

68. Jacques Lacan, "The Subversion of the Subject and the Dialectic of Desire in the Freudian Unconscious," in *Écrits*, trans. Sheridan, 319–20. See also Silverman, "The Lacanian Phallus," 97: "There is a good deal of slippage in Lacan not only between the phallus and the penis, but between the phallus in its symbolic capacity, and the phallus in its imaginary capacity." But, in contrast to most commentators, I am arguing that the slippage is what saves the phenomenon!

69. Gallop, "Phallus/Penis," 128.

70. Grosz, *Jacques Lacan*, 117.

71. Wendy Brown, *Manhood and Politics* (Totowa, NJ, 1988).

72. Gallop, "Phallus/Penis," 127.

73. For a similar perspective on Freud's account of women's sexual development and socialization, see Irigaray, *Speculum*, 49. There is another important corpus of Lacan that needs to be read in this context but for strategic reasons I am leaving for a future text, namely the XX Seminar, entitled *Encore*, on female sexuality.

74. I am using "theoretically correct" in the sense that the editors of the new Lacanian annual *SIC* use it.

75. Of course, we need to reckon with the historicity of the development over time of Lacan's own thoughts as well. Below, I shall be presenting an argument for a counter-strand *within* Lacan, a vitally important historicist motif.

76. Lacan, "Meaning," 82.

77. By referring to "the real" here, Lacan is implicitly associating the Phallus with the *objet a* (I am purposely anachronizing here with respect to the Lacanian corpus), which is a "piece" of the Real!

78. "The first piece of work that it fell to psychoanalysis to perform was the discovery of the instincts that are common to all men living today—and not only to those living today but to those of ancient and prehistoric times. *It called for no great effort, therefore, for psychoanalysis to ignore the differences that arise among the inhabitants of the earth owing to the multiplicity of races, languages, and countries*" (Sigmund Freud, "Dr. Ernest Jones (on His

50th Birthday) (1929)," in *The Standard Edition of the Complete Psychological Works of Sigmund Freud*, ed. and trans. James Strachey and Anna Freud, trans. Alix Strachey and James Strachey, vol. 18 [London, 1955], 249–50, my emphasis).

79. In my work, I distinguish between "symbolic" as used in cultural studies and "The Symbolic" as a term of art in Lacanian thought. For a similar distinction but a different typographical convention, see Charles Shepherdson, "The Role of Gender and the Imperative of Sex," in *Supposing the Subject*, ed. Copjec, 160.

80. Žižek, *Sublime Object*, 155–58.

81. Luce Irigaray, "The Poverty of Psychoanalysis," in *The Irigaray Reader*, ed. Margaret Whitford (Oxford, 1991), 82.

82. This is exactly the argument of Evans, "Historicism and Lacanian Theory," which I hope to be extending in this section of my presentation.

83. Lacan, *Écrits*, 285.

84. Jacques Lacan, *Écrits II* (Paris, 1971), 108.

85. I think that my interpretation of this passage is, however, quite different from that of Goux, "The Phallus," 43, who writes, "Psychoanalysis, therefore, does not determine a new object in naming the phallus. It operates an unveiling on its own account and by its own means, an unveiling that already ordained the mystical ritual," thus implying that psychoanalysis doubles an unveiling already ordained, while in my paraphrase it is the *veiling* that ordained the mystical ritual and which is being unmasked, demystified in the psychoanalytic encounter. Accordingly, Goux is led to doubt whether "the theoretical interpretation brings anything other than what exegesis [of the Mysteries], pushed to its limit, would have yielded." He takes theory as a redemptive interpretation of the Mystery, while I am taking it as a suspicious hermeneutic, which, of course then, reveals precisely what exegesis could not. See also Butler, "Lesbian Phallus," 151.

86. See discussion in Evans, "Historicism and Lacanian Theory," 36–37, on Lacan's 1938 support of Malinowski against Jones on the cultural relativity of the Oedipus complex.

87. There is another reading of Lacan possible, of course, one in which this is exactly what Lacan is claiming, namely that any unveiling only reveals—perhaps a stronger but surely a much more dispiriting reading.

88. "The *objet a* is something from which the subject, in order to constitute itself, has separated itself off as organ. This serves as a symbol of the lack, that is to say, of the phallus, not as such, but in so far as it is lacking": Lacan, *Four Fundamental Concepts*, 103. Once again, it is clear that the "Phallus" is being rendered here as "lack," but insofar as that lack is called the "Phallus" by Lacan and not clearly diagnosed as only being such owing to the Imaginary of a particular culture, Lacan is not acting as diagnostician but as symptom. Everyone lacking the Phallus then is equivalent to the early Hellenistic Jewish and Christian insistence that everyone equally needs to *become male!*

89. Lacan, *Four Fundamental Concepts*, 204. In the Hellenistic romance of Daphnis and Chloe, an old woman teaches Daphnis, the innocent, how to make love to Chloe. In a sense, the Greek romance is the opposite of *Blue Lagoon* in its assumptions about the naturalness of heterosex. Interestingly enough, in rabbinic myth, it is the human being who teaches the animals how to have sex. I thank Galit Hasan-Rokem who reminded me of this significant intertext.

90. Martha McCaughey, "Perverting Evolutionary Narratives of Heterosexual Masculinity; or, Getting Rid of the Heterosexual Bug," *GLQ* 3, nos. 2–3 (1996): 263.

91. I am grateful to Virginia Burrus for this wording.

92. Castelli, "'I Will Make Mary Male,'"; Michael W. Meyer, "Making Mary Male: The Categories 'Male' and 'Female' in the Gospel of Thomas," *New Testament Studies* 31 (1985): 554–70.

93. Shepherdson, "The Role of Gender," 160. Cf. in the same volume Copjec, "Sex and the Euthanasia of Reason," 23.

94. Monique Wittig, "The Category of Sex," in her *The Straight Mind and Other Essays* (Boston, 1992), 7.

95. Butler, *Gender Trouble*, 20.

96. Monique Wittig, "The Straight Mind," in her *The Straight Mind and Other Essays*, 32.

97. Ross Kraemer, "Monastic Jewish Women in Greco-Roman Egypt: Philo on the Therapeutrides," *Signs: A Journal of Women in Culture and Society* 14, no. 1 (1989): 342–70.

98. Meeks, "The Image of the Androgyne," 179; Macdonald, "Corinthian Veils," 289.

99. Of course, there are celibate men as well, but the point is that men do not have to renounce their sexuality in order to become "male," while women always do. One of the first to explore this issue was Clark, *Jerome, Chrysostom, and Friends*.

100. Verna E. F. Harrison, "Male and Female in Cappadocian Theology," *Journal of Theological Studies* 41, no. 2 (Oct. 1990): 441–71.

101. Jehuda Theodor and Hanoch Albeck, eds., *Genesis Rabbah* (Jerusalem, 1965), 54–55. In a recent and rather curious oversight, Judith Baskin has seriously misrepresented this text. After citing the view of Rabbi Samuel, she refers to the objection to it and concludes that his view has been refuted. However, the text clearly indicates that he responded—and one might add quite convincingly—to the objection, so, if anything, the implied authorship of the midrash ratifies and authorizes his view. In general, however—and in direct contrast to former strategies of mine as well as those of Baskin—I would prefer to insist on the irreducible heterogeneity of the talmudic/midrashic text and the manner in which it leaves multiple voices in play at the same time without resolution: Galit Hasan-Rokem, *The Web of Life—Folklore in Rabbinic Literature: The Palestinian Aggadic Midrash Eikha Rabba* (in Hebrew) (Tel Aviv, 1996). This seems to me the move that enables us to get past both polemic and apologetic. Judith R. Baskin, "Rabbinic Judaism and the Creation of Woman," in *Judaism Since Gender*, ed. Laura Levitt and Miriam Peskowitz (New York, 1996), 125–30.

102. Cf. the ancient Egyptian myth wherein a god who contained within himself [!] both male and female principles produced a pair of male and female deities who then generated all of the others: "Thus creation was conceptualized as the separation of male and female principles followed by their sexual interaction" (Gay Robins, "Dress, Undress, and the Representation of Fertility and Potency in New Kingdom Egyptian Art," in *Sexuality in Ancient Art*, ed. Natalie Boymel Kampen, Cambridge Studies in New Art History and Criticism [Cambridge, 1996], 27).

103. Luce Irigaray, *Je, Tu, Nous: Toward a Culture of Difference*, trans. Alison Martin (New York, 1993), 12.

104. Goux, "Luce Irigaray," 181.

105. Goux, "Luce Irigaray," 182.

106. Luce Irigaray, "Women's Exile," trans. Couze Venn, in *The Feminist Critique of Language: A Reader*, ed. Deborah Cameron (London, 1990), 51.

107. Carolyn Burke, "Irigaray Through the Looking Glass," in *Engaging with Irigaray*, ed. Burke, Schor, and Whitford, 43–44.

108. Naomi Schor, "This Essentialism That Is Not One: Coming to Grips with Irigaray," in *Engaging with Irigaray*, ed. Burke, Schor, and Whitford, 57–78.

109. Lloyd, *The Man of Reason*.

110. Interestingly enough, this constraint did not preclude public economic activity: Daniel Boyarin, *Unheroic Conduct: The Rise of Heterosexuality and the Invention of the Jewish Man*, Contraversions: Studies in Jewish Literature, Culture, and Society (Berkeley, 1997), xxii–xxiii and passim, but unfortunately this fact only disproves the hopeful contention of Schor in the name of de Beauvoir that "by leaving behind the unredeemed and unredeemable domestic sphere of contingency for the public sphere of economic activity, women too can achieve transcendence": Schor, "This Essentialism That Is Not One," 63.

111. Burrus, *Chastity as Autonomy*.

112. Boyarin, *Unheroic*, 143, 172–85.

113. Some of the following paragraphs have been adopted from Daniel Boyarin, *Carnal Israel: Reading Sex in Talmudic Culture*, The New Historicism: Studies in Cultural Poetics 25 (Berkeley, 1993). I have tried to rewrite them in a way that nullifies what is to me now an embarrasingly apologetic tone in the form in which I first published them.

114. R. Howard Bloch, "Medieval Misogyny," *Representations* no. 20 (Fall 1987): 11–12; Jacqueline Lichtenstein, "Making up Representation: The Risks of Femininity," *Representations* no. 20 (Fall 1987): 77–88.

115. Tertullian, "On the Apparel of Women," in *Fathers of the Third Century*, trans. and ed. Alexander Roberts and James Donaldson, The Ante-Nicene Fathers IV (Grand Rapids, MI, 1989), 17.

116. Tertullian, "Apparel," 14.

117. Clement of Alexandria, "The Instructor," 269.

118. Tertullian, "To His Wife," in *Fathers of the Third Century*, ed. and trans. Roberts and Donaldson, 41.

119. Clark, "Ascetic Renunciation"; Elizabeth Schüssler Fiorenza, *In Memory of Her: A Feminist Theological Reconstruction of Christian Origins* (New York, 1983), 90.

120. Burrus, *Chastity as Autonomy*.

121. This example is drawn from Boyarin, *Unheroic*.

122. I.e., these are the maximums that he is permitted to vow not to sleep with her. If he takes a vow for longer, he must divorce her and pay her the divorce settlement.

123. This is a difficult term that means something like idlers; it may mean those who spend all of their time in study.

124. A very recent rabbinic authority now "permits" talmudic scholars to sleep with their wives twice a week or even more often, because modern women need more sex than ancient women did!

125. For the full text and a discussion, see Boyarin, *Carnal Israel*, 114–15.

126. My own translation.

127. See also Carole Pateman, *The Disorder of Women: Democracy, Feminism and Political Theory* (Stanford, CA, 1989), 76.

128. Monique Plaza, "'Phallomorphic Power' and the Psychology of 'Woman': A Patriarchal Vicious Circle," *Feminist Issues* 1, no. 1 (1980).

2

Gender Irregularity as Entertainment: Institutionalized Transvestism at the Caliphal Court in Medieval Baghdad

Everett K. Rowson

One of the salient characteristics of medieval Islamic societies, especially in contrast to those of Europe, was their insistence—at least among the urban elite—on strict segregation of the sexes, through the institutions of the harem and the veil. Such societies might be expected to evince a correspondingly sharp, and simple, dichotomy between male and female sexual and gender roles, with little tolerance for those who broke the rules. In fact, however, our sources suggest a far more complex situation, at the level of both norms and realities. The recognized categories of sexual desire and behavior can by no means be reduced to variations on, or deviations from, a normative binary model of heterosexual identity, and the positive expression of male homoeroticism in particular was a major component of the poetic and belletristic traditions in all the primary Islamic languages. And at least equally striking is the accommodation these societies afforded to those who flouted the more public, non-sexual aspects of gender construction, such as dress, ornament, and mannerisms. Nowhere is this latter phenomenon more prominent than at the caliphal court in ninth-century Baghdad, where both male and female transvestism were not only tolerated, but institutionalized, and even salaried, as forms of professional entertainment.

Relatively abundant textual sources for both these institutions offer the opportunity to explore their place at court and in society, the nature of their appeal, and the underlying societal constructions of gender, as well as of sexuality, that make sense of them. In particular, a comparative analysis of what might appear at first to be parallel phenomena of cross-dressing, male to female and female to male, reveals some important asymmetries that suggest the centrality of questions of masculine gender and male sexuality for these societies.[1]

Cross-dressing and other cross-gender behavior are well-known phenomena in the Muslim Middle East, attested, in more or less institutionalized form, from the very beginning of Islamic history to the present. Unni Wikan has written extensively about the khanīths of contemporary Oman, that is, men who adopt a feminine persona, including clothing and perfume, and work as passive homosexual prostitutes. Wikan's choice of the word "transsexual" to translate the term khanīth, in conscious distinction to either "transvestite" or "homosexual," led to a lively interchange of letters in the journal Man, debating both the gender status of the khanīth ("third gender"? "pseudo-woman"?) and the relation between sexual and non-sexual aspects of his identity.[2] The nineteenth-century transvestite male dancers of Cairo are well known from E. W. Lane's Manners and Customs of the Modern Egyptians, where they are called khawals (a term whose meaning has since shifted to become a general— and highly abusive—word for passive male homosexuals) and ginks (now obsolete).[3] But the considerable evidence for institutionalized cross-dressing and other cross-gender behavior in pre-modern Muslim societies, among both men and to some extent women, has received less attention.

A recognized male cross-gender role, that of the mukhannath, is known from the time of the Prophet Muḥammad, who died in 632; and in the century following his death, under the Umayyad caliphs of Damascus, we hear of a high-profile group of such mukhannathūn (pl. of mukhannath) in the city of Medina. Appreciated primarily as musicians, they seem to have flourished there for some two generations, before being subject to a government crackdown in the year 717.[4] For some fifty years after this event our sources offer virtually no information on *mukhannathūn*, until the fall of the Umayyad caliphate and its replacement by that of the ʿAbbāsids, who founded a new capital at Baghdad in 762. The brilliant court life that developed there, notably under the celebrated Hārūn al-Rashīd (reigned 786–809),[5] is richly documented in a plethora of historical and literary sources, which also begin to speak again of *mukhannathūn*, now as court entertainers. Beginning with the reign of Hārūn's son al-Amīn (809–13), we also hear a great deal about *female* transvestites at court, known as *ghulāmīyāt* (sg. *ghulāmīya*). It is the questions raised by the simultaneous presence of these two forms of institutionalized transvestism at the ninth-century caliphal court in Baghdad that this essay is concerned to address.

Unlike the male *mukhannath*, the female *ghulāmīya* has no earlier history. The Prophet Muḥammad is reported to have condemned equally both male and female cross-dressers (implying that the latter as well as the former were a known phenomenon), and we do find occasional anecdotes about women who dressed as men in the Umayyad period;[6] but neither the Arabic terms used nor the phenomena described represent any precedent to this ʿAbbāsid institution. In fact, a famous anecdote offers us a precise explanation of the origin of the *ghulāmīyāt*. Speaking of Zubayda, the wife of Hārūn and mother of al-Amīn, the historian al-Masʿūdī says:

When her son [al–Amīn] succeeded to the caliphate [in the year 809], he favored the eunuchs and advanced their standing, notably Kawthar [his favorite], but others as well. When Zubayda saw how entranced he was by the eunuchs, and how he spent all his time with them, she took some of the slave girls who were well-built and had beautiful faces, and put turbans on their heads, arranged their hair in bangs and sidecurls, and cut short at the back, and dressed them in *qabāʾ*'s [a close-fitting robe], *qurṭaq*s [a close-fitting tunic], and *minṭaqa*s [a sash]; this attire gave them a svelte carriage, and emphasized their buttocks. Zubayda then sent them to al-Amīn, and they took turns serving him. He was pleased with them, and attracted by them, and brought them into public view, before both the elite and the commons. Then both elite and commons began to have slave girls with bobbed hair, whom they dressed in *qabāʾ*'s and *minṭaqa*s; and they called them *ghulāmīyāt*.[7]

The Arabic term *ghulāmīya* is an adjectival form, meaning approximately "*ghulām*-like." A *ghulām* is a "boy," especially a pre-pubescent or pubescent one; by extension, the word is also commonly used to refer to a male slave, of any age, and can be applied, as a euphemism, specifically to a eunuch. Despite this latter usage, however, and the tenor of al-Mas'ūdī's anecdote, other descriptions of the *ghulāmīyāt*, especially in poetry, make it abundantly clear that the intended effect was *not* the appearance of a eunuch, but rather that of an adolescent boy.[8] Besides *ghulām* itself, the two terms which appear most often in these descriptions are *amrad*, literally "beardless," and *shāṭir* (pl. *shuṭṭār*), meaning something like "rogue" or "swaggerer"—the *shuṭṭār* of Baghdad seem to have been essentially unruly teenagers. The tunic and sash were characteristic clothing of young men of this age group, and the *ghulāmīyāt* affected their wide sleeves, characteristic turbans, and sandals as well. In their haircuts, too, the *ghulāmīyāt* imitated young men's fashions, and we are told that the bobbed look was particularly characteristic of the "rogues," while the lengthened sidecurl on the cheek was considered one of the chief erotic attractions of the "beardless" male generally. Sometimes, in fact, the *ghulāmīyāt* simply painted sidecurls on their cheeks, using a compound of perfumes that served as both a black paint and an attractive scent. Or they went further, and used the same compounds to paint mustaches on their upper lips. The further step of writing names or even verses on their cheeks takes us beyond imitation of *ghulām*s to other stratagems for exercising their charms.[9]

It has often been pointed out that institutionalized male transvestism in most cases is not a matter of intended exact imitation of women's appearance, but rather a mix of male and female attributes. In the case of the *ghulāmīyāt*, however, the transformation seems to have been virtually complete, as evidenced by verses such as the following:

> Were it not for the down on his cheek, we would not know
> Which of the two youngsters is the boy.[10]

With due allowance for poetic hyperbole, this and numerous similar verses suggest at least that the *ghulāmīyāt* retained no specifically feminine clothing or other modifiable features. On the other hand, there is no reason to assume that they ever actually intended to "pass" as boys. The very use of painted mustaches argues more for a deliberately *obvi-*

ous imitation of the male, as does evidence that there was no attempt to disguise the swell of the breasts. In any case, it was surely intrinsic to the appeal of the *ghulāmīya* that she was a woman; otherwise, the fad would have had no point.

Two poems by Abū Nuwās, who was al-Amīn's poet laureate, will serve to round out this picture of the *ghulāmīya*'s appearance, as well as to suggest some of her characteristic activities. In the first, the poet describes the slave girl Maknūn ("hidden" or "cherished"[11]), with whom he had a brief, and for him uncharacteristic, affair:

> My eye this morning was given the best of "Good morning"s,
>> As it gazed on the face of the "Cherished" of every morning.
> Clad in a tunic, her supple waist unconstrained,
>> And with no flounces to be caught by the wind and disturb her ensemble,
> She shares her natural features with women, but has left to them
>> All types of ornament, except for the sash.
> Her hair is bobbed, neither hanging loosely down her back,
>> Nor gathered under a "crown" on top.
> The line of the sidecurl on her noble face resembles
>> A smudge of ink on a finger cleaning an inkwell;
> She summoned it with an infusion of musk until it came running to her
>> And settled in place between her ear and her shoulder.
> She is a boy *(ghulām)*, or if not a boy, then it is a boy who resembles her;
>> A worldly bounty is she, pleasure to the one who embraces her.
> She combines all that is lovely in both form and attire,
>> And no one's verbal description can do justice to her—
> With the sharp wit of a freethinker, the gaze of a singing slave girl
>> In the eyes of the one she loves, the quintessence of desire for one enamored—
> But pouting like a prisoner, contrary as a swaggerer *(shāṭir)*,
>> With the look of a genie and the appearance of a shameless hypocrite![12]

In the second poem, Abū Nuwās describes an anonymous *shāṭira:*

> A swaggerer, glorying in a face whose beauty
>> Is like a flash of light in the darkness of night—
> She found that the attire of a boy best perfected her beauty,
>> And was more appropriate for profligacy and sin.
> She kept working on the effect, until she managed
>> To imitate him in act and speech as well.
> She lords it over the (other) slave girls
>> Because she outdoes them so in roguishness and cheek.
> She rejects the tambourine out of pure contrariness and
> waywardness,
>> And plays with pigeons, just to be flippant;
> But her skill summons her to take up the long-necked lute
> *(ṭunbūr)*
>> When the old wine is passed round.
> She has her polo stick in hand every morning,
>> And practices archery and pellet-shooting as well.
> She wears her hair like a male, lets her sidecurl grow long,
>> And twists her sleeves like a boy.[13]

Polo and archery, as well as other sports such as cockfights and ram-fights, mentioned in other sources, are characteristic interests of idle young men; "contrariness" *(takrīh)* and "waywardness" *(fatk)* are also associated specifically with the *shuṭṭār.* Pigeon-fancying had a wider appeal, as we know from the ninth-century littérateur al-Jāḥiẓ's *Book of Animals,* but again was associated particularly with the young and the wayward.[14]

But more significant are the references here to musical instruments. While the *ghulāmīyāt* were not exclusively a court phenomenon, they were in fact mostly slave girls employed by the aristocracy (references to free *ghulāmīyāt* are rare), and very often as singers and dancers. Musical instruments were played by both sexes, normally as accompaniment to a singer, but there were distinctions made in the instruments used. Women generally played the tambourine, while prestigious male musicians most often played the standard lute *('ūd).* "Lighter" songs (cast in specifically "lighter" rhythms, and often with "lighter" themes in their words) were accompanied by the long-necked lute, or *ṭunbūr,* rather than the *'ūd;* and in this period, as we shall see, the *ṭunbūr* was particularly cultivated by the male transvestites *(mukhannathūn)*.

Before turning to the latter, however, it would be well to look a little more closely at the phenomenon of the *ghulāmīyāt* in terms of both personal identity and sex. First of all, the *ghulāmīya* identity was usually an imposed one, adopted at the behest of the slave girls' masters, although it could also be freely adopted. We are told that ʿArīb, the most celebrated female slave girl-musician of the ninth century, began her career as one of the caliph al-Amīn's *ghulāmīyāt*, but there is no evidence that she maintained that image in later years.[15] It would certainly be a mistake to see the *ghulāmīyāt* as either tomboys or lesbians, and in fact all three of these categories should be carefully distinguished. Zayyāt includes in his article a number of accounts, from both the Umayyad and ʿAbbāsid periods, of women who adopted male attire, wore swords, rode horseback, and so forth;[16] such women seem to have been generally admired— as "honorary men" if you will—but absolutely no corollaries were drawn about their sexual orientation, nor do we find any remarks upon their sexual attractiveness—which is clearly basic to the phenomenon of the *ghulāmīyāt*. We do find numerous references in our sources to lesbianism, and perhaps particularly among the slave girls—but that is because lesbianism is one recognized form of profligacy, and profligacy in general is associated with slave girls—as it is with *mukhannathūn, shuṭṭār,* eunuchs, musicians, and poets.[17] But no link is ever made, to my knowledge, between lesbianism and the phenomenon of the *ghulāmīya*, and none of the famous *ghulāmīyāt* are identified, even in passing, as having any lesbian interests.

In fact, it would seem to be abundantly clear that the institution of the *ghulāmīya* was a function of male sexual tastes, not female ones. And it is no accident that one of our chief sources on the *ghulāmīyāt* is the notorious pederastic poet Abū Nuwās—although he confesses to a certain limitation in their appeal, in a second poem of his on the *ghulāmīya* Maknūn, whom he did get to know a little better:

A woman with voluptuous breasts, one of the palace servants,
  Has captured my heart with the beauty of her neck, face,
  and bosom.
She is a *ghulāmīya*, her clothing scented with Barmakī
  perfume,[18]

With painted sidecurls and bobbed hair.
I have been entranced by gazing at the beauty of her face
    For some time now, although love of nubile girls is not
    my thing.
Every time I have seen her, I have used my poetry
    To break down her defenses, for poetry is one way to cast
    a spell.
Finally, she decided to meet me, and came to me
    In the afternoon, with no appointment.
I bade her welcome, and we shared a cup
    Of wine red like saffron or a burning ember.
But she said: Can this be wine? I am innocent before God
    Of associating with men in drinking wine!
I said: Drink! If this is forbidden,
    Let your sin, my gazelle, be on my neck, along with my
    own.
Then I asked her for something, and she said, with a tear in
    her eye,
    "But this would mean my death!"—and her tears began
    to flow.
I continued to speak sweetly to her, while saying to myself,
    "This little girl is a virgin, and these are a virgin's fears!"
And when we were finally united, I felt myself in a
    tempestuous sea,
    Drowning, O people, amidst its clashing waves.
"Help me, boy!" I cried, and he came to me
    When I had lost my footing and plunged into the depths
    of the well.
Had I not cried out for the boy, and had he not reached me
    With a rope, I would have sunk to the bottom.
Thus I swore that never again would I venture on a campaign
    by sea,
    Nor undertake any voyage except on the back of the earth.

Any hesitations we might have about the interpretation of this poem are obviated by the accompanying prose anecdote, in which Abū Nuwās states that "I became so involved in the act that I imagined her as a boy."[19]

Abū Nuwās was a pederast—a *lūṭī*—as was his patron al-Amīn—
and it is important here to be very clear about what this means. Essentially, a *lūṭī* was a man sexually attracted by pubescent boys; when sexual
activity resulted, this normally meant anal penetration of the boy by the
lūṭī.[20] A boy's motive for agreeing to this sexual act was not usually sexual desire; most commonly he was paid, although other considerations
could be involved as well. (One relatively common pattern, for instance,
was that of the *mubādil*, who would agree to be penetrated in exchange
for then taking the role of the penetrator himself.) Being known as a *lūṭī*
resulted in little or no loss of prestige: the public attitude towards *lūṭī*s
seems to have been the same as that towards *shuṭṭār*—a sort of clucking
disapproval not unmixed with envy. This is not to say that "masculinity"
was not an important value in this society; indeed, I would maintain
that it was a paramount value. But with regard to sexual conduct, this
society—in marked contrast to our own—defined "masculinity," not in
terms of "sexual object choice," but rather of "sexual act." In our society,
it is males who have sexual relations, of any kind, with other males who
are not "real men"; in ninth-century Baghdad, it was males who con-
sented to be penetrated anally who were not "real men."

Women—in both societies!—are of course not "real men," either;
and what is really going on here is a kind of expansion of the field of
natural "sexual object choice." Being a *lūṭī* was seen simply as profligacy,
a willingness to go beyond the limits of conventional morality, but in a
perfectly rational direction; and as such it was considered reprehensible,
to be sure, but neither demeaning nor perverted. Boys, our sources tell
us, are like women, in their physical softness, in their lack of emotional
restraint, and most obviously in their lack of facial hair; pubescent boys,
unlike prepubescent children, have a sexual identity, but still lack beards.
Even if the *lūṭī*'s partner was not expected to feel sexual pleasure in the
sexual act, it seems that this sexuality of his partner was important to
the *lūṭī*; and I would speculate that the ideal of the first down on the
cheeks, so omnipresent in Arabic poetry, reflects a sexual frisson sparked
by this touch of the exotic, and indeed the illicit, added to a pleasure
undisturbed by any apprehensions about the *lūṭī*'s own sexual identity.

Beards are the cardinal symbol of masculinity in traditional Islamic
culture, a fact clearly reflected in the long history of poetic controversy
over the effect of the beard on a boy's beauty. The insistence that a boy
with a full beard could still be beautiful became itself a minor topos in

Arabic poetry, although always dependent on its status as a protest against conventional wisdom; this controversy eventually spawned entire collections of "beard" poetry, pro and con. With the *ghulāmīyāt* one could have it both ways: the charms of both a boy and a girl simultaneously, with or without a beard (according to taste), and the whole perfectly legitimate if consummated, as the partner was biologically female—clearly irresistible. It may seem ironic, then, that institutionalized female cross-dressing here has everything to do with a variety of homosexual desire—not, however, of female, but of *male* homosexual desire.

It was to lure al-Amīn from his eunuchs that the *ghulāmīyāt* were first conceived, and the sources leave no doubt that his attraction was sexual, of the *lūṭī* variety. This is in fact explicitly stated in some satirical verses composed by an anonymous Baghdad wag on the incompetence and frivolity of the caliph al-Amīn and his vizier al-Faḍl b. al-Rabīʿ:

> The *liwāṭ* (active homosexuality) of the caliph is a marvel,
> And a greater marvel is the *ḥulāq* (passive homosexuality)
> of the vizier.
> The former crams, and the latter gets crammed—
> I swear, you never know!
> If only they would make use of each other,
> At least it could all be kept quiet;
> But the former plunges into Kawthar,
> While the latter wouldn't be satisfied if he got plugged by
> a mule![21]

Al-Amīn's taste in eunuchs was in fact rather unusual, although it is true that eunuchs shared the beardlessness and, usually, the bodily softness of boys and women. For information on the sexual status of eunuchs, we can turn to al-Jāḥiẓ, who seems to have been fascinated with them and wrote about them at length in several of his works. At one point, al-Jāḥiẓ seems to specify eunuchs as a third alternative to male and female as sexual object choice, stating explicitly that "Some women prefer women, others prefer men, yet others prefer eunuchs, and there are some who like all three equally well; and the same is true of men's preferences for men, women, or eunuchs."[22] Such a distinction would appear to conflict with the above characterization of al-Amīn's attraction to eunuchs as "*liwāṭ*," which would assimilate them as object choice to other males, whether boys or men (but as passive partners in any case); but such a conflict is probably more apparent than real. Al-Jāhiz's remarks are made in the context of an extended discussion of the peculiarities of eunuchs, in which it is useful for him to distinguish them—anatomically!—from both intact males and females, and thus treat them as a third sex; within the specific realm of sexual behavior, however, a distinct preference for eunuchs *rather than* intact males does not seem in general to have been remarked upon, and even in the unusual case of the caliph al-Amīn was likely more a function of availability than of taste.

As for eunuchs' own sexual preferences, al-Jāhiz informs us that these can vary as much as those of ordinary men, and include (active) *liwāt* and (passive) *hulāq* as well as heterosexual desire. Al-Jāhiz's comment that eunuchs share the emotionalism of women and young boys (or children: *sibyān*) may serve perhaps to reinforce the picture I am trying to draw of a gender configuration whose most basic distinction is that between men and not-men; but what most surprises him about eunuchs is that they are never—he claims—effeminates *(mukhannathūn)*. He says:

> What is astonishing is that, despite their transferral from the realm of male characteristics to that of females, they are not susceptible to effeminacy *(takhnīth)*. I have seen more than one Bedouin who was a *mukhannath,* so loose-limbed and effeminate that he dripped; I have seen madmen who were *mukhannathūn;* I have seen this occur among pure blacks, and I have heard someone claim to have met a Kurd who was a *mukhannath;* but I have never seen a eunuch who was a *mukhannath,* or heard of such a thing. I don't know why this should be; at first glance it would appear that it should be universal among them. And what is yet more astonishing about them in this connection is how common passive homosexuality *(hulāq)* is among them, despite the rarity of effeminacy, as well as the fact of their transferral from the realm of male characteristics to that of females.[23]

Whatever this passage may imply about eunuchs, it clearly shows that for al-Jāhiz's society we must be on our guard against conflating male homosexuality—or rather specifically passive male homosexuality *(hulāq)*, the quite distinct phenomenon of active homosexuality *(liwāt)* being not even in question here—with effeminacy *(takhnīth)*. Al-Jāḥiẓ is clearly using this latter term in its broad sense, signifying behavior—gestures, speech patterns, etc.—perceived as "effeminate"; but from our sources it is abundantly clear that it was also commonly used in a narrower sense, to refer to an institutionalized irregular gender role, represented by males who publicly adopted feminine modes of dress as well as behavior and felt it as an identity with both personal and corporate dimensions. It is this institution of male cross-gender behavior—the *mukhannathūn*—which offers a particularly instructive contrast to that of the female *ghulāmīya*.

Our fullest sources on the figure of the *mukhannath* refer to a century earlier, and to Arabia, not Iraq.[24] Under the reigns of the Umayyad caliphs ʿAbd al-Malik (685–705) and al-Walīd (705–15), in particular, a group—one might almost say a corporation—of male transvestite singers and musicians flourished in the city of Medina, attaining a prestige commensurate with, but distinct from, that of the male (free) and female (slave) singers and musicians. What distinguished the music of the *mukhannathūn* from both that of other men and that of women is not entirely clear, although it certainly included already the characteristic "lightness" attested later for the ʿAbbāsid period; the preferred instrument of the *mukhannathūn* was the *duff*, or woman's tambourine, not yet the *ṭunbūr*, or long-necked lute. The degree to which their dress was "effeminized" is also unclear; probably it was a mix of women's and men's garments, although they certainly wore women's jewelry. Unlike other men, they were admitted to the women's quarters and seem quite commonly to have functioned as marriage brokers. They were appreciated by the gilded society of aristocratic Medina as much for their wit and charm as for their music, although they shared the taint of presumed irregular living which depressed the status of all entertainers. They were not assumed to practice (passive) homosexual behavior. A general assumption of their lack of sexual interest in women does seem to have prevailed, although, according to a well-known tradition *(ḥadīth)*, the Prophet forbade their admission to the women's quarters specifically because he discovered that they were less impervious to women's charms than commonly assumed. (For the Umayyad period at least, the prohibition expressed in this *ḥadīth* seems to have been ineffective.) It is also attested that at least some of these *mukhannathūn* were married.

Mecca also produced some musical *mukhannathūn,* but they seem to have lacked both the musical distinctiveness and the corporate identity of the *mukhannathūn* of Medina. The latter phenomenon seems to have come to an abrupt halt under the caliph Sulaymān, in the year 717, when he issued an order that all the *mukhannathūn* of Medina were to be castrated. His motives in doing so are variously explained in our sources, but mostly they focus on the caliph's fears for the chastity of women tempted into immorality by the seductive songs the *mukhannathūn* composed; an alternative explanation has it that Sulaymān was appalled to hear that the *mukhannathūn* were exploiting their unique social position to indulge in illicit sexual relations with both women and men, and it was clearly the former that upset him. Neither homosexual behavior in itself nor any inherent immorality in the adoption of feminine dress and behavior is offered as an explanation.[25]

The *mukhannathūn* survived their castration, of course, and the *mukhannath* identity did not cease to exist as a social category, but after this calamity our sources offer little information about them for the rest of the Umayyad period, either in the Arabian Peninsula or elsewhere. We do begin to hear more about them again after the 'Abbāsids defeated and replaced the Umayyads as caliphs in 750, but in nothing like the detail we have for their Medinan predecessors, or indeed for the 'Abbāsid *ghulāmīyāt.* (The *mukhannathūn* were notably not the object of love poetry.) Their association with music continued, and at court, as noted, some of them specialized in playing the *ṭunbūr.* Yet while there were relatively well-known *ṭunbūrīs* at court who are identified as *mukhannathūn,* very little is made of their latter status in our sources. The importance of being a *mukhannath* seems now to lie elsewhere: it is their wit, not their musicianship, that makes them valued as *mukhannathūn.*

Certainly the best-known *mukhannath* of the ninth century was 'Abbāda, who functioned essentially as the court jester or buffoon of the caliph al-Mutawakkil (reigned 847–61).[26] (Al-Mutawakkil is also described in our sources as the caliph, after al-Amīn, who was fondest of the *ghulāmīyāt.*[27]) 'Abbāda was originally the son of a cook at the court of al-Ma'mūn (reigned 813–33), al-Amīn's brother and successor as caliph. After his father's death, we are told, he became a *mukhannath* and a profligate. The young al-Ma'mūn heard about him and had him brought before him. He was so entertained by 'Abbāda's jokes, mimes, and, perhaps, skits, that he sent him to his stepmother, Zubayda, to entertain

her as well. He became a fixture at court for many years thereafter, although with some long interruptions occasioned by the sharpness and
audacity of his humor, which induced more than one caliph, including
al-Mutawakkil, to banish him for a time.[28]

What is preserved of ʿAbbāda's humor ranges from the innocuous
to the savage to the lewd. An example of the innocuous is his explanation to an outraged Mutawakkil why he had slapped the prayer-leader of
a local mosque. While on his way to an errand, he had passed by the
mosque, and had decided to enter and get his obligatory prayer out of
the way before continuing on. But the *imām* had selected for his Qurʾān
text to recite during the first prostration of the prayer the Chapter of the
Cow *(sūrat al-Baqara)*, by far the longest chapter in the Qurʾān, which
he proceeded to recite in its entirety, rather than more conventionally se-
lecting a few verses; for the second prostration he then chose the Chapter of the House of ʿImrān *(sūrat Āl ʾImrān)*, the second longest chapter.
To top things off, he then turned to the assembled worshippers and said,
"You must repeat your prayers, because I was not in a state of proper ritual purity." The exasperated ʿAbbāda hauled off and gave him a sharp
slap on the back of the neck.[29] (It should be noted here that another category of court buffoon was the *ṣafʿān*, whose main duty was to be available to be slapped on the neck.[30])

Al-Mutawakkil was a violent opponent of the Shīʿa and harbored an
intense hatred for ʿAlī b. ʿAbī Ṭālib, the Prophet's nephew and son-in-
law whom Shīʿites revere almost as much as (and in some cases more
than) the Prophet himself. We are told that at al-Mutawakkil's pleasure
parties ʿAbbāda used to stick a pillow under his robe, bare his bald head
(ʿAlī was bald and fat), and dance before the drinking caliph, while the
musicians sang "The fat bald man has come, the caliph of the Muslims!"
At one of these sessions, al-Mutawakkil's son and heir, al-Muntaṣir,
stopped the proceedings and defended ʿAlī to his father, saying "Eat his
flesh if you wish, but do not feed it to this dog and his like!"[31] (Al-
Muntaṣir was later to assassinate his father in a palace coup—which
ʿAbbāda managed to survive.) Aside from its political implications, the
imitation or role-playing described in this anecdote is an activity persistently associated with the *mukhannathūn*.[32]

Most of ʿAbbāda's humor, however, was sexual, and much of it depended on his own presumed passive homosexuality. Such, for instance,
is his indignant remark when he was offered a eunuch as sexual part-

ner: "I don't board a ship without a rudder!"[33] Another time, asked his age, he said, "Ninety-five," and when asked why he'd never married, replied, "There just aren't any good men around any more!"[34] When al-Mutawakkil offered to give him a wife if he would give up his effeminacy *(takhannuth)*, he responded, "Are you a caliph or a marriage-broker?"[35] And when he was asked the interesting question, "Can there be a *mukhannath* who is not a passive homosexual *(bidūn bighāʾ)*?" he answered, "Yes, but it's like a judge without a judge's hat *(qāḍī bidūn dinnīya)*."[36]

The accounts of ʿAbbāda and other *mukhannathūn* make it abundantly clear that from this period on, in contrast to the earlier Umayyad period, they were automatically assumed to be passive homosexuals *(baghghāʾūn)*. It was not that the two categories became coterminous, however; rather, *takhannuth* went from being a category conceptually distinct from, but overlapping with, *bighāʾ*, to being a subset of it. The situation is clear in an eleventh-century literary anthology, in which three successive chapters are devoted to anecdotes about *mukhannathūn, lūṭīs*, and *baghghāʾūn*.[37] ʿAbbāda appears in both the first and the third of these chapters, but it is in the first that he, and other *mukhannathūn*, display their characteristic art of the rapid putdown. The general spirit of the *mukhannathūn* is perhaps best summarized in the oft-repeated boast of one of them: "We are the best of people: when we speak, you laugh; when we sing, you are ravished with delight; and when we lie down, you mount!"[38]

The shift in the *mukhannath*'s perceived sexual identity in the early ʿAbbāsid period is certainly connected with the emergence of public male homosexuality at the same time, a phenomenon of considerable importance in the history of Islamic society as well as Arabic literature but that cannot be gone into in detail here.[39] References to homosexuality are relatively rare in pre-ʿAbbāsid literature, and positive references are virtually absent. What is striking is the abruptness with which this situation changed in the second half of the eighth century, an abruptness that was remarked upon by contemporaries, notably al-Jāḥiẓ. Al-Jāḥiẓ attributes this phenomenon to the ʿAbbāsid armies of eastern Iran, who were sent out on long campaigns, contrary to previous practice, without taking their wives along, and learned to make do with their pages, faute de mieux; when they marched west to defeat the Umayyads, they imported this new practice to Iraq.[40] Other sources attribute a decisive role to Abū Nuwās and two of his masters, a view that I suspect should not be dismissed too lightly.[41] In any case, the idea quickly took root, at least among large segments of the upper classes, that a pubescent boy was a natural object of sexual interest to a mature male, if not necessarily a licit sexual partner. Correspondingly, the assumption that *mukhannathūn*, assimilated to women psychologically in a way ordinary pubescent boys were not, would inevitably also be assimilated to women in their sexual behavior, seems to have been a natural one. (About the psychology of the *mukhannathūn* themselves, it is of course more difficult to pronounce.)

A series of anecdotes about prominent members of the ʿAbbāsid court offers us a bit more information on non-sexual aspects of the *mukhannath* identity. For the caliph al-Amīn, we have an account of how two leading (non-*mukhannath*) male musicians were summoned by the caliph by night and ushered into a courtyard ablaze with candles, where al-Amīn was prancing about on a hobby-horse *(kurraj)*, surrounded by slave girls and *mukhannathūn* singing and playing drums *(ṭabl)* and flutes. The two were ordered to add their (professional) voices to the song, while the caliph continued to prance and dance, never flagging until dawn.[42] This "hobby-horse" (and the translation seems to be fairly close) is known already from the Umayyad period, and is almost always associated with *mukhannathūn*. To what extent it was simply a toy and to what extent a prop for a specific dance is unclear; certainly it was considered a frivolous activity, appropriate to the *mukhannathūn*, rather like pigeon-fancying.[43] They were also associated, very strongly, with drums *(ṭubūl)*—far more so in fact than with the *ṭunbūr*, which seems to have been strictly a court phenomenon, while the connection with drums is society-wide, as we shall see.[44]

Al-Amīn seems never to have been tempted actually to become a *mukhannath* himself, but one anecdote records that a son of his vizier al-Faḍl b. Al-Rabīʿ did. Al-Faḍl was upset by this and appointed, we are told, a boy to watch over the son and prevent him from plucking out his beard. One night, however, the son succeeded in doing so, and when the guard asked him the next morning, "Where is your beard?" he replied with a verse from the Qurʾān, originally referring to God's devastation of an orchard, "Then a visitation came upon it while they slept and in the morning it was as if plucked" (Qurʾān 68:19–20).[45]

Some years later, the caliph al-Wāthiq's (reigned 842–47) brother Jaʿfar, who was later to succeed as al-Mutawakkil, was in disfavor with the caliph, yet sent an intermediary to ask his permission to let his hair

grow long in back, "in the style of the *mukhannathūn*." Al-Wāthiq's response was to send a barber to him; when Ja'far arrived in a sumptuous
new black suit (the color of the 'Abbāsid dynasty), expecting to be told he
had the requested permission, the barber sat him down and cut his hair
without using an apron, thus spoiling the suit, and then slapped him in
the face with the cut hair.[46]

Earlier, from the very beginning of the dynasty, we have another
story about its first caliph, al-Saffāḥ (reigned 750–54). The caliph's half-
witted brother Yaḥyā was appointed governor of Mosul, and carefully
surrounded with advisers. This Yaḥyā, we are told, was notorious for his
drinking habits and his passion for the *mukhannathūn*. His very first act
upon arriving in the city of Mosul was to order drums *(ṭabl)* bought for
him immediately. The first of these arrived while he was on his mule, en
route from his palace to the mosque; when, overjoyed, he put it round
his neck and tried it out, the mule bolted and ran out of control into the
middle of the crowded mosque, the drum-playing governor on its back.
This led to his dismissal and an end to his being given any responsibility at all.[47] (The *ṭabl* of the *mukhannathūn* may have been a distinctive
sort of instrument; a tenth-century source distinguishes between "parade drums" *[ṭubūl al-mawākib]* and smaller "*mukhannaths*' drums" *[ṭubūl
al-makhānīth].*)[48]

According to another story, the poet Abū l'Atāhiya, who was Abū
Nuwās's chief rival, started out his career as a *mukhannath*, carrying
their characteristic provision-bag *(zāmilat al-mukhannathīn)*, and then
spent time as a pottery-seller, before becoming a poet. Years later, we are
told, someone saw Abū l'Atāhiya carrying such a provision-bag and reproached him, saying, "Does someone like you put himself in this position, given your age, your poetry, and your status?" But Abū l'Atāhiya
replied, "I just want to learn their tricks *(kiyād)* and memorize their
speech *(kalām)*."[49] The latter of these terms, *kalām*, "speech," probably
refers to a distinct vocabulary or argot of the *mukhannathūn*; the former
term, *kiyād*, plural of *kayd*, "guile," is less clear. *Kayd* is particularly associated with women, because of a famous Qur'ānic statement attributing it to them,[50] but in its frequent appearance in *mukhannathūn* stories
seems to have a somewhat different meaning, something more like
"mocking." (One should perhaps compare the modern colloquial meaning
in Egypt, "spite.") In some way it certainly does refer to the sharper side
of the *mukhannath*'s wit, and was feared; one is reminded of 'Abbāda's

performance as ʿAlī, as well as his recorded threat to the satiric poet Diʿbil: "If you compose an abuse poem about me, I will act out your mother in a skit!"[51]

Another aspect of the *mukhannathūn*'s sharp tongues is reflected in an anecdote consisting simply of an insult match between two of them, in which the first says, "You are nothing but a house with no door, a foot with no leg, a blind man with no stick, a fire with no firewood, a river with no ford, and a wall with no ceiling"; the much longer response of the other begins, "You viper's head, you donkey-renter's stick, you burnous of the Catholicus..." and goes on to, "you house-broom, who doesn't care where he gets put, what room he goes into, what inn he stays in, or what bath he works in..." etc.[52] This "genre," which is paralleled elsewhere, is strikingly similar to the phenomenon of mutual vituperation between traditional women in contemporary Cairo, called *radḥ*, and of which I have witnessed an uproarious parody by two members of the homosexual subculture, dressed in drag, in the context of a party; it would seem likely that the medieval *mukhannathūn* were also parodying women with their elaborate insults, although this is not explicit in the texts.[53]

But the milder or lighter side of the *mukhannath* personality is also stressed in our sources, as in this verse from an abuse poem:

> Abū l-Riḍā the Qurʾān reciter has an appearance
>   Which gives the impression of a feminine build;
> He is *mukhannath* in his (physical) nature,
>   But lacks the lightness of spirit of the *mukhannathūn*.[54]

More explicitly, the ninth-century poet and anthologist Ibn al-Muʿtazz, in his biography of a poet named Ibn Shāda, who was known as "al-Mukhannath," explains that "Ibn Shāda was not (really) a *mukhannath;* but he never composed abuse poetry about or defamed anyone, so he was called 'the Mukhannath' as a nickname; and he was the most well-mannered of people."[55] The temptation to see this as an ironic nickname should be resisted; it is the lack of aggressiveness of the *mukhannathūn* that is being thought of here, and its positive aspect stressed. In other contexts, such lack of aggressiveness is construed negatively, as cowardice, a particularly striking example being the sobriquet bestowed on the Muʿtazilite theologians by their enemies, "the *mukhannathūn* of the Khārijites," because they were seen as sharing some of the theological views of the latter without having the Khārijites' courage to embrace their drastic practical consequences, which included wholesale massacre of their opponents.[56] (Ibn al-Muʿtazz's source for his information on Ibn Shāda was, we may note, a son of the vizier al-Faḍl b. al-Rabīʿ, whom he names as Bādhinjāna, a feminine noun meaning "eggplant" and surely a nickname—it is extremely tempting to identify him with the *mukhannath*, described above, who managed to pluck his beard at night.)

One point it is extremely important to stress: the *mukhannathūn* had very little dignity, and their status in society, controversial even in the Umayyad period, sank noticeably under the ʿAbbāsids, possibly in part because they were henceforth assumed to be passive homosexuals. The latter assumption emphasized the degree to which they had voluntarily given up the distinctive gender markers of manliness, and joined the ranks of the not-male—boys, who would grow out of this status, and women, who could not help it. The resulting lack of dignity freed them, however, from numerous constraints, and enabled them to serve as clowns and entertainers of other sorts, who could be vastly amusing without having to be taken seriously.

The low status of the *mukhannath* is expressed poignantly in an anecdote recorded about Hārūn al-Rashīd. Having lost a son, the caliph was inconsolable, despite the best efforts of the religious scholars. Then a *mukhannath* came to him and said, "O Commander of the Faithful, I am a man who imitates women, as you see; what would you do, then, if your son were alive and looked like me?" From this, we are told, Hārūn took consolation, and dismissed the wailing women.[57]

Further evidence for this low status comes from two sources that offer perspectives from outside the literary tradition. In his *Art of Dispelling Sorrow*, the philosopher al-Kindī, a contemporary of the caliph al-Mutawakkil, describes four sorts of misguided people who rejoice in their own vices: the glutton, the gambler, the *shāṭir* (who seems to be here basically a brawler), and the *mukhannath*. Regarding the latter, al-Kindī says, "Despite his brazen indecency and his base morals, which are repulsive to everyone and rejected by any rational person, and his perversion of his appearance by plucking his beard and decking himself out as a woman, we find the *mukhannath* to be joyous and proud, thinking himself superior to everyone because of this and considering them to be deprived of the greatest of boons, for which he has been singled out, as the most precious and delightful of gifts."[58]

A century later, the philosopher Miskawayh was a bit less harsh, when responding to a question posed by his friend al-Tawḥīdī. Al-Tawḥīdī asked as follows:

> Why do some people make butts of themselves for others' humor? That is, why do they set themselves up to be laughed at and mocked, and to have their necks toyed with, putting up with this contentedly, while receiving little or no reward for it? How can they care so little about such an abhorrent thing? And yet some of them are even from noble and celebrated families in the cream of society! And in the same way, we see how another becomes a *mukhannath*, a singer, an instrumentalist—in general, how do people from great houses come to grow up to pursue demeaning paths?

In his rather lengthy reply, Miskawayh attributes such behavior ultimately to bodily temperament, which, however, only becomes an expressed personal trait as a result of the individual's failure to restrain his nature. Miskawayh opines that "treatment" of this condition can be successful—otherwise, he says, it would not be just to chastise or discipline him, or indeed to blame or praise him. But if he refuses treatment, imposition of the stipulated penalties upon him is incumbent. Miskawayh does not specify what these are, but compares them to the treatment imposed on a person suffering from a bodily ailment who refuses to undergo treatment voluntarily.[59]

Al-Tawḥīdī's question puts the *mukhannath* squarely in the public light: to parade oneself before an audience, as do entertainers generally, is clearly to sacrifice one's dignity at a very basic level. Subjecting someone to public display *(tashhīr)* was also a known form of punishment, and it is perhaps not surprising that *mukhannathūn* were associated with this phenomenon as well. In the late tenth century, for example, the historian al-ʿUtbī, describing the entry into Bukhara of some captives taken in battle, says they were met by *"mukhannathūn* with tambourines and spindles, rather than swords and spears"—apparently in a parody of what is known as the *taqlīs,* in which the townspeople went out to meet a victorious army.[60] A generation earlier, also in Bukhara, a baker convicted of treason was paraded through the streets behind a corps of *mukhannathūn*.[61] In eleventh-century Egypt, on the other hand, it is a *mukhannath* himself who is said to have been subjected to this punishment of *tashhīr*, apparently because he was acting as a procurer for five women out of his house.[62] Around the same time, another Egyptian *mukhannath* was murdered; we are told that he was a rich man and a musician, who maintained singing slave girls in his home but was himself enamored of beardless boys, on whom he spent much money.[63]

Much more evidence of this sort must be collected before it will be possible to trace the fortunes of the *mukhannathūn* in the Middle East after the period of the high ʿAbbāsid caliphate in the ninth century. In broad terms, however, it is apparent that—in contrast to the ninth-century fad for the *ghulāmīya*—the *mukhannath*, always associated with music, wit, and profligacy, persisted as a recognized figure for many centuries, and indeed still exists today, as the *khanīth* in Oman (and almost certainly elsewhere, even if unnoticed by western social scientists).

Finally, to return to the general question of parallelism between the sexes in cross-dressing and cross-gender behavior, it should be clear that any such parallelism is in fact extremely limited. Both the *ghulāmīyāt* and the *mukhannathūn* in the medieval Middle East were part of the demimonde of entertainers and persons of dubious morals—that is, the world of professional pleasure-givers. This function depended on their freedom from the constraining norms of respectable men and women, or, ultimately, on their lack of respectability. The *ghulāmīyāt* were not respectable because they were slaves and because they appeared in public, in contrast to respectable free women, kept in seclusion and veiled from public view. The *mukhannathūn* were not respectable because they had voluntarily relinquished their manhood. The gender strand within the social hierarchy, however, meant that the *ghulāmīya*'s status as such cost her no prestige relative to her more conventional slave girl peers, while the *mukhannath* lost a great deal relative to his more conventional peers, even if—I think—we take those peers to have been non-*mukhannath* jesters and buffoons.

It is in the realm of sex that the radical asymmetry between the *ghulāmīyāt* and the *mukhannathūn* is clearest—unless, that is, we consider the fact that both are intimately connected with male homosexuality as another point in common! But even if we were to do so, the ways in which they relate to male homosexuality are quite distinct. The point of the former was to charm the ordinary man through a combination of female and boyish sexual attractions; the latter offered entertainment to ordinary society that had nothing to do with sexual attraction, but depended on the freedom offered by gender inversion and the consequent abandonment of dignity. In the end, I suppose one could say, both subverted the rules of a rigidly hierarchical gender structure for the delectation of those belonging to the gender category securely established at the top of the hierarchy: sexually active—and bearded—adult males.

APPENDIX A: ARABIC TERMS

amrad (pl. *murd, murdān*): beardless
baghghāʾ (pl. *baghghāʾūn*): passive male homosexual, syn. *ḥalaqī*
bighāʾ: passive male homosexuality, syn. *ḥulāq*
ghulām: boy, slave, eunuch
ghulāmīya (pl. *ghulāmīyāt*): young female entertainer dressed as a boy
ḥalaqī: passive male homosexual, syn. *baghghāʾ*
ḥulāq: passive male homosexuality, syn. *bighāʾ*
khanīth: male transvestite (in contemporary Oman)
liwāṭ: active male homosexuality
lūṭī: active male homosexual
mukhannath (pl. *mukhannathūn*): male transvestite; effeminate
shāṭir (fem. *shāṭira,* pl. *shuṭṭār*): rogue, swaggerer, brawler
takhannuth: male transvestism; effeminacy
takhnīth: male transvestism; effeminacy
tashhīr: public exposure as a form of punishment
ṭunbūr: a long-necked lute
ʿūd: a standard lute

APPENDIX B: SOME CALIPHS

Umayyad Dynasty, 661–750

ʿAbd al-Malik, 685–705
al-Walīd I, 705–15
Sulaymān, 715–17

ʿAbbāsid Dynasty, 750–1258

al-Saffāḥ, 750–54
Hārūn al-Rashīd, 786–809
al-Amīn, 809–13
al-Maʾmūn, 813–33
al-Muʿtaṣim, 833–42
al-Wāthiq, 842–47
al-Mutawakkil, 847–61
al-Muntaṣir, 861–62

Notes

1. At one level, of course, this may seem tautological, since by "societies" we inevitably mean primarily the public world that was overwhelmingly dominated by men, and the sources on which we rely were without exception written by men. That more is involved than the skewed nature of our access to information should become clear, however, in what follows.

2. Unni Wikan, "Man Becomes Woman: Transsexualism in Oman as a Key to Gender Roles," *Man* 12 (1977): 304–19, with subsequent discussions in *Man* 13 (1978): 133 f., 322 f., 473–75, 663–71; Wikan, *Behind the Veil in Arabia: Women in Oman* (Chicago, 1982), esp. chap. 9, "The Xanith: A Third Gender Role?" My own use in this essay of the terms "homosexual" (usually preceded by either "active" or "passive") and "lesbian" is dictated by considerations of economy and ready intelligibility, and does not imply an "essentialist" stance on my part; I intend them to refer simply to same-sex sexual behavior and to those who participate in it, without any further implications regarding identity or, certainly, etiology. To the extent possible I prefer to reproduce the Arabic terms of my sources themselves, which I have listed and glossed in Appendix A.

3. E. W. Lane, *An Account of the Manners and Customs of the Modern Egyptians* (1860; reprint, New York, 1973), 381 f.

4. These *mukhannathūn* are the subject of my article, "The Effeminates of Early Medina," *Journal of the American Oriental Society* 111 (1991): 671–93; reprinted in *Que(e)rying Religion: A Critical Anthology*, ed. Gary David Comstock and Susan E. Henking (New York, 1997), 61–88. The present essay is intended in part as a sequel to this article, a brief summary of which appears below.

5. A chronology of the caliphs mentioned in this article appears in Appendix B.

6. For the Prophet's condemnation, see, e. g., al-Bukhārī, *Ṣaḥīḥ*, ed. L. Krehl and Th. W. Juynboll (Leiden, 1862–1908), *libās* 62 (4:94 f.) and *ḥudūd* 33 (4:308); full references in my "Effeminates," notes 12–14. For female transvestism in the Umayyad period, see note 16 below.

7. Al-Masʿūdī, *Murūj al-dhahab*, ed. Muḥammad Muḥyī al-Dīn ʿAbd al-Ḥamīd (Beirut, n. d.), 4:318; see also Nabia Abbott, *Two Queens of Baghdad: Mother and Wife of Hārūn al-Rashīd* (Chicago, 1946), 211 f. All translations from Arabic are my own.

8. The following discussion is based mainly on the wide-ranging study of the *ghulā-miyāt* by Ḥabīb Zayyāt, "al-Marʾa al-ghulāmīya fī l-Islām," *al-Machriq* 50 (1956): 153–92. Although his approach is not particularly analytical, Zayyāt has done a laudable job of ferreting out references to the *ghulāmīyāt* from an impressive range of sources.

9. For full documentation of these various aspects of the *ghulāmīya*'s appearance, see Zayyāt, "al-Marʾa al-ghulāmīya," passim. The best-known discussion of the use of writing (usually of provocative verses) on cheeks, foreheads, shoes, etc., is in the *Kitāb al-Muwashshā* of al-Washshāʾ (d. ca. 937), which is essentially a guide to becoming a fashionable person.

10. Zayyāt, "al-Marʾa al-ghulāmīya," 171, 191, attributed to a poet named "al-Ṭayyibī" or "al-Ṭībī," but without citation to a primary source. I have been unable to track the verse down elsewhere.

11. The form "Maknūn" is that of a *masculine* adjective, which is entirely typical of names given to the highly cultured and carefully trained slave girls, most of them singers and some of them notable poets, who were bought, sold, and enjoyed by the aristocracy of Baghdad in general and the caliphal court in particular in the ʿAbbāsid period. Probably the most typical type of name for such slave girls was a simple noun (whatever its grammatical gender), such as Nasīm ("Breeze") or Amal ("Hope"); but masculine adjectives as names certainly outnumbered both feminine adjectives and conventional feminine names, as can be seen, for example, from the thirty-one entries in the *Book of Slave Girl Poetesses* of Abū l-Faraj al-Iṣfahānī (d. 967), *al-Imāʾ al-shawāʿir*, ed. Jalīl al-ʿAṭīya (Beirut, 1984).

12. Abū Nuwās, *Dīwān*, vol. 3, ed. Gregor Schoeler (Wiesbaden, 1982), 90 f. Variant versions of this poem appear in Abū Hiffān, *Akhbār Abī Nuwās* ed. ʿAbd al-Sattār Aḥmad Farrāj, (Cairo, n.d.), 31, and Ibn Manẓūr, *Akhbār Abī Nuwās*, ed. Muḥammad ʿAbd al-Rasūl Ibrāhīm and ʿAbbās al-Shirbīnī (Cairo, 1924), 1:167–68; in the latter the slave girl's name is not Maknūn but Maʿshūq ("Beloved"—also in the masculine form).

13. Abū Nuwās, *al-Nuṣūṣ al-muḥarrama*, ed. Jamāl Jumʿa (London, 1994), 98, as part of a longer, multi-themed poem; a shorter version appears in *Dīwān Abī Nuwās* (Beirut, n. d.), 568. The lines translated here are quoted (with numerous variants) by Zayyāt, "al-Marʾa al-ghulāmīya," 164, and translated into German by Ewald Wagner, *Abū Nuwās: Eine Studie zur arabischen Literatur der frühen ʿAbbāsidenzeit* (Wiesbaden, 1965), 177 f.

14. Al-Jāḥiẓ, *K. al-Ḥayawān*, ed. ʿAbd al-Salām Muḥammad Hārūn, (Cairo, 1938–45), 3:147, 190. For a preliminary analysis of the persistent, and somewhat perplexing, hostility to pigeon-fancying in Islamic cultures, see H. Grotzfeld, "*Al-Laʿb bi-l-Ḥamām*," in *Die Islamische Welt zwischen Mittelalter und Neuzeit: Festschrift für Hans Robert Roemer zum 65. Geburtstag*, ed. Ulrich Haarmann and Peter Bachmann (Beirut, 1979), 193–97. The most commonly cited reasons for this hostility are the gambling associated with pigeon racing and the opportunities to spy inside other people's houses resulting from pursuing pigeons in urban environments.

15. Al-Shābushtī, *Kitāb al-Diyārāt*, ed. Gurgīs ʿAwwād, 3rd ed. (Beirut, 1986), 165 f. Nothing is said about her having been a *ghulāmīya*, however, in the extensive biographies offered by Abū l-Faraj al-Iṣfahānī in both his *Kitāb al-Aghānī* (Būlāq, 1868), 18:175–94, and his *al-Imāʾ al-shawāʿir*, 133–48.

16. Zayyāt, "al-Marʾa al-ghulāmīya," 156–61.

17. On lesbianism in general in the medieval Islamic world, see, provisionally, G. H. A. Juynboll's article, "Siḥāq," in *The Encyclopaedia of Islam*, 2nd ed. (Leiden, 1960), and Mitchke Leemans, "Siḥāq en Sekse: Lesbische Seksualiteit in Middeleeuws Arabische Literatur" (doctoral dissertation, University of Utrecht, 1996).

18. A scent associated with Jaʿfar al-Barmakī, vizier to Hārūn al-Rashīd; see Wagner, *Abū Nuwās*, 177, n. 5.

19. Ibn Manẓūr, *Akhbār Abī Nuwās* 1:169–70. The poem also appears (with numerous variants) in Abū Hiffān, *Akhbār Abī Nuwās* 1:169 f.; *Nuṣūṣ*, 104 f.; *Dīwān Abī Nuwās* (Beirut), 283. Abū Nuwās did also write straightforward love poetry about women, although much less of it than he did about boys; and a complex of anecdotes is preserved about his one alleged serious affair with a woman, the slave girl Janān (who was not a *ghulāmīya*). For a full discussion, see Wagner, *Abū Nuwās*, 39–51. Interestingly, Ibn Manẓūr in *Akhbār Abī Nuwās* 1:179, says that Janān "loved women and inclined toward them."

20. The only alternative envisioned by our sources is intercrural intercourse (between the thighs), known as *tafkhīdh*.

21. Al-Ṭabarī, *Taʾrīkh al-rusul wa-l-mulūk*, ed. M. J. de Goeje et al. (Leiden, 1879–1901), 3:805; cf. the translation by Michael Fishbein, *The History of al-Ṭabarī*, vol. 31: *The War between Brothers* (Albany, NY, 1992), 58.

22. Al-Jāḥiẓ, *al-Ḥayawān* 1:167.

23. Ibid. 1:136.

24. What follows here is a summary of my article "The Effeminates of Early Medina," see note 4 above.

25. It is true, however, as noted above (see note 6), that a group of traditions state that the prophet Muḥammad cursed both "men who imitate women" and "women who imitate men," and later discussions of these traditions generally assume that they are referring primarily to dress.

26. The sources on ʿAbbāda are very scattered. Some of the most important are al-Shābushtī, *al-Diyārāt*, 118–21; al-Ābī, *Nathr al-durr*, vol. 5, ed. Muḥammad Ibrāhīm ʿAbd al-Raḥmān and ʿAlī Muḥammad al-Bijāwī (Cairo, 1987), 277–92; and Ibn Shākir al-Kutubī, *Fawāt al-wafayāt*, ed. Iḥsān ʿAbbās (Beirut, 1973), 2:210–11.

27. Zayyāt, "al-Marʾa al-ghulāmīya," 190.

28. Al-Shābushtī, *al-Diyārāt*, 118–19.

29. Al-Ābī, *Nathr al-durr*, vol. 7, ed. Munīr Muḥammad al-Madanī (Cairo, 1991), 313–14.

30. On these slap-takers, see the information assembled by Shmuel Moreh, *Live Theatre and Dramatic Literature in the Medieval Arabic World* (New York, 1992), index s. v. *ṣafāʿina*.

31. Ibn al-Athīr, *al-Kāmil fī l-taʾrīkh*, ed. C. J. Tornberg (Leiden, 1851–76; reprint with new pagination, Beirut, 1965), 7:55.

32. Shmuel Moreh, in his *Live Theatre*, 25–27, discusses the *mukhannathūn* in this context, marshalling evidence to show that they were, in fact, actors. With regard to ʿAbbāda's career, for example, he translates the word *takhannatha*, which I have paraphrased above as "became a *mukhannath*," as "joined the actors and jesters." Although Moreh's citations, and his discussion, do bring out the close connection between the *mukhannathūn* and

miming throughout the medieval period in the Middle East, it seems to me that he has here, and throughout his book, pushed his interpretation of the evidence in the direction of "live theater" well beyond what it will bear. In any case, his interest in the *mukhannathūn* has very little to do with questions of gender or sexuality, which he deals with only tangentially.

33. Al-Ābī, *Nathr al-durr*, 5:279.

34. Ibid., 287.

35. Al-Shābushtī, *al-Diyārāt*, 119.

36. Ibid., 120.

37. Al-Ābī, *Nathr al-durr*, 5:277–313.

38. Al-Rāghib al-Iṣfahānī, *Muḥāḍarāt al-udabā'* (Beirut, n. d.), 2:255; al-Ābī, *Nathr al-durr*, 5:277; and many other sources.

39. I would stress again that my use of the term "homosexuality" here is not intended to carry any particular "essentialist" implications.

40. Quoted from al-Jāḥiẓ's lost *Book of Schoolmasters (Kitāb al-Muʿallimīn)* by Ḥamza al-Iṣfahānī in his recension of the collected poetry of Abū Nuwās, as part of his introduction to the section devoted to love poetry on males, see Abū Nuwās, *Dīwān*, ed. Schoeler, vol. 3:141 f.

41. See, e. g., the short biographies of Abū Nuwās's "mentors" Wāliba b. al-Ḥubāb and al-Khārakī in Ibn al-Muʿtazz, *Ṭabaqāt al-shuʿarā'*, ed. ʿAbd al-Sattār Aḥmad Farrāj, 4th ed. (Cairo, 1981), 86–89, 306 f.

42. Abū l-Faraj, *Aghānī*, 16:133. Cf. the variant (earlier) version in al-Ṭabarī, *Taʾrīkh*, 3:971–72; trans. Fishbein, *The History of al-Ṭabarī*, 31:247–48.

43. On the *kurraj*, see M. Gaudefroy-Demombynes, "Sur le cheval-jupon et al-kurraj," in *Mélanges offerts à William Marçais* (Paris, 1950), 155–60; Amnon Shiloah, "Réflexions sur la danse artistique musulmane au moyen âge," *Cahiers de civilisation médiévale* 5 (1962): 463–74; and most recently and extensively, Moreh, *Live Theatre*, 27–37. Moreh attempts to connect the *kurraj* with Central Asian shamanism, and again argues for "dramatic" connections.

44. For drums, see note 48 below. The connection of *mukhannathūn* with the *ṭunbūr* was related to their mutual connection to the "light" rhythm of *hazaj*; see Eckhard Neubauer, *Musiker am Hof der frühen ʿAbbāsiden* (Frankfurt, 1965), 38. Interestingly, there is a much-repeated tradition that the *ṭunbūr* was invented by the "people of Lot," as an aid to seducing beardless boys; see, e.g., the text by al-Mufaḍḍal b. Salama in ʿA. al-ʿAzzāwī, *al-Mūsīqā al-ʿIrāqīya fī ʿAhd al-Mughūl wa-l-Turkumān* (Baghdad, 1951), 82.

45. Al-Ābī, *Nathr al-durr*, 5:291. Humorous anecdotes turning on a frivolous use of Qurʾānic quotation constitute a well-known if minor subgenre of Arabic jokes, and it would be a mistake to overestimate the perceived severity of the sacrilege thereby committed.

46. Al-Ṭabarī, *Taʾrīkh*, 3:1372; trans. Joel L. Kraemer, *The History of al-Ṭabarī*, vol. 34: *Incipient Decline* (Albany, NY, 1989), 67–68; reproduced with variants in Ghars al-Niʿma, *al-Hafawāt al-nādira*, ed. Ṣāliḥ al-Ashtar (Damascus, 1967), 252 f. (no. 238). The first of these two sources is a sober historical one from the early tenth century; the second is an eleventh-century collection of anecdotes about faux pas.

47. Ghars al-Niʿma, *Hafawāt*, 100–101 (no. 113). I have not found this story in earlier, more serious sources, and as it stands its historicity is quite out of the question. Yaḥyā was indeed made governor of Mosul, but his actual claim to notoriety was the wholesale massacre he initiated among the town's inhabitants, for obscure reasons; see al-Azdī, *Taʾrīkh al-Mawṣil*, ed. ʿAlī Ḥabība (Cairo, 1967), 145–54. Some confusion regarding the protagonist of the story thus seems likely to have occurred.

48. Ikhwān al-Ṣafāʾ, *Rāsaʾil* (Beirut, 1957), 1:193. A poem cited in al-Tawḥīdī's *al-Imtāʿ wa-l-muʾānasa*, ed. Aḥmad Amīn and Aḥmad al-Zayn (Beirut, n. d.), 2:174, refers to an "ʿannāz," which the editors gloss as "a drum *[ṭabl]* which the *mukhannathūn* and professional singers hang around their necks," but without indicating their source for this information.

49. Abū l-Faraj, *Aghānī*, 3:122, 124.

50. Qurʾān 12:28, referring to Potiphar's wife's attempted seduction of Joseph: "This is an instance of your [f.pl.] *kayd;* indeed, your [f.pl.] *kayd* is great."

51. Al-Shābushtī, *al-Diyārāt*, 188. This anecdote, with several variants (in both protagonists and vocabulary), is discussed in detail by Moreh, *Live Theater*, 89, with specific focus on the "skit" *(khayāl, ḥikāya, laʿba)* and its implications for "drama."

52. Al-Tawḥīdī, *al-Imtāʿ wa-l-muʾānasa*, 2:59. The Catholicus was the head of the Nestorian Christian church, resident in Baghdad.

53. On contemporary *radḥ* in Cairo, see Afaf Lutfi al-Sayyid Marsot, "Mud-Slinging Egyptian Style," *Journal of the American Research Center in Egypt* 30 (1993): 189–92. The phenomenology of male imitation, or parody, of women, beyond strict transvestism, is an extremely interesting one cross-culturally and merits greater attention. That such stereotypically "effeminate" behavior in the modern West as the "limp wrist," lisping, and even "dishing" can be paralleled in medieval Arabic texts raises some obviously important questions. For an example of addressing a male in the feminine gender (in this case for satiric purposes), see the abuse poem (instigated by the caliph al-Mutawakkil) by Marwān al-Aṣghar against the poet ʿAlī b. al-Jahm, Abū l-Faraj, *Aghānī*, 11:3.

> O son of Badr, O ʿAli
>   You (fem.) claim to belong to the clan of Quraysh [the Prophet's clan],
> But you claim what is not true,
>   So shut up, you Iraqi mongrel *(Nabaṭīya,* fem.)!
> Shut up, you daughter of Jahm!
> Shut up, you passive homosexual *(ḥalaqīya,* fem.)!

The nonce word "*ḥalaqīya*," the feminine form of *ḥalaqī*, "passive male homosexual," conveys efficiently enough the gender implications of this sexual role in the society of the time.

54. Al-Thaʿālibī, *Tatimmat al-yatīma*, ed. ʿAbbās Eqbāl (Tehran, 1935), 1:9.

55. Ibn al-Muʿtazz, *Ṭabaqāt al-shuʿarāʾ*, 332.

56. ʿAbd al-Qāhir al-Baghdādī, *al-Farq bayn al-firaq* (Beirut, 1985), 82; Badīʿ al-Zamān al-Hamadhānī, "al-Maqāma al-Māristānīya," in *Maqāmāt*, ed. Muḥammad Muḥyī al-Dīn ʿAbd al-Ḥamīd (Beirut, 1979), 158.

57. Al-Tawḥīdī, *al-Imtāʿ wa-l-muʾānasa*, 2:130.

58. Al-Kindī, *Risāla fī l-ḥīla li-dafʿ al-aḥzān*, ed. Helmut Ritter and Richard Walzer, "Studi su al-Kindī II: Un scritto morale inedito di al-Kindī," *Atti della Reale Accademia Nazionale dei Lincei*, Memorie della classe de scienze morali, storiche e filologiche, Serie 6.8 (1938–39), 33–34.

59. Al-Tawḥīdī and Miskawayh, *al-Hawāmil wa-l-shawāmil*, ed. Aḥmad Amīn and al-Sayyid Aḥmad Ṣaqr (Cairo, 1951), 193 f.

60. Al-Minīnī, *Sharḥ al-Yamīnī al-musammā bi-l-Fatḥ al-wahbī ʿalā taʾrīkh Abī Naṣr al-ʿUtbī* (Cairo, 1869), 1:139. For *taqlīs* (derived, via Syriac, from Greek *kalōs*, "beautifully"), see, e. g., al-Balādhurī, *Futūḥ al-buldān*, ed. Raḍwān Muḥammad Raḍwān (Beirut, 1983), 137.

61. Moreh, *Live Theater*, 75, citing an unpublished text by the historian Ibn Ẓāfir.

62. Al-Musabbiḥī, *Akhbār Miṣr*, ed. W. G. Millward (Cairo, 1980), 187.

63. Al-Musabbiḥī, *Akhbār Miṣr*, ed. Aḥmad Fuʾād Sayyid and Thierry Bianquis (Cairo, 1978), 1:104.

3

RECONFIGURING THE PROPHET DANIEL: GENDER, SANCTITY, AND CASTRATION IN BYZANTIUM

KATHRYN M. RINGROSE

WHAT ABOUT THE PROPHET DANIEL?

In the twelfth century the Byzantine bishop, theologian, and essayist Theophylaktos of Ohrid wrote a fascinating essay in which he not only assumed that the prophet Daniel was a eunuch but also took the assumption so for granted that he used it to buttress the case he was building in favor of eunuchs as a group. The passage is found in an essay entitled *In Defence of Eunuchs*,[1] and prompts a complex and subtle examination of both gender constructs in Byzantium and the changing nature of those constructs over time. Written for his brother, a eunuch on the staff at Hagia Sophia, this work offers a window into a culture that acknowledged the existence of multiple gender categories, while openly articulating its ambivalence about the very existence of some of these categories. The world of Theophylaktos included sexually active men and women, ascetic men and women, and surgically altered men, commonly referred to as eunuchs. By the twelfth century these socially constructed categories were firmly established as part of the social structure of the Byzantine world. Theophylaktos's own family reflects the acceptance of eunuchism in both the court and the church. He was from an educated urban family, wrote extensively, and became an important bishop. He does not apologize for the fact that his brother was castrated as part of his preparation for a career in the church. Yet he does acknowledge the long tradition of pejorative rhetoric that surrounds eunuchs, particularly the eunuchs of the court and theater.

Theophylaktos's essay also reflects the ambivalence with which Byzantine society dealt with alternative gender categories. Eunuchs, because of their mutilation, were perceived to be effeminate and to share negative traits associated with women. Some eunuchs were believed to act as passive partners in same-sex relationships, and the degree to which they experienced sexual pleasure was the subject of endless conjecture. Yet eunuchs also were asexual, and as such, perhaps, untroubled by sexual desires, a trait that was the mark of the holy man in Byzantine society. Theophylaktos points out that by the twelfth century many eunuchs held high positions in the church and were celebrated in hagiographical writings.

The tension surrounding these multiple gender constructs is articulated with striking clarity in Theophylaktos's essay. Although his rhetorical goal is to present eunuchs as normal and worthy, Theophylaktos presents both sides of the polemic on the nature of the eunuch. His essay takes the form of a debate in which the protagonist is a eunuch. The antagonist, who speaks first, is not. The latter recites all of the traditional charges brought against eunuchs, including the charge that bodily mutilation is contrary to Mosaic law. The protagonist responds by reminding his opponent that the archbishops of Thessalonike, Pydna, Petra, and Edesse are all eunuchs, to say nothing of many of the lower clergy. As far as the Old Testament and Mosaic law are concerned, "Didn't God accord the eunuch honor in Isaiah? And what about the prophet Daniel?"[2]

GENDER AND BYZANTINE CULTURE

Well, what *about* the prophet Daniel? As we shall see, as early as the tenth century the Byzantines assumed that Daniel was a court eunuch, and this was clearly Theophylaktos's assumption. In countless subtle ways Daniel fulfilled roles assigned, in the Byzantine mind, to the court eunuch. His rearing and his relationship to the king of Babylon clearly fit a pattern characteristic of the Byzantine court eunuch. The facts about the historical Daniel, if, indeed, he ever existed, are unimportant in this context. What is of interest is the fact that the Byzantines assumed that he was a eunuch, and that by the twelfth century they were quite comfortable casting their favorite Old Testament figure in this role. This fact has more resonance than readily meets the eye, since Daniel was a major figure in Byzantine Christianity and was widely regarded as the most important precursor of Christ after John the Baptist.

Confronted with earlier attitudes about eunuchs, Theophylaktos's matter-of-fact presentation of Daniel as a court eunuch tells us that the status of the court eunuch was very different from what it had been in late antiquity. This is substantiated by the fact that by the twelfth century eunuchs were accepted as holy men and could hold the highest offices in the church, including that of patriarch of Constantinople. In following up on Theophylaktos's inference about the prophet Daniel, my research indicates that the status Theophylaktos attributes to eunuchs in the twelfth century was already established two hundred years earlier in the tenth century. We will see that eunuchs of the tenth century attempted to present themselves as spiritual figures and invented earlier "historical" eunuchs who had played spiritual roles in the lives of past emperors. The way that the tenth century portrays Daniel and his castrated companions, the boys in the fiery furnace, and the language used in connection with these figures illustrates important issues about the ways in which gender categories were constructed and reconstructed in the Byzantine Empire.

The discussion that follows explores these changing Byzantine assumptions about the gender of the prophet Daniel. It is based on the theoretical assumption that gender is a socially constructed category, and it is hoped that the following discussion will help to strengthen that proposition.

Gender construction included a relationship to sex and reproduction, but the cultural frame of reference was too complex for sex to be the single primary determinant of gender categories. For the purpose of this discussion, sexual categories are based on biological differences. We will see that late antique society often perceived eunuchs, because of their mutilation, as a third sex, half man, half woman, and biologically different from either one. By the tenth century eunuchs were perceived to be men as far as sexual classification was concerned, though men of a distinctly gendered sort.

By the middle Byzantine period (the ninth to the twelfth centuries) the socially constructed nature of the gender category of eunuch was well defined. Society not only imposed gendered standards of behavior, dress, and social roles but even physically mutilated individuals in order to assure their development as part of this specific gender group.

In addition to the assumption that gender was socially constructed in Byzantium, the discussion that follows is also based on the premise that this culture included multiple gender categories and that the construction of gender was not grounded in an oppositional male/female biological model.[3] Our culture is so thoroughly rooted in its bipolar gender framework that it is often difficult for us to escape assumptions of bipolarity. In order to show how the process of gender construction worked in the case of Daniel, we must first establish some generalizations about the cultural context within which gender construction took place.

It is my belief that Byzantine society was constructed hierarchically.[4] Human beings, men, women, and children, began as undefined, imperfect creatures until molded and perfected by society. Men were believed to be more suited, by nature, to perfection than women. Thus, out of the great mass of humanity, only physically whole men could achieve the highest peaks of physical and moral perfection. These men fell into two gendered groups. One was made up of aristocratic men who lived and procreated in the material world, the other consisted of men who consciously rejected their sexual natures. Both aristocratic men and ascetic men were biologically or physiologically "male," but they constituted distinctive gender groups because of the very different ways in which attitudes about sexuality and reproduction fitted into the gender construct of each group.

The ideal type of the ascetic male was the physically whole male who struggled to achieve holiness through denial of sexual urges and denial of the body. This type of holiness is presented as a trope in a variety of hagiographical sources and in cults associated with figures like St. Symeon the Stylite. This trope is important to an understanding of the Byzantine reconfiguration of the story of Daniel, but the category of this kind of holy man is distinct from the categories of those castrated eunuchs who served at court or in the church, though all were part of the social context.

Eunuchs were placed in a separately gendered group because of their mutilation. They could not achieve the status of aristocratic men. They also were denied the heights of ascetic achievement because they did not have to do battle with their own sexuality. As physiologically and biologically incomplete men, eunuchs shared many of the attributes of prepubescent boys, who were perceived to be in a state of formation and development that left their gender status ambivalent. Women, prepubescent girls, and young children are rarely mentioned in our sources and so will not play a role in this discussion. If we look at the Byzantine gender construct in this way, we see that eunuchs were not necessarily effeminate; rather they lacked full masculine status. The standards for achieving perfection within one's gender group were not based on opposing standards of masculinity and femininity, but on aristocratic masculine standards alone.

While this gender construct is hierarchical and is referenced to an ideal masculinity, either that of aristocratic men or that of ascetic men, some of our late antique and Byzantine sources express the construct using language that reflects bipolar, male/female traditions. This problem is compounded by modern translators and editors who reflexively translate "unmasculine" as "effeminate." As we look at sources after the ninth century, however, we find that many Byzantine sources move away from earlier bipolar linguistic traditions and acknowledge this hierarchical arrangement of gender groups by defining eunuchs in terms of those masculine qualities they lack, rather than those feminine qualities they are perceived to possess. Increasingly those desirable qualities that eunuchs lack are exactly those qualities that define ideal masculinity such as strength and courage.

As will be shown in the following pages, there is no question that in the Byzantine world eunuchs represent a distinct gender category, one that is defined by dress, assumed sexual behavior, work, physical appearance, quality of voice, and, for some eunuchs, personal affect. Because castration, when it is done at a young age, has definite physiological and developmental biological effects, it is always possible to find sources that support a modern argument that at least some eunuchs represent a third sex category based on biological change. It is important to remember, however, that late antique and Byzantine commentators did not attempt to unravel the complexities of sex and gender categories as modern scholars do. Many of the attributes of eunuchs that we would consider socially assigned aspects of gender our late antique and Byzantine sources would consider to be biological. For example, eunuchs are regularly criticized because they cry easily. A modern observer might suggest that if this is true it is probably related to the way they were reared. Perhaps they were allowed to express their emotions through tears. A Byzantine observer, however, would say that eunuchs easily cry because they have lost that important masculine quality, emotional self-control, and that this loss is a biological phenomenon that accompanies the loss of the testicles.

Conversely, we are dealing with a culture that is socially constructing a category with the aid of medical intervention that can lead to physiological change. Furthermore, if we look at this society in terms of our modern models for the organization of the categories sex and gender, it is quickly apparent that both categories are very fluid and socially dependent. For example, if male sexual organs and procreation are of critical importance to a society in its construction of a male sexual category, then eunuchs, because they lack full genitalia, will tend to be categorized as a third sex category. But if a society finds these biological sexual markers less important than other male qualities, like perfect service or lack of sexual distraction, then eunuchs will become a special gender category within a larger construct that is "men."

The complex gender constructs that are so evident in Theophylaktos's essay and in many other sources are rooted in the cultural inheritance of the Byzantine world. Byzantium inherited Roman patriarchal ideas that gave favored status to adult male heads of households, emphasized procreation and family formation, and established legal strictures against any sort of male genital mutilation. For the Romans male genitalia were important. In this Roman world men and women were assumed to differ morally, mentally, and physically. Aristocratic men, if properly trained and nurtured, were believed to rise above the level of women and children to become fully masculine heads of households. In this world, eunuchs were scorned as shameful, neither man nor woman, monstrosities, outsiders, pitiful, womanlike, etc.

Ideas about the construction of gender in the Byzantine world were also conditioned by Judeo-Christian traditions. The Jewish tradition regarding gender was rigidly bipolar and had little tolerance for intermediate gender categories. Early Christianity inherited this tradition and the legal structures that reinforced it. Yet throughout late antiquity, Christianity increasingly rejected sexuality and honored the celibate man. A man who could successfully suppress his own sexuality was a man particularly favored by God. There were endless discussions about where to draw the line between the celibate man who rejected his own sexuality and the eunuch who achieved celibacy with the aid of the surgeon's knife. Surely, the argument ran, eunuchs "cheat."

These "imported" traditions must be set against the realities of the structure of gender in the eastern Mediterranean and Middle Eastern world of late antiquity. These traditions accepted the existence of eunuchs as essential to the operation of aristocratic households and royal courts and were comfortable with these eunuchs' alternative gender status. In addition, the traditional thought patterns of this culture emphasized external appearances. The appearance of an individual's body gave the viewer information about the quality of his soul. A corrupt soul would eventually be revealed in a corrupt body. Similarly the physical body, especially in the castrated individual, was believed to affect his personality, his inner being.

As a result, the category constructed for eunuchs in late antiquity was based on real and assumed biological changes in both the appearance and personality of the individual, changes that were believed to be the direct result of castration. For example, since the testicles were believed to anchor man's physical nature, men whose testicles had been removed were assumed to be cool, weak, lax, irrational, unpredictable, and changeable, traits regularly associated with women.[5] Once an individual had been castrated he was reared within a framework appropriate to the category "eunuch."

The assumed construct for the eunuch's body was based on Galenic medical categories that were adopted by later Byzantine medical writers in their discussions of gender, health, the nature and development of the human body, and its nutrition. Galen, for example, taught that,

> The bodies of eunuchs, women and children are similar in that because of their nature or habit they are soft and moist, not hard and dry. When a doctor stretches the limb of a eunuch, woman or child in order to set a bone or treat a dislocation he is more likely to injure these individuals than is the case in the setting of a man's bone.[6]

Regarding the differences in temperature between men, women, and eunuchs Galen says, "Like women, eunuchs' flesh is cold."[7] Thus eunuchs
were situated within an elaborate Galenic universe in which women were
soft fleshed, cool, and moist, men were hard fleshed, warm, and dry,
and eunuchs, like prepubescent boys, lay on a continuum between the
masculine and feminine. The Galenic system treated the flesh of animals in the same way. The flesh of castrated and young animals was
moist, soft, and tender. The flesh of male animals was dry and hard
(tough) and muscular.[8] Within this structure the flesh of male animals,
and especially that part that surrounded the genital region, was considered to be unappetizing because of its strong smell and unhealthy because it was difficult to digest.[9]

Galenic teachings drew strong connections between the foods used
to nourish the individual and the qualities of the body that resulted from
eating particular foods. Later Byzantine medical writers followed Galenic
traditions, warning against "phlegm producing" foods like meat and shellfish. They provided detailed lists of foods that were dry, warm, moist,
and cool. These categories were comparable to those used to describe
the gendered bodies of men, women, children, and eunuchs. These concepts were embodied in the mental universe of the society, which assumed the logic of "gendered" eating habits: feeding each individual foods
that reinforced and nourished his or her particular physical makeup.[10]

The eunuch's body was assumed to be soft, cool, and fragile and
was categorized by doctors with the bodies of women and children. He
was reared among women and probably ate a bland diet of the kind rec-
ommended for women and children, a diet considered appropriate to
his body humors. His beard did not grow and his skin remained fine-
grained and soft, allowing him to retain an adolescent loveliness that
both men and women considered attractive. Like an aristocratic woman
he was expected to stay indoors and avoid sun tanning and the darken-
ing of his complexion. As he aged he retained his hair, a trait traditionally associated with eunuchs. Greek medical lore taught that baldness
was the result of active sexuality, while a full head of hair in an aging
man was a sign of celibacy or impotence. Depending on exactly how
and at what age a eunuch was castrated, lack of testosterone often caused
his body to elongate, producing an individual with unusually long, slen-
der limbs and hands, who was tall, elegant, lightly muscled, and grace-
ful. This characteristic physical appearance may not appeal to members

of societies whose taste is based on rigidly different male/female stereotypes because it is negatively associated with effeminacy, but it seems to have been accepted, even admired, at late antique and Byzantine courts where eunuchs played a prominent role in court ceremonial, standing like beautiful angels around the imperial throne, an image that is, perhaps, echoed in traditions in Byzantine painting. Eunuchs' altered physiology also affected their voices. The voice timbre remained high-pitched and light. As a result eunuchs were assumed to be talkative and gossipy, negative traits associated with women.

The very word "eunuch" can at times be ambiguous. In late antiquity the term εὐνοῦχος, "eunuch," was a broad term that was used for men who had lost the power to procreate, either through surgical intervention or accident or disease. In Byzantium after the tenth century the term "eunuch" usually referred to "cut" men, ἐκτομίας, surgically altered men whose testicles had been removed.[11]

In late antiquity almost all eunuchs came from servile backgrounds and were foreign born. This is an assumed part of their gender construct and contributes to their "otherness." Tradition claimed that they were either prisoners or slaves castrated outside the boundaries of the Roman Empire and brought to court. Later this idea was reinforced by referencing longstanding, though rarely enforced, legislation that forbade the making of eunuchs within the boundaries of the empire.[12] Eunuchs brought to court conventionally changed their names and associated themselves with the emperor's *familia*. These eunuchs had given up reproduction, family, and extended familial ties in order to become perfect servants. They were trained and shaped by their master to suit his needs. Some late antique sources suggest that these eunuchs were artificially created beings, as well as a third sex.

The sex and gender markers discussed above identified eunuchs throughout the late antique and early Byzantine periods. As we move into the ninth and tenth centuries, however, we find that there are other characteristics that establish the gender category "eunuch," and even divisions within the category itself, illustrating the ways in which socially constructed categories can change and develop over time.

In the tenth century we find that increasing numbers of eunuchs in Byzantium were drawn from the educated, propertied, freeborn classes within the empire and that these eunuchs were castrated within the boundaries of the empire. They often retained ties to their families and used their positions at court or in the church to elevate the status of their relatives. Traditionally eunuchs had served as teachers, doctors, guardians of women and children, body servants, entertainers, and singers. Now we find that these roles have been expanded; in fact, by the tenth century, some offices at court were reserved for eunuchs alone. They acted as keepers of sacred things, especially at court, and as all sorts of political and cultural intermediaries: between the emperor and God, between the emperor and the patriarch, between men and women, and between the sacred world of the court and the profane world outside.[13] An important part of their gender construct now centered on their perceived loyalty, trustworthiness, mediational activities, special intellectual powers, and spirituality.

In this period it is also possible to see a difference in the constructs attributed to court eunuchs and the eunuchs who served in church offices, differences that might support two distinct gender categories for these two groups. As will be seen in the following pages, the gender construct for court eunuchs carried with it a number of negative attributes, many of them part of a long historical tradition. Castrated servants at court were often assumed to achieve power and status through their positions as passive partners in sexual relationships with powerful men. Many commentators considered this an important part of their gendered construct. They also had access to wealth and did not hesitate to amass great wealth, often at the expense of the aristocracy. This left them open to charges of greed and worldliness. There is also veiled evidence that in their dress and manner they were easily recognizable, and that this contributed to the sense that they constituted a cultural "other." Much of their gender construct, as related to us by sources that are generally hostile, tends to be negative.

Despite this by the tenth century Byzantine court eunuchs also were acquiring other, more positive images. In this period we can begin to document the important roles that eunuchs played as guardians of sacred spaces. This is especially seen in the ceremonial book of the tenth century emperor, Constantine Porphyrogennetos. Only a eunuch or the patriarch could touch the imperial crown.[14] Only eunuchs or the patriarch could see the crown being removed from the imperial head. Only eunuchs, of all the royal servants, could escort the emperor when he engaged in the most sacred of religious ceremonies. Eunuchs were the only persons outside the conventional ecclesiastical hierarchy who were allowed to handle the candles that figured so prominently in these cere-monies. Eunuchs were closest to the imperial person, guarding his sa-cred person and his sacred space.[15]

Court eunuchs served as guardians of the emperor during the dan-gerous hours of darkness, and as such were immediately available to discuss and interpret dreams and portents of the night.[16] Finally, an im-portant part of the gendered construct of the Byzantine court eunuch was that he was trained to be a perfect servant, totally loyal and trust-worthy, undistracted by sexual desires or familial needs.[17] Eunuchs were perfect servants of the emperor and the aristocracy, just as angels were perfect servants of God. I have discussed these issues in greater detail in two recent articles.[18] This is a gender construct that has little to do with sexual desire or sexual object choice, despite the negative traditions men-tioned above. It is important to remember that men in the Byzantine world did not become eunuchs because they desired same-sex relation-ships. This is an erroneous modern assumption.[19] Thus the gender con-struct that tenth-century Byzantine culture assigned to court eunuchs was based on both formal and informal functions, external appearance, including both dress and mannerisms, and relationships to sexuality and reproduction. Equally important is the fact that by the tenth century almost all our sources assume that eunuchs are men, though of spe-cially gendered sort.

At the same time we see that by the tenth century eunuchs associ-ated with the church were being assigned a gender construct that was much more positive than that of the court eunuch. They were honored for their celibacy and asceticism, and the specific description of their gender construct represents the antithesis of the negative attributes tra-ditionally assigned to court eunuchs. The existence of this additional gender category is clearly evident in Theophylaktos's essay when he says that, despite negative opinion about the institution of "eunuchism" (a di-rect translation of his term), it is a valued and holy institution.[20] Those eunuchs who served in the church were castrated to aid them in remain-ing celibate and were not acculturated into the specialized gender status of the court eunuch. Chroniclers and hagiographers wrote about and often celebrated high churchmen who had been eunuchs. These in-cluded the Patriarch Germanos in the seventh century;[21] the infamous iconoclastic patriarch from the eighth century, Niketas;[22] the ninth-century patriarch, Ignatios;[23] and probably also the Patriarch Methodios;[24] and, from the tenth century, the Patriarchs Steven II[25] and Polyeuktos.[26] In addition to these patriarchs, hagiographers celebrated the lives of lesser eunuchs serving in both the church and at the court. Of special interest is the tenth-century life of St. Nikephoros the Bishop of Miletos,[27] who was castrated by his parents and then brought to Constantinople to be educated and trained to serve, probably in the royal court. He left the court to enter the church. Then there is Niketas who was also castrated by his parents, was trained, and then entered the household of the empress Irene. After a career as a civil servant and military commander he became a monk and specialized in healing men who were tormented by sexual desires.[28] Some scholars have suggested that Symeon the New Theologian might have been a eunuch.[29] Early in the twelfth century Symeon the Sanctified, an important eunuch at the Byzantine court, left the court and adopted the monastic life.[30]

By the tenth century some court eunuchs were engaging in activities that might help them acquire a reputation for sanctity. Powerful court eunuchs founded monasteries and sponsored hagiographical writings that celebrated their spirituality. For example, the court eunuch Constantine probably was responsible for the writing of the *vita* of his father, St. Metrios, a *vita* that celebrates Metrios's faith and honorable behavior for which he was rewarded by God with a son whom he could castrate and send to serve at court.[31] The eunuch Euphratas, an invention of the tenth century, is credited with converting the emperor Constantine I to Christianity and with designing and building the city of Constantinople.[32] In general, by the tenth century, the image of the court eunuch is becoming more positive and the virtuous ecclesiastical eunuch is almost a commonplace in Byzantine hagiography.

Clearly, in this society, gender was constructed very differently from the way we construct gender in modern western society. We have identified a separate gender category for eunuchs that is further divided into categories for court eunuchs and ecclesiastical eunuchs, and we have seen that there is considerable crossover between these categories.

In a more general sense, there is little evidence that individuals in the Byzantine world were placed in gender categories primarily because of sexual preference of any sort, an important way of assigning gender in some societies. The presence or absence of genitalia also does not elicit much comment in our Byzantine sources, though aristocratic authors express pity for eunuchs because they cannot procreate. In Byzantine society gender categories were determined in ways that remind one of some American Indian societies in the last century, where the primary determinants of gender were social roles and conventions dictating external appearances, physical mannerisms, facial expressions, and manner of dress.[33] Thus Byzantine court eunuchs constituted a socially constructed gender with characteristic patterns of appearance and behavior and characteristic training for very specific work. While their inability to procreate was part of the construct, their sexual preferences, while sometimes discussed by innuendo, were not. Eunuchs serving the church were gendered in accordance with the ascetic norms specified for celibate churchmen and holy men, placing such eunuchs in a larger group for which both sexuality and reproduction were inappropriate.

THEOPHYLAKTOS'S VISION OF DANIEL

The preceding theoretical framework makes it easier to understand Theophylaktos's rhetorical question, "What about Daniel?" The prophet Daniel presented Byzantine commentators with a major biblical figure who, in their minds, was associated simultaneously with the status of courtier and that of prophet. As a prophet, his story endowed him with all the attributes of a Byzantine religious ascetic, yet the context of his story identified him, to a Byzantine audience, unequivocally as a court eunuch, a category, as we have seen, conventionally associated with a great many negative stereotypes.[34] Thus the figure of Daniel provides an important example of the way in which the court eunuch was assimilating attributes of the ascetic holy man, uniting these two very different images in one single individual. The following pages examine the ways in which the tension between these two aspects of Daniel's story were treated in hopes that this will provide insight into the dynamics of gender in Byzantine society.

The traditional story of Daniel is familiar from the Book of Daniel in the Old Testament—how Jerusalem was defeated and Daniel and his three companions were among the children of noble birth carried off to Babylon.[35] King Nebuchadnezzar instructed his chief eunuch to select the best and brightest from among the captives for his own household.

Those selected had beautiful bodies and showed potential for training and education. Their names were changed and the king commanded that they be fed from his own table. The Septuagint never directly states that Daniel was a eunuch, yet the assumption lurks in the background, if only because Daniel and the three boys were turned over to the chief court eunuch for training.[36] In some commentaries on the Book of Daniel (the fourth-century commentary of Theodoret of Cyrrhus,[37] for example) and in some Byzantine historians who attempt to deal with historical events recorded in the Old Testament, it is routine to find the Daniel story accompanied, without comment, by the quotation from Isaiah 39, "And some of the sons who will be born to you, sons of your own begetting, shall be taken and shall be made eunuchs in the palace of the king of Babylon."[38]

It is not surprising that Byzantine society of the tenth century, a culture that was accustomed to having eunuchs at court, should assume that Daniel was a eunuch. After all he was a prisoner in a foreign land, his name was changed, he was reared in the king's *familia*, destined to be a courtier, and the king was concerned about his physical and intellectual formation. He was eternally youthful and lived outside the structure of the traditional aristocratic family—that is, he had no offspring. He was disassociated from any aristocratic or religious party and functioned as a moral control over the absolutism of the king. He was physically attractive and reared to present himself in ways that would bring honor to the court. He acted as an intermediary between his God and the king, between men and women (as in the story of Susanna),[39] and between the weak and the powerful. In this capacity he acted as a guardian of the weak, especially women and children, a role that is especially clear in his relationship to the three boys and to Susanna. He functioned as a guardian and purifier of sacred space (as in the story of Bal and the story of the Dragon).[40] He had "magical" properties, especially as an interpreter of visions and dreams.[41] Finally, and perhaps most importantly, he was the trusted servant of the king, loyal to him first of all after his God.

This was the context within which Daniel's story was read by the tenth century. Our perception of that context and of the dynamics of gender construction are brought into clear relief by the way in which the traditional story of Daniel was reconfigured to conform to tenth-century Byzantine conceptions of the court eunuch. At the same time, the figure of Daniel also retained the qualities of a holy man.

DANIEL AND ST. JOHN CHRYSOSTOM: THE STORY OF DANIEL IN THE FOURTH CENTURY

In the fourth century these two conceptions of Daniel, court eunuch and holy man, would have been so distinct that they would have been almost impossible to combine in a single individual. Court eunuchs were distasteful, worldly figures of ambiguous sexual status. Holy men were real men favored by God. In the tenth century, however, we will see that an attempt will be made to resolve this dichotomy, resulting in a new portrayal of Daniel that presents him as prophet, holy man, eunuch, and courtier.

While the following pages are based on a close reading of the Septuagint and several commentaries on the Book of Daniel, the two sources that offer the best opportunity for comparison are John Chrysostom's fourth-century *Commentary on the Book of Daniel*[42] and Symeon Metaphrastes' tenth-century *Life of Daniel*.[43] Both authors were certainly familiar with both religious ascetics and court eunuchs.

St. John Chrysostom, patriarch of Constantinople from 398 to 404, is a familiar fourth-century figure. He was born in Antioch at some time between 340 and 350 and died in 407. He was very well educated and became famous for his oratorical skills. During the time he was patriarch, John Chrysostom carried out an extended political battle with the powerful court eunuch, Eutropius. Chrysostom's *Homiliae in Eutropium Eunuchum Patricium,* which tradition says was delivered over Eutropius as he cowered beneath the altar in Hagia Sophia, seeking sanctuary, is familiar to most scholars of late antiquity and Byzantium.[44] Though Chrysostom never tells us that Eutropius is a eunuch, it would have been quite apparent to his audience. In his oration Chrysostom uses a wealth of words and verbal imagery traditionally associated with eunuchs. Chrysostom was a prolific writer, whose works are primarily exegetical homilies on the New and Old Testaments. His *Commentary on the Book of Daniel* is one of the latter. His works were widely read and held in high regard by his contemporaries.

Chrysostom, writing in the fourth century, faithfully recounted at least some of the story of the prophet Daniel as it appears in the Septuagint. The tension between Daniel's image as a holy man and Old Testament prophet and his position as a court official with functions associated with court eunuchs in Byzantium runs through the document. Chrysostom tells us how Daniel and the three boys were brought to Babylon, but never suggests in any way that they may have been eunuchs. The line that says that the boys were selected because they were beautiful in appearance, however, elicits a long and rather tortured gloss. "Everyone knows," he says, "that beauty is an impediment to chastity and the acquisition of wisdom, so why should the king require boys who had well-formed limbs and surpassed others in beauty?" Chrysostom was certainly aware of the sexual role played by the young eunuchs at court, and he needed to recast this biblical line.[45] "Beauty, in and of itself and as long as it is not connected with sexual sin, is not bad," he says, "and if the king, a barbarian, demanded beauty, then surely God, the lover of beautiful souls, also deserved beauty in his servants. Why," he asks, "would the king seek beauty when what he really ought to be looking for is wisdom and mental perception? He does so because he is a barbarian and as such is committed to the material world, a world in which the physical beauty of his servants brings him honor."[46]

Next Chrysostom discusses with approval Daniel's acculturation into the king's household. Daniel's studies will help him to do God's work and will make him effective in learned debate. Throughout this section Chrysostom regularly compares Daniel to Moses and Joseph, both of whom were boys from the royal house who were carried off to foreign countries and reared as part of a king's household, becoming prophets who served kings. Chrysostom then discusses the fact that Daniel and the three boys would not eat the food and drink the wine from the king's table.

Discussions of food are interesting because food is often gender linked in the late antique and Byzantine world. You were what you ate, and the foods that were considered healthy for aristocratic women, children, and eunuchs were different from the foods appropriate for aristocratic adult men, just as the resultant flesh of adult men was different from the flesh of eunuchs, children, and women.[47] Chrysostom's world thus assumed that the proper feeding of young eunuchs contributed to the physical changes in development brought about by castration. Chrysostom hedges on this problem. He says that Daniel rejected the wine because it might have been sacrificial wine, but that he had no such concern about the food. Rather he was following the law. "But," says Chrysostom, "what law? Laws governing ascetic dietary practice," he observes, "did not yet exist in Daniel's day."[48] Yet Chrysostom never suggests the obvious, that Daniel was following Jewish dietary laws. So Chrysostom tells us that Daniel and the three boys nourished themselves with a diet of raw grains and water. This conforms to the norms for the diet of a Byzantine religious ascetic, a diet that Chrysostom here projects backward on to an Old Testament prophet. Then he tells us that God miraculously made Daniel and the three boys plump and beautiful on this diet so that they would please the king. Here God is facilitating the physical changes in them that are required if they are to serve the king. This miracle, Chrysostom says, is beyond nature.

> Behold the Maker of the World who finally shows his effectiveness. For he, most of all, seems an image maker who not only is able to forge and form bronze, but also he, no less, who is able to correct the shape of a statue that has already been made. Likewise also in God and these boys he shall have recognized the same sort of thing. For that bodies, after such nourishment exhibit fat was no less an indication of the faculty of the creator than to have formed man from earth.[49]

By emphasizing this miracle, Chrysostom resolves the tension between Daniel's conflicting identities, holy man, prophet, and eunuch, and evades the possibility that Daniel was a eunuch.

DANIEL AND SYMEON METAPHRASTES IN THE TENTH CENTURY

Five hundred years later Symeon Metaphrastes tells the story in a way that highlights Daniel's dual identity far more openly than does Chrysostom. Our knowledge of Symeon Metaphrastes is meager considering his rich legacy of religious and hagiographical writings. He is believed to have died about the year 1000 and may have been a high official at court. He would almost certainly have known of the castrated illegitimate son of the emperor Romanus Lekapenos, Basil the *paracoemomenus,* who served as chief eunuch under Nikephoros Phokas, John Tzimisces, and Basil II, and was exiled in 985 when the emperor Basil II broke away from his tutelage. Basil the *paracoemomenus* may well have been a

model for Metaphrastes in his presentation of Daniel. Symeon Metaphrastes is best known for his collections of older saints' lives that he reworked to suit linguistic and thematic traditions of his day. His *menologion*,
or collection of saints' lives arranged in accordance with the ecclesiastical calendar, filled ten volumes and became the standard *menologion* for
the Byzantine ecclesiastical world. Though we know little about Symeon
Metaphrastes, it is clear that contemporary intellectuals admired and
commented on his work.

In Metaphrastes' version of the story of Daniel, he is openly portrayed as a court eunuch and holy man rather than as an Old Testament
prophet. Initially, as Metaphrastes recounts the story, he follows the Septuagint faithfully, explaining that it was necessary that Daniel and the
three boys be beautiful in body and soul so as to demonstrate their good
breeding and descent from the royal line. Symeon Metaphrastes then
goes on to say, "When the king had made them eunuchs [and here he
uses terminology, ἐκτομίας, or "cut man," that is the characteristic way
of referring to surgically altered eunuchs in the tenth century] and
arranged that they be fed from his own table, he turned them over to a
teacher so that they might learn foreign wisdom and the highest lore of the
Chaldeans. Their names were changed. The king loved them and looked
too favorably on them, praising their shrewdness, for not only were they
well disposed toward mathematics, but also each was very distinguished
because of his judgement and decorous behavior. Thus did the king be-
have toward the youths."[50]

This is interesting for two reasons. Metaphrastes' acceptance of Daniel
as a eunuch is unequivocal. It is assumed. More significantly, the roles
of king and chief eunuch are altered to parallel the realities of the Byzantine court. The chief eunuch assumes a secondary role and the real op-
erant relationship, from the time Daniel and the three boys arrive at
court, is between the king and the children. Thus it is the king who
takes direct responsibility for their castration and training.

For Symeon Metaphrastes the issue of the food that the boys eat is
more straightforward than in Chrysostom. They will not partake of anything that had life. That is, they will not eat animal flesh. This, they say,
is the way they were brought up. Daniel then asks the chief eunuch to
provide them with seeds, herbs, beans, and dates. A review of the diets
of holy men and women in Symeon Metaphrastes' other writings shows
that he considered this to be standard fare for ascetic men and women.[51]

Again the chief eunuch expresses concern that the children will become thin and unattractive, but, miraculously, this diet makes them look as though they live in great abundance and luxury. Ultimately the tension between the two images, eunuch and holy man, is resolved by a miracle, but does not require the circumlocutions of Chrysostom's discussion.[52]

According to the Septuagint tradition, Daniel's first encounter with King Nebuchadnezzar comes about when the king has a dream. The king remembers that it is important, but he cannot remember the details of the dream. When his wise men are unable to reconstruct it for him, he orders them put to death. Daniel prays to God and is granted insight into the nature of the dream, then retells it to the king and interprets its meaning. When he is finished he is rewarded by the king.

Chrysostom, in his fourth-century work, had explained Daniel's skill in interpreting the king's dream by saying that God made this happen in order for Daniel to appear wise.[53] His credentials had to be established before the Chaldeans in order to offset the fact that he was young, a captive, and a member of a foreign religion. Chrysostom then reminded us of Joseph's interpretation of Pharaoh's dream, again tying Daniel into the Old Testament tradition. For Chrysostom Daniel continued to be an Old Testament prophet. King Nebuchadnezzar was so astounded and grateful that he fell down at Daniel's feet and worshiped him, ordering that incense and offerings of bread be placed before him.[54]

Symeon Metaphrastes, in the tenth century, handles this story in a significantly different way. When Daniel discovers the nature of the dream he comes before the king. "Entering, at first he excused himself, not wishing to seem wiser than the other Chaldeans, and said that since none of them had been able to find the dream he would tell them." He could do this, not because of his own experience, not because of his intellect, but rather, he says, "I prayed to our merciful God whom we worship in danger of death, for my own soul and the souls of those who are of the same people, and he disclosed the meaning of the dream and its message. I did this no less for our pains than for your glory, oh king, who ordered such good and honest men to be unjustly put to death, since you were not trying to learn something within the realm of human reason, but rather an explanation of something that was the work of God alone."[55]

This is a very different scene from the parallel one in Chrysostom. Here Daniel is deferential to the king, although his criticism of the king's autocratic behavior is clear. After Daniel has revealed the meaning of the dream, the king "was astounded by Daniel's wisdom, and straightway setting aside all small things and the empire itself and the dignity of his rule, he got up off his throne and honored God with equal honors and he made Daniel guardian of all his kingdom."[56] In Metaphrastes' world, the chief court eunuch, for all his power, would have treated the emperor and his other advisors deferentially. The emperor certainly would never have bowed down to his chief eunuch or worshipped him. Here again the relationship between the king and the chief eunuch has been altered to reflect the world of the Byzantine court.

Additional differences emerge when we examine the tale of the three boys in the fiery furnace. Chrysostom asked why Daniel was not present and also cast into the furnace. He speculated that it was because the chief eunuch had given him the name of Balthazar, the name of the Babylonian's god, and therefore the Babylonians were afraid of being charged with having burned up their own god. Or else, Chrysostom wrote, perhaps the king had become too fond of Daniel and shielded him.[57] Chrysostom then recounted the traditional tale of the three boys cast into the fiery furnace, describing how "They sang and their singing was beyond nature. God honored them beyond nature. Behold a musical chorus singing hymns praising God as if from one mouth. Those who looked into the mouth of the furnace saw a theater of piety."[58] The last comment is a striking metaphor, given the way Chrysostom regularly fulminated against the theater. Can he be inadvertently referring to the eunuch singers and actors so regularly maligned by churchmen in the late antique world? Or, more likely, to the chorus of eunuch singers who provided music both at court and in the church? The evasiveness of Chrysostom's approach to Daniel's status as eunuch seems to emerge once again.

Symeon Metaphrastes introduces his version of the tale of the three boys in the fiery furnace with an addition to the Septuagint and to Chrysostom's story. In this passage Metaphrastes says that "a little while later it happened that these [the three boys] fell into danger because they offended the king in this way." Again, notice the concern for maintaining a proper relationship with the king. Metaphrastes continues by telling us that the king was "proud and puffed up" and as a result decided that he could "make an image of God in one day and try to do the work of God with his own hands."[59] Metaphrastes then returns to the traditional

text of the Septuagint to recount the refusal of the three boys to worship
the image. The author says that the boys refused both because they
would not disobey the sacred law that says that one cannot bow down to
a statue and because part of God's plan was that they should show how
unjust the king was. Metaphrastes' text continues, "Those who accused
the boys went forth and said, 'Oh king, those to whom you gave the
royal imperium, that is Sidrach, Misael and Abdenago, did not adore
the image or obey your order.'"[60] Notice that Metaphrastes does not specifically identify the boys as Jews, although the Septuagint and Chrysostom
do. When the king heard that the boys would not bow down to the image,
he could not believe that it was true. Their refusal "so angered the tyrant
that he ordered strong men to throw them, bound, wearing clothing and
leggings, into the furnace."[61] The king is here again being presented as
an individual who is capable of abusing his power. Here, too, the author
has modernized the text, for in the Septuagint the boys wear Persian
dress and their garments are named. In Metaphrastes, except for the
leggings, which are retained, the boys wear specifically Byzantine dress.

Symeon Metaphrastes' version of the story of Balthasar's feast presents interesting changes from the account in either the Septuagint or
Chrysostom. Here we again see Daniel reconfigured by Symeon Metaphrastes. When Balthasar's aunt suggests that he consult Daniel, she
describes him as "one of those who had been led from Judaea as a captive, a man who had the power to find out those hidden things known
only to God, who told king Nebuchadnezzar, when no one else was able
to answer his questions, what all good things meant and brought to
light those things he wondered about. If you tell him what you want to
know, you will soon find out." Before Daniel explains the meaning of
the writing on the wall, the king offers him great rewards, but Daniel
"asked that the king keep his rewards for himself, since a wise and divine man should not be motivated by rewards. He gets his reward from
helping those who are in difficulty." Later, when the king does not like
the explanation for the writings, he refuses to give Daniel the promised
reward, an interesting change from the Septuagint text.[62] Here Metaphrastes is underscoring Daniel's role as an intermediary, one who explains those hidden things known only to God. He is also telling us that
Daniel is committed to a life of service for his king, whoever he is, and
that, in his experience, kings and emperors don't always keep their
promises.

Chrysostom's version of the text put no emphasis on this service aspect of Daniel's life. For Chrysostom the explanation of the writing on the wall offered another opportunity for God to demonstrate his own and his servant's power to the king. In Chrysostom's version of the story the king keeps his promise.[63]

Chrysostom has little to say about Daniel's two sojourns in the lions' den or the story in which Daniel slays the dragon. Chapter Nine of Chrysostom's text begins with the arrival of the angel Gabriel. Here the theme is clearly salvation and the return of the Jewish people to their homeland. The commentary concludes with a few brief comments about Daniel's destruction of Bal, the killing of the dragon, and Daniel's second visit to the lion's den. Chrysostom makes it clear that God intervened to bring Habatuch and his food bowl from the Holy Land so that Daniel, whom God now treats like a prophet (and there is a certain implication here that he was not so treated at the beginning of the story), will not have to endure famine in the lion's den because unpolluted food is not available. God wants to avoid the problem with food that existed at the beginning of the story.

Symeon Metaphrastes offers a much more elaborate version of the destruction of Bal, the killing of the dragon, and Daniel's second stay in the lion's den, and then inserts a new chapter that is not in any other source. This chapter, Chapter Seventeen, seems to be an effort on Metaphrastes' part to bring Daniel into the lives of his readers in a concrete way. He tells us that "since Daniel was powerful and splendid he built a tower, beautiful and well made in Ecbatana of Media, which is saved even until this day. Those who see it think it is newly built, admire its beauty and marvel at its age. The kings of the Medes and Persians are buried there and a Jewish priest is in charge."[64] Perhaps Metaphrastes is here thinking of the great building projects of the powerful eunuchs of his day and their role in arranging for royal burials.

Metaphrastes then goes on to elaborate on the story of the cleansing of the temple of Bal, during which Daniel cleverly proves to the king that the priests of Bal are tricking him, followed by the story of the slaying of the great serpent worshipped by the Babylonians. Daniel tells the king that he can prove that the serpent is not a god, and that he will slay it without sword or staff. He then proceeds to kill it with a clever ruse, using a disguised pike and relying on the creature's gluttony. The fact that he will not use a sword or staff is Metaphrastes' addition to the story. This version is a clear echo of the Byzantine assumption that eunuchs, when they engage in active combat, almost always rely on cleverness, rather than on skill with military weapons. Daniel's act brings the wrath of the cult priests down on his head, and they demand that he be thrown into the lions' den for a second time. God again aids Daniel. He stops up the mouths of the lions and makes them act like well-minded εὖνοι bodyguards δορυφόροι, good and faithful πιστότατοι. The language of Metaphrastes' description of the lions' behavior is typical of the language routinely used to describe the eunuchs of the Byzantine court.[65] Again Metaphrastes is subtly connecting Daniel to court traditions, language, and imagery of his own day.

Metaphrastes continues with a discussion of Daniel's fasts in preparation for his visions about the future. Again, he uses language that is characteristic of his other *vitae*. Finally, he concludes with a chapter that is an addition to the text of the Septuagint:

> Not just from this vision but also from others Daniel seemed great in seeing oracles and marvelous at bringing things to light [explaining mysteries]. We have omitted other things regarding the judgement of Susanna, things done long ago when he was still a youth. What more remains that can surpass that? She had been faithful to her husband but was condemned to death because of the charges of those who looked upon her with unchaste eyes and was like to the suffering which Joseph suffered. Daniel admirably saved her, Daniel who, through his wise judgement defeated the evil of the elders and showed them more worthy of death and brought about their death. When one considers his great judgement σύνεσις, grace χάριτος and greatness of sight μεχέθους θεωριῶν, since he understood the hidden secrets of God and coming mysteries of the double word which was also made known to others and what would then happen and the resurrection of man and the glory of the saints and the fall of the impious which never ends and the depths of God, how much he, who is clothed in flesh, can learn about the holy spirit and finally, chains dissolved, turned over freed from the world to God whom he desired, a man freed from the desires of the flesh with his three child friends, always conversing with the prophets and not taking anything from us that might defend

and aid us. To the glory of the Father and Son and Holy Ghost
the divine Trinity that is above all, which deserves honor and
adoration in the ages to come.[66]

Here Metaphrastes is summing up his perception of Daniel's strengths,
both as a holy man and as a eunuch. He is an intermediary between
men and women, the weak and the powerful, the material and the spiritual worlds. He and the three boys can occupy this position because
they are freed from the desires of the flesh. In Metaphrastes' mind they
are gendered as eunuchs.

CONCLUSION

Both Chrysostom and Metaphrastes were confronted by the fact that,
while Daniel was an Old Testament prophet, in the context of Byzantine
assumptions about gender the traditional narrative had the potential for
placing Daniel simultaneously in two different categories, court eunuch
and holy man. The tension that this created shapes both versions of the
Daniel story in different ways. In general, Chrysostom treats Daniel as
an Old Testament prophet. The emphasis in Chrysostom's interpretation is on the development of Daniel as a prophet, the favor God shows
him, and the way God's will is fulfilled through Daniel. As far as
Chrysostom is concerned, the various kings of Babylon are fools and
very little time is expended on their relationship with Daniel. Chrysostom
is reluctant to present Daniel as a court eunuch, a category that was very
negatively perceived in his day.

   Yet Chrysostom is aware of the developing image of Daniel as a holy
man, and for him this is the more comfortable of the two available Byzantine categories. In one of the most beautiful passages in his account
Chrysostom describes the way Daniel mortifies his flesh, his fasting,
his tears, and his wearing of sackcloth. Chrysostom says that Daniel
does this in order that his body should remain fair, and that the ashes
remind him of his own mortality. The sackcloth presses him down with
its roughness. The fasting reminds him of the way things were in para-
dise. These were the customs of this holy man. Then he puts these words
into Daniel's mouth: "I am not worthy of the earth," he said, "nor clothing, nor things which exist *in accordance with nature*, but am oppressed
by a *heavier punishment*, I who am *dressed in Persian garments and wear a*

Persian headdress."[67] Chrysostom is certainly aware that traditionally, in art, Daniel is always shown as youthful and beardless wearing Persian clothing and a Persian-style headdress.

I believe that the unspoken message here is that Daniel has rejected the material world yet must bear a heavier punishment. He must wear the costume of a Persian courtier. Though I cannot yet prove this, I suspect that wearing this kind of an eastern costume may also have been associated with eunuchs in Chrysostom's mind. In any case, Chrysostom evades the probability that Daniel was a court eunuch, though he is aware that Daniel might well be viewed as a eunuch even in the fourth century. This is confirmed both by his treatment of Daniel's beauty and by the inadvertent use of images that were applied to eunuchs in his day. Given the negative attributes ascribed to eunuchs in late antiquity, Chrysostom prefers to present Daniel as an Old Testament prophet and holy man.

For Symeon Metaphrastes both images are well developed, and he rather baldly presents Daniel as both a court eunuch and a holy man. Metaphrastes eases the tension between the two by downplaying the older image of Daniel as prophet and by reframing the context so that it resembles the Byzantine court. Daniel's dominant image becomes that of court eunuch, and his function is to provide moral guidance to an emperor before whom he is always deferential. The complications inherent in eating the wrong gender-specific food are still solved by a miracle, but the contextualization and reliance on familiar Byzantine categories allow Metaphrastes to merge the two images.

What larger generalizations are possible from this brief exploration of these two accounts of the life of Daniel? The fact that these contradictory images could both be taken for granted and successfully merged indicates that gender categories, at least in tenth-century Byzantium, were far more complex than we are inclined to assume. The strength of the ascetic image at the expense of the image of Daniel as a Hebrew prophet certainly supports what we know to be the increasing importance of ascetic holy men and monks in Byzantium.[68] The development of the image of Daniel as a eunuch in Metaphrastes' account suggests a clarification or cultural codification of the status of eunuch, especially at court. Indeed, it seems likely that, in the prophet Daniel, Metaphrastes was offering a model for the "good eunuch." Such positive stereotypes of court eunuchs are relatively scarce, but this model certainly matches the rather specific one offered by Theophylaktos of Ohrid in the twelfth century.

Finally, is all this smoke and mirrors? Did aristocrats outside the highly refined world of the church even dream of associating court eunuchs with the prophet Daniel? I think they did and offer this vignette from the chronicle of Skylitzes to illustrate my point. Skylitzes, an eleventh-century chronicler who worked from earlier sources, tells us (and it is the telling of the tale that is important) that when one of Basil II's court eunuchs was disloyal and tried to poison him, Basil threw him into a den of lions.[69] I doubt that Basil actually did this. The real point is that authors of the Byzantine chronicle tradition thought it an appropriate way for an emperor to discipline a eunuch.

Byzantium was a Christian, post-Roman society that was also rooted in the longstanding cultural traditions of the eastern Mediterranean. Inevitably it had to reconcile or ignore the contradictory assumptions about gender construction embedded in those traditions. The preceding examination of the ways in which the story of Daniel was reworked between the fourth and twelfth centuries amply illustrates the complexity and multiplicity of gender categories in Byzantine culture. It was constantly necessary to reconcile the tensions between the bipolar and multiple-gender constructs that coexisted in this eastern Mediterranean world.

Byzantine society is often described as static and unchanging, yet, as we have seen, basic assumptions about the structure of gender, and specifically about eunuchs, changed significantly between the fourth and twelfth centuries. This is dramatically illustrated by the way in which Byzantine culture reconfigured one of its most popular religious figures, the prophet Daniel, as a court eunuch and holy man. In the earlier period Daniel was cast as a holy man. By the tenth century, however, the part of the biblical narrative that presented Daniel as a courtier made little sense to a Byzantine audience unless Daniel were also presented as a eunuch, a perfect servant of the emperor.

NOTES

1. Theophylacte d'Achrida, *Discours, traités, poésies, et lettres*, ed. Paul Gautier, 2 vols. (Thessalonike, 1980–86), 1:291–331, hereafter cited as *Defense of Eunuchs*.

2. *Defense of Eunuchs*, 301, line 8. All translations are my own unless otherwise specified.

3. Thomas Laqueur, in his book *Making Sex: Body and Gender from the Greeks to Freud* (Cambridge, MA, 1990), 22, argues convincingly for a single-sex model for antiquity

and suggests that as a result the female body is always constructed relative to a male point of reference.

4. On this point, see Peter Brown, *The Body and Society: Men, Women, and Sexual Renunciation in Early Christianity* (New York, 1988), 10.

5. Both Aristotle and Galen frequently compare the human body to a loom. In this construct the testicles are the loom weights and the veins and arteries act like the warp of the loom. When the weights are removed, the warp threads spring upward. By analogy, when a man's testicles are removed, the inner connections that maintain the harmonious balance of the body roll up and stop functioning optimally. See Aristotle, *Generation of Animals*, trans. A. L. Peck (Cambridge, MA, 1942), 20 and 548; Galen, *Opera Omnia*, ed. C. G. Kuhn, 20 vols. (Leipzig, 1829), 18:574.

6. Galen, *In Hippocratis de officina medici commentariorum*, trans. Malcolm Lyons (Berlin, 1963), 334.

7. Galen, *Opera Omnia*, 18:41.

8. Galen, *De alimentorum facultatibus*, ed. G. Helmreich (Berlin, 1923), 334.

9. Ibid., 334.

10. Galen tells us that women, boys, and eunuchs must be careful of consuming phlegm, φλέχμα, in their food, because phlegm can upset the humors in these cool individuals. Galen, *Opera Omnia*, 13:662. These ideas are still subscribed to in the Byzantine period: *De alimentia*, in *Physici et medici Graeci minores*, ed. J. L. Idler (Berlin, 1841–42; reprint, Amsterdam, 1963), 268–69. The anonymous author of this text lists foods that make phlegm—meat, internal organs, and shellfish—and categorizes vegetable foods into traditional Galenic boxes. Ibid., 269. Thus foods are, in a sense, gendered. Men are encouraged to eat those foods that correspond to their warm, dry flesh, women those that correspond to their cool, moist flesh. Ascetic men and women were expected to avoid those foods that might incite them to sexual activity. This elaborate gender structuring of food is very complex and yet so thoroughly assumed within the culture that it is rarely discussed in our sources.

11. There are few discussions of the precise nature of these mutilations in either late antique or Byzantine sources. With two exceptions I have found no references in Byzantine sources to eunuchs who have had both penis and testicles removed. The first of these exceptions is the passage in Liutprand of Cremona in which the author describes youths whom he buys in the West and brings to the emperor as a special gift. These youths were doubly castrated, but the surgery was done in the West. The second exception, from tenth-century legal sources, indicates that laws punishing sexual crimes by removing all genitalia were still retained on the books: J. D. Zepos, ed., *Jus Graecoromanum* (Athens, 1931), 2:58. Our best description of castration procedures can be found in the writings of the seventh-century physician, Paul of Aegina, *Chirugia*, in *Paulus Aegineta*, ed. I. L. Heiberg, 2 vols., Corpus medicorum Graecorum 9.1, 9.2 (Leipzig, 1921–24), 111. He describes two forms of castration, the crushing of the testicles in infants and the excision of the testicles in older individuals. He considers the latter method to be preferable. He also describes techniques for the surgical removal of a diseased penis and the insertion of a lead tube to keep the urethra open. While this resembles surgical techniques used for castrations in cultures that practice double castration, Paul of Aegina never suggests that this second type of surgical

technique is used for anything but healing disease. All of this suggests to me that in the Byzantine world techniques for making eunuchs were simple and relatively safe, and making eunuchs to serve the emperor and society was a very different matter from making eunuchs as a punishment.

12. Anne Hadjinicolaou-Marava, *Recherches sur la vie des esclaves dans le monde byzantine* (Athens, 1950); G. A. Rhalles and M. Potles, *Syntagma ton theion kai hieron Kanonon* (Athens, 1852–59), 1:53; 2:676. By the early tenth century the law code of Emperor Leo the Wise reflects the prevalence of castration in Byzantine society and the need to adjust the law to current practice. While Leo acknowledges that castration creates a creature "far different from what God intended," he objects to the severity of past punishments for those who perform castrations, while acknowledging that it is wrong to castrate. His new law punishes imperial servants who castrate with removal from court and large fines. For those outside the court, punishments are reduced to fines, tonsuring, confiscation of goods, and exile. Victims if slaves are compensated with their freedom; if free they receive no compensation. Leo the Wise, *Law Codes of Leo the Wise, Patrologia cursus completus, series graeca*, ed. J.-P. Migne, (Paris 1857–66), 10:886–910; hereafter *Patrologia cursus completus* cited as *PG*. This and other evidence makes it clear that by the tenth century castrations were taking place within the empire, and many eunuchs were Romans, not foreigners. Old legislation stayed on the books but was not enforced.

13. Kathryn M. Ringrose, "Eunuchs as Cultural Mediators," *Byzantinische Forschungen* 23 (1996): 75–93.

14. For book 1 of the ceremonial book of Constantine Porphyrogennetos, see Constantine VII Porphyrogenete, *Le livre des ceremonies*, ed. A. Vogt (Paris, 1935), hereafter cited as *De Cer.* 1. For book 2, see J. Reiskié, *PG* 112:972–1416, hereafter *De Cer.* 2. The Reiskié text can also be found in *Constantini Porphyrogeniti Imperatoris De ceremoniis aulae byzantinae libri duo*, ed. J. J. Reiskié, 2 vols. (Bonn, 1829–30). For examples of ceremonials in which the emperor is crowned or his crown is removed in private by the *praepositus sacri cubiculi*, or chief eunuch, in an unseen ceremony see *De Cer.* 1:6, 57, 58, 63, 92, 135, and 156. The most interesting example of this is found in the description of the observances on the day of the feast and procession celebrating the Ascension of Christ. Sometimes the emperor goes to this ceremony by boat. On these occasions, when the boat lands, the emperor must be crowned in the open. The text says, "The emperor commands the *praepositus* to command that the princes of the *cubiculum* [that is, the personal body servants of the emperor, assigned to work in his private quarters, and almost always eunuchs] carrying a purple cloak, stand in a circle. The emperor goes into the middle of the circle and is crowned by the *praepositus* because he cannot be crowned before the faces of bearded men. For this reason the prefects of the *cubiculum* stand in a circle." *De Cer.* 1:101 and 2:85, 98.

15. The sanctity of the body of the imperial person is evident throughout the *De Ceremoniis*. The emperor is kissed on the hands or knees by high dignitaries as part of well-established ritual. The emperor hands regalia, decorations, etc. to high dignitaries as part of rituals. Yet, when the emperor takes something into his own hand he always takes it from the hand of a eunuch, usually the *praepositus sacri cubiculi*.

16. I suspect that it is no accident that one of the most popular "dream books" of both the medieval East and West was one attributed to the prophet Daniel. After having a

dream one would consult a dream book to find out what that dream meant. Granted it can be argued that Daniel's connection here is one of prophesy, and the prophesies contained in the Old Testament under his name became models for later prophetic constructions, but I think one can also argue that since the Byzantines associated Daniel with eunuchism they also associated him with the eunuchs' function as intermediaries between the worlds of reality and those of dreaming, and saw him as an individual who might hold the key to correctly intepreting divine messages coming from God. For the text of the dream book of Daniel, see E. de Stoop, "Onirocriticon du prophete Daniel," *Revue de philologie* 33 (1909) (Reprint, Amsterdam, 1975): 93–111.

17. *De Cer.* 2:1159 ff. outlines the ceremonial for the promotion of a eunuch to the position of *cubicularius*, or personal servant who serves the emperor in his private quarters. It illustrates the importance of the service aspect of the court eunuch's gender construct. The *praepositus* delivers "the customary advice," warning and exhorting the new *cubicularius* not to lay his hands on another who is bearded without the emperor's order and not to be a drunkard and a braggart and not to concern himself with affairs that are not his business and not to have sexual relations with or be friendly with men who are lacking in moral worth or who plot against the emperor's authority and not to reveal to them any of the emperor's secrets. He should honor all those of the first rank in office and his equals in office, and all the senate and most of all the *praepositus*.

18. Kathryn M. Ringrose, "Living in the Shadows: Eunuchs and Gender in Byzantium," in *Third Sex, Third Gender: Beyond Sexual Dimorphism in Culture and History*, ed. Gilbert Herdt (New York, 1994), 85–110, 504–18; and Ringrose, "Eunuchs as Cultural Mediators."

19. Since eunuchs were generally castrated as young children, this act cannot have been a voluntary act or one influenced by individual sexual preference. Some Byzantine sources do, however, refer to a category of eunuchs who are "eunuchs by nature." For example, in the tenth-century life of St. Andrew Salos we find that such a eunuch befriends the saint's disciple, Epiphanios. See François Halkin, ed., *Bibliotheca Hagiographica Graecae* and *Bibliotheca Hagiographica Graecae: Actuarium* (Brussels, 1957 and 1969) (hereafter referred to as BHG and cited by entry numbers), 117. This eunuch is τῇ φύσει εὐνοῦχος and the saint accuses him of trying to seduce his disciple: *The Life of Saint Andrew the Fool*, ed. and trans. Lynnart Rydén, 2 vols. (Uppsala, 1995), 1:82, and 2:315. Also in *Acta Sanctorum* (hereafter *AASS*) (Brussels, 1910), May, vol. 6, 30. In the life of St. Basil the Younger (BHG 264b) there is a long diatribe against the powerful court eunuch, Samonas. He is called a eunuch by nature, φύσει ὁ Σαμωνᾶς εὐνοῦχος, and accused of engaging in acts of sodomy. S. G. Vilinskii, *Zitie sv. Vasilija Novago v russkoj literaturi*, Zapiski Imp. Novsiossijskago Universiteta 7 (Odessa, 1911), 285–90. In the life of St. Niphon of Konstantiane, which was probably written some time after the tenth century, we find the demons debating over the soul of a eunuch who is called a sodomite. He is a eunuch by nature, δὲ φύσει εὐνοῦχος, both in spirit, ψυχῇ, and in body, σώματι. In this case the saint saves the eunuch's soul. In the same life we are told of another eunuch, τῇ φύσει εὐνοῦχος, who loved money and beat his servants. Even the Virgin could not save him. A. V. Rystenko and P. O. Potapow, *Materialien Zur Geschichte der Byzantisch-Slavischen Literatur und Sprache*, Zentrale-Wessenschaftliche Bibliothek Zu Odessa (Odessa, 1928), 111, line 9. Byzantine sources often assume that eunuchs act as passive partners in same-sex relationships,

without assuming that this is a matter of personal choice. In fact, the official lecture on duties that the chief court eunuch gives to new eunuchs inaugurated into service in the imperial private quarters states that a eunuch must not be friendly with or have sexual relations with a ruined man or one who is involved in political scheming. Sexual behavior that we would label homosexual is not forbidden, or even mentioned. Instead the eunuch is being told to be careful with whom he has sexual relations. I suspect that "eunuch by nature" may be a code phrase used to refer to those castrated men who actively seek out sexual relations with other men. See *De Cer.* 2, *PG* 112:1162.

   20. Theophylaktos of Ohrid presents eunuchism as an established institution of value in that it guards men's chastity during morally difficult times. Valued eunuchs who belong to this category include those who are castrated as children and not of their own volition. See *Defense of Eunuchs*, 305–09.

   21. Lucian Lamza, ed., *Patriarch Germanos I. Von Konstantinopel (715–730)* (Würzburg, 1975).

   22. Nicetas was hated in his own time because of his iconoclastic policies, not because he was a eunuch: C. de Boor, ed., *Theophanis Chronographia*, 2 vols. (Leipzig, 1883–85). The twelfth-century chronicler, Michael Glycas, however, uses the fact that Nicetas was a eunuch to heap abuse on him, using traditional negative rhetoric: Michael Glycas, *Annales*, ed. I. Bekker (Bonn, 1836), 527.

   23. Life of Ignatios the Patriarch (BHG 817), *PG* 105:487–574. See also John Skylitzes, *Synopsis Historiarum*, ed. A. Thurn (New York, 1973), 106, line 18.

   24. The tale of Methodios's sterility appears in almost all the historians who discuss his patriarchate: I. Bekker, ed., *Theophanes Continuatus* (Bonn, 1838), 4:158; John Skylitzes, *Synopsis Historiarum*, 86, line 52. The story is a version of a common "discovery" tale in which a holy person, man or woman, is accused of fathering a child and then found to be incapable of doing so. In the case of a woman, who is typically posing as a young man, she is found to be a woman. In the case of a man, he is found to be a eunuch.

   25. George the Monk, *Georgius Monachus, Chronicon*, ed. C. de Boor, 2 vols. (Leipzig, 1904), 902; Bekker, *Theophanes Continuatus*, 410.

   26. Leo the Deacon, *Historiae libri X*, ed. C. B. Hase (Bonn, 1828), 32, says that Polyeuktos "had elected from childhood the monastic and unencumbered life.... It was not just his nature that made him this way. He was a eunuch and had come to extreme old age, but also he had given up all worldly goods...." John Skylitzes, *Synopsis Historiarum*, 244, says that, "He made Patriarch Polyeuctes the monk, who came from Constantinople and grew up and was educated there, and was castrated by his parents and lived the monastic life for a long time with praise."

   27. "Vita Sancti Nicephori, Episcopi Milesii," ed. Hippolyte Delehaye, *Analecta Bollandiana* 14 (1895): 129–66 (BHG 1338).

   28. D. Papachryssanthou, "Un Confesseur du Second Iconoclasm: La vie du Patrice Niketas," *Travaux et mémoires* 3 (1968): 309–51.

   29. Rosemary Morris, "The Political Saint of the 11th Century," in *The Byzantine Saint*, ed. Sergie Hackel (London, 1981); A. J. Van der Aalst, "The Palace and the Monastery in Byzantine Spiritual Life c. 1000," in *The Empress Theophano: Byzantium and the West at the Turn of the First Millennium*, ed. Adebert Davids (Cambridge, MA, 1995), 326–27. Symeon's origins in Paphlagonia, a common source of eunuchs in this period, suggests that he might have been a eunuch, as does the fact that, as a student, he was sponsored by his uncle, a powerful eunuch courtier in the service of Basil II and Constantine VIII. Symeon also served as a *spatharokoubikoularios* (ceremonial spear carrier assigned to the emperor's personal service) at court, an office often held by eunuchs. We are far from certain, however, about whether St. Symeon was a eunuch. In her recent book, *Monks and Laymen in Byzantium 843–1118* (Cambridge, MA, 1995), Morris no longer makes this claim for him. In fact, many provincials who came to the city from Paphlagonia were not eunuchs, and many powerful eunuchs at court sponsored young scholars—one thinks immediately of the eunuch Theoctistus's sponsorship of Constantine/Cyril. The palace employed both bearded and eunuch *spatharokoubikoularii*. I suspect that this question can only be settled by a detailed analysis of St. Symeon's writings.

30. Morris, *Monks and Laymen*, 279–80.

31. Life of St. Metrios (BHG 2272), *AASS*, November, Propylaeum, Synaxaria Ecclesiae Constantinople, 721–24. Another similar story that celebrates the holiness of the eunuch Constantine's father can be found in the writings of one of the continuators of Theophanes, sometimes referred to as Symeon Magister. I. Bekker, ed., *Theophanes continuatus; Ioannes Cameniata; Symeon Magister; Georgius Monachus* (Bonn, 1828), 713.

32. The eunuch Euphratas appears in a number of scattered ninth- and tenth-century sources. Sometimes he is presented as a eunuch, at other times he is not. See F. Halkin, "L'empereur Constantin converti par Euphrates," *Analecta Bollandiana* 78 (1960): 5–17; H. G. Opitz, "Die Vita Constantine des Codex Angelicus 22," *Byzantion* 9 (1934): 535–90; A. Kazhdan, "'Constantin Imaginaire': Byzantine Legends of the Ninth Century about Constantine the Great," *Byzantion, Revue Internationale des Études Byzantines* 57 (1987): 196–250; F. Halkin, "Une nouvelle vie de Constantin dans un légendier de Patmos," *Analecta Bollandiana* 77 (1959): 63–107; F. Halkin, "Les deux derniers chapitres de la nouvelle vie de Constantin," *Analecta Bollandiana* 77 (1959): 370–72. The eunuch Euphratas also appears in the *Patria*. See Theodore Preger, ed., *Scriptores Originum Constantinopolitanarum*, 2 vols. (Leipzig, 1901–07; reprint, New York, 1975), fasc. 2, 147. See also G. Dagron, *Constantinople imaginaire: Études sur le recueil des "Patria"* (Paris, 1984).

33. See Harriet Whitehead, "Institutionalized Homosexuality in Native North America," in *Sexual Meanings: The Cultural Construction of Gender and Sexuality*, ed. Sherry B. Ortner and Harriet Whitehead (Cambridge, MA, 1981), 97.

34. St. John of Damascus reflects early-eighth-century negative stereotypes about eunuchs in his collection of ecclesiastical commentary on eunuchs (*PG* 95, no.2:1563). He begins with biblical commentary, then proceeds to repeat a letter that he attributes to St. Basil, which contains one of the most vitriolic passages on eunuchs we have: "The race of eunuchs is evil and hateful. Such a one is neither woman nor man, mad for women, envious, stingy, willing to receive anyone, insatiable. Such a one weeps into his food, is quick to anger, mad for gold, evilly paid, harsh, effeminate and a slave to his belly. What can I say? Such a one is damned by the knife. For how can such a one have sound judgement when his feet are twisted? For he remains chaste without reward because of the knife and burns with passion without bearing children because of his most private obscenity."

35. Greek authors would have known one of several versions of the Septuagint or would have relied on Origen's text of the Pentateuch. These would have included the sections on Susanna and on Bel (otherwise spelled Bal) and the Dragon, now in the Protestant Apocrypha. For an excellent summary of the Greek textual tradition and the problems it presents, see Louis F. Hartman and Alexander A. Di Lella, *The Book of Daniel*, in *The Anchor Bible*, ed. W. F. Albright and D. N. Freedman (New York, 1978), vol. 23, chap. 12. The edition of the Septuagint used here is A. Rahlfs, *Septuaginta*, 2 vols. (Stuttgart, 1952). Hereafter, *Septuaginta*. The Book of Daniel begins on page 870 of the second volume.

36. *Septuaginta*, 870–73.

37. Theodoret, Bishop of Cyrrhus, "Interpretatio in Danielem," *PG* 81:1256–1546. See also the early sections of the writings of George Cedrenus that reflect Byzantine perceptions of events before the time of Christ in his *Historiarum Compendium* (Bonn, 1838), 1:199.

38. Mathew S. Kuefler in his article "Castration and Eunuchism in the Middle Ages," in *Handbook of Medieval Sexuality*, ed. Vern L. Bullough and James A. Brundage (New York, 1996), 295, suggests that the assumption that Daniel was a eunuch has roots in Jewish tradition and from there was transmitted to the West by Jerome. He cites evidence for this in both the Babylonian Talmud and Jerome's own writings. As far as the Babylonian Talmud is concerned, we cannot assume a connection between Isaiah 39:7 and Daniel that dates before the sixth century. Jerome, however, writing in the early fifth century, seems aware of Jewish traditions that link Isaiah 39:7 and Daniel and the three boys. In both passages cited by Kuefler, Jerome suggests that Daniel and the three boys are eunuchs. See Jerome, *Adversus Jovinianuum*, *Patrologia cursus completus, series latina*, ed. J.-P. Migne, 221 vols. in 222 pts. (Paris, 1844–80), 23:255, and Jerome, *Commentarius in Danielem* l.l.3, Corpus christianorum, series latina 75A, (Turnholt, 1964), 778–79. As I have shown, early Byzantine authors make this same connection between Isaiah 39:7 and the story of Daniel and the three boys, though they are reluctant to openly call them eunuchs as Jerome does. A further problem that remains to be solved is exactly what the Talmud or Jerome means by "eunuch." In the context of Jerome's writings it certainly means courtier, but whether a castrated or simply celibate courtier is unclear. I am indebted to Prof. David Goodblatt of our faculty for his help in dealing with the multilayered complexities of the dating of the Babylonian Talmud.

39. *Septuaginta*, 864–70.

40. *Septuaginta*, 936–41.

41. *Septuaginta*, 874–76.

42. John Chrysostom, "Interpretatio in Danielem Prophetam," *PG* 56:194–245 (hereafter "in Danielem").

43. Symeon Metaphrastes, "Vita S. Prophetae Danielis," *PG* 115:371–403 (hereafter "V. Danielis").

44. John Chrysostom, *Homilia*, *PG* 52:391. Chrysostom's themes point to the vanities of worldly pleasures and power and the changes and ambiguities that afflict the natural world. Eutropius is accused of abusing food and drink, despoiling widows and orphans, unlawfully seizing wealth and property, wearing silk robes, and displaying himself. These are all classics of the pejorative literature aimed at eunuchs. Images used of Eutropius include the dry fruitless tree and the ephemeral drying rose, both familiar images used about eunuchs. Chrysostom is clearly familiar with the gender construct that surrounds the eunuchs of his day. His dislike of eunuchs is also apparent.

45. The suggestion that young, beautiful eunuchs served as passive sexual partners for powerful men in society runs through our sources. It is difficult to know how much truth lies in these accusations since they are deeply imbedded in pejorative literary stereotypes.

46. Chrysostom, "in Danielem," 194.

47. Holy men tend to eat diets that emphasize well-balanced foods like bread. They avoid foods like meat and organ meats that cause sexual appetite. They mainly eat foods that "dry" their humors—lentils, pulse, cabbage, cooked vegetables, mustard, and greens— and a selection of approved "warm" foods including grains, dates, fruits, garlic, and onions. An excellent discussion of the importance of food and the body can be found in Brown, *The Body and Society*, 181–82.

48. Chrysostom, "in Danielem", 197.

49. Ibid., 199.

50. Metaphrastes, "V. Danielis," 372.

51. A survey of the diet of holy men in Symeon Metaphrastes' other *vitae*, which can be found in *PG*, vols. 114–16, indicates that St. Lucian (BHG 997), 114:400, eats only bread and water; St. Theodosius the Caenobiarcha (BHG 1778), 481, eats only dates, pods, cooked vegetables, and date pit meal; St. Euthymius (BHG 649), 672, eats bread, water, dates, and wine once each week; St. Clement of Ancyra (BHG 353), 824, eats only vegetables and specifically never touches meat. Symeon Metaphrastes rather specifically tells us that for St. Clement, "Vegetables were his only food. He didn't eat anything that moved, always remembering the three boys whose bodies, sharpened by abstinence, could not be defeated by the fire of debauchery nor by the flames of the furnace." St. Kyriacos the Anchorite (BHG 464), *PG* 115:929, eats only wild onions; St. Aberkios (BHG 4), 1236, eats only bread, wine, olives and oil. John the Abbot, *PG* 116:44, eats only herbs; St. Melanà (BHG 1242), 769, eats only harsh food and hard bread, as do Sts. Inda and Domna (BHG 823), 1041.

52. Metaphrastes, "V. Danielis," 373.

53. Chrysostom, "in Danielem," 199.

54. Ibid., 209.

55. Metaphrastes, "V. Danielis," 375.

56. Ibid., 378.

57. Chrysostom, "in Danielem," 210.

58. Ibid., 211.

59. Metaphrastes, "V. Danielis," 378.

60. Ibid., 379.

61. Ibid., 379. By the time Symeon Metaphrastes is writing, the image of the boys in the fiery furnace is frequently used as a metaphor for overcoming sexual desire. We see this in Metaphrastes' other writings, for example, in the life of St. Theophanes (BHG 1789), *PG* 115:16, where he tells us that just as the angel saved the boys from the flames of the furnace so, also, an angel saved St. Theophanes and his bride from the flames of sexual desire.

62. Metaphrastes, "V. Danielis," 387.

63. Chrysostom, "in Danielem," 225.

64. Metaphrastes, "V. Danielis," 389.

65. In the Byzantine period, the etymology of the word eunuch, which probably comes from εὐνή, a bed or sleeping place, was falsely believed to come from εὔνοος, or well-minded, and to reflect the intelligence and loyalty of eunuch servants. The term δορυφόρος is specifically used for a king's personal bodyguard or spear carrier. Eunuchs served this function in Byzantium, and the use of eunuchs in this role at court can be traced back to the Assyrian Empire. The same word is also used for satellites revolving around planets. There is clearly an association between eunuchs and personal body servants and body-guards, individuals who were allowed to share the king or emperor's most intimate personal space. See Metaphrastes, "V. Danielis," 397.

66. Metaphrastes, "V. Danielis," 401.

67. Chrysostom, "in Danielem," 238 (my emphasis).

68. Morris, *Monks and Laymen*, 30.

69. John Skylitzes, *Synopsis Historiarum*, 367, line 69.

4

NEGOTIATING GENDER IN
ANGLO-SAXON ENGLAND

❊

CAROL BRAUN PASTERNACK

It is the argument of this book that even in the Middle Ages, which has
in the modern imaginary often represented a period of harmonious
Christian ideology, there was no single, fixed idea of the masculine and
the feminine as essential qualities. Rather, gender was inflected by other
systems of difference, including social status, religion, and sexuality.
This essay contributes to the book's thesis by focusing on conflicting
aristocratic and Christian constructions of gender in early Anglo-Saxon
England. It does so by reading two documents from the early period of
Christianization, the laws of Æthelberht (d. 616) and the Penitential of
Theodore (Archbishop of Canterbury, 669–90).

These texts show two different ways that leaders responded to Christianization and the cultural influences that accompanied it. The penitential is, of course, more explicitly doctrinal, more precisely about conversion and what it meant for someone to attempt to follow the dictates of
this radically different religion. The laws reflect more broadly the cultural
changes of the seventh century, of which conversion to Christianity was
one component. Both texts negotiate conflicts between new cultural and
religious ideas and the practices long considered appropriate to elite pagan culture, and both texts define choices and their consequences in ways
that contribute to definitions of gender. The definitions implied by the
two texts, however, are not consonant with each other, and the differences

do not seem to derive solely from the genre and scope of the texts. Rather they point to the fluidity and conflictual nature of gender definitions in a culture undergoing profound changes.

Christian ideals and the sexual practices and the systems of gender appropriate to elite pagan culture differed in deeply significant ways. In brief, the traditional culture understood moral and legal responsibility in the corporate terms of the family and the tribe. A person's legal relationships extended to both his or her mother's and father's families. By contrast, Christianity, especially in its late antique and early medieval manifestations, introduced an emphasis on the responsibility of the individual soul and a preference for the dissociation of the individual from familial entanglements. While the family and the tribe were fostered by the pursuit of wealth and offspring, late antique and early medieval Christianity taught that spiritual and bodily purity, especially chastity, were among the highest virtues. So, teachings that were central to this stage of Christianity were also destructive of the Germanic family structure and the social structures based on the family.[1] Even the sexuality of marriage was at issue. As James A. Brundage points out, the Roman-Christian concept focused on the consent of the partners while in the Germanic concept consummation was the constitutive element. Though in the ninth century Hincmar, Archbishop of Reims, "propounded a theory of marriage" that included both the Roman-Christian concept of consent of the partners and the Germanic concept of consummation as essential to the social institution, in this way "harmoniz[ing] Roman and Christian concepts of marriage with traditional Germanic practice," nevertheless, as Brundage also makes clear, the tension regarding the significance of sexual reproduction persisted.[2] Faithful, monogamous marriage, or better yet chaste marriage, or better yet virginity endured as the sexual practices signifying Christian virtue.

The system of practices and concepts related to reproductive organs and erotic desires—whether or not these further reproduction—are at the heart of gender definition. Whether we conceive of gender as a binary system (masculine vs. feminine) or as multiple sites along a continuum or within a matrix, the capacity to give birth or to inseminate and the choices of whether to copulate and with whom contribute to one's classification as masculine, feminine, queer, virginal, aristocratic, or slave.[3] I hope to make clear that the construction of these categories— not just which but what each is—is subject to negotiation.

Also important to gender formation is the individual's relation to the corporate body. Roman Christianity stressed the individual will and acts and the well-being of the individual soul, and also, in elevating chastity and virginity and in its definitions of incest,[4] stressed sexual practices that reinforced the ideology of a person narrowing connections with natal and conjugal families in favor of monastic and heavenly families. Since in some practices and texts, such as the laws discussed below, men and women occupied distinctively different positions in corporate bodies, the shifting relation of the individual to the corporate body also affected gender formation.

Although theorists and scholars commonly credit later periods with the discovery of the "individual," perhaps in part because of economic and class considerations, the Christian demand for individual responsibility conflicted with the familial responsibility that was characteristic of Germanic family life and helped to produce the ideology and psychology of the individual. Indeed, the responsibility of the individual person for his or her own deeds and will (or shaping of desire) is a profound point of rupture brought by Roman Christianity to Anglo-Saxon culture. I speak of "rupture" here even though the break was never complete and there was always tension and struggle between the two social formations and ideologies, as well as a certain cross-influence.[5] In short, after the arrival of the Roman mission in Britain in 597, things—including gender— were never the same again.[6] Even though it did not successfully banish the old, in introducing an alternative formation that it preached as true and necessary to the everlasting salvation of the soul, the Roman mission altered the symbolic through which an aristocrat in Anglo-Saxon England became a person and a social being.

At the center of my analysis of gender, then, is the historicity of the subject. According to Lacan, the linguistic system of a culture and the larger symbolic system within which it operates have a deep relationship with the development of the individual psyche because, at the point at which the young child recognizes its self as distinct from its mother, it begins to desire union with a (m)Other *and* it is through the symbolic structures of its culture that it necessarily speaks that desire and its identities (to itself and to others). Through this separation, desire, and speaking the young child becomes a subject, subjected within its culture's symbolic system. I would add that a true conversion enacts a new subjection of a spiritual infant, attempting to replicate the processes of subject formation within the new symbolic system.[7] In "The Agency of the Letter in the Unconscious or Reason Since Freud," Lacan posits that language and culture are subject to radical, historical change. Lacan cites the Reformation and Freudianism as such ruptures exemplifying "that the slightest alteration in the relation between man and the signifier... changes the whole course of history by modifying the moorings that anchor his being."[8] In this essay I argue that Christianization produced such a rupture for the Anglo-Saxons, but I also contend that altering "the whole course of history" does not involve a wholesale wiping out of an old system in favor of a new but the introduction of a new set of struggles. Specifically, the social and cultural disruptions brought to the Anglo-Saxons by the Roman mission reenacted the struggle in the origins of Christianity, which Daniel Boyarin elaborates in this volume, between, on the one hand, a gendering of masculine and feminine based in part on the procreative functions of both genders and, on the other, a gendering that subdues procreation to an ideal of chastity.

A quick look at a problem posed to aristocratic masculinity by the conversion will make the conflict more concrete. In Anglo-Saxon society, the prestigious male often developed his sphere of influence and his property through his *wif*—a word identical in its singular and plural forms in both the nominative and accusative. (The ambiguous quantity of this word seems appropriate to the practice of high-status men, who acquired multiple conjugal relations, and it allows me a useful ambiguity in this discussion.) As well as generating children, a prestigious male generated networks of influence through the natal families of his *wif*, adding the political powers of these families to his own. Although a *wif* maintained legal connections with her natal family and its political status and even maintained control over some property, some documents, such as the laws discussed below, also situated her as the object of her husband's subjectivity, the object of his protection, and the property through which he generated more property as progeny.[9] The man's identity then expanded through marital associations and procreation. Christian doctrine opposed these practices at two levels. First it preached virginity as a primary virtue, which threatened to cut off these avenues to prestige, leaving open only the lesser byways of nieces and nephews. Second, it promoted faithful monogamy, which severely limited an individual's possibilities for acquiring status, political power, and property.

For centuries, on the Continent as well as in England, high-status males and representatives of church doctrine came into conflict over questions relating to monogamy, especially in later centuries when dynastic continuity was at stake.[10] While the church influenced royal law, it was less successful with aristocratic behavior. In 695, as punishment for *unriht hæmed*, "illicit unions," King Wihtred of Kent imposed penalties of excommunication, expulsion for foreigners, and heavy fines for nobility and commoners.[11] In the 740s Boniface, the Anglo-Saxon missionary to the Continent, succeeded in convincing the Frankish ruler Pepin to enforce church laws forbidding subsequent marriages when a repudiated spouse was still alive.[12] He also directed his attentions to the behavior of English kings, but with less effect. In 746–47, he chastised King Æthelbald of Mercia vigorously and at length because he had not taken "a lawful spouse nor observed chastity for God's sake" but rather pursued his "adulterous lust," even violating "holy nuns and virgins consecrated to God."[13] In his request to the priest Herefrid to deliver and explain his letter to Æthelbald, Boniface broadened beyond the king himself his concern regarding chastity, lamenting, "We suffer from the disgrace of our people whether it be told by Christians or pagans that the English race reject the usages of other peoples and the apostolic commands—nay, the ordinances of God—and refuse to hold to one wife, basely defiling and mixing up everything with their adulterous lusts, like whinnying horses or braying asses."[14] Similarly, when he wrote to Archbishop Egbert of York for his stylistic advice on the letter to Æthelbald, Boniface advised the archbishop to watch for similar "evils" among his "own people." "It is," he asserted, "an evil unheard of in times past and, as servants of God here versed in Scriptures say, three or four times worse than the corruption of Sodom, if a Christian people should turn against lawful marriage contrary to the practice of the whole world—nay, to the divine command—and should give itself over to incest, lust, and adultery, and the seduction of veiled and consecrated women."[15] Whether or not this "evil" practice was "unheard of in times past," it certainly remained a problem for some time to come. So, Alcuin wrote in 797 to Osbert, who had been an advisor to Offa of Mercia and now was in a position to counsel Cenwulf, that he should advise Cenwulf as well as Eardwulf of Northumbria (Alcuin's king) "that they keep close to divine goodness, avoiding adultery, not slighting the wives they already have by affairs with women of the nobility, but in the fear of God keeping their own wives or agreeing to live in abstinence." He continued, "I fear our king Eardwulf must soon lose his throne for the affront to God involved in putting away his wife and openly living with his mistress, as is reported."[16] And although adultery was strictly outlawed in Cnut's laws, the laws did not stop him (or others) from polygynous practices.

From the language of these letters, one would never construe that such practices might from another perspective be seen as normal components of high-status masculinity, but research, most notably of Margaret Clunies Ross and Pauline Stafford, has shown the prominence of "concubinage" and other multiple conjugal alliances in Anglo-Saxon England.[17] It may well be that the stubborn persistence of polygynous practices (whether serial or simultaneous) had to do with the intimate way in which they were imbricated with deep components of gender definition and subjectivity for the noble male. In fact, the ideology of Christian marital relations is so deeply imbricated in our language that we have no neutral term to designate the several *wif* of high-status, Anglo-Saxon males (even "concubine" carries a connotation of licentiousness, as do "mistress" and "paramour"). To an even greater degree than the Anglo-Saxons, we have been subjected to this aspect of Christianity by the language of Anglo-Saxon documentary culture. So, it is particularly important that we read these documents to discover complexities and contestations that have been written over.

Understanding Christianization as a complex and contested process has the advantage of focusing us on struggles that took place by means of documents, making richer and more complicated our sense of social and cultural history, and of providing a model for how cultural systems impinge on each other and complicate people's lives, even today. Understanding gender as impacted by such a complex and contested process similarly casts light on the variety of ways people attempted to cope with the ideological conflicts concerning sexuality and kinship that resulted from the introduction of Christianity and on the array of gender formations constructed in documents. While we cannot see with any clarity what the gender constructions were for the Germanic peoples in Britain prior to the introduction of Christianity,[18] we can see how each document attempted to settle issues of gender and subject its readers or other objects of its work to a particular resolution of the conflicts. We can see the historicity of the gendered subject. Socially, however, the conflicts remained unresolved—or resolved only by individuals—and remained continually subject to renegotiation.

Æthelberht's laws and Theodore's Penitential function well as foils for each other, shedding light on how deeply and broadly gender and the family were being negotiated during this era. The texts are also both from Kent and from the first century following the Roman mission to Canterbury. Though seemingly produced by two distinct milieu, royal and ecclesiastical, the boundaries between these two are highly permeable: the royal clerks and advisors were most often ecclesiastical in their professions. Indeed, church doctrine concerning marriage is an explicit part of a subsequent Kentish code bearing Wihtred's name, which, as mentioned above, gives a prominent place to penalties for "illicit unions." (Though Hlothere and Eadric's and Wihtred's codes are more contemporaneous with Theodore's Penitential, they are not as full as Æthelberht's, functioning as supplements to preceding codes; hence, my choice to analyze the earlier text.[19]) Nonetheless, the goals and scopes of the documents do differ, and, because of their different genres and different purposes, one finds different ways of negotiating the cultural conflicts concerning gender and family.

Æthelberht's law code is the earlier of these documents: although its only extant manuscript is quite late—twelfth century—it was a production of King Æthelberht of Kent at the beginning of the seventh century, subsequent to Augustine of Canterbury's arrival. Scholars vigorously debate the degree to which the code represented native pagan practices or was derived from Continental models and was the gesture of a king newly converted to Christianity, who wanted to make the most of that new association with the Roman church.[20] Those scholars who have studied the laws for traces of marital practices and women's rights have tended to view this earliest of the Anglo-Saxon law codes as a fairly pure reflex of pagan Germanic culture. For example, Stephanie Hollis writes, "there is no trace of [Augustine's] influence in the law codes of his royal convert, Æthelberht of Kent," and she like others turns to it as a source for "indigenous custom" in marital practices.[21] The tendency of these investigations has also been to examine individual provisions in the code in relation to those in other Germanic law codes, both on the Continent and in the Anglo-Saxon kingdoms. While this method has done a great deal to clarify the often elliptical language of the laws, it will be my argument here that some aspects of the ways in which the laws construct gender appear only when considering the way in which the text functions as a whole.[22] As a whole, while following Continental models, Æthelberht's law code incorporates native practices and also functions as a monarchical gesture of a self-consciously Christian king. This last factor shapes the document's construction of family and gender. In the tension between its individual provisions that seem to derive from native practice and the thrust of the document as a whole toward a monarchical and Christian construction of family, we can see one way in which documents negotiated differences between native and Christian ideologies concerning gender.

The preface and the initial laws, along with Bede's later evaluation of the code, point toward the document's function as the gesture of a Christian king. Æthelberht's laws begin:

> These are the decrees which King Æthelberht established in the lifetime of Augustine. [Theft of] God's property and the church's shall be compensated twelve fold; a bishop's property eleven fold; a priest's property nine fold; a deacon's property six fold; a clerk's property three fold. Breach of the peace shall be compensated doubly when it affects a church or a meeting place.[23]

The preface thus associates Æthelberht's decrees with the Christian mission of Augustine, and the first laws provide against theft of church property. The subsequent provisions turn to the king's prerogatives, providing for protection of the king's council. But evaluating this beginning is complicated by the fact that the only extant manuscript for these laws is *Textus Roffensis*, a text produced in the twelfth century by Bishop Ernulf of Rochester Cathedral. Æthelberht's laws appear here following three Norman law codes in Latin, as the first of an extensive collection of Old English codes arranged in chronological order.[24] The rubric or preface to the laws, "These are the decrees which King Æthelberht established in the lifetime of Augustine," certainly could have been provided as part of the manuscript's framework for the series of codes, although Richards points out in her discussion of "Anglo-Saxonism in the Old English Laws" that such a preface is common in Continental Germanic codes.[25]

In any case, Bede, only about a century after Æthelberht and long before the *Textus Roffensis*, associated Æthelberht's code with his position as Christian king:

Among other benefits which he conferred upon the race under his care, he established with the advice of his counsellors a code of laws after the Roman manner. These are written in English and are still kept and observed by the people. Among these he set down first of all what restitution must be made by anyone who steals anything belonging to the church or the bishop or any other clergy; these laws were designed to give protection to those whose coming and whose teaching he welcomed.[26]

This commentary provides a reasonably contemporary affirmation of the originality of the initial laws in the code and an evaluation of their practical and symbolic value.[27] Bede identifies four points as significant: that the laws were "established . . . after the Roman manner," that they were written, that they have had staying power, and that they "were designed to give protection" to the Christian missionaries. In addition, Bede states that that protection and the laws themselves were a gesture of "welcome," implying that Æthelberht through this legislation legitimated the cultural takeover initiated by their teaching.

In producing the legislation, Æthelberht also raised his status as king by connecting himself to the emperors of Rome and the patriarchs of the Bible who provided written laws for their people. As Patrick Wormald argues, the codes of Germanic barbarian kings were symbolic gestures designed to produce an "image of king and people as heirs to the Roman Emperors, as counterparts to the Children of Israel, or as bound together in respect for the traditions of the tribal past."[28] Bede's characterization of Æthelberht's laws as "in the Roman manner" could refer to the tradition of barbaric law codes written in Latin and following in the footsteps of Roman imperial law and also to the traditions of biblical legislation transmitted through the Roman Church.[29] In Æthelberht's code itself, in Richards's words, "traditional materials, both Frankish and pagan Germanic, are thus reworked, expanded, and given an ecclesiastical overlay."[30] This particular combination set up an alliance between the monarchy and the church that could well have served Æthelberht in asserting authority over powerful tribal families at the same time as they served to recognize the church's right to property and a certain dominion.

As a text, Æthelberht's code emphasizes the monarchy and the individual, almost entirely eclipsing the functions of the bilineal kinship systems recognized as intrinsic to pre-Christian Germanic peoples.[31] This emphasis would have been useful to Æthelberht as a *bretwalda,* an over-king whose domain encompassed a number of tribal kingdoms, insofar as it would have implied his domination over the powerful extended families of tribal aristocracies.[32] It also would have been useful to the church in complementing its teachings regarding individual rather than familial responsibility for sin, its push towards patriliny and monogamy, and its own design to be an institution that transcended and superceded divisions between families, tribes, and even kingdoms.[33] Though I concur with Wormald and Wallace-Hadrill that these laws probably did not function as resources for practice by the people or by judges, I suggest that in addition to the laws being designed "to impress [the legislators] themselves,"[34] they were also designed to impress the church officials who helped produce them,[35] admittedly not by legislating a whole slate of Christian doctrines such as monogamous marriages but rather by implying that the king and his people even within the scope of native custom were fit for such doctrines.

The laws themselves set forth an ordered, documented hierarchy of rank and gender, thereby implying that the Anglo-Saxon people and family conformed to this hierarchy and system of relations. The laws are concerned with property and with people valued as a kind of property. They give categories and names to elements as parts of this system. Whether or not these were derived from customary, oral law and practice, these categories and names became a part of documentary culture through Æthelberht's act. After the single law pertaining to theft of church property, the laws proceed through a social hierarchy, addressing first injuries to the king's property, then to a nobleman's, then to a commoner's. A great number of the laws—numbers 33 to 72, out of a total of 90, according to modern numeration—address injuries to the bodies of freemen (bones, skulls, ears, eyes, etc.).[36] As a symbolic system, the laws abstract injuries to the body and property into a monetary system of exchange, and people attain their value through their relationship to others, within a system of social stratification.

The laws contribute to a system of difference between masculine and feminine in three important ways. First, while both men and women have property value and their loss can be compensated through money, men but not women occupy and are valued according to social rank. A man is a king, a nobleman, a freeman, a commoner, a servant, a slave *(cyning, eorl, frigman, ceorl, esne, ðeow)*, but, with the possible exception of the *friwif* (free woman) and the *mægþ* (maiden), the woman is always valued in relation to a man, never the man in relation to a woman.[37] Second, men and women are situated similarly in that the laws make little mention of natal kin groups in relation to either. The rankings of the men seem to devolve evenly down from the king without any competing allegiances to kin. But this social complication of the natal kin group does appear in the series of laws that is concerned principally with women. While it is evident in the laws that men and women are concerned in producing issue, it is clear from this series that women are valued primarily in relation to their ability to produce progeny and are the objects of masculine protection.[38] Third, and perhaps most significantly, in almost all of these laws except those concerning childbearing, men are in the subject position and women the object.

The social hierarchy begins, significantly, with the king's property, implying his sovereignty. Women first enter the laws as attachments to the king's household and then as the property of men in descending rank, being cited among the objects that might be injured or killed. "If someone lies with the king's maiden, he shall pay as compensation 50 shillings"[39] begins a series on violations of such women. The compensation is the same amount as that specified for violation to the king's protection[40] and, presumably for that reason, it is the same as the compensation for killing someone "on the king's premises" or for injury to the king's lordship if someone kills a freeman.[41] But for lying with a "grinding slave" of the king a man pays 25 shillings; for a woman of the third rank 12 shillings.[42] The compensation varies according to the value of the woman as property and, as these provisions are among those specifying other compensations to be paid to the king, presumably is to be paid to the king, not to the woman or her natal family. The compensation for lying with the servant of someone other than the king depends on the class of the person owning her; so, a nobleman is compensated with twelve shillings, a commoner with six shillings (in both cases the same amount as for violations to their *mund,* property under their "protection"), a man of the second rank with fifty sceattas (there seem to have been twenty sceattas in a Kentish shilling), a man of the third with thirty sceattas.[43] (The laws are silent regarding who gets the compensation.) This ranking ignores any sense that the woman has an identity that derives from her natal family and ignores any kind of competition or conflict between kin groups and thus creates a picture of monarchically controlled order.

Families appear only in connection with laws concerning offspring and marriage. The importance of reproduction comes across clearly in law 64, which designates that in compensation for destruction of the penis, one must pay three times the *leudgeld*, *leudgeld* being the payment designated in this code for cases of homicide.[44] Significantly, *leod* refers to someone who is a member of a people, a leader of a people, or to the people itself (though this term is feminine rather than masculine and usually in the plural form), and so *leudgeld* implies payment for injury not just to an individual man but to a member of a people.[45] The penis is called here the *gekyndelice lim*, *gecynd* being the term for "offspring" as well as "generation."[46] Consequently, the value of the destroyed *gekyndelice lim*, as with that of the slain man, relates to the continuation of the people, and both of these, the law implies, are intrinsic to the masculine subject.

The issue of reproduction and the perpetuation of family comes to the foreground in the laws that focus on marital arrangements. While most of these come in a single series near the end of the code, one appears in the first sequence, the socially hierachical provisions against violations of property and protection (items 1–32). Law 31 provides, "If a freeman lies with the *wif* [woman/wife] of another freeman, he must pay with his *wergeld* and obtain a second *wif* with his own money and bring [her] to that other [man] at home."[47] This law has sometimes been read as indicating a mechanism through which a woman might obtain a different husband, in a manner analogous to divorce.[48] In attempting to determine the status of the woman in this law, scholars have focused on the payment of *wergeld*, specifically whose *wergeld* is to be paid as a penalty: that of the adulterer (the first "freeman"), of the husband (the second "freeman"), or of the first *wif*. For, if the *wif* has her own *wergeld*, then she has an identity independent of her mate's. There is a comparable provision in the Lex Baioariorum, which indicates that the woman does have her own *wergeld: Si quis cum uxore alterius concuberit libera, . . . cum weragildo illius uxoris contra maritum componat* (cap. VIII, line 10: "If anyone beds down with the free wife of another, . . . with the wergeld of that wife he allays the husband").[49] But the context of Æthelberht's law code in general and of this law in particular point to a different interpretation. In Æthelberht's laws, as discussed above, injuries are paid in relation to the value of the injured party, and all the preceding laws that provide against "lying with" a woman are ordered according to the status of the man, the freeman's serving maid being worth less than the nobleman's. This particular series of laws (items 15–32) concerns the destruction of life or property related to freemen and commoners (referred to as *man, friman,* and *ceorl*). The laws edited as 27–32 specifically seem to be a related set of penalties providing for instances of violating a man's *edor* ("enclosure" or "dwelling").[50] They begin with *edorbrecþe* ("enclosure-breaking"), then provide against someone taking property from within, against entering the *edor,* against slaying another man, against lying with the freeman's *wif* (item 31), and finally against damaging the protection for the home proper.[51] The woman in this context is part of the man's household, and damage to her is one kind of damage to the household. Consequently, I conclude that the freeman who possessed the *wif* is compensated with his own value, since it is his *mund* that is violated and his reproductive power that is injured. In addition, that *wif* is to be replaced with *oþer wif* (the issue of how easy the husband is to please, mentioned by Attenborough, is irrelevant in this context because the topic of the laws is property, not love or attractiveness[52]). The law, then, does not recognize that either woman has an identity apart from her position within the man's property. Neither does it recognize any familial structures outside of the man's own *edor.*

The woman's natal family enters the picture for the first time in the series edited as 73–85. This series primarily addresses concerns related to women. Significantly, it is not parallel to the preceding laws concerning damage to men's property in that the women are given no hierarchical positions independent of men and are named in relation to marital status, a situation comparable to that found in canonization records of thirteenth-century Paris, discussed by Farmer in this volume.[53] The principal family in these laws is the man's and the principal concern the security of his marriage and the production of his offspring. Nevertheless, the woman's natal family plays a part because it must in relation to marital arrangements, though because the laws are a system of recompense for injuries, the woman's natal family enters this documentary system only in relation to failed marriages. Further, despite the fact that the woman's natal family is addressed here, in general this series contributes to the work of narrowing systems of identity for a woman.

The first two laws in this series, while not about marriage per se, contribute to a documentary "independence" of women. Directly after the provision for the loss of a toenail (valued at twenty *sceattas*) is a single law that has as its subject the *friwif*, the term probably designating a woman married to a freeborn man rather than a woman freeborn by birth, since the *mægþ* (maiden or "unmarried woman," as Attenborough translates the word) is the subject of the next law.[54] The law is difficult to interpret because of its singularity as well as its elliptical nature. According to Christine Fell, however, this law concerns the financial responsibility of the *friwif* for certain possessions of the household. As in certain later laws in which the wife is exempted from financial responsibility if goods her husband has stolen "were not brought under his wife's lock and key," so here the wife is responsible for some sort of dishonesty if she controls the lock.[55] Generally, though this law names the woman as a *friwif*, it seems to point to some sense of responsibility separate from husband, as well as separate from her natal family. The next law, also, indicates—or perhaps attempts to create—independence from natal family. It declares "A maiden's compensation shall be as a freeman's."[56] While as an unmarried woman she cannot be valued by her relation to a husband, her independence from family is striking in that the law does not recognize her *fæderingmagas* ("father's relatives"), who are mentioned below in relation to the marriage that fails to produce offspring.

The next provisions attempt to negotiate the *mund* for widows (the fine for violating their protection), defining the widows in relation to their late husbands' families.[57] The initial designations for violations of their protection follow a seemingly unproblematic order comparable to that for men, setting up a scale for compensation that begins with the "best" widow, who is from noble kindred *(mund þare betstan widuwan eorlcundre)*, and proceeding down through the second, third, and fourth ranks. The final provision, however, introduces a term that appears anomalous to this system and might gesture towards social practices not recognized in most of the laws. Law 76 designates, *Gif man widuwan unagne genimeþ, II gelde seo mund sy* ("if someone seizes an unowned widow, the *mund* will be paid double").[58] While the preceding designations of *mund* for widows do not recognize "ownership" as a factor, implying a legal independence, this provision insists on its importance and recognizes the "unowned" condition as the exception and as a condition requiring special protection. As a condition that is largely unrecognized in the laws, we cannot know ordinarily to what group or person the widow would belong, her natal or her marital family or some lord, but we can tell from the anomalous nature of this law in relation to the others that in the social relations that existed outside of the legal code such relationships of legal ownership were assumed. But in their silences the laws work counter to those assumptions.[59]

The next laws, which directly address marriage, show the importance for women of these systems of belonging and the complexities for the woman in her shifting allegiance from natal to marital families, as well as showing the importance for men of dominating these relationships and of keeping offspring within their families rather than their wives' natal families. As a system oriented towards compensation for damages, these laws pertain to failures in marital unions: deception in marital arrangements, dispositions of property when the husband has died, and abductions of women, unmarried and married. The series begins with the initial stage in marital arrangements by providing against dishonesty. The law maintains the terminology of ownership applied to the widow by specifying, "If a man buys [gebigeð] a maiden [mægþ], the bargain shall stand [ceapi geceapod sy], if it is without deceit [unfacne]; if there is deceit [facne], then the girl is brought to her home and the man gets his payment back: the bargain is cancelled."[60] The emphasis here is on legal arrangements for the transfer of the mægþ from her "home" to the person negotiating to obtain her.

That these negotiations are in pursuit of offspring is implied by the four provisions that immediately follow, which concern the consideration of such issue in the case of the man's death. They divide into two parts, the first concerning the situation of the woman who bears a living child (Gif hio cwic bearn gebyreþ, item 78) and the second that of the woman who does not bear a child (Gif hio bearn ne gebyreþ, item 81). The first provision specifies that the woman who bears a living child gets half the goods, if her husband dies. Then the laws express a particular concern about the shape of a family. They affirm that if the woman lives with her children, she will get half the goods (item 79), and then they specify if she desires to have a ceorl (another husband), she will inherit "as a child" (swa an bearn, item 80).[61] These provisions, then, encourage the woman to remain a part of the family into which she initially married. If a woman doesn't have a child, her father's kin are to have her goods (fioh) and the "morning gift" (morgengyfe) that was given to her by her husband as part of the marital arrangements.[62] Although the laws do not say who then provides her mund, the disposition of property implies that she returns to her place among her father's kin. After that, the laws turn from the negotiated marriage to the maiden forcibly seized. The law calls for the perpetrator to pay fifty shillings ðam agende ("to her owner" or "to her protector"), the same payment that would have been a part of a negotiated match, plus whatever is needed to obtain the agendes consent.[63] If she is already betrothed, an additional payment of twenty shillings is necessary. Who this agend is, however, is not specified—perhaps her father's kin, perhaps a lord or protector of some other kind. That agend is probably not the king, in any case, for when the law provides against gængang (perhaps abduction or rape on the highway), it specifies two payments, one of thirty-five shillings, presumably to the agend, and another fifteen to the king.[64] The injury of someone lying with the woman of a servant (mid esnes cwynan) while that man is alive provides a transition at that point to other injuries involving servants.

In sum, this series implies that the appropriate way to achieve progeny is to negotiate the transfer of a maiden from her father's kin to the ceorles kin and for the woman thereafter to remain with the ceorl if she has children. The importance of her fæderingmagas appears only in the instance of dishonesty in the arrangements and in the instance of no children resulting from the match by the time of the man's death. But in these instances we may get a glimpse of a status before or concurrent with the laws in which a strong and persisting relationship existed between daughter and natal kindred. Significantly, in all of these laws except those concerning childbearing, men are always in the subject position and women the object. Even the childbearing laws might be read as provisions subordinate to the initiating condition, "Gif mon mægþ gebigeð" ("if someone 'buys' a maiden"). We see here also concern for value of procreation, primarily through marital property laws, though also through law compensating injury to the penis, and we see the woman primarily as genetrix, subjected within the marital family as producer of offspring.[65] When she is not in that procreative subjectivity, she is either part of her father's family or unagen and perhaps without mund (a term with a legal as well as a common sense, meaning "protection" and also the fine paid for violation of that protection; possibly the "money paid by a bridegroom to bride's father, [or the] bridegroom's gift to bride").[66] Perhaps because of this document's association with the Christian mission, the laws make no specific provisions for women who are the second or third *wif* of a high-status man or for the relative rights of their offspring, though these issues did impact contemporary politics[67] and even appear in the penitential tradition, as will be discussed below. As these laws are silent regarding whether relationships are monogamous or outside of certain degrees of kinship, they do not confront conflicts between aristocratic practices and Christian teaching regarding reproductive strategies. The appearance of a comfortable coexistence is enhanced by the nature of the document as a seemingly total description and comprehensive casting of disruptions into order.

The particular negotiation of gender in Æthelberht's laws produces a masculine whose legal identity is bodily and individual in relation to other individuals who might injure him or whom he might injure and in relation to the king and also, in the first provisions of the code, to the church and its officials. Masculine identity incorporates certain objects of possession that are within the scope of injury and compensation to him, namely *wif* and his property within his enclosure *(edor)*. The laws do not explicitly recognize second or third *wif* or their progeny (though they do not explicitly exclude them either). The feminine produced in this code is virtually without subjectivity. In terms of her legal identity she is the object of the male, whether in terms of ownership or protection. The laws treat her specifically only when that object position becomes problematic because others have intruded into the position of the subject by lying with that *wif* or by abducting her or because of the delicacies of transferring her from the protection of her father's family to her husband's or because widowhood has put into question where she fits as an object of protection or ownership. The masculine and feminine identities produced here are not Christian per se; in fact, other explicitly Christian documents, such as the Penitential discussed below, work hard to put the woman in the subject position as an individual responsible for her own acts. The masculine and feminine identities constructed in Æthelberht's laws may rather in part be the unwitting result of eliminating as much as possible the family from the network of responsibility and focusing on legal responsibility in a hierarchy that descends from the king, both aspects that I have suggested are related to the Roman mission.

The differentiations between masculine and feminine take on a different configuration in Theodore's Penitential.[68] The Penitential constructs the feminine as well as masculine in the subject position, and bodily purity appears as a standard for both though it is more of a problem for the feminine than the masculine, especially in regard to the procreative functions of the female. In addition, though the Penitential emphasizes individual responsibility and eclipses any legal and moral responsibilities that family often bore for a member's acts,[69] in the course of dealing with the practices of marriage and family, the Penitential positions masculine and feminine within the nuclear family. Although the Penitential appeared a generation or two after Æthelberht's laws, approximately 668–690, "with later elements," the different view of gender given by the two documents has at least as much to do with their genres as with their dates. The Penitential did not serve the political or religious aspirations of a king or kingdom but rather the aspirations of persons interested in learning how to practice Christianity. It functioned as a site of negotiation between the practices of people's lives and Christian doctrines on various points of purity. Sexuality, procreation, and marriage were among the areas subject to such negotiations.[70] It was also a mechanism or discipline for willing subjection to a new symbolic as well as the practices related to that symbolic system. Unlike Æthelberht's laws, which functioned more as a gesture regarding the relationship between the king and his people and the missionary church than as a resource for practice, the Penitential was meant to be used as a guide for reforming specific behaviors.[71] Whereas in Æthelberht's laws any conflicts between Christianity and indigenous practice were occluded, in the Penitential such conflicts were addressed directly. The implied goal within this system was chastity for both men and women. But because penitentials must recognize present practices in order to reform them, certain practices emerge in this document that did not in the laws, including multiple marriages. Hence, the generic differences between the Penitential and the laws contribute substantially to broadening our understanding of the cultural negotiations of gender in the process of conversion.

Theodore's Penitential seems to be a document that resulted from the enthusiasm of Anglo-Saxon Christians for learning how to practice their still relatively new religion. As Thomas Charles-Edwards argues, this document is an artifact of a dynamic process in which pupils were trying to understand teachings regarding penance and canons of behavior. The anonymous compiler of the text worked from information from oral traditions of his immediate pupils and the texts that were circulating.[72] Indeed, the anonymous compiler of the Penitential described the book as an attempt to sort out the "confusing and conflicting digest" of Theodore's oral discourse that resulted from the enthusiasm of "... not only many men but also women, enkindled by him through these [decisions] with inextinguishable fervor, burning with desire to quench this thirst, [who] made haste in crowds to visit a man undoubtedly of extraordinary knowledge for our age."[73] This desire does not seem to have been one imposed by a priest on an unwilling person dragging his or her heels on the way to confession but may instead have been the eagerness of those attempting to follow an exotic new religion, in many ways at odds with their customary way of life.

The Penitential would have functioned, then, as an instrument of conversion. Though not intended to be read by or recited to the laity, its provisions show us points of struggle for a person attempting to turn from one discourse and way of life to a radically different one, casting off the old through penance. The text proceeds through Theodore's "judgments" concerning the appropriate penance for various offenses, beginning with "excess and drunkenness," proceeding to "fornication," "thieving avarice," "manslaughter," "heresy," and so on. In addition to the book of penance, the text includes a book of canons, or acceptable practices, which covers some of the same territory in terms of assertions of proper conduct rather than penalties for sins. The text as a whole gives an impression of how complicated it was to practice Christianity in Anglo-Saxon England and how much will or desire was required by men and women in making this commitment. That such teachings were culturally contentious emerges in an epilogue, contained in just two manuscripts, in differing fragments. Here the writer speaks defensively in response to those who have "abus[ed]" the work of Jerome, Isidore, Pope Gregory I, "our apostle," and even Moses.[74] He indicates that to some, including "a certain gross follower of heathen fables," Christian texts were an outrage, worthy of "calumny."[75] So we see, then, that some refused this conversion, while others attempted to remake themselves.

The remaking involved an interface between the symbolic of Christian teachings—in all their multiplicity and variability—and the practices of people who participated to some degree in a prior and competing symbolic system and resulted in its own particular amalgamation of practices and its own particular symbolic system.[76] As part of its implied symbolic, the document enacts an equivalent ideal of purity for

masculine and feminine subjects, both ideally chaste or at least faithfully monogamous and both subject to penalties for fornication. The
origin of this equality is impossible to determine,[77] but here it is expressed by making women as well as men individually responsible for
their own sins. In the section "Of the Penance for Special Irregularities
in Marriage," for example, both the man and the woman are held account-
able together or separately for the marriage itself, for adultery, for vows
of virginity and "foolish vows" taken after marriage,[78] for neglect in bap-
tizing a weak infant, and for slaying an unbaptized child.[79] Only a woman
is held responsible for making a vow (presumably of chastity) without
her spouse's permission, for entering church in an impure state, for
love potions, for aborting a fetus, and for slaying her child after birth or
in the womb.[80] Only men, however, are held responsible for marrying
twice or more, for setting aside a wife, and for having intercourse that is
improper because his wife is impure at the time, the day is forbidden,
the position is unnatural, or his partner is an animal.[81]

As these differences in responsibilities imply, masculine and feminine identities are constructed differently with regard to many social
and moral aspects related to marriage and family. In many respects, the
man is the one who dominates the marriage. He marries twice or more,
he does or does not put aside his wife, and he is the one who bears responsibility for the timing (and the object) of intercourse. He also chooses
whether to put away an adulterous wife and how to punish her if he
chooses to remain married.[82]

The woman's social role as procreator contributes directly to the differences in the masculine and feminine subjects. The man occupies
only one classification whether married or not. The woman, however—
much like the women in the thirteenth-century sermon literature discussed by Farmer in this volume—is either married, widow, virgin, or
slave. Here this classification affects the penalties for fornication for the
woman and for the man. So, if a man commits adultery with a married
woman or with a girl avowed to God (puellam Dei), his penalty is greater
(three years) than if he does so with a virgin (one year) or his slave (six
months of fasting and manumission of the girl). Similarly, a married
woman has a greater penalty for fornication than a widow or a girl.[83] In
addition, the married woman's penalty for adultery is greater than the
man's (seven years instead of three years or less).[84] Frantzen very plausibly asserts that "the canons concerning adultery are not about the act or

the person who performs it; rather they are about the husband's status and his vulnerability to [his wife's]."[85] The husband's status depends on the wife's value as procreator within the man's family, as appears in Æthelberht's laws, and this aspect of masculinity in the Penitential reveals traces of the indigenous symbolic with which the Penitential is struggling.[86]

The Penitential also shows the woman's association with procreation in that she is the one culpable for acts of abortion and infanticide and the use of love potions. Here issues of purity enter into the mix of concerns related to a woman's procreative function. As indicated above, a woman—lay or nun—is not permitted to "enter a church or communicate" when she is in "menstruo tempore" and "before purification after childbirth."[87] Hence, in the Penitential, in spite of the attempts to develop the subjectivity of the feminine on a par with the masculine, in part through making men and women culpable for adultery, the feminine body is the locus for procreation and as such the feminine body is also a site of pollution.

The differences between the masculine and the feminine here relate in part to that struggle between two different symbolic systems (each, no doubt, including variants) and between the new symbolic system and, in Hollis's words, "the raw material of life" of the late seventh and early eighth century in England.[88] Marriage appears for the man and the woman both as a sanctified institution and as a violation of purity in that "in a first marriage the presbyter ought to perform Mass and bless them both, and afterward they shall absent themselves from the church for thirty days" and also "do penance for forty days, and absent themselves from the prayer."[89] The Penitential recognizes the reality of the man who is married twice, three times "or more, that is in a fourth or fifth marriage, or beyond that number," and imposes penance of a year in length on that man for marrying twice and seven years in length for the other marriages, and yet the code insists that "he shall not put away his wife" and "they shall not be separated."[90] Similarly, a few provisions later the text asserts, "He who puts away his wife and marries another shall do penance with tribulation for seven years or a lighter penance for fifteen years."[91] At the least, polygyny in the form of serial monogamy seems to have been practiced and to some degree, this penitential recognizes, had to be accommodated in the process of reforming behavior and changing gendered relationships.

In addition, the unpredictability of early medieval life intrudes on the attempts to maintain faithful monogamy. In the canons of Book II, there are provisions for when someone can remarry if his or her spouse has been taken captive or enslaved and what to do if that spouse returns after marriage (for example, "If after this the former wife comes again to him, she ought not to be received by him, if he has another, but she may take to herself another husband, if she has had [only] one before").[92] Additionally, if a woman can prove that her husband is impotent, she may take another.[93] In these provisions and many others, the church is forced through the genre of the penitential to recognize elements of the indigenous family structure including the practice of high-status men to expand their social and psychological identity through polygyny and the importance of procreation for both feminine and masculine subjectivity.

Considering the entire range of the Penitential's provisions on marriage and related matters, we get a sense of the process of subjection involved in conversion and of the interrelationship of conversion and gender. Conversion appears not as an easy change brought about by "nurturing first with milk," as Alcuin suggested,[94] but as a process of two steps forward and one back and of complex interactions between symbolic systems and between the symbolic and practice. In showing the complex interactions of the two ideologies, the Penitential also recognizes the strength of traditional masculinity in its incorporation of ample opportunities for procreation in or out of marriage, and in single, double, triple, or more marriages. In addition, the Penitential shows how firmly the masculine was ensconced in the subject position in documentary culture: despite the efforts in the Penitential to recognize the woman's subjective responsibility for error, the man's identity was less tied to his marital state, and he was more often responsible for marital matters. So, even while certain provisions (and simple logic) show that a woman could marry more than once under certain circumstances, the statement pronouncing the penance for such marriages addresses the man who marries a second or third time and whether he sends away his wife. Finally, the Penitential includes in this mix the implication that the procreative functions of women's bodies were impure. This concern for the pollution of procreative functions may well have been a byproduct of the ideals of chastity and virginity.

The conflicts between Christian and elite pagan systems of gender continued throughout the Anglo-Saxon period. In the tenth century, high-status males continued their practices of concubinage and polygyny, serial and otherwise. Edgar the Elder had three wives; Edgar the Younger also three, at least one repudiated; Æthelred II (aka "Unræd") two wives, the second being Emma, who became the second wife of Cnut. Both of Cnut's wives confusingly were named Ælfgifu: Ælfgifu of Northampton, his first wife and the mother of at least two sons, and Ælfgifu-Emma, queen first to Æthelred and mother of two sons and a daughter with him, and then queen to Cnut and mother of a son. This same king who employed the renowned Archbishop Wulfstan as his chief advisor maintained relationships with both women concurrently and for a time employed Ælfgifu of Northampton as regent of Norway with her son, Swein, at the same time that he employed Ælfgifu-Emma as regent of Denmark with her son, Harthacnut. Both women had their allies in England, and when Cnut died, for complex political reasons Ælfgifu of Northampton's son, Harold, ruled before Emma's son, Harthacnut, even though modern scholarship has identified Ælfgifu of Northampton's marriage with Cnut as "irregular." Harold ruled until he died of an illness in 1040, at which point Harthacnut was already on his way back from Denmark with a fleet of sixty-two warships.[95] Harthacnut ruled England until his death in 1042 and was succeeded at his designation by Edward, the son of their mother and Æthelred. The relative strengths of the women's paternal families and of the allies of those families played a significant role in the success of their sons, showing the continuing importance of the Germanic bilateral kinship system.

In sum, the social functions of men and women remained complex and the differentiations of the masculine and the feminine remained under negotiation in relationship to the relative success of the conversion process in each particular social and textual situation.

Notes

My sincere thanks to Sharon Farmer and L. O. Aranye Fradenburg (formerly Louise O. Fradenburg) for their thoughtful and detailed assistance with this essay. My thanks also to the contributors to this volume for enlivening my thinking about gender in the Middle Ages through the vigor of their ideas and great range of their learning. This essay has also benefitted from the very worthwhile work on women in Anglo-Saxon England and in Germania, more abundant than what I have been able to cite below, and also from the much smaller body of work on gender in Anglo-Saxon, as distinct from scholarship on women and men. For discussions of this distinction and an account of work in both areas, see Clare A. Lees, "At a Crossroads: Old English and Feminist Criticism," in *Reading Old English Texts*, ed. Katherine O'Brien O'Keeffe (Cambridge, 1997), 146–69.

1. As James A. Brundage, *Law, Sex, and Christian Society in Medieval Europe* (Chicago, 1987), similarly states: "Germanic custom and Christian teaching saw the role of marital sex quite differently.... The Germans considered sexual relations essential to the definition of marriage, whereas Christian teachers, under the influence of patristic authorities, distrusted sex: they saw it as unclean, and incompatible with their ascetic values" (135–36).

2. Brundage, *Law, Sex, and Christian Society,* 136–37. Dyan Elliott discusses a similar contradiction between the church fathers' view of marriage as the single arena appropriate to sexual reproduction and the development of "spiritual marriage," marriage without sexual relations, a practice that arose in response to the Fathers' own emphasis on the virtue of virginity: *Spiritual Marriage: Sexual Abstinence in Medieval Wedlock* (Princeton, NJ, 1993), 4–5.

3. Sexuality I define as including those practices that do not further reproduction, such as chastity and homosexuality. Gender, in my usage, is a term that defines one group in relation to another including as a defining component aspects of sexuality but also other aspects of behavioral expectations and social parameters. Gender can be conceived of as binary in structure or as occupying multiple sites along a continuum or within a matrix.

4. Christian doctrine forbade marriage within certain kin relations, perhaps most vehemently a son's marriage to his father's widow. Bede, for example, found scandalous that Æthelberht's son married his stepmother, possibly the same Frankish Bertha who brought priests with her when she came to Kent in order to practice her Christian religion (Bede of course does not make explicit the connection between Eadbald's stepmother and Bertha). Bertram and Colgrave point out, however, that this practice is the topic of Augustine's fifth question to Pope Gregory and that Eadbald "put her away" when he became Christian: *Bede's Ecclesiastical History of the English People,* ed. Bertram Colgrave and R. A. B. Mynors (Oxford, 1969), II.5 and III.6, p. 151, n. 5. Referred to below as *EH* or Colgrave and Mynors. See also the account of Alfred's elder brother marrying Judith after their father's death, in *Asser's Life of King Alfred,* ed. William Henry Stevenson (Oxford, 1904), 17.5, p. 16.

5. For a good example of both the cross-influence and the struggle, see Patrick Wormald's discussion of Bede's disapproval of the "family monasteries" that transported blood relationships into what Roman Christianity conceived of as entirely spiritual relationships, "Bede, *Beowulf,* and the Conversion of the Anglo-Saxon Aristocracy," in *Bede and Anglo-Saxon England,* ed. Robert T. Farrell, British Archaeological Reports (Oxford, 1978), 32–95.

6. While the arrival in Kent in 597 of Augustine of Canterbury's entourage serves as a handy point of reference, it was not the first Christian mission. In addition to British Christian communities that may have survived from the time of the Roman settlement of Britain, there were converts and monastic settlements from the Irish Church. Furthermore, Augustine's mission was preceded by the marriage of King Æthelberht of Kent to Bertha, the Christian daughter of Charibert, a Merovingian king of Paris. She brought the bishop Liudhard with her to help her practice her religion. See *EH* I.25.

7. In his correspondence with Charlemagne, Alcuin discusses the difficulties of conversion, likening new converts to infants. See Stephen Allott, ed. and trans., *Alcuin of York* (York, 1974), letter 56. For the Latin, see "Alcuini Epistolae," ed. E. Dümmler, in *Mon-*

umenta Alcuiniana, Bibliotheca rerum Germanicarum 6, ed. Philipp Jaffé (1873; reprint, Darmstadt, 1964), letter 67, p. 308. For a discussion of medieval understandings of conversion as a life-long process, see Karl F. Morrison, *Understanding Conversion* (Charlottesville, VA, 1992), and Morrison, *Conversion and Text: The Cases of Augustine of Hippo, Herman-Judah, and Constantine Tsatsos* (Charlottesville, VA, 1992).

8. Jacques Lacan, "The Agency of the Letter in the Unconscious or Reason Since Freud," in *Écrits: A Selection*, trans. Alan Sheridan (London, 1977), 146–78, at 174. I draw here on my discussion of Lacan in "Post-Structuralist Theories: The Subject and the Text," in *Reading Old English Texts*, ed. O'Keeffe, 177–79. For a discussion of the multiplicity and lack of closure in Lacan's oeuvre, see Daniel Boyarin's essay in this volume and Anika Lemaire, *Jacques Lacan*, trans. David Macey (London, 1977), 113–14.

9. Stephanie Hollis, *Anglo-Saxon Women and the Church: Sharing a Common Fate* (Woodbridge, Suffolk, 1992), 63, makes a similar point, that legal provisions for compensating a man for sexual transgressions with his wife "suggest... that women were not recognized as individual entities in law and were, presumably, thought of as in some way incorporated in the identity of their kindred or husband."

10. Perhaps the most famous instance is the conflict resulting from Henry VIII's desire to attain papal permission to set aside his first wife. For a discussion of medieval examples, see Georges Duby, *Medieval Marriage: Two Models from Twelfth-Century France*, trans. Elborg Foster (Baltimore, MD, 1978), and Frances Gies and Joseph Gies, *Marriage and the Family in the Middle Ages* (New York, 1987), 88–96.

11. "Illicit unions" are the topic of articles 3–6, directly following laws for the protection of church property. For a convenient text, see F. L. Attenborough, ed. and trans., *The Laws of the Earliest English Kings* (New York, 1963), 24–31.

12. See Suzanne Fonay Wemple, *Women in Frankish Society: Marriage and the Cloister 500 to 900* (Philadelphia, 1981), 77. My thanks to Sharon Farmer for pointing out this contrast.

13. *The Letters of Saint Boniface*, trans. Ephraim Emerton (Morningside Heights, NY, 1940), 124–30, referred to hereafter as "Emerton." For the Latin, see *Die Briefe des heiligen Bonifatius und Lullus*, ed. Michael Tangl, Monumenta Germaniae Historica, Epistolae Selectae 1, 2nd ed. (Berlin, 1955), referred to hereafter as "Tangl." "... numquam legitimam in matrimonium uxorem dixisses"; "sed libidine dominante in scelere luxoriae et adulterii"; "cum sanctis monialibus et sacratis Deo virginibus per monasteria commissum sit" (147–48). This letter is sometimes cited for Boniface's reference to Germanic pagan practices of chastity, but we should keep in mind two things regarding his statement that "even... pagans... punish fornication and adulterers": his ethnography may be as shaped by his own rhetorical purposes as Tacitus's was, and his examples of pagan punishments all involve women who are forced to hang themselves or are flogged through the town until left for dead or who, in Boniface's example of virtue among the Wends, after a husband's death, commit suicide (Emerton, 127–28). Though Boniface states that these are all signs of the importance of "the mutual bond of marriage" among the pagans, the Germanic law codes punish only women for adultery.

14. Emerton, 131. "Obprobrium namque generis nostri patimur sive a christianis sive a paganis dicentibus, quod gens Anglorum spreto more ceterarum gentium et despecto

apostolico praecepto, immo Dei constitutione legitimas uxores dedignentur habere et hin-nientium equorum consuetudine vel rudentum asinorum more luxoriando et adulterando omnia turpiter fedet et confudat" (Tangl, 156).

15. Emerton, 132–33. "Inauditum enim malum est preteritis seculis et, ut hic servi Dei gnari scripturarum dicunt, in triplo vel in quadruplo Sodomitanam luxoriam vincens, et gens christiana contra morem universe terrae, immo contra preceptum Dei despiciat le-gitima matrimonia et adhereat incestis luxoriis adulteriis et nefanda stupra consecratarum et velatarum feminarum sequatur" (Tangl, 158). Evaluating Boniface's accusations regard-ing the violation of nuns is complicated by a number of social factors, including the obla-tion of noble children at a young age, the fact that monasteries were often seen as royal property, and the possible custom of marriage by abduction (see below).

16. Allott, *Alcuin of York*, 46. "ut se apud divinam contineant pietatem, adultera de-vitantes; nec despiciant uxores priores propter adulteria feminarum nobilium; sed sub timore Dei vel proprias habere vel etiam se cum consensu in castitate continentes. Timeo quod Ardwulfus rex noster cito regnum perdere habeat propter contumeliam, quam in Deum gerit, propriam dimittens uxorem publice se socians concubinae, ut fertur" ("Al-cuini Epistolae," ed. Dümmler, 79). Hollis, *Anglo-Saxon Women*, suggests a contrasting perspective for Alcuin's prediction, that putting aside a wife who came from a powerful family might provoke war or other sanctions from that family (62). As I think she would concur, the two contemporary analyses were compatible.

17. Margaret Clunies Ross, "Concubinage in Anglo-Saxon England," *Past and Present* no. 108 (1985): 3–34; Pauline Stafford, *Queens, Concubines, and Dowagers: The King's Wife in the Early Middle Ages* (Athens, GA, 1983), and Stafford, *Queen Emma and Queen Edith: Queenship and Women's Power in Eleventh-Century England* (Oxford, 1997). Ross prefers the term "concubinage" to "polygyny" because "the institution of concubinage presupposes the institution of legal marriage for the concubine differs from the wife because her sexual services are not rewarded by a defined legal status and automatically recognized rights for herself and her children" ("Concubinage," 6). The status of particular women, however, is not always that clear. Particularly in the earlier period, when bilateral, cognatic kinship pat-terns dominated inheritance practices, as Ross herself recognizes, the concubine "has cer-tain traditionally determined privileges and her children are often able to inherit from their father" (6). Because of the murkiness of divisions in many cases and because the dis-tinction between wife and concubine *(riht wif* and *cyfes)* appears only in ecclesiastically generated documents, I prefer the undifferentiated term *wif.* See Ross, "Concubinage," 18–23, for a discussion of Old English terminology of conjugal relations. David Herlihy, *Medieval Households* (Cambridge, MA, 1985), uses the term "resource polygyny" to refer to the social practice of multiple marital relationships among the Germanic peoples. See Wemple, *Women in Frankish Society,* 38–41, for a survey of polygynous kings and nobility among the Merovingians and 78–88 for marital complications in the Carolingian period.

18. I propose such a "prior time" for simplicity's sake, even though there may have been no such prior time. A number of scholars are now imagining that some traces of the British church remained from the time of the Roman settlement, and the Germanic tribes on the Continent prior to their migration may well have had meaningful contact with Christianity as the theory that the runic alphabet derives from the Roman implies.

19. Patrick Wormald points to the statements in the prologues to the codes of Hlothere and Eadric and of Wihtred that their laws "supplemented the general body of law whereby society lived," which may have been codified in Æthelberht's Laws: *The Making of English Law: King Alfred to the Twelfth Century*, vol. 1 (Oxford, 1999), 101–02.

20. See the work of Hollis, *Anglo-Saxon Women*; Mary P. Richards, "Anglo-Saxonism in the Old English Laws," in *Anglo-Saxonism and the Construction of Social Identity*, ed. Allen J. Frantzen and John D. Niles (Gainesville, FL, 1997), 40–59; H. G. Richardson and G. O. Sayles, *Law and Legislation from Æthelberht to Magna Carta* (Edinburgh, 1966); J. M. Wallace-Hadrill, *Early Germanic Kingship in England and on the Continent* (Oxford, 1971); Patrick Wormald, "*Lex Scripta* and *Verbum Regis*: Legislation and Germanic Kingship, from Euric to Cnut," in *Early Medieval Kingship*, ed. P. H. Sawyer and I. N. Wood (Leeds, 1977), 105–38; and Wormald, *The Making of English Law*, 93–101.

21. Hollis, *Anglo-Saxon Women*, 54, 61–65. General studies of the laws in relation to Anglo-Saxon women and marriage include Anne L. Klinck, "Anglo-Saxon Women and the Law," *Journal of Medieval History* 8, no. 2 (June 1982): 107–21; Christine Fell, *Women in Anglo-Saxon England* (Oxford, 1984), esp. 56–89; Mary P. Richards and B. Jane Stanfield, "Concepts of Anglo-Saxon Women in the Laws," in *New Readings on Women in Old English Literature*, ed. Helen Damico and Alexandra Hennessey Olsen (Bloomington, IN, 1990), 89–99. For a similar study on Germanic laws, including Anglo-Saxon, see Brundage, *Law, Sex, and Christian Society*, esp. 124–45.

22. Richards and Stanfield, "Concepts of Anglo-Saxon Women," while pulling together provisions concerning women from a wide range of law codes, encourage us to consider the laws "as written texts . . . compiled for specific purposes" in imitation of those produced on the Continent (90–91).

23. "Þis syndon þa domas, þe Æðelbirht cyning asette on Augustinus dæge. Godes feoh 7 ciricean XII gylde. Biscopes feoh XI gylde. Preostes feoh IX gylde. Diacones feoh VI gylde. Cleroces feoh III gylde. Ciricfriþ II gylde. Mæthl friþ II gylde" (Introduction and item 1). All citations of Æthelberht's laws are from Attenborough, *Laws of the Earliest English Kings*; the translations are mine, though I consult Attenborough (pp. 4–5). I omit in the quotation the numbers of the law(s) because they are not in the manuscript and provide an editorial system of grouping provisions that at times may be misleading. The scribe separates provisions with a point and a large capital. Some lines are also out-dented, but these differences do not seem to correspond to topic divisions; for example, after two provisions for "loss of the regenerative member" and piercing all the way through it, an out-dented *Gif* introduces the provision for the penis that is pierced part-way through (top of 3r). For ease of reference, however, I often refer to and list in the notes the numbers of the laws introduced by modern editors, as found in Attenborough's edition. I have checked his edition against the facsimile of *Textus Roffensis*, ed. P. H. Sawyer (Copenhagen, 1957–62).

24. For the authoritative study on this manuscript, see Mary P. Richards, *Texts and Their Traditions in the Medieval Library of Rochester Cathedral Priory*, Transactions of the American Philosophical Society 78, no. 3 (Philadelphia, 1988).

25. Richards, "Anglo-Saxonism," 43. Assertions doubting the authenticity of the preface include Wallace-Hadrill, "The rubric is not original, though it may embody material from a prologue (now lost) such as was common in the continental laws" (*Early Germanic*

Kingship, 39); and Richards, "Anglo-Saxonism," who is interested, as I am, in the way the "rubric to Æthelberht's law code . . . links its origin to St. Augustine" but acknowledges in parentheses that the rubric "may be a later scribal addition" (44). Wormald points out in a footnote to "Inter Cetera Bona . . . Genti Suae: Law-Making and Peace-Keeping in the Earliest English Kingdoms," *La Giustizia Nell'Alto Medioeve (Secoli v–vii), Settimane di Studio del Centro Italiano di Studi Sull'Alto Medioevo* 42 (1995): 963–93, that similar rubrics appear in the *Textus Roffensis* for the law codes of Hlothere and Wihtred; he believes that the rubric derives from Bede (983 and n. 28). While the phrase "in Augustine's day" points toward a retrospection that could indicate a later addition to the manuscript, it might also be a way of honoring Augustine shortly after his death in 604 (for this date, see Bede, *EH* II.3; Colgrave and Mynors, 144).

26. "Qui inter cetera bona quae genti suae consulendo conferebat, etiam decreta illi iudiciorum iuxta exempla Romanorum cum consilio sapientium constituit; quae conscripta Anglorum sermone hactenus habentur et obseruantur ab ea. In quibus primitus posuit, qualiter id emendare deberet, qui aliquid rerum uel ecclesiae uel episcopi uel reliquorum ordinum furto auferret, uolens scilicet tuitionem eis, quos et quorum doctrinam susceperet, praestare." English and Latin from Colgrave and Mynors, 150–51. Attenborough points his readers to this passage in his edition of the laws (*Laws of the Earliest English Kings*, 2).

27. Nevertheless, Richardson and Sayles assert that these clauses are an "interpolation" (*Law and Legislation*, 2). They believe that they "may represent, in a distorted form, a genuine piece of Kentish legislation in the later seventh century" (2), but doubt their authenticity because they constitute the only part "which in any way purports to affect the Roman mission or the band of uncertain and unstable converts," because the penalty for stealing from the king is only nine-fold in comparison to a twelve-fold compensation for the church's property and eleven-fold for the bishop's, and because they do not believe that Æthelberht ever converted to Christianity and that the introduction of writing to Kent and the production of the laws were, then, unrelated to the king's conversion (3 and 157–69). The relative rates of compensation have troubled many scholars, among them William A. Chaney, "Aethelberht's Code and the King's Number," *The American Journal of Legal History* 6 (1962): 151–77.

28. Wormald, "*Lex Scripta*," 136. I depart from Wormald, however, in that he believes that Æthelberht's "legislation was pressed by churchmen on a disinterested or reluctant kingship," apparently because so few of the provisions pertain specifically to Christian practice (131). I argue below that not only did the laws function as a gesture indicating that Æthelberht and his people were joining a tradition of an alliance between empire and the "religion of the Book" (Wormald, "*Lex Scripta*," 131), but that the shape of the laws as a whole—their inclusions and exclusions—implies a new constellation of king and family more consistent with Christian views than pagan family structures. In this way, the laws worked out a compromise between "traditions of the tribal past" and the teachings of the Roman Church that also served the interests of a more powerful monarchy. See also the arguments of Wallace-Hadrill, *Early Germanic Kingship*, esp. 36–40.

29. Wormald, "*Lex Scripta*," and Richards, "Anglo-Saxonism."

30. Richards, "Anglo-Saxonism," 44.

31. See Alexander Callander Murray, *Germanic Kinship Structure: Studies in Law and Society in Antiquity and the Early Middle Ages,* Studies and Texts 65 (Toronto, 1983), for the definitive study establishing bilineal rather than agnatic kinship as dominant among the Germanic peoples, and David Herlihy, *Medieval Households,* for a study of change in the structures of lineage and households in the Middle Ages. See also Lorraine Lancaster, "Kinship in Anglo-Saxon Society," *British Journal of Sociology* 9 (1958): 230–50, 359–77, abridged and reprinted in *Early Medieval Society,* ed. Sylvia L. Thrupp (New York, 1967), 17–41; and H. R. Loyn, "Kinship in Anglo-Saxon England," *Anglo-Saxon England* 3 (1974): 197–209, esp. 204–05.

32. Loyn argues that in Anglo-Saxon England "the formal institutional life of the kin was atrophied, if not stifled at birth, by the strength of territorial lordship and Christian kingship" ("Kinship," 209), though "kinship remained immensely strong in ordinary social life," carrying on such functions as defining a man's status, marital arrangements, and inheritance of land (199–202). For a recent discussion that modifies Loyn's argument, see Thomas Charles-Edwards, "Anglo-Saxon Kinship Revisited," in *The Anglo-Saxons from the Migration Period to the Eighth Century: An Ethnographic Perspective,* ed. John Hines (Woodbridge, Suffolk, 1997), 171–204 (I obtained this book too recently to consult this essay). See James W. Earl, "The Role of the Men's Hall in the Development of the Anglo-Saxon Superego," *Psychiatry* 46 (1983): 139–60, esp. 142–47, for a different analysis of the dominance of "lordship ties" over those of tribal "kinship."

33. See Kevin MacDonald, "The Establishment and Maintenance of Socially Imposed Monogamy in Western Europe," *Politics and the Life Sciences* 14, no. 1 (February 1995): 3–23, for a discussion of how the church and the monarchy were allied in their interests to subdue the powers of the "extended family" of the aristocracies, in part through the encouragement of "socially imposed monogamy."

34. Wormald, "*Lex Scripta,*" 136. See also Wallace-Hadrill, *Early Germanic Kingship,* 37.

35. *Pace* Richardson and Sayles, *Law and Legislation,* who believe that Æthelberht's laws are pre-Christian (7–9).

36. Mary P. Richards, "*Lex Salica,*" in *Sources of Anglo-Saxon Literary Culture: A Trial Version,* ed. Frederick M. Biggs, Thomas D. Hill, and Paul E. Szarmach (Binghamton, NY, 1990), 134–35, and Wallace-Hadrill, *Early Germanic Kingship,* 38, indicate the resemblance between this list of fines and those in the *Lex Salica,* the Frankish code first produced for Clovis (d. 481), with its last major recension at the time of Charlemagne.

37. Yet we know from other documents, such as wills, records of legal disputes, and marriage settlements, that women could own property, including the slaves and thanes associated with estates. See, among others, discussions by Lancaster, "Kinship in Anglo-Saxon Society," 359–67; Fell, *Women in Anglo-Saxon England,* 56–88; and Marc A. Meyer, "Land Charters and the Legal Position of Anglo-Saxon Women," in *The Women of England: From Anglo-Saxon Times to the Present,* ed. Barbara Kanner (Hamden, CT, 1979), 57–82. Sharon Farmer, "Manual Labor, Begging, and Conflicting Gender Expectations in Thirteenth-Century Paris," in this volume, discovers a similar system in *ad status* sermons, in which men are defined according to rank or employment, and women according to their marital status.

38. Klinck similarly asserts, "In the earliest Anglo-Saxon period, women, whatever their rank in society or stage in life, remain in the guardianship of men. This situation is reflected in the fines payable for violation or abduction of women, offences which are regarded as committed against the guardian/master, rather than the woman herself" ("Anglo-Saxon Women and the Law," 109). Klinck cites specifically Æthelberht items 10 ff. and 75–76.

39. "Gif man wið cyninges mægdenman geligeþ L scillinga gebete" (item 10).

40. "Cyninges mundbyrd L scillinga" (item 8).

41. "Gif in cyninges tune man mannan ofslea, L scill' gebete" (item 5); "Gif man frigne mannan ofsleahþ, cyninge L scill' to drihtinbeage" (item 6).

42. "Gif hio grindende þeowa sie, XXV scillinga gebete. Sio þridde XII scillingas" (item 11). "*Þridde* ("third") stands as an absolute term, as elsewhere in Æthelberht's laws does *oþre* ("second"), and *feorðan* ("fourth"). Attenborough fills in the term "class" for these words to modify, for which I have substituted "rank" so as not to confuse this system of differentiating status from "class" in later, capitalist societies. For a discussion of systems of rank in Anglo-Saxon England, see H. Munro Chadwick, *Studies on Anglo-Saxon Institutions* (1905; reprint, New York, 1963), 76–126. Æthelberht's laws imply that at least at this period in Kent, the ranks of *eorl* (nobility), *ceorl* (commoner), and even types of slaves were broken down into ranks of the first, second, third classes, etc. All of these ranks were related to the amount of the person's *wergeld* (the standard for determining fines against a person) and the fine for violation of a person's *mund* ("surety" or "protection") (see Chadwick, *Studies on Anglo-Saxon Institutions*, 115–16).

43. "Gif wið eorles birele man geligeþ, XII scill' gebete" (item 14); "Gif wið ceorles birelan man geligeþ, VI scillingum gebete; aet þære oþere ðeowan L scætta; aet þare þriddan XXX scætta" (item 16). Cf. Klinck, "Anglo-Saxon Women and the Law," 109.

44. "Gif man gekyndelice lim awyrdeþ, þrym leudgeldum hine man forgelde" (item 64). See John R. Clark Hall, *A Concise Anglo-Saxon Dictionary,* 4th ed. with supplement by Herbert D. Merritt (Cambridge, 1960), referred to hereafter as "Clark Hall," and Joseph Bosworth, *An Anglo-Saxon Dictionary,* ed. and enlarged by T. Northcote Toller (Oxford, 1898), hereafter referred to as "Bosworth-Toller," *s.v.* "leodgeld." The term here, however, seems to be derived from glosses to the *Lex Salica* (see Richards, "*Lex Salica,*" 134; and Wallace-Hadrill, *Early Germanic Kingship,* 38). Cf. Æthelberht items 7 and 21–23.

45. In this code *wergeld* is used only in law 31. For discussion of this law, see below. For the uses of *wergeld* in the language, see Bosworth-Toller *s.v.* "wer-, were-gild," which defines the term generally as "the price set upon a man according to his degree," and points out that it could be used as the payment for homicide or for certain crimes as well as for simple designation of rank.

46. Bosworth-Toller *s.v.* "gecynd" II, III. An alternative word for penis is *wæpen* and for male *wæpned.*

47. "Gif friman wið fries mannes wif geligeþ, his wergelde abicge, 7 oðer wif his agenum scætte begete 7 ðæm oðrum æt ham gebrenge" (item 31).

48. See Fell, *Anglo-Saxon Women,* 64, who characterizes the law as "a straightforward statement of the rights of divorce, remarriage and financial compensation." Richards and Stanfield, "Concepts of Anglo-Saxon Women," state, "the emphasis in Æthelberht 31 is on the wrongdoer's responsibility to cover all expenses involved in a new marriage if the parties are willing" (94). Theodore John Rivers, "Adultery in Early Anglo-Saxon Society: Æthelberht 31 in Comparison with Continental Germanic Law," *Anglo-Saxon England* 20 (1991): 19–25, analyzes the law as designating a fine for a violation of marriage, that is "adultery."

49. Attenborough: "The word *his* is ambiguous. Schmid and other scholars understand the word to refer to the wife's wergeld, in favour of which may be compared the Lex Baioariorum, cap. VIII, l. 10.... Liebermann takes *his* to refer to the wergeld of the adulterer, and urges that otherwise the neuter *his* would not be used, but the changes of gender in cap. 11 and cap. 83 cited by him are hardly conclusive parallels, since in both cases the pronoun *hio* occurs in a new sentence" (*Laws of the Earliest English Kings*, 177, n. 31.1). See also Rivers, "Adultery in Early Anglo-Saxon Society," 22–24.

50. Clark Hall *s.v.* "eodor"; Bosworth-Toller *s.v.* "edor" and "eodor" I.

51. *Rihthamscyld* translated literally is "protection for the home proper": see in Bosworth-Toller "riht" IV and "hamscyld." The nature of the damage is termed provocatively with the same term used for injury to the penis, *þurhstinð* ("pierces"): "Gif man rihthamscyld þurhstinð, mid weorðe forgelde" (item 32).

52. Attenborough, *Laws of the Earliest English Kings*, p. 177, n. 31.1.

53. Farmer, "Manual Labor."

54. Christine Fell, "A 'Friwif Locbore' Revisited," *Anglo-Saxon England* 13 (1984): 157–65, states that "it cannot now be determined" whether *friwif* "applied specifically to single women of free-born status, or whether it could also be used of wives and widows" (159). According to Patrizia Lendinara, "The Kentish Laws," in *The Anglo-Saxons*, ed. Hines, it is a hapax legomenon (word that is attested uniquely here) (223).

55. Item 73 reads: "Gif friwif locbore leswæs hwæt gedeþ, XXX scll' gebete." As Fell indicates in her discussion, "locbore" has customarily been translated as "with long hair," indicating the woman's free status, and "leswæs hwæt gedeþ" as "misconducts herself" ("A 'Friwif Locbore'"; see Attenborough, *Laws of the Earliest English Kings*), indicating sexual misconduct, but *locbore* is attested only in this one law and *leswæs* quite general in its scope of "loss" or "dishonesty." The comparable law Fell cites is Cnut, chaps. 76–76.1a. For a sense of how volatile interpretations of *friwif* and *friwif locbore* are, see the comment by Giorgio Ausenda in the "Discussion" following Lendinara's paper "The Kentish Laws": "In my opinion, instead [of Attenborough's interpretation of the term as 'free-born'], this expression refers *without a doubt* to an unmarried woman, presumably a virgin" (my emphasis). He cites the Latin term *in capillo* from the Longobardic law as a parallel, where it "is in complementary distribution with 'married woman'" (233). In Æthelberht, however, as I have stated, the term appears to be distinguishing this case from those for the maiden and the widow, which follow.

56. "Mægþbot sy swa friges mannes" (item 74).

57. See Klinck, "Anglo-Saxon Women and the Law," 109.

58. Attenborough interprets *unagne* as indicating a widow "who does not [of right] belong to" the man who seizes her (see his translation of the law), but this interpretation introduces a redundancy since one would not seize someone already belonging to him.

59. Marc A. Meyer cites these laws concerning the *mund* for widows as indications that in this period "a widow was still under the protection of her *mægþ*," or kin-group:

"Land Charters," 65 and n. 61. Meyer further indicates that the *mund* for the widow shifted so that "by the tenth century, with the increasing power of the king's law, the widow was placed under royal protection" (65). Æthelberht's laws are already working toward this shift by obscuring the relationships of property and law between the individual and his or her *mægþ*.

60. Æthelberht item 77: "Gif mon mægþ gebigeð, ceapi geceapod sy, gif hit unfacne is. Gif it þonne facne is, eft þær æt ham gebrenge, ond him man his scæt agefe." Klinck argues that we should take the terms indicating "purchase and ownership" at face value. Though she cites arguments to the contrary, that the wording of these laws is misleading, she points out that "there is no hint in these earliest laws themselves that what looks like purchase and ownership is actually something different" ("Anglo-Saxon Women and the Law," 109). We have no explicit information regarding the nature of the "deceit," which is as likely to be a deceit in the financial arrangements as much as in any bodily quality of the woman; note that it is the *ceapi* or "bargain" that is *facne* or *unfacne*.

61. I accept here Carole Hough's very learned and important argument that *bugan* does not mean "departs" but rather "live with." Carole A. Hough, "Early Kentish 'Divorce Laws': A Reconsideration of Æthelberht, chs. 79–80," *Anglo-Saxon England* 23 (1994): 19–34. Klinck, among others, interprets this provision as indicating that "divorce is entirely accepted" ("Anglo-Saxon Women and the Law," 110). Similarly, Fell believes that this law gave women "the right to walk out of a marriage that did not please her. . . . Since, if she took the children with her, she was also entitled to take half the property, she seems to have had reasonable independence and security" (*Women in Anglo-Saxon England,* 57).

62. "Gif hio bearn ne gebyreþ, fæderingmagas fioh agan 7 morgengyfe" (item 81). In the case of high-status families, the morning gift could be a substantial amount of property, even entire estates including their thanes.

63. "Gif mægþmon nede genimeþ: ðam agende L scillinga 7 eft æt þam agende sinne willan ætgebicge" (item 82). This law has been discussed in the context of "marriage by abduction" provisions in barbaric law. See Rebecca V. Colman, "The Abduction of Women in Barbaric Law," *Florilegium* 5 (1983): 62–75.

64. There has been considerable discussion concerning the meaning of *nede genimeþ*, specified in item 82 and perhaps implied in items 83 and 84 as well, as to whether it means abduction or rape as well. See Carole Hough, "A Reappraisal of Æthelberht 84," *Nottingham Medieval Studies* 37 (1993): 1–6; and Christine Fell, "An Appendix to Carole Hough's Article A 'Re-appraisal of Æthelberht 84,'" *Nottingham Medieval Studies* 37 (1993): 7–8.

65. As Klinck points out, "In Ethelbert's laws, a woman has a claim on her husband's property only by virtue of being the mother of his children" ("Anglo-Saxon Women and the Law," 109–10).

66. The definition pertaining to bridal payments is listed in Clark Hall as a masculine noun, citing only the poem *Christ,* line 93, as an example (*s.v.* "mund" II); Bosworth-Toller, usually considered the more authoritative dictionary, perhaps because of its fuller examples (their first editions were published about the same time, in 1894 and 1898), does not list this definition, only those pertaining to protection (*s.v.* "mund" III and IV) and more literally "hand" (*s.v.* I) and the hand as a measure (*s.v.* II), all of these with feminine forms only.

67. Among other discussions, see Jo Ann McNamara and Suzanne Wemple, "The Power of Women through the Family in Medieval Europe: 500–1100," in *Clio's Consciousness Raised*, ed. Mary S. Hartman and Lois W. Banner (New York, 1974), 103–18; Stafford, *Queens, Concubines, and Dowagers;* Janet L. Nelson, *Politics and Ritual in Early Medieval Europe* (London, 1986), which includes Nelson's groundbreaking essay, "Queens as Jezebels: Brunhild and Balthild in Merovingian History."

68. For a different discussion of the relationship between sexual practices and Theodore's Penitential, among other documents of the conversion, see Anthony Davies, "The Sexual Conversion of the Anglo-Saxons," in *A Wyf Ther Was: Essays in Honour of Paule Mertens-Fonck*, ed. Juliette Dor (Liège, 1992), pp. 80–102.

69. Allen J. Frantzen, *The Literature of Penance in Anglo-Saxon England* (New Brunswick, NJ, 1983), points out that the handbooks for penance "amplified the penitential's emphasis on the individual and his need to assume responsibility for his spiritual welfare," and that this perspective was "a turning point in early medieval spirituality" (13). Frantzen's book remains the best study on Anglo-Saxon penitentials in terms of its fullness and its thoughtfulness. He argues that Theodore with his Penitential initiated "[a]n 'English' as opposed to an 'Irish' disciplinary system" as part of his efforts to consolidate the English church (62–63). On the influence of the Penitential, see 68–69.

70. Hollis, *Anglo-Saxon Women*, also sees the text as a kind of cultural negotiation, but evaluates the whole process of negotiation as a positive evolution "producing an ideal of marriage union as a one-ness and likeness of identity, a sharing of the same fate that persisted beyond physical separation, in life and in death" (50).

71. On their tentative and yet probable relationship to "social practice," see Allen J. Frantzen, "Between the Lines: Queer Theory, the History of Homosexuality, and Anglo-Saxon Penitentials," *Journal of Medieval and Early Modern Studies* 26, no. 2 (Spring 1996): 255–96, at 270. Clare A. Lees and Gillian R. Overing, *Double Agents: Women and Clerical Culture in Anglo-Saxon England* (Philadelphia, 2001), briefly discuss the role of penitentials in the "patristic symbolic," in which they perceive a privileging of "sacerdotal male bodies" and "equally strict terms of containment" for both laymen and -women (165–66).

72. Thomas Charles-Edwards, "The Penitential of Theodore and the *Iudicia Theodori*," in *Archbishop Theodore: Commemorative Studies on His Life and Influence*, ed. Michael Lapidge, Cambridge Studies in Anglo-Saxon England 11 (Cambridge, 1995), 141–74.

73. "Multi quoque non solum viri, sed etiam feminæ de his ab eo inextinguibili feruore accensi sitim hanc ad sedandam ardenti cum desiderio frequentari hujus nostri nimirum sæculi singularis scientiæ hominem festinabant, unde et illa diversa confusaque degestio regularum illarum cum statutis causis libri secundi conscripta inventa est apud diversos. . . . Quibus communiter omnibus absque invidia prout possum, laboro ex cunctis quæ utiliora invenire potui, et singillatim titulos præponens congessi": *Poenitentiale Theodori*, in *Councils and Ecclesiastical Documents Relating to Great Britian and Ireland*, ed. Arthur West Haddan and William Stubbs, vol. 3 (Oxford, 1871), 176–77; referred to hereafter as "Haddan and Stubbs." Translation from John T. McNeill and Helena M. Gamer, *Medieval Handbooks of Penance: A Translation of the Principal "Libri Poenitentiales" and Selections from Related Documents* (New York, 1938), 182–215, at 183; referred to hereafter as "McNeill and Gamer."

74. Pope Gregory I sent Augustine of Canterbury to King Æthelberht and in this way became inscribed as the special apostle to the Anglo-Saxons.

75. McNeill and Gamer, 214; this last portion of the Epilogue is available only in Vatican, Palatinus Latinus 554, and edited by Paul Willem Finsterwalder, *Die Canones Theodori Cantuariensis und ihre Ueberlieferungsformen* (Weimar, 1929).

76. I do not anywhere in this discussion mean to imply that Christian teachings were ever uniform on any issue at any point in the Middle Ages, except perhaps the impermissability of polygyny. Theodore's Penitential is a case in point regarding the many strands of medieval Christianity since Theodore himself came from Tarsus, not Rome, and the private penitential from Ireland. In addition, the content incorporates Old Testament law regarding such issues as adultery and menstrual uncleanness and New Testament ideas regarding marriage, as well as aspects of Germanic and perhaps even Greek practices. Nevertheless, the text necessarily poses its combination of teachings as Christian and as in opposition to an array of social practices that can be understood not as fallings away from Christianity but as part of an indigenous symbolic system that was the target of conversion. For discussions of how "Anglo-Saxon" Theodore's Penitential is, see Frantzen, *The Literature of Penance*, esp. 59–69; and Charles-Edwards, "The Penitential of Theodore," passim; for Irish influence, see T. O'Loughlin and H. Conrad-O'Briain, "The 'Baptism of Tears' in Early Anglo-Saxon Sources," *Anglo-Saxon England* 22 (1993): 65–83.

77. Hollis, *Anglo-Saxon Women*, suggests that the quality of companionship in a marriage derives from the model of a relationship between warriors (49–50), whereas Paul's writings encouraged the man to act as the "head" of the family body, including the wife. Others argue that Christian teachings encouraged making women responsible for their own sins and even made possible their ownership of book-land (land held in perpetuity and independently from family and hence land that it would be possible for women to deed or bequeath to the church); for one discussion, see Meyer, "Land Charters."

78. The phrase is "votum . . . virginitatis" (Haddan and Stubbs, 190). It is not clear whether the provision is describing someone marrying who has already taken a vow of virginity or someone who is already married and takes a vow of celibacy.

79. See items 1, 5–6, 13, and 29–30 in I.xiv.

80. See items 6–7, 14–18, and 24–27 in I.xiv.

81. See items 2–4, 8–12, and 19–23 in I.xiv. In case you are keeping count, item 28 sets a penalty for the "presbyter" who has failed to baptize an infant who dies. See McNeill and Gamer, 195–98, and Haddan and Stubbs, 187–89, for all of these sections.

82. II.xii.5–6 and 12 in McNeill and Gamer, 208–09; II.xii.5–6 and 11 in Haddan and Stubbs, 199–200.

83. I.xiv.9–12 and I.ii.14.

84. See I.xiv.9–14, but also see I.ii.1, where the penalty for fornication with a married woman is four years. Also pertinent to this discussion, but a topic that I do not address in this essay for lack of space, is fornication with the same sex, which is more heavily penalized for men than heterosexual fornication, but for women same-sex fornication is less heavily penalized than heterosexual (see I.ii.2 and 12 and I.xiv.14–15). For a discussion of the terminology of same-sex intercourse in the penitentials and its implications for historical

discussions of homosexuality, gay studies, and queer theory, see Frantzen, "Between the Lines" and *Before the Closet: Same-Sex Love from "Beowulf" to "Angels in America"* (Chicago, 1998).

85. Frantzen also states, "These regulations show how the church protected the social order that bound men to each other, not just the social order that bound men to women. They also suggest that the male can be seen as occupying the weaker role, for his status is subject to his wife's behavior; her misconduct is more heavily assessed because her wrongdoing damages her husband's prestige and defies his power over her" ("Between the Lines," 272). In Germanic legal texts, as Frantzen notes, typically women and not men are targeted for penalties in consequence of adultery (ibid., 271–72). This fact is widely noted by scholars; Frantzen cites Brundage, *Law, Sex, and Christian Society*, 132, and Brundage, "Adultery and Fornication: A Study in Legal Theology," in *Sexual Practices and the Medieval Church*, ed. Vern L. Bullough and Brundage (Buffalo, NY, 1982), 129–34.

86. Thomas Pollock Oakley, *English Penitential Discipline and Anglo-Saxon Law in Their Joint Influence*, Columbia University Studies in the Social Sciences 242 (New York, 1923; reprint New York, 1969), long ago proposed that the penitential disciplines and the laws reinforced each other in Anglo-Saxon England, pointing to the codes later than Æthelberht's that called for doing penance for certain violations in addition to the penalties imposed by the secular laws. While Oakley was interested in the ways the laws encouraged Christian morality, here we can see ways in which the penitentials could reinforce pre-Christian practices and symbolic structures.

87. I.xiv.17: "Mulieres autem menstruo tempore non intrent in æcclesiam, neque commonicent, nec sanctimoniales, nec laicæ; si presumant, IIIbus. ebdomadibus jejunent." 18: "Similiter peniteant, quæ intrant æcclesiam ante mundum sanguinem post partum, id est, XL. diebus" (Haddan and Stubbs, 188–89). Trans. McNeill and Gamer, 197.

88. Hollis, *Anglo-Saxon Women*, 56.

89. "In primo conjugio presbiter debet missam agere et benedicere ambos et postea abstineant se ab æcclesia XXX. diebus; quibus peractis peniteant XL. diebus, et vacent orationi; et postea communicent cum oblatione" (I.xiv.1; Haddan and Stubbs, p. 187). Trans. McNeill and Gamer, 195.

90. I.xiv.2: "Digamus peniteat I. annum . . . ; non separentur, non dimittat tamen uxorem." 3: "Trigamus et supra, id est, in quarto aut quinto vel plus, VII . . . ; non separentur tamen" (Hadden and Stubbs, 187–88). Trans. McNeill and Gamer, 195–96.

91. II.xiv.8: "Qui dimiserit uxorem suam, alteri conjungens se, VII. annos cum tribulatione peniteat, vel XV. levius" (Haddan and Stubbs, 188). Trans. McNeill and Gamer, 196. There is some slippage evident between xiv.2–3 and 8, which cannot be definitively explained. Perhaps the sequent marriages of 2–3 were subsequent to previous wives' demise or vows of celibacy whereas 8 involved an out-and-out divorce. In any case, it is notable that the penance for putting aside a wife and marrying another was longer than for the man committing adultery, but the same as for a woman committing adultery.

92. II.xii.24: "Si iterum post hæc uxor illa venerit ad eum, non debet recipi ab eo, si aliam habet; sed illa tollat alium virum sibi, si unum ante habuerat" (Haddan and Stubbs, 201). Trans. McNeill and Gamer, 210, numbered II.xii.25.

93. II.xii.32 in Haddan and Stubbs (p. 201); II.xii.33 in McNeill and Gamer (p. 211).

94. In his correspondence with Charlemagne, Alcuin instructs that he "provide good preachers for the people" who should follow the example of the apostles: "For they gave their hearers milk, that is gentle teaching, when they were beginners in the faith . . . meaning that new converts to the faith must be fed on gentler teaching as babies on milk, lest minds too weak for harder teaching vomit what they have imbibed" (Allott, *Alcuin of York*, letter 56). "Sed nunc praevideat sapientissima et Deo placabilis devotio vestra pios populo novello praedicatores; moribus honestos, scientia sacrae fidei edoctos et euangelicis praeceptis imbutos; sanctorum quoque apostolorum in praedicatione verbi Dei exemplis intentos. Qui lac—id est suavia praecepta—suis auditoribus in initio fidei ministrare solebant . . . significavit: ut nova populorum ad fidem conversio mollioribus praeceptis quasi infantilis aetas lacte esset nutrienda; ne per austeriora praecepta fragilis mens evomat, quod bibit" ("Alcuini Epistolae," ed. Dümmler, letter 67, p. 308).

95. F. M. Stenton, *Anglo-Saxon England* (Oxford, 1947), p. 416. The facts on Cnut and his two marriages I have gleaned from Stenton, though others have written on this topic as well, most notably Pauline Stafford, *Queen Emma and Queen Edith,* who addresses in detail the issue of "irregular" marriages.

PART II

DISCOURSES OF DOMINATION

5

MALE FRIENDSHIP AND THE SUSPICION OF SODOMY IN TWELFTH-CENTURY FRANCE

MATHEW S. KUEFLER

Scholars have long recognized the attention paid in the literature of the twelfth century to intimate bonds between men. There are numerous instances, on the one hand, of the favorable depiction of men whose loyalty and devotion to each other overcomes all obstacles. There is, on the other hand, a concerted effort to condemn men whose intimacy involved a sexual component. Attempts to historicize this double reaction have not been successful, however, mostly because literary scholars tend to focus on the narrative role played by depictions of male friendships and their implied homoeroticism, while religious scholars tend to emphasize the prohibition of sexual connections between men and the intellectual background from which that prohibition emerged. The key to contextualizing both the homoerotic implications of male friendships and the hostility to sodomy, though, is to understand the traditions of male solidarity and friendship among the military aristocracy of medieval France and the reasons that existed for undermining those traditions in the twelfth century. I will argue that throwing suspicion on male friendships as breeding grounds for sodomitical behavior suited the goals of the men of the ecclesiastical and royal hierarchies, who were attempting large-scale social and political reforms that required the subversion of male solidarity and the abandonment of earlier patterns of men's friendships in favor of new patterns of support for lineage and obedience to authority.

Almost two decades ago, historian John Boswell described what he called an "efflorescence" of gay male culture in the period before the twelfth century, using the term "gay" to refer "to persons who are conscious of erotic inclination toward their own gender as a distinguishing characteristic or, loosely to things associated with such people, as 'gay poetry.'" He also documented the end of this gay culture in the period after the twelfth century, and a shift from tolerance of sexual difference to intolerance. Nonetheless, he was unable to historicize the pattern he perceived, and unable to explain why this shift occurred in the twelfth century. His hypothesis was that it was related to urbanization, yet even he described such a hypothesis as "largely unsatisfactory," and expressed the opinion that "advances in knowledge in many disciplines will probably be necessary to clarify the nature of so large and complex a development."[1]

Since that time, few scholars have taken up Boswell's challenge. Most historians have contented themselves with undermining the first part of Boswell's thesis, dismissing Boswell's claim that certain historical individuals can be characterized as "gay" and rejecting the evidence for a "gay" culture in the Middle Ages.[2] Indeed, in a book on the theological development of the notion of sodomy in the eleventh and twelfth centuries, historian of theology Mark Jordan maintains forcefully that his work "is not a social history of 'medieval homosexuality'" and doubts "whether such a history is possible ... [or] desirable."[3] Historian Robert Moore stands apart in accepting Boswell's claim for the disintegration of a subculture based on homoeroticism and in attempting an explanation of that disintegration. Moore argues that:

> during the eleventh, twelfth and thirteenth centuries, Jews, heretics, lepers, male homosexuals and in differing degrees various others were victims of a rearrangement ... which defined them more exactly than before and classified them as enemies of society. But it was not only a matter of definition. In each case a myth was constructed, upon whatever foundation of reality, by an act of collective imagination. A named category was created—Manichee, Jew, leper, sodomite and so on—which could be identified as a source of social contamination, and whose members could be excluded from Christian society and, as its

enemies, held liable to pursuit, denunciation and interrogation,
to exclusion from the community, deprivation of civil rights and
the loss of property, liberty and on occasion life itself.[4]

It is a powerful and compelling argument—that society defined itself
through a process of social exclusion—but it still does not explain why
male homoeroticism should be listed among the categories for exclusion.
As Jordan so neatly demonstrates, "the category 'sodomy' had been viti-
ated from its invention by fundamental confusions and contradictions,"
and the "sodomite" as represented by Christian theologians did not and
could not exist.[5] Even as historians generally have repudiated the possibility of a sexual identity based on homoeroticism and any premodern
conscious recognition of erotic difference that Boswell defined as "gay,"
however, literary scholars increasingly point to homoerotic elements in
writings about male friendship of the twelfth century.[6]

My project is to try to cut through this Gordian knot, precisely by attempting to historicize these literary and theological expressions of male
intimacy, praised as friendship or condemned as sodomy, and to situate
them among the inhabitants of the twelfth century and within a period
of social change. Indeed, I maintain that such a project is key to understanding both the nature of those expressions of male intimacy and their
implications for a history of sexuality, and also key to taking up Boswell's
unanswered question of explaining the rise of intolerance of male homoeroticism.[7] I would also argue, *pace* Jordan, that the uncovering of the
historical context in which the "invention of sodomy" took place is a pre-
requisite for denaturalizing that invention, a denaturalization that I deem
both possible and desirable.[8]

As part of that historicizing process, moreover, the relationships between men need to be seen within a broader context than the clerical
subculture that forms the basis for much of both Jordan's and Boswell's
work. Any attempt to historicize must include the connections between
that subculture and the aristocratic military culture around it. For even if
virtually all of the writings that survive from the twelfth century come
from clerical or monastic hands, these writings form part of a larger relationship between the religious and the secular, in which the former was
not only critical of but also deeply influenced by the latter. As part of that
relationship, the twelfth-century clerical and monastic writers on male
friendship and on sodomy replied directly to the traditions of masculinity

among the military aristocracy, even if they attempted to parody or to subvert those traditions.

In particular, these ecclesiastical writers worked to weaken the bonds
of male solidarity encouraged by military culture in favor of ties of obedience to church and state, a movement well recognized by historians
and often called the "taming" of the nobility. As part of that "taming,"
ecclesiastical writers of the twelfth century problematized male friendships in a new way, using the suspicion that these friendships were nothing more than a cover for sodomy as a means of undermining their social
importance. Moreover, as will be shown, this suspicion was also associated with the performance of male gender identity among the military
aristocracy to the extent that to be a sodomite was to be no longer a
man, linking the suspicion of sodomy with men's misogynistic fears of
effeminacy.

The literary tradition of male friendship may seem an odd place
from which to begin a "historicizing" account of men's relationships,
but for the twelfth century, literary sources provide the clearest images
of those relationships, images that can then be supplemented by and
verified against other sources. Northern France both provides a rich de-
posit of literary and other historical sources, and forms a culturally co-
hesive unit. By using a variety of the texts spanning the twelfth century,
moreover, we can more easily mark the progress of the suspicion of
sodomy in male friendships over the course of that century. While it is
impossible to pinpoint an exact date at which men's friendships became
suspect, it is possible to demonstrate a broad shift in attitudes from early-
twelfth-century texts to later twelfth-century ones, and it is in several
mid-century texts that the new problematics of male intimacy can first
be seen.

Many early-twelfth-century sources from northern France preserve a
record of emotional intimacy between men. John Boswell documented
numerous examples in his study, including such ecclesiastical figures as
Anselm of Bec, Baudri of Bourgeuil, and Marbod of Rennes.[9] These are
among the writers who have fallen under the scrutiny of scholars after
Boswell.[10] Stephen Jaeger, who rejects Boswell's argument that the writings of these men demonstrate a physical eroticism, suggests that the
"language of the erotic shows innocently that the illicit is proximate
[proche] but avoided or ignored, . . . mastered, controlled, maintained in
its place."[11] Such language, he counters, owes more to the epistolary and

philosophical traditions of ancient writers than to a "gay" identity. The erotic could not have been articulated if it had been physicalized.

Jaeger is certainly correct in asserting that before the middle of the twelfth century love between men might be depicted without awkwardness or embarrassment. Consider Peter Abelard's early-twelfth-century poetic version of the lament of the biblical King David for Jonathan, a traditional model of male friendship:

> Jonathan, more than a brother to me, one in spirit with me, what sins, what crimes have sundered our hearts? . . . For you, my Jonathan, I must weep more than for all the others. Mixed in all my joys there will always be a tear for you. . . . Alas, why did I agree to the wretched advice that I not defend you in battle? Stabbed like you, I should have died happily, for love can do nothing greater than this, and to outlive you is to die at every moment: half a soul is not enough for life. I should have paid friendship's single obligation then, at the time of greatest need; as sharer in victory or companion in ruin, I should have either rescued you or fallen with you, ending for you the life you so often saved. Then death would have joined us even more than it parted us.[12]

His poem borrows not only from biblical antecedents but also from classical ones, such as the lament of Nisus for Euryalus in Virgil's *Aeneid,* another traditional model of male friendship.

By the end of the twelfth century, however, writers of northern France displayed a new awkwardness in depicting male friendships, and a new desire to downplay the devotion between male friends. The erotic was no longer so "innocent." The praise of male friendship continued, but only when it insisted on its spiritual and not carnal nature.[13] Take, for instance, the example of Alain of Lille, writing near the end of the twelfth century, whom we will have occasion to discuss in greater detail below. Alain put the praise of male friendship in the mouth of personified Nature herself:

> Indeed, she desires that he be thus embraced by love *[amor]* and by inviolate loyalty *[fides],* that his love might gain the love of another. . . . She desires that he might believe anything of him,

wish to declare himself to him, and to reveal to him all of his thoughts. Let him commit to him the secrets hidden in his heart, so that to him, keeping the treasure of his mind in him, there is no secret that might not be revealed to him, that his friend might measure by such a sign the weight of his friendship, which might equally be weighed in return.[14]

When Alain remarked on the devotion between David and Jonathan and between Nisus and Euryalus, he admitted the possibility of real intimacy between men:

For David and Jonathan are two there but yet are one; although they are separate individuals, they are not two in soul but one; they halve their souls and each gives part to the other.... Another Nisus appears in Euryalus and another Euryalus flourishes in Nisus; thus either one of them reflects the other and from one of these companions a judgment can be made on both.[15]

Nonetheless, Alain also made sure to clarify that he was writing about "those whom chaste love, uncomplicated friendship, unclouded trust, true affection have joined together."[16] Significantly, Alain dedicated another treatise, his *De planctu naturae* ("Nature's Lament"), to personified Nature's condemnation of sodomitical relationships between men. Alain thus demonstrates that the awkwardness of twelfth-century writers about male friendships was directly connected to the suspicion of sodomy between men.

The anonymous reworking of Virgil's *Aeneid,* written shortly before the mid-point of the twelfth century in the Norman French dialect and called the *Roman d'Énéas,* serves as an excellent example of the suspicion of male friendship and as a useful starting point. The *Roman d'Énéas* is a particularly interesting source because it was situated in both the past and the present: set in a distant Roman past and borrowing from an ancient Latin literary tradition, but also written in the midst of the changes of the twelfth century and in the new written vernacular. As such, its anonymous redactor had both a model for male friendship and the liberty to manipulate that model. The figure of Eneas, moreover, was already marked with a certain effeminacy even in the Latin text because of his eastern Mediterranean origins, a typical Roman conceit, and as we will see, the accusation of effeminacy formed an integral part of the accusation of sodomy in the twelfth century.

Male friendship is at the heart of the *Roman d'Énéas*. The text includes the story of the male companions Nisus and Euryalus, and even elaborates on Virgil's description of the men's devotion to each other:

> They loved each other with such a love that they might not have a greater. Never was there a truer love than theirs, as long as they lived. One did not know anything without the other, nor had any joy nor good thing.[17]

Another episode of male intimacy in the *Roman d'Énéas*, also borrowed from Virgil, involves Eneas himself and a young man named Pallas, who was killed in the conquest of Italy. Eneas holds the dead youth in his arms, uttering a long and poignant lament before fainting away from grief:

> Pallas, said he, flower of youth *[jovente]*, . . . you were so handsome yesterday morning, that under the sky there was no more comely youth *[meschin]*, but in a short time I see you changed. . . . Handsome figure, comely thing, just as the sun withers the rose, so has death quickly all defeated and all withered and changed you.[18]

Eneas's grief is reiterated through physical description:

> After that he was silent, he could say no more, in his heart was grief and very great anguish, he fell on the deceased in pain, and when he rose back up, all weeping, he kissed the corpse.[19]

Indeed, Eneas exhibits more grief and more emotion here than at any other place in the text.

The *Roman d'Énéas* also complicates male friendship. Later in the text, in an episode barely present in Virgil's poem but much elaborated by the twelfth-century author, Eneas falls in love with Lavine, who is betrothed to his political rival. Their love is opposed by Lavine's mother, who attempts to dissuade Lavine from her love for Eneas in a manner worth quoting at length, because it makes clear how the suspicion of sodomy within male friendship worked:

This villain is of such a nature *[de tel nature]* that he has never a care for women. He prefers the opposite practice *[mestier]*. He does not want to eat the female animal *[biset]*, for he loves very much the flesh of a male one *[char de maslon]*. He would rather take a boy *[garçon]* than be near to you or any other. . . . How is that that you have not heard that he treated Dido badly? No woman had any good from him, nor will you have, if he is, as I think, a traitor and a sodomite *[sodomite]*. Always he will announce that he is leaving you, if he has any debauched young thing *[godel]*, and it will seem to him good and well that he leave to seek his pleasures *[druz]*. And if he can use you to attract the boy, he will not find it too strange to let the boy do his thing *[son bon]* with you so that the boy will let him do it to him *[lo sofrist de soi]*; he will let the boy mount you, if he can in turn ride the boy.[20]

When Eneas abandons Lavine for the male companionship of a military campaign, she begins to have her own doubts about him:

It is the truth, said she, what my mother told me about him. A woman is very little to him, he would rather sport with a boy *[deduit de garçon]*, he loves none but male whores *[males putains]*. His Ganymede he has with him, little of me is enough for him. He has been rutting for a very long time, in the middle of sporting with a boy. . . . He has enough boys with him, and loves the worst of them better than me. He makes their clothes ripped *[fandue trove lor chemise]*. Many of them he has in his service, and their breeches are lowered: thus they earn their wages.[21]

It is not only Lavine who is forced to reevaluate the virtue of Eneas's relationship with Pallas, however, but the audience of the poem along with her, and this is reinforced by her words that generalize this episode:

Be cursed today such a type of man *[tel nature d'ome]* who has no care for women; and he who is all accustomed to that. For this practice *[mestiers]* is very bad, and he is thinking very much like a fool who leaves a woman and takes a man.[22]

Here is a new and self-conscious admission of the possibility of a sexual element in male friendships.

The *Roman d'Énéas* also demonstrates that what was being challenged in the twelfth century, through the suspicion of sodomy, was military culture and the bonds of solidarity between men that were necessary for the cohesion of military culture. The anonymous redactor of the *Roman d'Énéas* was asserting that the service of young warriors to a war leader might be as much a sexual as a military service. If we accept, at least for the moment, the assertion of the anonymous redactor of the *Roman d'Énéas* that sodomy might have formed part of military culture, and if we also accept that the redactor was commenting not only about the ancient conventions of pederasty but also about contemporary society and its sexual mores, we now have a point from which to begin to historicize sexual relations between men and to consider, in the words of Jonathan Goldberg, "the ways in which normative bonds that structured society also allowed for sexual relations."[23]

How often sexual relations may have resulted from the cohabitation of men during times of military service is of course impossible to say. Many writers of the twelfth century implied a real physical intimacy between men of the military class, and sources throughout the period describe the erotic charms of youthful males, or what Sally North calls a "combination of manly stature and strength with a girlish face."[24] This physical intimacy certainly included an appreciation of male beauty. The *chanson de Roland*, for example, which survives from the beginning of the twelfth century, describes the warrior Ganelon in these words: "Noble was his body and his torso was broad, and so handsome was he that all his peers stare at him."[25] Likewise, the physical side to male intimacy included touches and embraces between men. The *Couronnement de Louis*, for example, written in the mid-twelfth century, includes this description of the meeting of two aristocratic friends: "The noble count embraced him on both sides and kissed him four times on his face."[26] Physical intimacy between men is also directly connected to their emotional intimacy, as depicted in the French legend of two knights, called *Ami et Amile*, written probably at the very end of the twelfth century:

> And he saw him who had already recognized him. Toward him
> he turned when he had also recognized him in turn. With such

sweetness *[vertu]* did they greet each other, so forcefully did they
kiss and so softly did they embrace, that not long after they were
done in and overcome.[27]

In other words, a physical component to male friendship was expected
and celebrated.

It would be a mistake simply to read these expressions of physical
intimacy in male friendships as overtly homoerotic, however, in part because men continued to share physical intimacy beyond the twelfth century in an age conscious of sodomitical sin.[28] Nonetheless, writers of
the twelfth century seeking to undermine the solidarity between men by
accusing them of sodomitical practices may have used these physical
expressions of friendship as part of their attack. And it is not difficult to
imagine that these physical expressions may also have reflected a type of
homoeroticism that might sometimes have included sexual intimacy.
Indeed, sexual intimacy between men must sometimes have happened,
if the accusations made by the author of the *Roman d'Énéas* and other
writers of the twelfth century hoped to carry any real weight. So we are
left to interpret in a variety of possible ways the ambiguous statements
of the twelfth century, such as that by the anonymous author of the mid-
century *Prise d'Orange,* who remarks that better than the love of a beautiful woman was that of "a young bachelor *[bacheler]* with his first beard,
who knows how to live well in fun *[deport]* and in arms."[29]

The adolescent male, the "bachelor with his first beard," figures
prominently in virtually all twelfth-century discussions of sexual intimacy between men. Georges Duby has discussed the sexual adventur-
ousness of the bands of adolescent males, but assumes it to have taken
place entirely within a heterosexual framework. "The sexuality of the
bachelors had always been meandering," he writes.

> They freely availed themselves of peasant women, servant girls,
> and the many whores who were apt to relieve the champions of
> most of their winnings on the night after the tournament; they
> also took advantage of the widows whom they consoled and the
> "maidens" who so graciously received the heroes of the Breton
> romances at each nightly pause of their wanderings.[30]

Duby implies that the bachelors indulged their sexual needs entirely
with women, but contemporary writers—and not only the author of the

Roman d'Énéas—suggested otherwise. Hildebert of Lavardin, archbishop of Tours in the middle of the twelfth century, used the classical myth in which Jove abducted the youth Ganymede for his sexual and domestic service as the basis for his attack against the sexual arrangements of the military aristocracy. Hildebert railed against what he called *Ganymedes crimen* ("Ganymede's sin") in his own society:

> A boy *[puer]* is not at all a safe thing; do not devote yourself to any of them. Many a house is reported to have many Joves. But you should not hope for heaven through Ganymede's sin: no one comes to the stars through this type of military service. A better law consecrates heavenly castles to Junos alone: a male wife *[masculus uxor]* has the underworld.[31]

If Hildebert is to be believed, these sexual practices were rampant throughout the noble households of northern France:

> Above all other sexual crimes is the sodomitical plague, and males *[mares]* give to males *[maribus]* the debts due their spouses. Innumerable Ganymedes tend innumerable hearths, and that which she was used to enjoying, Juno grieves. Boys *[puer]* and men *[vir]* and even frail old men *[senex]* debase themselves with this vice and no manner of life *[conditio]* ceases from this vice. Whoever of you change the honor of nature to this practice *[mos]* and neglect the licit Venus for the forbidden, do you not remember that you are taught by [the example of] Sodom that you should beware this crime, lest you perish by sulphur?[32]

About the same time, Bernard of Cluny also complained about the "innumerable Ganymedes" of his day.[33] It is impossible to gauge the extent to which the comments of Bernard and Hildebert reflected the realities of male sexuality and how much was exaggerated for rhetorical effect. Still, the suspicion of sexual relationships between men and adolescent boys was reinforced by worries about its prevalence among the military aristocracy.

If male sexuality involved some sexual experimentation with other males within the war band and noble household, and if it took the form of an older man's sexual interest in a younger man, as these sources imply, the likeliest site for such sexual behaviors was in the institution of fostering. Through fostering, groups of noble sons were raised in the household of a military associate of their father, learning the arts of war and serving as his companions and assistants. In the twelfth century, foster sons remained with their foster fathers until they reached adulthood and were given their own arms, an event that typically occurred at about the age of fifteen.[34] Fostering is well attested in the sources of the eleventh and twelfth centuries. In the early-twelfth-century romance of *Tristan* by Béroul, for example, the hero says that he should have "a hundred young men *[danzeaus]* with me, who serve me in order to take arms and who render me their service."[35] In many ways, fostering formed the backbone of early medieval military culture, since the loyalties established and cultivated through fostering provided the cohesion to the military band. Fostering also provided much of the social context for male friendship in the period before the twelfth century.

The institution of fostering also provided the context for attacks on male intimacy by writers, beginning in the middle of the twelfth century. The guardianship of Pallas and the other young men by Eneas in the *Roman d'Énéas*, for example, was implied to be that sort of fostering arrangement. Hildebert's complaint against "this type of military service" *(hac modo militia)* also relies on a play on words linking pederasty and fostering. The image of Jove and Ganymede itself depends on the parallels between the mythical rapture of the adolescent male by an adult male for domestic and sexual service and the contemporary "theft" of boys into the military household as foster sons. In fact, several writers of the twelfth century refer to the younger partners in alleged sexual relationships as *catamitae* ("catamites"), a medieval Latin variant of Ganymede.

Even writers who do not attack the homoeroticism of the fostering household seem to have considered the adult male's appreciation of adolescent male beauty as one of the characteristics of the institution. Consider the remark made regarding the arrival of Richard, the future duke of Normandy, at the court of King Louis IV of France, a twelfth-century reference from the *Gesta Normannorum ducum* ("Deeds of the Dukes of the Normans") to a tenth-century event:

> Sending for the boy *[puer]* Richard he had him presented for his inspection, and, having seen that he was endowed with handsome features *[egregia forma perspiciens decoratum]*, decided that

he should be brought up with other boys of his own age *[cum coetaneis pueris]* in his own court.[36]

Consider also the description of the fostering of Amicus and Amelius, two young men of a hagiographical legend from the early twelfth century, but again, referring to an earlier age, the age of Charlemagne:

> The two pledged their faith to each other and made their way together to the court of Charles the king, where he perceived them to be modest, wise, and very handsome *[pulcherrimi]* young men, peers alike in their education as in their appearance *[vultus]*, loved by all and honored by all. What more can I add? Amicus was made the king's treasurer and Amelius his cup-bearer *[dapifer]*.[37]

Amelius as cupbearer to Charlemagne cannot help but bring to mind the myth of Ganymede and Jove. It is not impossible to view these descriptions of the role played by physical attraction in fostering in earlier eras as part of the critique by twelfth-century writers, although the appreciation of the boys' beauty may also be related to medieval notions of the connection between physical beauty and moral goodness.

We have yet to understand why it was in the twelfth century that male intimacy became so problematic. As I see it, the problem was twofold. First was a social problem. Loyalty and intimacy between men, of the sort described as typical for men of the warring classes and encouraged by the institution of fostering, distracted men from what was being promoted as their primary responsibility to the family. Men's duties to the lineage were an obsession of twelfth-century writers. The requirements of the family included first and foremost its perpetuation through the fathering of male heirs to take up its titles and lands, and were interpreted as necessitating a single-minded pursuit of procreation.[38] These requirements reflected in turn the shift of the economic bases of western Europe, from wealth derived from the capture and circulation of booty stolen by the warring band, to a wealth calculated on the incomes of cultivated lands and the inheritance of those lands. The delayed ages of marriage of men in the noble classes and their long absences away from their wives in the warrior band to support the earlier system of wealth had to be brought to an end for the sake of family continuity, which supported the new system of wealth.[39]

One sees how commonplace the concern for lineage was in the writings against sodomy from the twelfth century, which frequently condemned the "sterile unions" between men. In an anonymous poem of debate from the end of the twelfth century, Helen, who represents the love of women, provokes Ganymede, who represents the love of boys, with these words: "Venus mixes males [masculi] in sterile unions."[40] Alain of Lille complained of the sodomitical male that "he hammers on an anvil which issues no seeds," and that "his ploughshare scores a barren strand."[41] The same concern for lineage can also be seen in the *chansons de geste*. The central theme of the *Roman d'Énéas*, like that of Virgil's *Aeneid* on which it is based, is the descent of Eneas, but in the twelfth-century version, this descent is made possible only by Eneas's abandonment of the military band and his "sodomitical tendencies" for the love of Lavine. Her mother clarifies the issues at stake, after calling Eneas a sodomite:

> It would be all over with this age if all men [home] were like this throughout the world. Never would a woman conceive, there would be a great loss of people, no one would ever have children. The age would fail in a hundred years.[42]

The very existence of such arguments implies that the emphasis on lineage did not necessitate an abandonment of the homosocial war band, but ecclesiastical writers of the twelfth century worked hard to link the one with the other.

In place of the devotion that men offered each other, moreover, twelfth-century writers offered to men the possibility of an equal devotion to women through the promotion of courtly love. As modern scholars have pointed out, to love a woman became such a central focus of male identity beginning in the twelfth century that not to love a woman brought into question a man's right to call himself a man.[43] This idea is sprinkled throughout the twelfth-century literature of courtly love. Chrétien de Troyes had a knight say that

> Whoever kisses a woman and does nothing more, when they are all alone together, then I think there is something remiss [remaint] in him.[44]

But this idea was also closely linked with the contemporary attack on intimacy between men and the accusation of sodomy. In the *Lai de Lanval,* Marie de France had Guinevere give this retort to a man who rejects her sexual advances:

I have been told often enough that you have no inclination *[talent]* toward women. You love young men *[vaslez]* who are well built *[bien afaitiez]* and you sport *[dedulez]* together with them.[45]

A man's refusal to devote himself to a woman is here linked to his illicit devotion to other men.

A recurring theme in all of these texts praising the love of women is the unnaturalness of sex between men. Lavine's mother includes it in her harangue against Eneas: "he who acts against nature, who takes men *[homes]*, who leaves women, undoes the natural coupling."[46] In the debate between Helen and Ganymede, the same accusation is made: "You openly despise sex with women *[sexum mulieribus]*. The order of things is overturned and its law perishes through you."[47] To call sexual relations between men unnatural was to imply that a natural form of sexual relations existed, and twelfth-century writers worked hard to assert a sexual complementarity between men and women, part of a larger reformulation of gender relations in that period that has been skillfully delineated by Jo Ann McNamara.[48] It is true that courtly love sometimes worked counter to the support of the lineage. Even then, however, courtly love furthered the project of the reorientation of men's affections away from each other to someone outside the "system" of male solidarity. If that someone, moreover, was a woman with lands of her own or was heiress to her father's lands, lineage might still be promoted. Most importantly, through the conventions of courtly love, writers of the twelfth century insisted that every man give his love, both devotion and sexual interest, to a woman. In the *Roman d'Énéas,* Eneas moves from his homosocial band and his devotion to the boy, Pallas, to the love of the woman, Lavine. Even Ganymede, in his debate with Helen, eventually accepts her viewpoint that love of a woman is better than love of a boy.

The legend of Amicus and Amelius serves as an excellent example of the twelfth-century shift from devotion to male friendship and the military band to devotion to a woman and the lineage. According to the earlier, hagiographical form of the legend, written anonymously in the early twelfth century, Amicus and Amelius begin their friendship when they are baptized together as children, and strengthen that friendship when they serve together as young men in Charlemagne's army, although they eventually separate to marry and raise families. When Amicus is stricken with leprosy, however, he approaches his former companion with a story that an angel has appeared to him and told him that he will be cured only by being bathed in the blood of his friend's sons. After some deliberation, Amelius's loyalty to Amicus overcomes his loyalty to his family: he slaughters his children, bathes his dear friend in their blood, and his dear friend *(carissimus)* is healed. But because of God's mercy, his sons are brought back to life, and in thanksgiving the two men leave their wives and take vows of chastity. They rejoin Charlemagne's army and are killed together in battle. Even in death their devotion to each other is affirmed by means of another miracle:

> Those whom God had joined in the concord of one spirit and in love *[unanimi corcordia et dilectione]* in life, so in death he did not want them to be separated.... There were made therefore two churches ... [and t]he remains of their bodies were buried, the one here, the other there. In the morning, however, and done according to divine disposition, the body of Amelius was found with his sarcophagus next to the sarcophagus of Amicus in the king's church. What an admirable association of these two friends, what ineffable love between them *[o admiranda duorum societas amicorum, o ineffabilis caritas amborum]*, which not even in death deserves separation![49]

Near the end of the twelfth century, however, a new version of this legend was written in the vernacular. The lives of the two men, now called Ami and Amile, follow roughly the same pattern, but after the miraculous cure from leprosy, the story takes a new turn. Amile remains with his wife and his resurrected sons, and Ami, who is now free of the pollution of leprosy, is able to rejoin his wife and son. In this version, notably, it is not the male bond that is reinforced by the divine intervention, but the family bond. The final episode of their death and burial together is entirely omitted. Reginald Hyatte, who has examined the theme of friendship in the later version, remarks that the two men's "pursuit of absolute friendship . . . does not have a place in the social order of family and feudal state."[50] Although the exact relationship between the two versions of the legend is uncertain, it is tempting to see the latter as a redaction of the former more in keeping with the sentiment of the later twelfth century, when traditions of male friendship were being subverted in favor of familial ties.

Male friendship was not only a social problem, however, but a political one. The devotion of men of the military classes to each other also undercut their loyalty to the church and state. Placing suspicion on male solidarity as sodomitical also suited a larger agenda of reorienting the personal loyalties of the male nobility away from each other and towards their obligations of obedience as subjects of royal and ecclesiastical power, both of which were being greatly extended in the twelfth century. R. I. Moore, for example, argues that accusations of sexual and religious unorthodoxy were "means of suppressing resistance to the exercise of power . . . and of legitimizing the new regime in church and state."[51] Christopher Baswell also sees the extension of royal power behind the suspicion of sodomy in the *Roman d'Énéas*.[52] The numerous ecclesiastical regulations on marriage of the twelfth century have also been typically seen as attempts by church leaders to control the sexuality of the noble classes and as part of the efforts to "tame" them. Simon Gaunt, for example, sees the twelfth century as a "historical flashpoint" for the "renegotiation of sexuality amongst the French aristocracy which may well be related to the impact of the church's attempt to control the adjudication of marriage," in which the antipathy to homoeroticism in texts such as the *Roman d'Énéas* provided "a means of regulating male homosocial bonds, of imposing normative models of heterosexuality and gender on all men."[53]

The accusation of sodomy was useful to both royal and ecclesiastical authorities. Given the right political circumstances, any man's friendships might be accused of being a cover for unnatural acts, and this accusation would then justify the regulations of men's lives that both church and state imposed. This is not to say that church and state worked in concert. Indeed, they often worked against each other, but both used the same methods since both were also working within the same cultural context, and implicated even as they complicated each other. Alan Bray has noted the political uses of the suspicion of male intimacy at work in texts of the sixteenth century, but it can also be seen as early as the twelfth.[54]

The accusation of sodomy was also politically useful on another level, by deflecting anxiety about its prevalence away from the clergy and monastic orders and onto the secular nobility. The anonymous clerical writer who penned the *Roman d'Énéas,* as well as the other ecclesiastical writers of the twelfth century, were doubtless aware of the campaigns of the Gregorian reformers, men like Peter Damian, who believed that sodomy was a serious problem for the clergy and that men guilty of the offense should be permanently removed from clerical ranks.[55] In the wake of the Gregorian reforms, moreover, especially after the imposition of clerical celibacy in the early twelfth century, clerics faced accusations that they were sodomites, forbidding to other priests sexual relationships with women only because they themselves were uninterested in them.[56] Serlo of Bayeux, for example, writing at the beginning of the twelfth century, called the celibate clerics "men of foul, adulterous, and sodomitical *[turpis, mechi, sodomite]* lives."[57] Linking sodomy with military culture, then, also served to refocus the accusation of sodomy and to acquit the clergy of the charge that they were the twelfth century's true sodomites.

An excellent example of these varied social and political uses of the suspicion of sodomy is Orderic Vitalis's account of the Norman king of England, William Rufus, from his *Historia ecclesiastica* ("Ecclesiastical History"). According to Orderic, who wrote before about 1140 from his monastery in Normandy, William was an undisguised enemy of the Christian religion, a fact that made all of his interactions suspect on some level. It was the group of young men at William's court, however, that triggered Orderic's fiercest denunciations. William's courtiers were purely wicked, he wrote:

> They rejected the traditions of honest men, ridiculed the counsel of priests, and ... frivolled away their time, spending it as they chose without regard for the law of God or the customs of their ancestors. They devoted their nights to feasts and drinking-bouts, idle chatter, dice, games of chance, and other sports, and they slept all day.[58]

It was hardly surprising, Orderic seemed to suggest, that at that same court sodomy was rampant:

> Then the effeminates *[effeminati]* throughout the realm ruled supreme, and carried on their debaucheries without restraint, and loathsome Ganymedes *[catamitae]*, who ought to be consumed by flames, abused themselves with foul sodomite-things *[sodomitica]*.[59]

It is true that William Rufus never married, despite being over forty years of age at the time of his death in 1100, and he seems to have preferred to spend his time in the company of young men, hunting and warring with them. William was by no means unique in these pursuits, but such a lifestyle could serve to raise suspicions of sodomitical behavior, given the right circumstances, as Orderic attempted to do in his history. William Rufus thus served as an excellent if negative example, according to Orderic, of the sodomitical dangers inherent in this unmarried and impious lifestyle. Through his presentation of William, Orderic advocated for both a conscious dedication to family and lineage and a conscious devotion to ecclesiastical authority. Through William, Orderic also presented the risk to those who refused such dedication and devotion: the descent into effeminacy, that combination of gender and sexual perversion.[60]

If William is placed alongside one of his contemporaries, Geoffroi, the count of Perche, whom Orderic depicts as a model of manhood, the contrast that Orderic implied becomes much starker:

> He was a distinguished count, handsome and brave, God-fearing and devoted to the church, a staunch defender of the clergy and God's poor; in time of peace he was gentle and lovable and conspicuous for his good manners; in time of war, harsh and successful, formidable to the rulers who were his neighbours, and an enemy to all. He stood out among the highest in the land because of the high birth of his parents and his wife Beatrice, and kept valiant barons and warlike castellans in firm subjection to his government. He gave his daughters in marriage to men of high rank ... from whom sprang a worthy line of noble

descendants. So Count Geoffrey, being blessed with such descendants and supported by arms and men, wealth and friends, and, most important of all, filled with the fear of the Lord, feared no man and advanced [into battle] bold as a lion.[61]

Geoffroi is obedient to God and his church and careful of his lineage, and it was this obedience and care as much as his prowess in war that distinguished him as a real man in Orderic's eyes. Orderic included Geoffroi's marriage and the resulting children as part of his masculine "success"; the role of aristocratic wives in the "taming" process advocated by ecclesiastical writers such as Orderic should not be underestimated, and served as yet another reason for encouraging marriage among the noble classes.[62] Orderic had another good reason for praising Geoffroi: he was allied through marriage with the closest neighbor and greatest benefactor of Orderic's abbey.[63]

It is true that there were other men disliked by Orderic Vitalis, men not painted as sodomites by him. Hugh of Chester, for example, was "a great lover of the world and worldly pomp," and was "always surrounded by a huge household [familia], full of the swarms of boys [numerosa puerorum] of both high and humble birth."[64] Hugh was married, but also had many concubines. Indeed, Hugh seems yet another example of the "untamed" sexuality of the military aristocracy. Still, Hugh had several children, even if all but one of them were by his concubines and not by his wife. Hugh, moreover, permitted good priests like Gerold of Avranches to preach freely and to win converts for the ascetic life from among the young men attached to his household.[65] So Hugh had a fecundity, both physical and spiritual, that William Rufus lacked.

William Rufus's brother, Robert Curthose, who became duke of Normandy, narrowly escaped a condemnation at Orderic's hands similar to that of his brother. In his history, Orderic included a holy man's prophecy that Robert would "give himself up to lust and indolence," and that "Ganymedes and effeminates [catamitae et effeminati] will govern [in his duchy], and under their rule vice and wretchedness will abound."[66] And indeed, when Robert became duke, Orderic continued, he was at first "led astray by the evil counsel of degenerate youths [peruersi iuuenes]."[67] But Robert repented of his evil ways, sought the advice of churchmen, and later even participated in the First Crusade, being transformed in the process from Christian retrobate to Christian hero. Ultimately, as the example of Robert Curthose demonstrates, Orderic's vituperation against the nobility formed part of a larger ecclesiastical project: the pacification of military culture, or at least its redirection toward more acceptable ends.

The means by which the prohibition against sodomitical relations between men and youths was enforced was by associating such sexual activity with effeminacy, which in the twelfth century implied the perversion of sexuality and gender. For if to be a man necessitated devotion to a woman or to the lineage that marriage to her might provide, men who were devoted to each other could hardly be men. To reject these social aims, then, was not only to make oneself vulnerable to attacks of sexual unorthodoxy but also of gender unorthodoxy. Such an association can be seen in Orderic Vitalis's writing against the "effeminates," but he was not the only twelfth-century writer to do so. Bernard of Cluny, when attacking sodomy, linked the two in this fashion:

> The law of kind [genus] perishes, and common custom is destroyed by this plague. It is unknown to cattle, or dogs, or horses, but to man [homo] entirely [alone]. I call them half males [semimares] and judge them half men [semivires], polluting themselves, giving to each other—alas!—what they owe to the inferior sexes [sexibus inferioribus].[68]

The nature that was violated by sodomy, Bernard implied, was not only human nature but also especially masculine nature. Helen describes it in this way in her debate with Ganymede:

> Males [masculi] should blush, nature should mourn; of nature's binds, no concern is shown by men [vires]. . . . You who attach yourselves, males to males [maribus mares], who wastefully unman men [devirare vires], at night you pollute yourselves and boys [pueri].[69]

Nowhere was the objection to sodomy on the basis of the natural order more clearly linked to the loss of masculinity than in one of the twelfth-century's greatest advocates of nature, the churchman Alain of Lille. His De planctu naturae begins:

> I turn from laughter to tears, from joy to grief, from merriment to lament, from jests to wailing, when I see the decrees of Nature

fall silent, when a shipwrecked multitude perishes by a monster
of Venus, when Venus fighting with Venus makes "hes" into
"shes," and when she unmans men *[devirare vires]* with magic
art. . . . The sex of the active gender *[activi generis sexus]* trembles
thus to degenerate shamefully into the passive gender *[passivum
genus]*. A man *[vir]* is made female *[femina]*. He blackens the
honor of his sex. The art of magic Venus hermaphrodites *[her-
maphroditare]* him. . . . He denies being a man *[vir]*.[70]

Alain's use of grammatical similes to back up his argument about the
unnaturalness of same-sex coupling has been carefully analyzed by Jan
Ziolkowski, who compares them with those of several other contemporary authors.[71] Nevertheless, the similes work not because human corre-
spondences should follow grammatical rules—in fact, the opposite argument is being made—but because in both, masculine and feminine
are separate categories and there should be no confusion between the
two. Indeed, Gautier de Coincy in his *Miracles de Nostre Dame* argued for
the distinction between grammar and sex:

Grammar couples "him" to "him" *[hic a hic]*, but nature curses
this coupling. Eternal death is born to him who loves the masculine gender *[masculin genre]* rather than facing the feminine,
and God effaces him from his book. Nature laughs, it seems to
me, when "him" and "her" join together, but "him" and "him"
is a lost cause *[chose perdue]*. Nature is so aghast, she beats her
fists and wrings her hands.[72]

Curiously, the same authors who condemned men becoming women
also described women becoming men in praiseworthy tones and without concern for the damage done to the natural categories of gender.
Even Alain of Lille, in another work, congratulated the goddess Minerva
for her virile wisdom: "a man in mind *[sensus]*, a woman in body *[sexus]*,
thus both a man and a woman, and in spirit *[anima]* not a she but a
he."[73] The *Roman d'Énéas* also celebrates the manly martial prowess of
the warrior-woman, Camille.[74]

The gap left between the condemnation of men-who-become-women
and the praise of women-who-become-men reveals much about the categories of gender as understood by twelfth-century writers. Obviously it

was not the crossing of gender boundaries that defined the transgressive act; indeed, women who so behaved were seen as improving themselves. Rather, it was because the boundary between gender and sexual difference was situated on an incline: women who became men elevated themselves, but men who became women degraded themselves. The underpinnings of this belief are obvious: the misogyny of twelfth-century culture that assumed the inferior status of women, and the "deep-seated ambivalence" toward women, such as Penny Gold describes for the period.[75] As so often has been demonstrated about many medieval writers, women represented carnality and men spirituality. Sexual desire was always therefore effeminizing to men on some level, at least according to ecclesiastical writers. But twelfth-century writers regarded sodomy as particularly abhorrent because men were believed to take on feminine sexual roles, in addition to giving in to an effeminizing desire. Behind this idea is the assumption that a man who interacts sexually with another man must do so by acting as a figurative woman, and behind that idea, another assumption, that there can be no sexual relations without a gendered hierarchy. Neither of these were new ideas of the twelfth century, and both were as entrenched in western culture as misogyny and tied directly to it.[76]

Writers of the twelfth century exploited these ancient fears to lend weight to their prohibitions. They maintained that masculine identity itself depended on the rejection of affectional solidarity between adult and adolescent males in favor of devotion to women. There was a certain irony to suggesting that fostering, the institution whose primary purpose was to initiate a boy into manhood, was instead the occasion for the perversion of masculine identity and the making of the boy into a woman, it is true. But linking the loyalty that these young men had for each other with the perversion of masculine nature resulting from sodomy was part of the "taming" of the military nobility.

Associating male intimacy with the loss of masculine identity worked both at the level of external prohibition and that of internal self-regulation. The one subjected to the power of surveillance became the principle of his own subjection and assumed responsibility himself for the constraints of that power.[77] Probably the most famous treatise on courtly love, that written by Andreas Capellanus near the end of the twelfth century, serves as an excellent example of this self-policing trend. He began his treatise with the declaration,

Now, in love you should note first of all that love *[amor]* cannot exist except between persons of different sexes. Between two males *[mares]* or two females *[feminae]* love can find no place, for we see that two persons of the same sex are not at all fitted for giving each other the exchanges of love or for practicing the acts natural to it. Whatever nature denies, love blushes to embrace.[78]

Here is both the argument of the complementarity of men and women, and the claim of the unnaturalness of love between men. Andreas repeated the idea later in his treatise, to support his claim that all men long for sexual union with a woman:

And if you want to deny the truth of this, you will be forced to admit that two males *[masculi]* can give each other the solaces of love, a thing which would be disgraceful *[nefandus]* enough to speak of and criminal *[criminosus]* to practice.[79]

Nevertheless, and even before this declaration, Andreas stated in the dedicatory prologue that

I am greatly impelled by the continual urging of my love *[dilectio]* for you, my revered friend Walter, to make known by word of mouth and to teach you by my writings the way in which a state of love *[amor]* between two lovers may be kept unharmed. . . . Because of the love *[affectus]* I have for you I can by no means refuse your request.[80]

Despite Andreas's careful choice of synonyms for love—*dilectio* and *affectus*—this prologue must surely undo on some level Andreas's subsequent remarks insisting that men can only love women. Andreas, moreover, ended his treatise by undermining the "naturalness" of courtly love altogether and by affirming that true affection is best found between male friends, concluding that true love was impossible between men and women, in part, because by it

one friend *[amicus]* is estranged from another and serious unfriendlinesses grow up between men *[homines]*. . . . For what do we find so necessary or so useful to men *[homines]* as to have reliable friends?[81]

Andreas returned to the praise of marriage at the end of his treatise, it should be noted, bringing his work into conformity with the new emphasis on family and lineage. Nonetheless, the tension caused by Andreas's ambivalent recognition of male intimacy remains.

The suspicion of sodomy in the twelfth century by no means put an end to male friendship, as is obvious, even if it questioned the purpose of male intimacy. Because even in the midst of attacks against sodomitical desire, erotic desire for men could still be expressed, if in indirect ways. Chrétien de Troyes frequently described the masculine appeal of his heroes, for example, and placed an appreciation of their beauty in the minds of other men:

> Meleagant was extremely noble [genz] and capable, and well built [bien tailliez] in his arms, legs, and feet; and his helmet and shield which hung from his neck suited him perfectly. But at [first sight of the] the other [knight, who was Lancelot], all fell silent, even those who wished to see him shamed, and all said that Meleagant was nothing compared to him.[82]

Alain of Lille also paused longingly on the image of the ideal man as he appears before his mystical wedding to the personification of nature, even in the midst of his treatise against sodomy and while ostensibly repudiating that longing:

> On his face there showed no signs of feminine softness [feminea mollitia]; rather the authority of manly dignity [virilis dignitas] alone held sway there.... [H]is hair lay in orderly fashion to prevent it from appearing to degenerate into feminine softness.... His face, as manly dignity demanded, was missing in no grace of beauty [pulchritudinis gratia].[83]

This passage suggests the same sort of ambivalence in Alain of Lille's writing about the relationship between nature and homoeroticism that Jordan has described in Alain's writings.[84] But it shows an equal ambivalence about the meaning of a gendered sexuality, since if the man has no *feminea mollitia*, which might be translated as "effeminacy" as easily as "feminine softness," then what is most desirable about him is his masculinity, which lies at the heart of his *pulchritudinis gratia* ("grace of beauty").

The fear of male intimacy beginning in the mid-twelfth century did mean, however, that it became impossible to represent openly passionate friendships between men. In some ways, the only truly unproblematic passion that could be shared between men was a mutual desire for the same woman, because it lay beyond the suspicion of sodomy. Eve Sedgwick has pointed out that in nineteenth-century literature "the bond that links the two rivals is as intense and potent as the bond that links either of the rivals to the beloved," and Marjorie Garber has discussed the polymorphous sexuality of the love triangle in modern literature.[85] Such potent configurations of desire were not unknown to medieval writers. Andreas Capellanus suggested that the passion of rivalry even improved love:

> If you know that someone is trying to win your beloved away from you, that will no doubt increase your love and you will begin to feel more affection for her. I will go further and say that even though you know perfectly well that some other man is enjoying the embraces of your beloved, this will make you begin to value her solaces all the more.[86]

Nothing typifies the vestiges of homoeroticism in this new relationship of rivalry better than Le chevaliers au lyeon ("The Knight of the Lion"), the legend told by Chrétien de Troyes of Yvain and his longtime companion, Gawain. Despite their sincere devotion to each other, they come to blows in defending a woman's honor, ignorant of each other's identity. Chrétien detailed at length how they both love and hate each other with equal passion at that moment.[87] The passage parallels an earlier description of the love and hate between Yvain and his lady.[88] When Chrétien began his depiction of the battle between the two men, he could not resist returning to the irony of their ignorance of each other's identity, saying that if they had known who they were fighting, "they would have permitted each other to kiss and embrace and not to bruise, they who were bruising and wounding each other."[89] When the two men finally recognize each other, they do exactly as Chrétien had predicted: "each threw his arms around the other's neck and they embraced."[90] Yvain and Gawain had been fighting over a woman, and her presence inserts itself between them as the cause of their breach. Nevertheless, the two men surmount this obstacle to their love and regain it in the end. As this example demonstrates, male intimacy was rescued some-what by being recast as rivalry, and this sort of love triangle proved an especially fruitful conjunction for writers from the twelfth century on.[91]

It is important, finally, to add something about the consequences of the ambivalence surrounding male friendships for male sexual identity. For the reluctance to address devotion between men in literary sources after the twelfth century, as seen in the love triangle, can also be histori-cized, situated in the historical aftereffects of the problematization of male friendships. Even as the promotion of the lineage and the conven-tions of courtly love made men's sexual desire for women an essential component of male identity, it also constructed its opposite, the sodomite, the "other" that a man could never permit himself to be and still be a man. R. I. Moore briefly alludes to the formation of a sodomite identity in this period, but it was John Boswell who first suggested that *some-thing* important happened in this period, even if he did not understand what that *something* was.[92] Boswell's work has been dismissed by some as essentialist; that is, presupposing a transhistorical gay identity without which his interpretation of homoerotic texts is meaningless.[93] Nonethe-less, it is possible to view the writings that condemned male intimacy in the twelfth century as part of the construction of a new sexual identity for men.

Indeed, concomitant to the historical changes of the twelfth century was a major shift in the categories of male sexuality. A magnifying glass had been turned on men's relationships, both social and sexual. Alain of Lille could, as a result of this intensified examination of men's sexual roles, desire to make the following precise classifications, again by using a grammatical metaphor:

Of those men *[homines]* who acknowledge the grammar of Venus, some closely embrace those of masculine gender *[genus]* only, others, those of feminine gender, others, those of common, or indiscriminate *[promiscuus]* gender. Some, indeed, if belonging to the heteroclite gender, decline irregularly, in the winter with the feminine, in the summer with the masculine gender. There are some, who, disputing in the logic of Venus, in their conclu-sions get [*sortiri,* to obtain by chance] a law of interchangeability of subjects and predicates. There are those who take the part of the subject and cannot function as predicate. There are some who function as predicates only but have no desire to have the legitimate subject submit to them.[94]

These are odd categories of sexual identity from a modern perspective, perhaps, but the attempt at classification itself is not unfamiliar to us.

Not even the detailed groupings of sexual acts in penitential literature, which provides the best precedent to Alain's remarks from an earlier age, demonstrate an equivalent desire to create different categories of identity based on sexual preferences. The *Decretum* of Yves of Chartres, for example, which collected together different opinions on penances for sin at the turn of the previous century also in northern France, only alludes to such classificatory possibilities, and with a much more limited scope of vision. The *Decretum* suggests harsher penances for someone who is "in the habit of" *(in consuetudine est)* committing sodomy, and for a cleric or monk who is "a pursuer of boys" *(parvulorum insectator)* or one who "plays with boys and has friendships [with boys] of tender age" *(ludere cum pueris et habere amicitiae aetatis infirmae)*.[95] Sodomy has by no means the same implications as in the texts we have examined, where it functions as much as a violation of masculine identity as of sexual morality, and where being a sodomite represented a male person who was a failure as a man.

Appreciating the historical context of the twelfth-century literary sources, we can now see that the fluidity of sexual identities in premodern Europe, emphasized in much of the current historiography on the history of homosexuality, began to be lost in the twelfth century. We are not viewing the creation of a "sexual minority" or the construction of a "third sex," by any means, but the writers of the twelfth century did begin to open a conceptual space for such later developments through their notion of a man who became an "unman" by means of his sexual practices. Indeed, the very content of masculinity, what it meant to be a man, was changed by this fear of intimacy between men and its new notions of men who fell out of the category of men. Jordan's documentation of a terminological shift from "Sodom" to "sodomy" to "sodomite" is particularly useful, when situated in this context, because it confirms the development of a new sexual identity for men, if only as a mental image, as he suggests in his conclusion.[96] Such a conclusion also parallels that of R. Howard Bloch, who demonstrates the complex interplay between the courtly and misogynistic literature of the later Middle Ages and its central role both as response to and in the construction of a new social identity for women.[97] Gender, one's sense of oneself as "male" or "female" and the social meaning attached to that sense, and sexuality, the spectrum of desires between love and sexual pleasure, thus regulated each other in turn.

NOTES

Earlier versions of this paper were presented at the conference of the Society for French Historical Studies in Boston in March 1996, at a Colloquium on Medieval Sexuality at the University of California at Santa Barbara, and at a meeting of the Medievalist Club at San Diego State University. I am very grateful for the assistance of all those who have read and commented on the ideas in this paper at various stages, including Randolph Trumbach, Noah Guynn, Elizabeth A. R. Brown, David Nirenberg, Ulrike Wiethaus, Kathryn Ringrose, and Everett Rowson. The editors of this volume also went far beyond the call of duty in offering suggestions about improvements and reshaping of sections. Any errors that remain, however, are entirely my own. This paper is dedicated to Joanne Ferraro, my colleague and friend at San Diego State University.

1. John Boswell, *Christianity, Social Tolerance, and Homosexuality: Gay People in Western Europe from the Beginning of the Christian Era to the Fourteenth Century* (Chicago, 1980), 44 and 243–44.

2. On this debate, see the various essays collected in *Forms of Desire, Sexual Orientation and the Social Constructionist Controversy*, ed. Edward Stein (New York, 1990).

3. Mark D. Jordan, *The Invention of Sodomy in Christian Theology* (Chicago, 1997), 8.

4. Robert I. Moore, *The Formation of a Persecuting Society: Power and Deviance in Western Europe, 950–1250* (Oxford, 1987), 99.

5. Jordan, *Invention of Sodomy*, 9.

6. See, for example, Reginald Hyatte, *The Arts of Friendship: The Idealization of Friendship in Medieval and Early Renaissance Literature* (Leiden, 1994), chap. 3, 130.

7. In this project, I am grateful to the groundbreaking research of Eve Kosofsky Sedgwick, who in her study of men in nineteenth-century English literature, created a useful new terminology for writing about male intimacies, "homosociality." She called a similar suspicion of male friendships in the nineteenth century a "homosexual panic," and linked it to new gender arrangements that brought into question men's "homosocial desires." I argue that a similar process was at work in the twelfth century, a process one might even call "sodomitical panic." See Sedgwick's *Between Men: English Literature and Male Homosocial Desire* (New York, 1985).

8. Jordan never asks, for example, why it was in the eleventh century that Peter Damian coined the term "sodomy," nor why it was used by so many theologians after him in the twelfth as a helpful category. Still, Jordan's is a fascinating and innovative work of intellectual history and one grounded in a profound knowledge of the intellectual history of the Middle Ages.

9. Boswell, *Christianity, Social Tolerance, and Homosexuality*, esp. chaps. 8 and 9.

10. See, for example, Gerald A. Bond, *The Loving Subject: Desire, Eloquence, and Power in Romanesque France* (Philadelphia, 1995).

11. C. Stephen Jaeger, "L'amour des rois: structure sociale d'une forme de sensibilité aristocratique," *Annales E.S.C.* 46 (1991): 547–71: "le langage de l'érotique montre innocemment que l'illicite est certes proche mais évité ou ignoré. Il est maîtrisé, contrôlé, maintenu à sa place." Unless otherwise indicated, all translations are mine.

12. Peter Abelard, *Dolorum solacium*, in *Medieval Latin Poems of Male Love and Friendship*, ed. and trans. T. Stehling (New York, 1984), lines 45–48, 61–64, 69–92: "Plus fratre mihi, Ionatha, / in una mecum anima, / quae peccata, quae scelera, / nostra sciderunt viscera! / ... / Tu mihi, mi Ionatha, / flendus super omnia, / inter cuncta gaudia / perpes erit lacrima. / ... / Heu, cur consilio / adquievi pessimo, / ut tibi praesidio / non essem in proelio? / vel confossus pariter / morerer feliciter, / cum, quid amor faciat, / maius hoc non habeat, / et me post te vivere / mori sit assidue, / nec ad vitam anima / satis sit dimidia. / Vicem amicitiae / vel unam me reddere / oportebat tempore / summae tunc angustiae, / triumphi participem / vel ruinae comitem, / ut te vel eriperem / vel tecum occumberem, / vitam pro te finiens / quam salvasti totiens, / ut et mors nos iungeret / magis quam disiungeret."

13. See Jean Leclercq, *Monks and Love in Twelfth-Century France* (Oxford, 1979); Hyatte, *Arts of Friendship*, chap. 2.

14. Alain of Lille, *Anticlaudianus*, in *The Anglo-Latin Satirical Poets and Epigrammatists of the Twelfth Century*, ed. T. Wright, vol. 2 (1872; reprint, Wiesbaden, 1964), 7.7: "Quaeret quem vero sic complectatur amore, / Illaesaque fide, quod amor lucretur amorem / Alterius.... / ... / Quaerat cui possit se totum credere, velle / Declarare suum, totamque exponere mentem. / Cui sua committat animi secreta latentis, / Ut sibi, conservans thesaurum mentis in illo, / Nil sibi secretum, quod non develet eidem, / Ut suus in tali signo mensuret amicus / Pondus amicitiae, quam lance rependat eadem."

15. Alain of Lille, *Anticlaudianus*, translated here by J. Sheridan (Toronto, 1980), 2.4: "Nam David et Jonathas ibi sunt duo, sunt tamen unum; / Cum sint diversi, non sunt duo mente, sed unus. / Dimidiant animas; sibi se partitur uterque, / ... / Alter in Euryalo comparet Nisus, et alter / Eurialus viget in Niso, sic alter utrumque / Reddit, et ex uno comitum pensatur uterque."

16. Alain of Lille, *Anticlaudianus*, trans. Sheridan, 2.4: "quos castus amor, concordia simplex, / Pura fides, vera pietas, conjunxit."

17. *Énéas, roman du XIIe siècle*, ed. J.-J. Salverda de Grave, 2 vols. (1925; reprint, Paris, 1983), lines 4913–18: "amoient soi de tele amor / qu'il ne pooient de greignor: / unques plus voire amor ne fu / que d'aus, tant com il ont vescu; / l'uns ne savoit sanz l'autre rien, / ne ne avoit joie ne bien." I have based my translation of *Énéas* here and below in part on the translation of J. Yunck, *Énéas: A Twelfth-Century French Romance* (New York, 1974).

18. *Énéas*, lines 6147, 6187–89, 6193–96: "'Pallas,' fait il, 'flor de jovente, / ... / tant estïés biaus ier matin, / sos ciel n'avoit plus gent meschin, / en po d'ore te voi müé, / ... / Bele faiture, gente chose, / si com soloil flestist la rose, / si t'a la morz tot tost plessié / et tot flesti et tot changié.'"

19. *Énéas*, lines 6209–13: "Atant se tolt, ne pot plus dire, / au cuer ot duel et molt grant ire, / desor lo mort chaï pasmez, / et quant il s'an fu relevez, / lo mort baisa tot an plorant."

20. *Énéas*, lines 8567–73, 8578–92: "Cil cuiverz est de tel nature / qu'il n'a gaires de femmes cure; / il prise plus lo ploin mestier; / il ne velt pas biset mangier, / molt par aimme char de maslon; / il priseroit mialz un garçon / qui toi ne altre acoler; / ... / N'as tu oï comfaitemant / il mena Dido malemant? / Unques feme n'ot bien de lui, / n'en avras tu, si com ge cui, / d'un traitor, d'un sodomite. / Toz tens te clamera il quite; / se il avoit alcun godel, / ce li seroit et bon et bel / quel laissasses a ses druz faire; / s'il lo pooit par toi atraire, / nel troveroit ja si estrange / qu'il ne feïst son bon de toi / por ce qu'il lo sofrist de soi; / bien lo lairoit sor toi monter, / s'il repueit sor lui troter."

21. *Énéas*, lines 9130–38, 9159–64: "'Ce est,' fait ele, 'verité, / que ma mere m'a de lui dit; / de feme lui est molt petit, / il voldroit deduit de garçon, / n'aime se males putains non. / Son Ganimede a avec soi, / asez li est or po de moi; / il est molt longuement an ruit, / a garçon moine son deduit; / ... / Il a asez garçons o soi, / lo peor aime mialz de moi, / fandue trove lor chemise; / maint an i a an son servise, / lor braies sovant avalees: / issi deservent lor soldees.'"

22. *Énéas*, lines 9165–70: "Maldite soit hui tel nature / d'ome qui de femme n'a cure; / il est de ce toz costumiers. / Molt par est malvés cist mestiers / et molt par a fol esciant / qui feme let et homo prent."

23. Jonathan Goldberg, *Sodometries: Renaissance Texts, Modern Sexualities* (Stanford, CA, 1992), 23. He calls this project "reading for sodomy—and for sodomites."

24. Sally North, "The Ideal Knight as Presented in Some French Narrative Poems, c.1090–c.1240: An Outline Sketch," in *The Ideals and Practice of Medieval Knighthood*, ed. Christopher Harper-Bill and Ruth Harvey (Bury St. Edmunds, 1986), 123.

25. *Chanson de Roland*, ed. P. Jonin (Paris, 1979), lines 284–85: "Gent out le cors e les costez out larges; / tant par fut bels tuit si per l'en esguardent."

26. *Couronnement de Louis*, ed. E. Langlois (Paris, 1965), lines 1766–67: "Li gentilz cuens par mi les flans l'embrace, / si le baisa quatre feiz en la face."

27. *Ami et Amile*, ed. P. Dembowski (Paris, 1969), lines 177–81: "Et cil le vit qui l'ot ja avisé. / Vers lui se torne quant il l'ot ravisé, / Par tel vertu se sont entr'acolé, / Tant fort se baisent et estraingnent soef, / A poi ne sont estaint et definé."

28. See Yannick Carré, *Le baiser sur la bouche au moyen âge: Rites, symboles, mentalités* (Paris, 1992).

29. *Prise d'Orange*, ed. C. Régnier (Paris, 1970), lines 625–26: "Un bacheler juene de barbe prime, / Qui de deport et d'armes set bien vivre."

30. Georges Duby, *Medieval Marriage: Two Models from Twelfth-Century France*, trans. Elborg Forster (Baltimore, MD, 1978), 13. See also Georges Duby, "Youth in Aristocratic Society: Northwestern France in the Twelfth Century," in *The Chivalrous Society*, trans. Cynthia Postan (Berkeley, 1977), 112–22.

31. Hildebert of Lavardin, *Ad S. nepotem*, in *Hildeberti Cenomannensis episcopi carmina minora*, ed. A. Brian Scott (Berlin, 1969), 20–21: "Res male tuta puer, nec te committe quibusdam; / multa domus multos fertur habere Joves. / Non tamen expectes Ganimedes

crimine coelum; / hac modo militia nullus ad astra venit. / Consecrat aethereas solis ju-
nioribus arces / lex melior; manes masculus uxor habet."

32. Hildebert of Lavardin, *De malitia saeculi*, in *Medieval Latin Poems of Male Love
and Friendship*, ed. Stehling, lines 35–44: "Omnibus incestis superst est sodomitica
pestis, / dantque mares maribus debita conjugibus. / Innumeras aedes colit innumerus
Ganymedes, / hocque, quod ipsa solet sumere, Juno dolet. / Hoc sordent vitio puer et vir
cum sene laeno, / nullaque conditio cessat ab hoc vitio. / Quisquis ad hunc morem naturae vertis honorem / et Venerem licitam negligis ob vetitam, / nonne recordaris quod per
Sodomam docearis / hoc scelus ut caveas, sulphure ne pereas?"

33. Bernard of Cluny, *De contemptu mundi*, in *Medieval Latin Poems of Male Love and
Friendship*, ed. Stehling, line 15: "Lex Sodomae patet, innumerus scatet heu! Ganymedes."

34. Jean Flori, *L'essor de la chevalerie, XIe–XIIe siècles* (Geneva, 1986), 15. See also
Maurice Keen, *Chivalry* (New Haven, CT, 1984), 66–69.

35. Béroul, *Tristan*, ed. N. Lacy (New York, 1989), lines 2174–76: "Et cent danzeaus
avoques moi, / Qui servisent por armes prendre / Et a moi lor servise rendre."

36. *Gesta Normannorum ducum*, ed. and trans. E. van Houts, vol. 1 (Oxford, 1992),
4.2: "Mittens enim Ricardum puerum suis iussit aspectibus presentari, quem egregia
forma perspiciens decoratum cum coetaneis pueris in suo palatio decreuit educandum."

37. *Vita Amici et Amelii carissimorum*, in *Amis and Amiloun*, ed. E. Kölbing, Al-
tenglische Bibliothek, vol. 2 (Heilbronn, 1884); trans. M. Kuefler, *Life of the Dear Friends
Amicus and Amelius*, in *Medieval Hagiography: An Anthology*, ed. T. Head (New York, 2000):
"utrique fidem inter se spoponderunt et ad curiam Karoli regis simul ingrediuntur, ubi
cerneret juvenes moderatos, sapientes, pulcherrimos, pares uno cultu et eodem vultu, ab
omnibus dilectos et ab omnibus honoratos. Quid referam? Factus est Amicus thesaurarius
regis et Amelius dapifer." Note that Kölbing's edition, which contains numerous typographical errors, has *cerneres* where I read *cerneret*.

38. An early study is that by Georges Duby, "Lineage, Nobility and Knighthood: The
Mâconnais in the Twelfth Century—A Revision," in *The Chivalrous Society*, 59–80. For a
recent examination, see Theodore Evergates, "Nobles and Knights in Twelfth-Century
France," in *Cultures of Power: Lordship, Status, and Process in Twelfth-Century Europe*, ed. T.
Bisson (Philadelphia, 1995).

39. The contemporary shift in land inheritance from partitive inheritance to primogeniture did not detract from this emphasis on procreation and family continuity. First,
primogeniture did not always and everywhere triumph over other forms of inheritance. See the example of continued competing systems of land inheritance in Blois-
Chartres by Amy Livingstone, "Kith and Kin: Kinship and Family Structure of the Nobility
of Eleventh- and Twelfth-Century Blois-Chartres," *French Historical Studies* 20 (1997):
419–58. Second, even when younger sons were excluded from the primary landholding
of the family, they were often given secondary landholdings, from maternal, dotal, acquired, or border estates. See Andrew W. Lewis, *Royal Succession in Capetian France: Studies on Familial Order and the State* (Cambridge, MA, 1981), esp. 29–32, 37–42, and 162–63.
Third, younger sons might be needed to take up the primary landholding of the family
in the event of the death of the eldest son and principal heir, a not infrequent event in the
period.

40. *Altercatio Ganymedis et Helene,* in *Medieval Latin Poems of Male Love and Friendship,* ed. Stehling, line 155: "Miscet Venus masculos sterili iunctura."

41. Alain of Lille, *De planctu naturae,* in *Anglo-Latin Satirical Poets and Epigrammatists,* ed. Wright (trans. Sheridan), 1.1: "Cudit in incudem quae semina nulla monetat, / Torquet et incudem malleus ipse suam. / Nullam materiam matricis signat idea, / Sed magis et sterili litore vomer arat."

42. *Énéas,* lines 8596–8602: "De cest sigle seroit tost fin, / se tuit li home qui i sont / erent autel par tot lo mont; / ja mes feme ne concevroit, / grant sofraite de gent seroit; / l'an ne feroit ja mes anfanz, / li siegles faudroit ainz cent anz."

43. For discussion of the assumption of sexual desire and devotion to women as an integral part of masculinity by later medieval writers, see David Aers, "Masculine Identity in the Courtly Community: The Self Loving in *Troilus and Criseyde,*" in *Community, Gender, and Individual Identity: English Writing, 1360–1430,* ed. Aers (New York, 1988); or Susan Crane, *Gender and Romance in Chaucer's Canterbury Tales* (Princeton, NJ, 1994), chap. 1.

44. Chrétien de Troyes, *Li contes del Graal,* ed. R. Pickens (New York, 1990), lines 3826–28: "Qui beise fame et plus n'i fet, / Des qu'il sont seul a seul andui, / Dons cuit ge qu'il remaint an lui."

45. Marie de France, *Lai de Lanval,* ed. K. Warnke (1925; reprint, Geneva, 1974), lines 281–84: "Asez m'e la hum dit sovent, / que de femme n'avez talent. / Vaslez amez bien afaitiez / ensemble od els vus dedulez."

46. *Énéas,* lines 8606–08: "et qui se fet contre nature, / les homes prent, les fames let, / la natural cople desfait."

47. *Altercatio Ganymedis et Helene,* lines 114–15: "sexum mulieribus invides aperte. / Ordo rerum vertitur et lex perit per te." See also Boswell, *Christianity, Social Tolerance, and Homosexuality,* 381–89.

48. Jo Ann McNamara, "The *Herrenfrage:* The Restructuring of the Gender System, 1050–1150," in *Medieval Masculinities: Regarding Men in the Middle Ages,* ed. Clare A. Lees (Minneapolis, 1994).

49. *Vita Amici et Amelii carissimorum,* cix–cx: "Quos Deus sicut unanimi concordia et dilectione in vita coniunxit, ita et in morte eos separari noluit.... Fabricate sunt ergo due ecclesie ... reliqua vero corpora hic atque illic sepulta sunt. Mane autem facto dispositione divina inventum est corpus Amelii cum suo sarchofago juxta sarchofagum Amici in ecclesia regali. O admiranda duorum societas amicorum, o ineffabilis caritas amborum, que nec in morte dividi meruit!"

50. Hyatte, *Arts of Friendship,* 130. On the versions of the legend, their dating and relationships, see the introduction to MacEdward Leach, *Amis and Amiloun* (London, 1937), ix–xxxii.

51. Moore, *Formation of a Persecuting Society,* 144.

52. Christopher Baswell, "Men in the *Roman d'Énéas:* The Construction of Empire," in *Medieval Masculinities,* ed. Lees, 162. Baswell explores these questions further in his *Virgil in Medieval England: Figuring the Aeneid from the Twelfth Century to Chaucer* (Cambridge, 1995), 200–210.

53. Simon Gaunt, *Gender and Genre in Medieval French Literature* (Philadelphia, 1995), 74, 81. See also the earlier work of Georges Duby, *The Knight, the Lady, and the*

Priest: The Making of Modern Marriage in Medieval France, trans. B. Bray (New York, 1983); and Christopher Brooke, *The Medieval Idea of Marriage* (Oxford, 1989), 56–60.

54. Alan Bray, "Homosexuality and the Signs of Male Friendship in Elizabethan England," *History Workshop* 29 (1990): 1–19.

55. See Jordan, *Invention of Sodomy*, chap. 3.

56. See Anne Llewellyn Barstow, *Married Priests and the Reforming Papacy: The Eleventh-Century Debates* (New York, 1982), esp. 112–14, 120, and 134–36.

57. Serlo of Bayeux, *Defensio pro filiis presbyterorum*, in *Libelli de lite imperatorum et pontificum*, vol. 3, Monumenta Germaniae Historica (Hannover, 1891), 580–83; quoted in Barstow, *Married Priests*, 240: "homines vite turpis, mechi, sodomite." Barstow also provides information on the authorship of the text, information not provided in the MGH edition, 240, n. 53. Cf. the anonymous *Nos uxorati*, quoted and translated in Boswell, *Christianity, Social Tolerance, and Homosexuality*, 398–400.

58. Orderic Vitalis, *Historia ecclesiastica*, ed. and trans. M. Chibnall, vols. 3–4, (Oxford, 1972–73), 8.3.324 (vol. 4): "Ritus heroum abiciebant, hortamenta sacerdotum deridebant.... Omne tempus quidam usurpabant, et extra legem Dei moremque patrum pro libitu suo ducebant. Nocte comesationibus et potationibus uanisque confabulationibus aleis et tesseris aliisque ludibriis uacabant, die uero dormiebant."

59. Orderic Vitalis, *Historia ecclesiastica* (my translation here), 8.3.324: "Tunc effeminati passim in orbe dominabantur indisciplinate debachabantur sodomiticisque spurciciis foedi catamitae flammis urendi turpiter abutebantur."

60. See also Frank Barlow, *William Rufus* (Berkeley, 1983), esp. chap. 3, "The Bachelor King and His Domestic Servants," for his discussion of the accusation of sexual unorthodoxy made against William.

61. Orderic Vitalis, *Historia ecclesiastica* (trans. Chibnall, vol. 4), 8.3.302: "Erat idem consul magnanimus, corpore pulcher et ualidus, timens Deum et aecclesiae cultor deuotus, clericorum pauperumque Dei defensor strenuus, in pace quietus et amabilis bonisque pollebat moribus; in bello grauis et fortunatus, finitimisque intolerabilis regibus et inimicus omnibus. Hic nobilitate parentum suorum et coniugis suae Beatricis inter illustres spectabilis erat; strenuosque barones et in armis acres oppidanos suae ditioni subditos habebat. Filias quoque suas consularibus uiris dedit in matrimonio ... ex quibus orta est elegans sobolis generosae propago. Goisfredus itaque comes tot stemmatibus exornabatur; et armis animisque cum diuitiis et amicis fulciebatur; et quod est super omnia timore Domini stipatus neminem timens ut leo progrediebatur."

62. See Sharon Farmer, "Persuasive Voices: Clerical Images of Medieval Wives," *Speculum* 61 (1986): 517–43, esp. 522–23 on Orderic Vitalis.

63. See Marjorie Chibnall, *The World of Orderic Vitalis* (Oxford, 1984), 24–26. A similar description is given of Helias of Maine: see Orderic Vitalis, *Historia ecclesiastica*, 8.3.332; 10.4.35–39.

64. Orderic Vitalis, *Historia ecclesiastica* (trans. Chibnall, vol. 3), 6.3.4: "Hic nimirum amator fuit seculi seculariumque pomparum quas maximam beatitudinum putabat esse portionem humanarum. Erat enim in militia promptus in dando nimis prodigus gaudens ludis et luxibus, mimis, equis et canibus aliisque huiusmodi uanitatibus. Huic maxima

semper adherebat familia in quibus nobilium ignobiliumque puerorum numerosa per-strepebat copia."

65. See Orderic Vitalis, *Historia ecclesiastica*, 4.2.220 on Hugh's children and 6.3.4–17 on the preaching of Gerold and its effects.

66. Orderic Vitalis, *Historia ecclesiastica* (trans. Chibnall, vol. 3), 5.2.385: "Ipse uelut uacca lasciuiens libidini pigriciaeque seuiet, et ipse primus aecclesiasticas opes diripiet spurcisque lenonibus aliisque lecatoribus distribuet. Talibus principatum suum porriget et ab his consilium in necessitatibus suis exiget. In ducatu Rodberti catamitae et effemi-nati dominabuntur sub quorum dominatione nequitia et miseria grassabuntur." I have re-placed Chibnall's "catamites" with "Ganymedes."

67. Orderic Vitalis, *Historia ecclesiastica* (trans. Chibnall, vol. 3), 5.2.388: "Prauo per-uersorum monitu iuuenum Rodbertus iuuenis male deceptus est et inde multis ingens discrimen et detrimentum exortum est."

68. Bernard of Cluny, *De contemptu mundi*, lines 31–34: "Lex genii perit, usus et in-terit hac lue notus; / nescit ea pecus, aut canis, aut equus, ast homo totus. / Semimares voco, semiviros probo, se maculantes; / debita sexibus inferioribus heu! sibi dantes."

69. *Altercatio Ganymedis et Helene*, lines 153–54, 209–11: "Erubescant masculi, doleat natura; / de nature vinculo non est viris cura. / . . . / Vos qui vobis maribus mares appli-catis, / qui prodigialiter viros deviratis, / nocte vos et pueros fede maculatis."

70. Alain of Lille, *De planctu naturae*, 1.1: "In lacrimas risus, in luctus gaudia verto, / In planctum plausus, in lacrimosa jocos, / Cum sua Naturae video decreta silere, / Cum Veneris monstro naufraga turba perit; / Cum Venus in Venerem pugnans illos facit illas; / Cumque suos magica devirat arte viros. / . . . / Activi generis sexus se turpiter horret / Sic in passivum degenerare genus. / Femina vir factus, sexus denigrat honorem, / Ars magi-cae Veneris hermaphroditat eum. / . . . / Se negat esse virum." I have relied in part here on Sheridan's translation.

71. Jan Ziolkowski, *Alan of Lille's Grammar of Sex: The Meaning of Grammar to a Twelfth-Century Intellectual* (Cambridge, MA, 1985).

72. Gautier de Coincy, *Les miracles de Nostre Dame*, ed. V. F. Koenig, vol. 2 (Geneva, 1961), lines 1233–43: "La grammaire *hic* a *hic* acopple, / Mais nature maldist la copple. / La mort perpetuel engenre / Cil qui aimme masculin genre / Plus que le feminin ne face / Et Diex de son livre l'esface. / Nature rit, si com moi samble, / Quant *hic* et *hec* joinnent en-sanble, / Mais *hic* et *hic* chose est perdue; / Nature en est tant esperdue, / Ses poins debat et tuert ses mains."

73. Alain of Lille, *Anticlaudianus*, 3.4: "vir sensu, femina sexu; / Sic vir, sic mulier, animo non illa, sed ille est."

74. See *Énéas*, lines 3959–76.

75. Penny Schine Gold, *The Lady and the Virgin: Image, Attitude, and Experience in Twelfth-Century France* (Chicago, 1985), 3.

76. For examples of the fear of effeminacy in men from late ancient texts, see the Christian author Prudentius (*Amartigenia*, ed. and trans. H. J. Thomson [Cambridge, MA, 1949], lines 279–307) or the pagan author Ammianus Marcellinus (*Res gestae*, ed. W. Sey-farth [Leipzig, 1978], 14.6.9–10). A useful overview of the ambivalence toward women

and sexuality in the western Christian tradition is provided by Uta Ranke-Heinemann, *Eunuchs for the Kingdom of Heaven: Women, Sexuality, and the Catholic Church*, trans. Peter Heinegg (London, 1990).

77. This social-psychological process is discussed by Michel Foucault, *Discipline and Punish: The Birth of the Prison*, trans. A. Sheridan (1975; reprint, New York, 1995), 202–03.

78. Andreas Capellanus, *De amore*, ed. P. Walsh (London, 1982), trans. J. Parry, *The Art of Courtly Love* (New York, 1990), 1.2: "Hoc autem est praecipue in amore notandum, quod amor nisi inter diversorum sexuum personas esse non potest. Nam inter duos mares vel inter duas feminas amor sibi locum vindicare non valet; duae namque sexus eiusdem personae nullatenus aptae videntur ad mutuas sibi vices reddendas amoris vel eius naturales actus exercendos. Nam quidquid natura negat, amor erubescit amplecti."

79. Andreas Capellanus, *De amore* (trans. Parry), 1.539: "Et si huic vultis resistere veritati, necessitatis cogit ratio profiteri duos masculos sibi adinvicem posse amoris solatia exhibere, quod satis esset narrare nefandum et agere criminosum."

80. Andreas Capellanus, *De amore* (trans. Parry), *praefatio:* "Cogit me multum assidua tuae dilectionis instantia, Gualteri venerande amice, ut meo tibi debeam famine propalare mearumque manum scriptis docere qualiter inter amantes illaesus possit amoris status conservari. . . . propter affectum quo tibi annector, tuae nullatenus valeo petitioni obstare."

81. Andreas Capellanus, *De amore* (trans. Parry), 3.9: "Nam exinde unus ab altero divertitur amicus, et inimicitiae inter homines capitales insurgent. . . . Quid enim tam necessarium tamve utile hominibus invenitur quam amicos habere securos?"

82. Chrétien de Troyes, *Le chevalier de la charette*, ed. W. Kibler (New York, 1981), lines 3540–49: "Molt estoit genz et bien aperz / Meliaganz, et bien tailliez / de braz, de janbes, et de piez; / et li hiaumes et li escuz / qui li estoit au col panduz / trop bien et bel li avenoient. / Mes a l'autre tuit se tenoient— / nes cil qui volsissent sa honte— / et dïent tuit que rien ne monte / de Meliagant avers lui."

83. Alain of Lille, *De planctu naturae* (*Patrologia cursus completus, series latina*, ed. J.-P. Migne, 221 vols. [Paris, 1841–66], 210:471–72), 16.8: "Hujus in facie nulla femineae mollitie vestigia resultabant, sed sola virilis dignitatis regnabat auctoritas. . . . moderatae tamen comptionis libramine jacebat ornata, ne si comptionibus vagaretur anomalis, in femineam demigrare videretur mollitiem. . . . Hujus facies, prout virilis dignitas exposcebat, a nulla pulchritudinis gratia deviabat." This passage is omitted in the Wright edition without explanation.

84. Jordan, *Invention of Sodomy*, chap. 4.

85. Sedgwick, *Between Men*, 21; Marjorie Garber, *Vice Versa: Bisexuality and the Eroticism of Everyday Life* (New York, 1995), chap. 18.

86. Andreas Capellanus, *De amore* (trans. Parry), 2.2: "Sed et, si cognoveris aliquem ad tuae amantis subversionem laborare, illico tibi sine dubio augmentatur amor, et maiori eam incipies affectione diligere. Immo amplius tibi dico: etsi manifeste cognoveris quod alius tuae coamantis fruatur amplexu, magis ex hoc eius incipies affectare solatia." Andreas later contradicts himself, ibid., 2.6.16, but this is not unusual.

87. See Chrétien de Troyes, *Le chevaliers au lyeon*, ed. W. Kibler (New York, 1985), lines 6002–27.

88. Chrétien de Troyes, *Le chevaliers au lyeon*, lines 1453–65.

89. Chrétien de Troyes, *Le chevaliers au lyeon*, lines 6119–21: "entrebeisier et acoler / s'alassent einz quë afoler, / qu'il s'antr'afolent et mehaingnent."

90. Chrétien de Troyes, *Le chevaliers au lyeon*, lines 6316–17: "s'a li uns a l'autre tandu / les braz au col, si s'antrebeisent."

91. The homoerotic element of men's rivalry over a woman in thirteenth-century romance texts is skillfully described by Christiane Marchello-Nizia, "Amour courtois, société masculine et figures du pouvoir," *Annales E.S.C.* 36 (1981): 969–82.

92. See also Colin Morris, *The Discovery of the Individual, 1050–1200* (1972; reprint, Toronto, 1987), 96, who also seems to link in a vague way the new attitude toward male friendship and sexual love: "The growth of a keen self-awareness was naturally accompanied by a fresh interest in close personal relationships. The twelfth century has been called the century of friendship, and it occupies an important, if controversial, place in the history of the Western idea of sexual love."

93. Boswell defended his position in his final book, *Same-Sex Unions in Premodern Europe* (New York, 1995), but refused to see it as essentialist.

94. Alain of Lille, *De planctu naturae*, 8.4: "Eorum siquidem hominum qui Veneris profitentur grammaticam, alii solummodo masculinum, alii femininum, alii commune, sive genus promiscuum, familiariter amplexantur. Quidam vero, quasi hetrocliti genere, per hiemen in feminino, per aestatem in masculino genere, irregulariter declinantur. Sunt qui, in Veneris logica disputantes, in conclusionibus suis subjectionis praedicationisque legem relatione mutua sortiuntur. Sunt qui vicem gerentes suppositi, praedicari non norunt. Sunt qui solummodo praedicantes, subjecti termini subjectionem legitimam non attendunt." Again, I have relied in part here on Sheridan's translation.

95. Yves of Chartres, *Decretum* (*PL* 161:682), 9.92–95: "Qui fornicatus fuerit sicut Sodomitae, si servus est, scopis castigabitur et 2 annos poeniteat; si liber est conjugatus, 10 annos; si privatus, septem annos poeniteat. Puer 100 dies, si in consuetudine est; laicus conjugatus, si in consuetudine habet, 15 annos poeniteat. . . . Clericus vel monachus ut parvulorum insectator, vel qui osculo vel aliqua occasione turpi deprehensus fuerit, publice verberetur, et comam amittat, decalvatusque turpiter sputamentis oblinitus in facie, vinculisque arctatus ferreis, carcerali 6 mensibus angustia maceretur, et triduo per hebdomadas singulas ex pane hordeaceo ad vesperam reficiatur. . . . Si deprehensus fuerit aliquis frater ludere cum pueris, et habere amicitias aetatis infirmae, tertio commoneatur ut memor sit honestatis, atque timoris Dei; si non cessaverit, severissime corripiatur."

96. Jordan, *Invention of Sodomy*, passim. Jordan writes (163–64): "The invention of the homosexual [in the nineteenth century] may well have relied on the already familiar category of the Sodomite. The idea that same-sex pleasure constitutes an identity of some kind is clearly the work of medieval theology, not of nineteenth-century forensic medicine." This is much like the conclusion that I also reached (independently), although I would emphasize the interplay of social and political forces with theological categories.

97. R. Howard Bloch, *Medieval Misogyny and the Invention of Western Romantic Love* (Chicago, 1991).

6

CRUCIFIED BY THE VIRTUES:
MONKS, LAY BROTHERS, AND
WOMEN IN THIRTEENTH-CENTURY
CISTERCIAN SAINTS' LIVES

MARTHA G. NEWMAN

In the eighth book of his *Dialogue on Miracles,* Caesarius of Heisterbach explained to a Cistercian novice why he reported more visions of Jesus' passion than his resurrection. "There is no sacrament which is so powerful an incentive for divine love as the reproaches of the passion," he wrote;

> Christ is the book of life ... which the apostles, with the great glory of miracles, carried like a crown through the whole world. When first they offered it to the literate, that is to the Jews, and they rejected it as if sealed, they next offered it to the illiterate, that is, to the Gentiles, and when they could not understand it, they explained it to them. ... Christ wrote this book because he suffered by his own will. The small and black letters were written by the bruising blows of the scourge on the parchment of his body; the red letters and capitals by the piercing of the nails; and the full stops and commas by the pricking of the thorns. Well had that parchment already been polished with a multitude of beatings, whitened by blows and spit, and erased with the reed.[1]

In this remarkable description of Jesus' body as a parchment inscribed by bleeding wounds and then expounded to the unlearned Gentiles by the apostles, Caesarius articulated themes that, in recent years, modern scholars have associated with the religious behavior of late medieval women. It has become common to hear of the physicality of female religious practice, to study how women wrote their identification with Jesus on their bodies, and to analyze the ways in which female behaviors were explained and interpreted by their clerical friends and confessors.[2]

Hagiographical writings from the Cistercian monastery of Villers in the Brabant demonstrate that these themes of corporeality, inscription, and interpretation are neither limited to representations of female spirituality nor fully characteristic of it. A thirteenth-century *vita* of a lay brother from Villers draws parallels between its subject's self-tortures and the sufferings of the male body of Christ; the author described lay brothers in ways usually reserved for women while portraying religious women as he did the monks. My reading of this *vita*, along with other hagiographical texts from Villers, suggests that their Cistercian authors complicated a binary separation of male and female spirituality by emphasizing distinctions based instead on literacy and social status.

Underlying our analyses of late medieval female spirituality is the medieval association of woman with body and man with spirit. Caroline Walker Bynum used this set of dichotomies to argue that the particularly somatic behaviors shown by late medieval women demonstrate not a hatred of the body but an exploration of its religious potential, especially in forging an identification with the human Jesus.[3] Although Bynum was careful to show that men as well as women could identify with Christ's suffering body, her conclusions have implied that such physicality was a distinguishing characteristic of female spirituality: late medieval women were perceived as body, and they expressed themselves through their bodies. While most scholars of female spirituality use Bynum's conclusions as a starting point, recently they have further contextualized medieval ideas about the female body and gender.[4] They remind us not to take gender as a given, but to examine the various ways in which medieval people used gendered language and expressed their expectations of sexual difference.

Scholars studying the religious ideas and practices of medieval women have either explicitly or implicitly used the behavior and ideas of literate and clerical men as foils for female austerities. But they have only briefly noted that late medieval hagiographers also attributed extreme bodily mortification to men, especially to men of low status.[5] There has been little work exploring how this male behavior complicates our picture of medieval constructions of gender.[6] By recognizing the malleability of thirteenth-century gender categories, we can uncover ways in which medieval elites defined themselves so as to maintain their positions of privilege.[7]

A comparison between Cistercian lay brothers and choir monks illuminates the variations in male spirituality. The lay brothers did not leave written records of their own, but they appear as subjects in both miracle stories and hagiography. The hagiographical writings by the monks of Villers are especially fruitful for analysis, for they allow a three-way comparison between monks, lay brothers, and religious women—whether Beguines or Cistercian nuns—who lived in the vicinity of the monastery. By making such a comparison, we find at least three explicitly gendered positions within the extended Villers community. The first was that of the monks, whose own use of nuptial imagery placed them in a feminine position relative to the divine. The second was that of the lay brothers, about whom the monks used virile images to portray a masculine spirituality based on the mortification of the flesh in imitation of the suffering of Jesus. The third was that of the religious women. The monks initially described them using nuptial imagery similar to that which they used for themselves, but they later associated these women with the virile language and bodily mortification already attributed to the lay brothers.

For the most part, the monks of Villers controlled these constructions of gender. However, the monks' efforts did not occur in a vacuum; they responded to the behaviors and ideas of the lay brothers and the women whose religious practices they described. Thus, we can periodically glimpse the ways in which both lay brothers and religious women explored the potential in their own social positions.[8] Here, however, I am concerned primarily with the monks and the ways in which they constructed gender categories to define themselves in relation to others and to assert their own holiness. The early-thirteenth-century hagiographical texts from Villers suggest that their Cistercian authors were more concerned about maintaining differences based on literacy and monastic status than about emphasizing distinctions based on sex. They used gendered imagery to reinforce the differences between the choir monks and the lay brothers. Only gradually did they use the same language to distinguish themselves from religious women by attributing to these women a suffering body in imitation of the body of Christ.

Whereas the religious ideas of Cistercian monks have been much studied, lay brother spirituality remains relatively unexplored. Historians have debated whether the Cistercian lay brotherhood was a form of lay piety or a replication of social divisions in a "feudal" mode of production.[9] To a degree, the lay brothers compensated for the monks' refusal to accept manorial revenues: the Cistercians had established the lay brotherhood to help with agricultural labor, especially on lands distant from the cloister. Some lay brothers had been peasants in villages whose lands were gradually accumulated by the monks.[10] Yet, despite an 1188 ruling of the Cistercian Chapter General that required all professing aristocrats to become choir monks, there was not always a firm status distinction between the lay brothers and the monks. In the early thirteenth century, Caesarius of Heisterbach still told stories about knights who became lay brothers.[11]

The most rigid distinction between lay brothers and monks was not dependent on social status but on literacy. Monks could read; lay brothers could not and were forbidden to learn. Thus, while the monks shared with the lay brothers the spiritual benefits of the Cistercian order, the lay brothers held an ambiguous place in the ritual expressions of Cistercian unity. They followed a different horarium with a shortened liturgy, lived in a separate dormitory or in granges, participated in their own chapter, and wore a distinctive habit.[12] They occasionally joined the monks and novices in processions and in rituals such as the Maundy Thursday foot washing that demonstrated the three distinct groups that comprised the male order, but they were excluded from most of the monks' liturgical ceremonies. On the eve of the Nativity, for instance, the lay brothers cleaned the church while the monks and novices prayed.[13]

Our best glimpse into the life of the lay brothers comes not from regulatory documents but from stories of visions and miracles that Cistercian monks collected in the last decades of the twelfth century and the first decades of the thirteenth. These collections drew on both oral and written traditions within the order: some stories retold classic exempla in a Cistercian context while others related the experiences of the authors and the religious men and women whom they knew.[14] These collections appear to have addressed audiences both within and without the order: they provided lessons and encouragement to the Cistercians themselves, and they presented Cistercian arguments for the order's continued holiness at a time when the monks felt their preeminence to be under attack. Since these stories were written by monks, occasionally citing a lay brother as an oral source, those that describe the lay brothers tell us more about the monks' views of the lay brothers than they do about the lay brothers' own ideas. They demonstrate, on the one hand, the monks' attempts to keep the lay brothers content with their position despite the inequities in the monastery, and, on the other hand, the monks' concern for maintaining their own privileged position within the community.

The collections contain stories in which lay brothers miraculously lost the characteristics that distinguished them from the monks. One lay brother, for example, learned the entire liturgy in a dream and retained this knowledge once he awoke; another had a vision in which a young woman taught him to read; a third was miraculously transported from the fields to the cloister so he could participate in the hymns for the feast of the Assumption.[15] Even a story about the lay brothers' revolt at Schönau in 1168 presents the lay brothers as more than just agricultural workers within a monastic community. According to this story, the lay brothers objected that the monks had received new shoes while they had not. Complaining that their "arduous and harsh work was intolerable," they plotted to sneak into the monks' dormitory to slash the new shoes. The monks quelled the rebellion after one of its leaders died and the abbot refused him prayers and a burial in holy ground until the other conspirators relented. The monks used this story about material inequities to claim that the lay brothers still trusted in the spiritual benefits of the order. In general, these stories imply that the illiterate lay brothers sought to participate in the monastery's spiritual life even though they recognized that they lived in an environment in which literacy shaped the dominant expressions of contact with the divine.[16]

Other stories suggest that the lay brothers, or the monks who wrote about them, located religious possibilities in the lay brothers' daily routines and tasks. According to one story, a plowman saw Jesus walking next to him, holding the whip and pole used to prod the oxen.[17] Other stories associated the lay brothers' perseverance in their work with the "exemplary virtues": that is, the virtues of humility, obedience, and patience that Jesus demonstrated while on the cross. The monks used tales about lay brothers to illustrate these virtues. In a sermon in the monks' chap-

ter, the abbot Bernard of Clairvaux praised the patient suffering and re-
pentance of a lay brother who had endured a painful bone disease.[18]
Similarly, he celebrated an anonymous *homo rusticus* whom he had initially rebuked for overconfidence about salvation but who then reminded Bernard that the kingdom of God was acquired by the virtue of
obedience alone, not by nobility of body or possession of earthly wealth.
After this lay brother's death, the abbot recounted the story of this encounter in chapter and "all were wonderfully moved to the love of obedience by his example."[19] Even the story of the lay brother transported to
the choir to participate in a feast day liturgy illustrated lay brother obedience: according to the author, the lay brothers were overjoyed at the
miracle for it demonstrated that the work they did out of obedience
would not hinder their desire to serve God, even if they missed liturgical
celebrations as a result.[20]

The association of the lay brothers' labor with the exemplary virtues
shown by Jesus on the cross echoes other Cistercian writings linking
labor and the passion. In his only extant sermon for Good Friday, Bernard
of Clairvaux argued that it was not only Jesus' pain but also his labor
that transformed human labor and pain and made salvation possible.[21]
However, Bernard left ambiguous whether the labor he praised was that
of the lay brothers as well as that of the choir monks, for he also stated
that those who labored out of necessity, rather than voluntarily, did not
conform to the image of God. Such a comment suggests that the voluntary labor of the monks was a form of penance but implies that the lay
brothers' not-entirely-voluntary labor was not. As we will see, however,
the early-thirteenth-century authors from Villers removed the ambiguity
by suggesting that a laboring lay brother could embody Jesus' patient,
obedient, and humble sufferings on the cross.

The Cistercian miracle and vision stories also leave ambiguous the
lay brothers' position in the Cistercian community. These stories might
smooth over the divisions between lay brothers and choir monks but
they still demonstrate fundamental differences between the two groups.
Whereas there are stories about monks who labored, stories about labor
most frequently concern the lay brothers; whereas there are stories
about monks who demonstrate the exemplary virtues of patience, obedience, and humility, again these virtues are most frequently displayed by
the lay brothers. Even more markedly, lay brothers do not appear in stories that demonstrate the benefits of monastic prayer or describe visions

of bridal ornaments being prepared for the monks' souls.[22] When lay brothers had visions of Jesus, Jesus shared in their labors or appeared at their death bed. When monks had such visions, Jesus embraced them and they prepared to become Christ's bride.[23]

The choir monks' visions of Jesus reflect a pervasive message of Cistercian culture: that the monks should reject male power, male authority, and male desire and, by transforming their wills, place themselves in a feminine position vis-à-vis their God.[24] But for Cistercian authors, "woman" was not a symbol with a single set of meanings. The monks described themselves with an array of feminine images that provided a multiplicity of associations. At times, for instance, Bernard of Clairvaux compared his monks to the maidens in the Song of Songs, emphasizing a female weakness that characterized the early stages in their process of reform.[25] At other times, he emphasized the maternal qualities of his abbots, suggesting that they, like Jesus, should nurture those under their charge.[26] And at yet other times, he described the monks' souls as the bride of the Song of Songs who desired contact with the divine and occasionally received the gift of a divine embrace.[27] In all such cases, the Cistercians' use of female imagery derived from their reading of the Song of Songs and from their use of this text as the foundation for their monastic sermons. As Brian Stock has suggested, it was the Cistercians' common interpretation of the Song of Songs that ultimately bound the monks together into what he calls a "textual community."[28]

The lay brothers' exclusion from visions of the soul as Jesus' bride or lover suggests that they were only marginally a part of this textual community. Since they were only allowed into the monks' chapter when they offered their vows of profession and on selected feast days during the year, they had little opportunity to hear chapter talks and sermons; they instead received instruction in their own chapter.[29] We do not know the content of this instruction. It is possible that such talks repeated the themes of the vision and miracle stories that associated the lay brothers with the exemplary virtues, suggested that Jesus participated in the lay brothers' tasks, and implied that the lay brothers' life of manual labor could be a form of *imitatio Christi*. We find these themes again in the hagiographical material produced at the monastery of Villers in the thirteenth century, and these texts make explicit what the vision collections had only implied: that lay brothers could find within the Cistercians' culture elements that encouraged them to identify with Jesus by embodying Jesus' patient, obedient and humble sufferings on the cross.

The first, longest, and most influential of these lay brother *vitae* is that of brother Arnulf. Its author was probably Goswin, a cantor at Villers, who composed his account shortly after Arnulf's death in 1228 and claimed to rely on information supplied by one of Arnulf's intimates.[30] The author emphasized Arnulf's unique qualities. Some people, he wrote, received from God particularly miraculous gifts not found in others; Arnulf's gifts were his ability to inflict and endure extreme self-mortification and his willingness to use his sufferings for the spiritual benefit of himself and his friends.[31] Arnulf's behavior enacted the ideas that Caesarius of Heisterbach had explained to his novice interlocutor: that meditation on Jesus' passion was a spur to divine love. Just as Caesarius had described Jesus' body as a text on which the wounds of the passion were inscribed, so Arnulf marked his own body in imitation of Jesus' love, marks that were then read and interpreted by his biographer, Goswin.

The *vita* is divided into two books. The first depicts Arnulf's afflictions: the knotted ropes with which he lacerated his flesh, his tight leather belts, his shirts made of hedgehog pelts, his repeated flagellation with thorny branches. The second book portrays Arnulf's virtues, his visions, and his care for others, all of which had their source in his asceticism. Modern scholars have tended to view Arnulf's self-tortures with uneasiness: they have labeled him insane, considered him a curiosity, and treated Goswin's account with skepticism.[32] Brian Patrick McGuire's study, however, reverses these interpretations by placing Arnulf within a Cistercian tradition that found in community and in affective ties a path toward the divine.[33] McGuire leaves unexplored the relation between Arnulf's behavior and his status as a lay brother, and he does not speculate about the reasons behind Goswin's willingness to celebrate the life of such a difficult, even disruptive, man.[34] Goswin's life drew on earlier Cistercian ideas about the lay brothers and became a model for a distinctive lay brother spirituality. Goswin enhanced the distinctiveness of this spirituality by describing it with gendered images that contrasted with those the monks used to describe their own desire for God. Whereas the choir monks strove to become female, transforming their souls to become worthy brides of Christ, Goswin's Arnulf instead remained male, identifying his body with the body of Christ.

Arnulf's self-mortification does not fit easily into a Cistercian religiosity that placed more emphasis on the transformation of the physical than on an opposition between body and spirit. As I have argued elsewhere, the Cistercians found a potential goodness in both their own bodies and the physical world; their project was not to reject the physical but to try to bring it into harmony with the divine will.[35] Arnulf's extreme asceticism, in contrast, seems at first glance to be motivated by a hatred of the body. According to Goswin, even some of Arnulf's contemporaries found his practices disturbing and suggested that for the sake of Christ he should have mercy on his flesh, "flesh that was poor and fragile, without which he could not live." But Arnulf could not be persuaded. "My flesh is my enemy," he replied.[36] Goswin wrote about Arnulf's self-imposed sufferings with a fascinated horror that emphasized his subject's ingenuity in creating instruments of torture out of whatever objects he had at hand. He made ropes out of horsetails and bound them around his waist; he made clothes from horsehair and out of hedgehog pelts supplied by the community's shepherds. He found three iron chains that he wore around his midsection, and he wore a coat of mail next to his skin.[37] But, as we will see, Goswin found a religious potential in Arnulf's physicality, albeit in a form more extreme than that to which his Cistercian contemporaries were accustomed.

Although Goswin professed his shock and unease with Arnulf's self- . torture, he nonetheless made Arnulf's behavior familiar to his audience by classifying it according to the same virtues of humility, patience, and obedience that had dominated earlier accounts of lay brother behavior. Goswin stressed Arnulf's humility and patience, noting his simplicity and his honest customs and claiming that he considered himself small and vile so that he could be great before God.[38] Not only was Arnulf's self-mortification a sign of his humility and patience but so was his refusal to be provoked into anger, even when unjustly accused. Goswin related a story in which Arnulf secretly received the abbot's permission to give bread to the poor but was then accused by some monks of stealing monastic goods. Not wanting to cause a scandal by admitting that he had acted with the abbot's permission, Arnulf accepted punishment and spent eleven days at the door of the monastery.[39] Goswin also emphasized Arnulf's obedience, especially his willingness to descend from contemplation whenever a brother summoned him to a task or someone wished to visit with him.[40] Arnulf's obedient response to these requests meant that he willingly prayed for the souls of others, both living and dead, and his obedience and patient suffering made his prayers seem particularly effective.[41]

Goswin placed Arnulf's unusual behavior in the familiar context of the exemplary virtues. At the same time he made more explicit than did the miracle collections the association of these virtues with an *imitatio Christi*. Goswin was not the only early-thirteenth-century Cistercian to do so; his contemporary, Caesarius of Heisterbach, described the exemplary virtues of patience, obedience, and humility as the very nails of the passion. Monks who possessed such virtues became like Christ on the cross:

> Obedience without grumbling nails the right hand of the monk; patience without hypocrisy nails the left. . . . True humility nails his feet, so that for Christ's sake he subjects himself not only to his superiors but also to his brothers.[42]

For Caesarius, monks with these virtues underwent a symbolic crucifixion through the everyday austerities of Cistercian life: long vigils, rough food, scant clothing, and strict obedience. Goswin's Arnulf, in comparison, displayed these virtues by his heroic sufferings in imitation of Christ on the cross. Goswin repeatedly wrote of Arnulf's focus on the crucifixion, claiming "he manfully followed the Lord Christ to the passion."[43] After describing Arnulf's extraordinary self-flagellation with a wooden rod wrapped in hedgehog pelts, Goswin called Arnulf a man "wisely unlearned in the virtue of the holy cross, who avidly learned it by beating himself"; he then suggested that Arnulf offered the blood from the perforations in his body to Christ, "who at the time of his passion had offered his blood to God the Father."[44] Similarly, Arnulf flagellated during Lent from terce to vespers; when his brothers tried to limit his self-torture by reminding him that Jesus had died at nones, Arnulf responded that Jesus had hung on the cross until vespers, and that he would not lay down his own cross until then.[45] Even Arnulf's death invoked the passion. Goswin noted that Arnulf died on a Friday around sext, which corresponded with the time during which "the majestic Lord hung on the cross."[46]

Goswin's picture of Arnulf's imitation of Jesus' sufferings differs from the choir monks' response to the passion. In his second sermon for Palm Sunday, the Cistercian abbot Guerric of Igny spoke of monks carrying the cross, but he portrayed their crucifixion as part of a process of extinguishing sin, and he considered the nails to be the fear of God and not the virtues.[47] In another sermon for Palm Sunday, Guerric articulated a theme also used by other Cistercians. He portrayed Jesus on the cross as a figure who protected and nurtured the monks: the monks were to meditate on Jesus' wounds, shelter themselves within them, and enter the gash in his side so that "the blood of the wound might give [them] life, the warmth of his body revive [them], the breath of his heart flow into [them]."[48] When the choir monks imitated the passion, their suffering was interior or symbolic; it aroused them to love but not to self-mortification.[49] The monks adored Jesus but they did not become him: if he was their mother, they were his children; if he was their bridegroom, they became his bride.

Goswin's descriptions of Arnulf's desire for divine contact also differed from the language and imagery used by the choir monks. The monks' use of nuptial imagery to describe their longing for divine contact is well known.[50] The language of the Song of Songs permeated their sermons and presented their souls in a feminine position as the brides of Christ. Goswin stressed Arnulf's love of God but, although he occasionally quoted from the Song of Songs, he did not portray Arnulf's soul as Christ's bride nor use erotic language of longing and desire to describe Arnulf's search for God. Instead, he used images of edification. According to Goswin, Arnulf's flagellation and self-torture taught him the virtues of the holy cross and filled him with a divine love that made him not the bride of Christ but Christ's student.[51] Arnulf was a "disciple of his Lord and Master who had offered his most holy flesh to the lacerations of whips," and he learned from Jesus simplicity of heart, humility, and the "art of arts, the art of love."[52]

Arnulf's most dramatic vision of God also situated him as Christ's student. In this vision, Jesus initially responded to Arnulf's desire to know God by asking him why his understanding of the crucifixion was not sufficient. "Is it not enough for you," Jesus asked, "that for you I deigned to assume flesh, that for you I endured hatred, spittle, blows, beatings, a crown of thorns, and nails, and . . . was hung nude on the gibbet of the cross?"[53] Arnulf replied that it was not enough, "not because he denied that the passion of the Lord was sufficient for his own redemption and that of the entire world, but because he demonstrated with his most ardent heart that he eagerly desired a most blessed vision of the holy Trinity."[54] As a result, Jesus showed him first his own face, then the celestial choirs, and then Mary in her glory, but each time Arnulf demanded more. Finally, Jesus showed him the Trinity. As a result of this vision, Goswin concluded, "this man of true simplicity was taught by grace; he learned in a school of highest divinity what the wise of this world could not find through their knowledge."[55]

Goswin's use of educational metaphors to describe Arnulf's contact with the divine both reinforced Arnulf's subordinate position and suggested ways in which this position was subverted. The lay brothers' life of labor and their enforced illiteracy reflected a prevalent clerical assumption that low-status men, like women, could not master intellectual knowledge and were thus more suited to physical than intellectual labor.[56] Goswin's stress on Arnulf's suffering body and somatic spirituality, which contrasted with the nuptial imagery that the monks used to describe their own spirituality, suggests that Goswin accepted this clerical assumption. At the same time, his description of Arnulf as a student of Christ, whose extreme austerities gave him the ardent love that inspired his presumptuous demands of Jesus and whose visions made him more knowledgeable than those wise in book learning, implies that Goswin, and possibly Arnulf himself, found religious potential in the physicality associated with the position of lay brother. The knowledge Arnulf could not attain through literacy he achieved through the physical suffering and labor of his body.

The monks' presentation of their souls as the brides of Christ implied that their process of conversion and spiritual growth required a symbolic reversal of gender. The monks used feminine imagery both to describe their new position of weakness as they embarked on a path of reform and to portray the relation with God that became possible once they had achieved their reformation. Such use of gender dichotomies and reversals was common in the writings of religious men in the later Middle Ages. Many religious men, aware of the associations that linked maleness with spirit and divinity were also deeply conscious of their own human state. By portraying themselves using images with female associations, they were able to express their bodily humanity while also insuring that the gospel message promising the redemption of the humble and lowly could apply to them.[57]

Goswin's descriptions of Arnulf, however, suggest that such male reversals were not universal. Rather than using imagery that placed

Arnulf in a feminine position, Goswin instead emphasized Arnulf's maleness. He portrayed Arnulf as strong and manly; he was "the strongest of knights," an "athlete who competed manfully."[58] Arnulf's own ideas seem to be akin to Goswin's, although he described himself as striving to become strong and manly rather than as having achieved such a state. According to Goswin, people heard Arnulf chanting as he scourged himself, saying "I must act bravely; I must act manly; manly I must be for my friends need it badly. Take this blow for this friend, that blow for that friend, in the name of God."[59] As he became virile, he became increasingly able to suppress any temptations, to endure and transcend his pain, and to become more like Christ.

The use of gendered language to mark the differences between Arnulf's spirituality and that of the choir monks is especially apparent in one of Goswin's most dramatic accounts of Arnulf's asceticism. In the midst of a description of the elaborate cords with which Arnulf bound himself and the way in which they tormented his putrefying flesh, Goswin interjected a comment about Christ's circumcision:

> Oh truly happy boy, whose gracious mother is so solicitous about his recent birth that she not only feeds him on sweet milk but also offers him myrrhed wine to drink; then she binds him in his infant's cradle with bands of prickly cord and, with the sharpest knife, cuts away his wanton flesh.[60]

Such an interruption implicitly compares Arnulf's torments with Jesus' circumcision and, because of the exegetical association of the circumcision with the crucifixion, it again points toward Arnulf's reenactment of the passion. At the same time, this passage serves to emphasize Arnulf's maleness and Goswin's association of Arnulf with the male Jesus. In recent years, there has been debate over the meaning of Jesus' circumcision—did a medieval interest in Jesus' foreskin and an iconographic emphasis on his penis signify Jesus' fully sexual masculinity or, more generally, his fleshly humanity?[61] Although Caroline Bynum makes a convincing argument that late medieval people were more likely to associate the circumcision and Jesus' penis with pain, blood, and salvation than with sexuality, Goswin's text makes a direct connection between circumcision and overcoming sexual desire. Jesus' circumcision may have been a symbol of the suffering flesh that provided redemption, but in this case at least, the suffering flesh was specifically male, allowing the pain of the male lay brother Arnulf to be identified with the pain of the human Jesus.

Goswin's story of Arnulf's symbolic circumcision again contrasts with stories about the choir monks. Arnulf may have endured a symbolic circumcision, but some choir monks, in contrast, underwent symbolic castration. In one story from the last third of the twelfth century, a monk who had long been tormented by the demons of sexual desire received a visitation by an angel who offered to remove the organ that had been the source of his temptations. When he awoke, he found his body whole but his desires gone.[62] Even more dramatically, a late-thirteenth-century chronicle entry about William, the abbot of Villers from 1221 to 1236, describes his body after death:

> There did not appear in that place any vestige of genitals except for a clear smooth area, bright and pure, striking the eyes of the observers with its great brightness.[63]

William had developed close friendships with religious women during his life; his lack of genitals may have reflected the chronicler's unease about this.[64] Both these stories suggest that, when monks conquered sexual desire, they became emasculated. Arnulf also battled sexual temptation, but he remained fully male.

Goswin's picture of Arnulf as a man who identified with the male body of the suffering Christ complicates what many scholars have identified as a medieval association between woman, body, and the crucified Christ.[65] The scholars analyzing the implications of this association have tended to create a binary comparison between religious women on the one hand and clerical men on the other and have not considered how the addition of lower-status men might complicate their picture.[66] Goswin's identification of Arnulf with the crucified Christ suggests that Christ's body did not necessarily carry female associations but instead could be a multivalent symbol, providing a model for both men and women who found in Christ's suffering flesh a meaning for their own physicality. At the same time, Goswin's emphasis on Arnulf's maleness reinforced the lay brothers' subordinate position in the monastery. The choir monks' use of feminine language to describe their own spirituality not only asserted that they had voluntarily renounced worldly power and prestige, but it also suggested that they were the most humble and thus the most deserving of redemption. In comparison, by imputing masculine characteristics to Arnulf, Goswin implied that Arnulf, like the other lay brothers, never had any power to renounce. Through his self-mortification, Arnulf made himself virile, but the other less heroic lay brothers remained in a position of involuntary weakness that contrasted with the choir monks' voluntary assumption of a feminine weakness vis-à-vis their God.

Goswin's picture of Arnulf as a man identifying with the male body of the suffering Christ was not unique. Instead, it established a pattern for other shorter descriptions of lay brothers at Villers. These *vitae* appear in the *Gesta sanctorum Villariensium,* a late-thirteenth-century compilation that contains stories about lay brothers, choir monks, and monastic officials.[67] Although there is great variation in the behavior and experiences of the subjects of these *vitae,* a basic pattern distinguished choir monks from lay brothers. The choir monks, while sometimes visionaries and often living lives of poverty and simplicity, did not practice bodily self-mortification; the lay brothers did. Thus Nicholas, who served as a shepherd in one of Villers's granges, "punished his flesh" to the extent that a witness compared him to the ancient hermits. As with Arnulf, Nicholas's biographer associated this self-torture with charitable actions toward others: Nicholas performed works of charity and mercy, and people came to him for instruction and advice.[68] Similarly, Peter, whose *vita* was written by a master of the lay brothers at Villers, flagellated, wore hair shirts, and pressed hot iron against his chest; his biographer described him as crucifying his flesh for Christ.[69] Like Arnulf, Peter had visions of both Jesus and Mary, and like Arnulf, he demonstrated his love for God externally on his body rather than through an internalized longing of his soul.

It is difficult, if not impossible, to know whether these lay brothers actually practiced these harsh austerities or whether they were the creations of their biographers. What is clear is that the authors drew on ideas common in Cistercian writings—the association of the lay brothers with the virtues shown by Jesus on the cross, the association of labor with the passion—and from them they described a distinctive lay brother spirituality. In the process, they expressed the already existing status differences in the monastery as differences in gender identity. Whereas the literate choir monks explored the possibilities of assuming a feminine position as they prepared their souls for a divine embrace, the illiterate lay brothers instead strengthened their male bodies, making them into parchments on which they wrote their identification with Christ.

Goswin may have described Arnulf's self-imposed suffering as making him manly, but he imputed to Arnulf behaviors that mirrored those attributed to religious women. Both regular and extra-regular communities of women flourished in the diocese of Liège in the early thirteenth century, and the *vitae* of these women describe penitential behavior, physical self-mortification, and an identification with Jesus similar to that of Villers's lay brothers. Thomas of Cantimpré's life of Christina of St.-Trond, for example, describes Christina as hiding in ovens and throwing herself into freezing rivers in order to take on the sufferings of others in purgatory; Jacques de Vitry's life of Mary of Oignes recounts Mary's self-mutilation in imitation of Christ's wounds.[70] Many of these *vitae* also describe heroic fasts through which these women offered their extreme hunger as expiation for the sins of their fellow Christians.[71] Simone Roisin suggests that the parallels between the lay brothers and these religious women might have resulted from a common social background and the contacts they might have formed with one another.[72] It is possible also that we are seeing in these extreme physical behaviors a form of piety developed by both men and women who had been excluded from the religious rituals of literate and priestly men, and who found religious possibilities in the characteristics that the literate clergy imputed to them.[73] However, we must be careful that we not treat the biographers who described these women and lay brothers as transparent transmitters of actual behavior.[74] It is perhaps more pertinent to ask why Cistercian monks developed models for their lay brothers that replicated the behaviors attributed to religious women by clerical biographers.

Studies of the interactions between religious women and their clerical, often mendicant, confessors and biographers suggest a symbiotic relation between the two. The male associates provided these women with access to the sacraments and with institutional support while the women offered evidence of an immediate experience of the divine that these men, for all their sacramental powers and schooling, could not experience themselves.[75] Unlike the mendicants, however, early-thirteenth-century Cistercian choir monks did not experience the same contrast between a learned, office-based Christianity and a charismatic, mystical one. They thus had less reason to use either religious women or their holy lay brothers for a vicarious experience of the divine.

They did, however, use their stories about lay brothers to reinforce their sense of the holiness of their order. Late-twelfth- and early-thirteenth-century Cistercian monks had need for such reinforcement for they experienced challenges from a number of directions. Other monks and clerics criticized their wealth and power, mystical women and friars developed new forms of religious life that reinterpreted ideas of religious weakness and poverty, and some lay brothers violently protested the inequities of their position.[76] Stories about holy lay brothers provided a monastic response to these revolts by suggesting that the brothers should be content with the traditional organization of the Cistercian community and find religious possibilities in their subordinate position and in the physicality of their manual labor. At the same time, the increasing size of Cistercian communities and the lay brothers' growing separation from the monks may have given the two groups fewer opportunities for shared discussions of internal thoughts and experiences; if the monks were to acknowledge lay brother sanctity, such sanctity had to be externalized on the lay brothers' bodies. Finally, the lay brothers' asceticism allowed the monks, who were often concerned about counteracting charges of novelty, to assert that they were the true heirs of Benedict and the Desert Fathers. In describing Arnulf's creations from hedgehog pelts, Goswin claimed that Arnulf's austerities surpassed even those of Benedict and the ancient martyrs, while the lay brother Nicholas's biographer claimed that his bodily mortification made him seem like one of the ancient hermits.[77]

Goswin incorporated into his life of Arnulf forms of behavior that clerical and mendicant hagiographers attributed to religious women, but Goswin himself did not associate such behavior with women. Whereas Arnulf and the other lay brothers expressed their spirituality in an exterior and physical fashion, the subject of another of Goswin's *vitae*, the Cistercian nun Ida of Nivelles, did not.[78] Goswin's life of Ida, written soon after her death in 1231 or 1232, does have strong parallels with the life of Arnulf: like Arnulf, Ida had visions of the Trinity and of the Christ child; like Arnulf, Ida empathized with Jesus' passion and pain; like Arnulf, Ida helped promote the salvation of others and even rescued a

woman from purgatory.[79] As he had with Arnulf, Goswin emphasized
Ida's virtues of patience, obedience, and humility.[80] However, such similarities only make the differences more striking. Ida showed no signs of
the self-induced mutilation that Arnulf so reveled in and, unlike Arnulf,
she developed a relation with the divine that followed the pattern established by the Cistercians' interpretation of the Song of Songs.

Goswin portrayed Ida's desire for the divine in much the same fashion as the choir monks who wrote of their own desire: as an internal
longing of the soul as bride for the bridegroom Christ. Repeatedly, Goswin
described Ida as receiving kisses and embraces from Jesus.[81] After receiving communion, for example, Ida would "cross over into a spiritual
dormitory in which, alienated from her senses, she would quietly and
most happily be lulled to sleep in the arms of her bridegroom."[82] Another time during communion she viewed the host as a young man who
kissed and embraced her.[83] Even when Ida had visions resembling those
of Arnulf, Goswin described them differently. Both Ida and Arnulf had
visions in which Mary handed them the baby Jesus, but whereas Arnulf
trembled and immediately handed the baby back, Ida kissed him and
spent the day mothering him.[84] And unlike Arnulf, who experienced his
vision of the Trinity as Jesus' student, Ida experienced hers in her soul
and connected it with her spiritual growth. As Goswin wrote, "her soul
was imprinted by the glue of most ardent love for the holy Trinity, so
that it made her spirit one with the spirit of the Lord."[85] Repeatedly,
Goswin called Ida either the "maid of Christ" or the "bride of Christ";
nowhere in Ida's *vita* was the masculine imagery that Goswin had used
to describe Arnulf.

By depicting Ida's experiences with the same interiorized language
that the choir monks used to portray their own contact with the divine,
Goswin refused to distinguish male and female spirituality in the same
way that he had separated the choir monks from the lay brothers. Nor
was Goswin alone in this. Caesarius of Heisterbach's stories in his *Dialogus miraculorum* not only show friendships between Cistercian monks
and religious women, they also demonstrate that these men and women
offered one another much the same sorts of aid: they prayed for one another, offered each other spiritual instruction, and had visions that confirmed the sanctity of their friends.[86] Unlike the mendicant *vitae* of religious women that contrast an official male religiosity with a charismatic

female one, early-thirteenth-century Cistercian monks and nuns seem to have shared a common religious culture, one that was based, at least in part, on a shared interpretation of the Song of Songs.[87]

These men and women did not long share a culture that transcended gender differences. By mid-century, friendships between Cistercian monks and religious women begin to disappear from the sources; if such friendships continued, they were no longer celebrated with the enthusiasm of the previous decades.[88] Why this change occurred is still a matter of speculation. Although the female literacy that had allowed the Cistercian monks and nuns to share a similar culture did not disappear, other factors such as the further clericalization of the Cistercian order, the monks' increased university training, and their rivalry with the Dominicans may have taken precedence over this shared textual culture and encouraged the monks to distance themselves from the women.[89]

As Cistercian monks distinguished their spirituality from that of religious women, they began to do what their mendicant contemporaries had already done: to see female sanctity displayed externally on women's bodies. The late-thirteenth-century Cistercian *vitae* of religious women are not identical to the earlier lives of the lay brothers: their subjects' bodies were more likely to undergo miraculous transformations, and the women were still more likely to be described using the erotic language from the Song of Songs.[90] But the women's self-imposed suffering in imitation of Jesus' passion resembled that of the lay brothers, so much so, in fact, that Beatrice of Nazareth's biographer borrowed one of Goswin's accounts of Arnulf's self-mortification to describe Beatrice's practices.[91]

Not only did the Cistercian hagiographers from the later thirteenth century begin to describe a female somatic spirituality that resembled that of the lay brothers, but also they began to use images of virility and strength similar to those that Goswin had used in his life of Arnulf. The biographer of Ida of Lewis, who may well have been a monk from Villers, described Ida as "like a man seizing his weapons"; she fought the devil "manfully, not in a womanly way."[92] Similarly, the Cistercian author of the life of Ida of Leuven reported that Ida "was not a woman or fainthearted, but driven by a strong and manly constancy"; the devil was frustrated by her "manly boldness."[93] As we have already seen, the association of virile imagery with lay brother sanctity reinforced the lay brothers' subordinate position; the same effect occurred with women. By depicting holy women and saintly lay brothers as strong and manly, the monks managed to reaffirm the special holiness of their own feminized humility.

For a brief period in the early thirteenth century, however, some Cistercian monks did not employ descriptions of a somatized spirituality to separate themselves from women but instead used it, and the gendered language associated with it, to reinforce distinctions within their male communities. They presented the spirituality of religious women as similar to their own and used gender to differentiate themselves from other men. Their creation of three explicitly gendered positions, those of the monks, the lay brothers, and the religious women, suggests that religious divisions were only partially determined by sexual difference and were also dependent on social status and literacy.

When Caesarius described Christ's body as a book inscribed by the passion and interpreted by the apostles to the illiterate Gentiles, he did not assume that these illiterates were women. Goswin's life of Arnulf explores issues raised in Caesarius's passage: it demonstrates how an illiterate man read Christ's passion by enacting it on his own body, and it illustrates how the monks shaped this reading, both by defining the social environment within which Arnulf acted and by interpreting Arnulf's behavior for a wider audience. At the same time this and other hagiographical texts from Villers show that the themes of corporeality, inscription, and interpretation neither apply to all representations of thirteenth-century female spirituality nor apply only to the spirituality of women. Writing on the body may have been a form of expression for voiceless men and women who found religious potential in their illiteracy and their subordinate positions. Writing about these bodies, however, was a form of self-definition for literate elites whose emphasis on the physicality of their subjects only furthered a distinction between literate and illiterate and reinforced their sense of their own holiness.

NOTES

1. "Liber vitae Christus est, secundum Johannem septem signaculis signatur... quem Apostoli cum multa gloria miraculorum, quasi coronam portaverunt per universum mundum. Quem cum primo obtulissent scienti litteras, id est Judeao, et respuisset illum tanquam signatum, obtulerunt illum nescienti litteras, scilicet gentilitati, et cum illum intelligere non posset, exposuerunt ei.... Librum hunc Christus ipse scripsit, quia propria voluntate passus est. In pelle siquidem corporis eius scriptae erant litterae minores et

nigrae, per lividas plagas flagellorum; litterae rubeae et capitales, per infixiones clavorum; puncta etiam et virgulae, per punctiones spinarum. Bene pellis eadem prius fuerat multiplici percussione pumicata, colaphis et sputis creata, arundine liniata." Caesarius of Heisterbach, *Dialogus miraculorum* 8.35, ed. Josephus Strange (Cologne, 1851), 1:108–09. Unless noted, all translations are mine.

2. See especially Caroline Walker Bynum, *Holy Feast and Holy Fast: The Religious Significance of Food to Medieval Women* (Berkeley, 1987). See also the essays by Jo Ann McNamara, John Coakley, and Elizabeth Robertson in *Images of Sainthood in Medieval Europe*, ed. Renate Blumenfeld Kosinski and Timea Szell (Ithaca, NY, 1991); Amy M. Hollywood, *The Soul as Virgin Wife: Mechthild of Magdeburg, Marguerite Porete, and Meister Eckhart* (Notre Dame, 1995); Karma Lochrie, *Marjorie Kempe and Translations of the Flesh* (Philadelphia, 1991); Elizabeth Alvilda Petroff, *Body and Soul: Essays on Medieval Women and Mysticism* (Oxford, 1994); Ulrike Wiethaus, ed., *Maps of Flesh and Light: The Religious Experience of Medieval Women Mystics* (Syracuse, NY, 1993); Danielle Régnier-Bohler, "Voix littéraires, voix mystiques," in *Histoire des femmes en occident: Le moyen âge*, ed. Christiane Klapisch-Zuber (Paris, 1991), 443–500; Jeffrey Hamburger, *The Rothschild Canticles: Art and Mysticism in Flanders and the Rhineland circa 1300* (New Haven, CT, 1990); and *Gendered Voices: Medieval Saints and Their Interpreters*, ed. Catherine M. Mooney (Philadelphia, 1999).

3. Bynum, *Holy Feast and Holy Fast*, esp. 288–96; and Bynum, *Fragmentation and Redemption: Essays on Gender and the Human Body in Medieval Religion* (New York, 1991), chaps. 5 and 6.

4. Karma Lochrie, for example, disassociates "body" and "flesh," arguing that the association of medieval women with "flesh" gave them a powerful but potentially disruptive voice unavailable to men (*Marjorie Kempe*, 3–5, 13–55). Similarly, Amy Hollywood emphasizes that gender differences lay more in the hagiographers' reception of religious behaviors than they did in the subjects' own religious expression (*Soul as Virgin Wife*, 27–39). See also Hollywood, "Suffering Transformed: Marguerite Porete, Meister Eckhart, and the Problem of Women's Spirituality," in *Meister Eckhart and the Beguine Mystics*, ed. Bernard McGinn (New York, 1994), 87–113. For works that debate the binary sex/gender distinctions, see Miri Rubin, "The Person in the Form: Medieval Challenges to 'Bodily Order,'" in *Framing Medieval Bodies*, ed. Sarah Kay and Miri Rubin (Manchester, 1994), 100–122; R. N. Swanson, "Angels Incarnate: Clergy and Masculinity from Gregorian Reform to Reformation," in *Masculinity in Medieval Europe*, ed. D. M. Hadley (London, 1999), 160–77; Karma Lochrie, Peggy McCracken, and James A. Schultz, eds., *Constructing Medieval Sexuality* (Minneapolis, 1997); Joan Cadden, *Meanings of Sex Difference in the Middle Ages: Medicine, Science, and Culture* (New York, 1993); and for non-medieval discussions, Gilbert Herdt, ed., *Third Sex, Third Gender: Beyond Sexual Dimorphism in Culture and History* (New York, 1994).

5. André Vauchez, *La sainteté en occident aux derniers siècles du moyen âge d'après le procès de canonisation et les documents hagiographiques* (Rome, 1981), 450–55. See also Donald Weinstein and Rudolph M. Bell, *Saints and Society: The Two Worlds of Western Christendom, 1000–1700* (Chicago, 1982), 153–57, 236–38; and Giles Constable, "The Ideal of the Imitation of Christ," in his *Three Studies in Medieval Religious and Social Thought* (Cambridge,

1995), 194–217. Scholars of female spirituality often cite Vauchez and Weinstein and Bell but then continue to compare women to clerical men. See, for example, Hollywood, *Soul as Virgin Wife*, 30.

6. The study of the construction of masculinity is a rapidly growing field. For studies of medieval masculinities, see Dyan Elliott, "Pollution, Illusion, and Masculine Disarray: Nocturnal Emissions and the Sexuality of the Clergy," in *Constructing Medieval Sexuality*, ed. Lochrie, McCracken, and Schultz, 1–23; and the essays in *Medieval Masculinities: Regarding Men in the Middle Ages*, ed. Clare A. Lees (Minneapolis, 1994) and *Masculinity in Medieval Europe*, ed. Hadley.

7. For the idea that constructions of gender signify relations of power, see Joan Wallach Scott, "Gender: A Useful Category of Historical Analysis," in *Feminism and History*, ed. Scott (Oxford, 1996), 152–80.

8. For studies that try to uncover female religious expressions from the accounts of male hagiographers, see the essays in *Gendered Voices*, ed. Mooney.

9. Historians have given various dates for the institution of the Cistercian lay brotherhood. Jacques Dubois believes it unlikely that the lay brotherhood was established before 1115; see "L'institution des convers au XIIème s., forme de vie monastique propre aux laïcs," in *I laïci nella "societas christiana" dei secoli XI e XII*, Settimana internazionale di studio 3 (Milan, 1968), 183–261. Kassius Hallinger suggests that the lay brotherhood began before 1119; "Woher kommen die Laienbrüder?" *Analecta Sacri Ordinis Cisterciensis* 12 (1956): 10 (hereafter *ASOC*). For the spiritual motivations of the lay brothers, see Hallinger, "Woher kommen die Laienbrüder?" 84–95; for the idea that the lay brotherhood continued the class divisions of feudalism, see Ernst Werner, "Bemerken zu einer neuen These über die Herkunft der Laienbrüder," *Zeitschrift für Geschichtswissenschaft* 6 (1958): 355–59; and Isabel Alfonso, "Cistercians and Feudalism," *Past and Present* no. 133 (1991): 3–30. For a summary of the historiographical debates concerning the lay brothers, see Bruce Lescher, "Laybrothers: Questions Then, Questions Now," *Cistercian Studies* 23 (1988): 63–85. Constance Berman's *The Cistercian Evolution: The Invention of a Religious Order in Twelfth-Century Europe* (Philadelphia, 2000) raises important questions about our understanding of the first half century of the Cistercian movement. I will continue to use the phrase "Cistercian order" to refer to Cistercians before 1160, however, because I find that both Cistercian monks and non-Cistercian observers saw the Cistercians as bound by common observances and a general meeting of abbots.

10. For a possible example of this at Cîteaux, see J. Marilier, ed., *Chartes et documents concernant l'abbaye de Cîteaux, 1098–1182* (Rome, 1961), 143–45. Constance Berman has found evidence of this in southern France. See her *Medieval Agriculture, the Southern French Countryside and the Early Cistercians*, Transactions of the American Philosophical Society 76 (Philadelphia, 1986), 55–57. It is unclear what happened to the wives and families of these men.

11. *Statuta capitulorum generalium ordinis cisterciensis ab anno 1116 ad annum 1786*, ed. Joseph-Marie Canivez (Louvain, 1933), 1:108; Caesarius of Heisterbach, *Dialogus miraculorum*, 1.37, pp. 45–46. In the early years of the order, some lay brothers, such as Bernard of Clairvaux's uncle, Milo of Montbard, clearly came from the aristocracy while, even after 1188, the monks told stories about priests who hid their ordination and entered monasteries

as lay brothers in order to live a life of greater humility. For Bernard's uncle, see *De illustri genere S. Bernardi*—*Probationes* 99, *Patrologia cursus completus, series latina* (hereafter *PL*), ed. J.-P. Migne (Paris, 1878–90) 185:1461. For others, see R. Ducourneau Othon, "De l'institution et des us des convers dans l'ordre de Cîteaux," in *Saint Bernard et son temps*, Association Bourgignonne des Sociétés Savantes (Dijon, 1928), 161 n. 2. It is possible that, at least in the early years of the order, illiterate aristocrats became lay brothers rather than monks. For priests who became lay brothers, see Caesarius of Heisterbach, *Dialogus miraculorum*, 1.39, pp. 46–47.

   12. Chrysogonus Waddell, ed., *Cistercian Lay Brothers: The Twelfth-Century Usages with Related Texts* (Brecht, Belgium, 2000), 57–64, 69–70, 73–76.

   13. Bruno Griesser, ed., "Die *'Ecclesiastica officia Cisterciensis ordinis'* des Cod. 1711 von Trient," *ASOC* 12 (1956): 199, 200, 195, 212, 100.

   14. See the works of Brian Patrick McGuire: "A Lost Clairvaux Exemplum Collection Found," *ASOC* 39 (1983): 27–62; "Structure and Consciousness in the *Exordium magnum cisterciense*," *Cahiers de l'Institut du Moyen Age Grec et Latin* 30 (1979): 31–91; "Written Sources and Cistercian Inspiration in Caesarius of Heisterbach," *Analecta Cisterciensia* 35 (1979): 227–82; and "Friends and Tales in the Cloister: Oral Sources in Caesarius of Heisterbach's *Dialogus miraculorum*," *Analecta Cisterciensia* 36 (1980): 167–245.

   15. Herbert of Clairvaux, *De miraculis*, 1.16, 1.31, *PL* 185:1292, 1304; Conrad of Eberbach, *Exordium magnum*, ed. Bruno Griesser (Rome, 1961), 4.13, pp. 238–39.

   16. Conrad of Eberbach, *Exordium magnum*, 5.10, pp. 292–98.

   17. Herbert of Clairvaux, *De miraculis*, 1.15, *PL* 185:1291–92.

   18. Herbert of Clairvaux, *De miraculis*, 1.17, *PL* 185:1292–93.

   19. Herbert of Clairvaux, *De miraculis*, 1.29, *PL* 185:1301–03.

   20. Conrad of Eberbach, *Exordium magnum*, 4.13, pp. 238–39.

   21. Bernard of Clairvaux, *Sermo feria iv hebdomadae sanctae*, in *Sancti Bernardi opera* (hereafter *SBO*), ed. J. Leclercq, C. H. Talbot, and H. Rochais (Rome, 1957–77), 5:56–67.

   22. Some stories about monks also emphasized their humility, patience, and obedience, but a much smaller proportion of stories about monks than stories about lay brothers. In many cases, when a story emphasizes a monk's humility or simplicity of heart, it turns out he is only barely literate. See, for example, Herbert of Clairvaux, *De miraculis*, 1.11, *PL* 185:1287–90. In the *Exordium magnum*, of the eighteen stories about lay brothers, eight portrayed lay brothers with the exemplary virtues, another two portrayed lay brothers possessing a "simplicity of heart," and three more portrayed the dangers of disobedience.

   23. Herbert of Clairvaux, *De miraculis*, 1.15, 1.18, *PL* 185:1291–94.

   24. See Caroline Walker Bynum, *Jesus as Mother: Studies in the Spirituality of the High Middle Ages* (Berkeley, 1982), esp. chap. 4, and *Holy Feast and Holy Fast*, 284, in which Bynum argues that male use of feminine imagery portrayed a fundamental characteristic of male spirituality—the desire for role reversals that rejected standard forms of male power. See also David Damrosch, "*Non alia sed aliter:* The Hermeneutics of Gender in Bernard of Clairvaux," in *Images of Sainthood in Medieval Europe*, ed. Kosinski and Szell, 181–95.

   25. Bernard of Clairvaux, *Sermones super cantica canticorum*, 12.8–9, 21.10–11, *SBO* 1:65–66, 127–28.

26. For a list of examples, see Bynum, *Jesus as Mother*, 113–25. See especially, Bernard of Clairvaux, *Sermones super cantica canticorum*, 10.3, 23.2, *SBO* 1:49–50, 139–40. See also Guerric of Igny, Sermon 8.4–5, in *Liturgical Sermons*, trans. the monks of Mount St. Bernard Abbey (Spencer, MA, 1971), 1:198.

27. This is the central theme of Bernard's sermons on the Song of Songs.

28. Brian Stock, *The Implications of Literacy: Written Language and Models of Interpretation in the Eleventh and Twelfth Centuries* (Princeton, NJ, 1982), 90, 329, 405.

29. Waddell, *Cistercian Lay Brothers*, 69–70, 183–85.

30. *Vita Arnulfi* (hereafter, *VA*), in *Acta sanctorum quotquot toto orbe coluntur* (Paris, 1867), June 7, 556–79. For its dating, see Simone Roisin, *L'hagiographie cistercienne dans le diocèse de Liège au XIIIe siècle* (Louvain, 1947), 32–34; it appears to have been written before 1236. The edition in the *Acta sanctorum* is based on three thirteenth-century manuscripts.

31. "Divisiones enim gratiarum sunt sicut dicit beatus Apostolus; et unusquisque proprium donum habet ex Deo, alius sic, alius vero sic. Sed licet Deus noster omnipotens, quandoque in aliquo servorum suorum operetur quaedam singulariter mirabilia et mirabiliter singularia, quae in multis aliis inveniri non possunt." *VA praefatio*, p. 558.

32. E. de Moreau, *L'abbaye de Villers-en-Brabant* (Brussels, 1909), 104; Thomas Merton, *Modern Biographical Sketches of Cistercian Blesseds and Saints*, cited in Brian Patrick McGuire, "Self-Denial and Self-Assertion in Arnulf of Villers," *Cistercian Studies Quarterly* 28 (1993): 242; and Roisin, *L'hagiograhie cistercienne*, 33.

33. McGuire, "Self-Denial and Self-Assertion," 241–59.

34. Roisin, in *L'hagiographie cistercienne*, 96, also noticed that it was primarily the lay brothers (Arnulf, Peter, and Nicholas) who demonstrated "les excès d'austérité."

35. See my *The Boundaries of Charity: Cistercian Culture and Ecclesiastical Reform, 1098–1180* (Stanford, CA, 1996), esp. chap. 3.

36. "Obsecramus pro Christo miserere carnis tuae, carnis pauperis et fragilis, sine qua vivere non potes.... Nequaquam, inquit ille, nequaquam ad effectum perducetur hujusmodi persuasio, cum caro mea hostis meus sit." *VA* 1.14, p. 561.

37. *VA* 1.9, 1.17, 1.20, 1.36, pp. 560, 561, 562, 565.

38. *VA* 2.6, p. 567.

39. *VA* 2.8, p. 567.

40. *VA* 2.6–10, pp. 567–68.

41. His willingness "to leave God for God's sake," Goswin emphasized, made his prayers especially effective, for according to Augustine, a single prayer made in obedience was better than ten thousand made with disdain; *VA* 2.10, p. 568.

42. "Manum monachi dextram configa obedientia sine murmuratione; sinistram patientia sine simulatione.... Pedes illius vera humilitas configat, ut non solum praelatis, sed et fratribus se propter Christum subiiciat." Caesarsius of Heisterbach, *Dialogus miraculorum*, 8.19, p. 97.

43. "sequebatur viriliter Dominum Christum ad passionem," *VA* 1.31, p. 564. See also 1.22, p. 562.

44. "et in virtute sanctae crucis sapienter indoctus, arripiens illam, flagellavit se," *VA* 1.15, p. 561; "ut merito offerres Domino majestatis sanguinem tuum, qui tempore passionis suae gratanter obtulit pro te Deo Patri sanguinem suum." *VA* 1.16, p. 561.

45. *VA* 1.35, p. 565.

46. "qua Dominus majestatis in cruce pependit," *VA* 2.68, p. 579.

47. Guerric of Igny, Sermon 30, in *Liturgical Sermons*, 2:59–65.

48. Guerric of Igny, Sermon 32.5, in *Liturgical Sermons*, 2:77–78. For similar images, see Bernard of Clairvaux, *Sermones super cantica canticorum*, 61.4, *SBO* 2:150–51, and Gilbert of Hoyland, Sermon 2.7, *PL* 184:21.

49. See Constable, "The Ideal of the Imitation of Christ," 204, 212–13. One exception may be Humbert of Igny: Bernard's sermon at his death suggests that Humbert bore stigmata but it is unclear if these stigmata were real or metaphorical. See Constable, ibid., 213.

50. See Jean Leclercq, *Bernard of Clairvaux and the Cistercian Spirit*, trans. Claire Lavoie (Kalamazoo, 1976); Michael Casey, *Athirst for God: Spiritual Desire in Bernard of Clairvaux's Sermon on the Song of Songs* (Kalamazoo, 1988); and my *Boundaries of Charity*.

51. "in virtute sanctae crucis sapienter indoctus," *VA* 1.15, p. 561.

52. "... ostendens verum se esse discipulum Domini et Magistri sui, qui sanctissimam carnem suam flagellis laniandam praebuit. Sub cujus magisterio proficiens de die in diem in simplicitate cordis, didicit ab ipso mitis esse et humilis corde; didicit etiam artem artium, artem amoris," *VA* 1.11–12, p. 560.

53. "Sufficitne tibi, inquit, quod propter te carnem dignanter indui, propter te sustinui opprobria, sputa, colaphos, flagella, spineam coronam, clavos: et ut majorem sustinerem confusionem, in patibulo crucis nudus pependi?" *VA* 2.17, p. 569.

54. "Cum autem hoc dixit, non ideo utique dixit, ut negaret passionem Domini sibi et universo mundo sufficere ad redemptionem; sed demonstrabat se corde ardentissimo anhelare ad beatissimam sanctae Trinitatis visionem." *VA* 2.17, p. 569.

55. "vir equidem simplex, a gratia instructus, in schola summae divinitatis didicit, quod mundi hujus sapientes per sapientiam suam invenire non potuerunt," *VA* 2.19, p. 569.

56. See the chapter by Sharon Farmer in this volume.

57. Bynum, *Holy Feast and Holy Fast*, 282–88.

58. "Miles fortissimus" and "pugnans ... novus athleta viriliter"; *VA* 1.15, 1.6, pp. 561, 559.

59. "Agendum est mihi fortiter, agendum viriliter; viriliter, inquam, agendum: quia valde necessarium est amicis meis: adjiciebatque; Ictus istos et istos, pro illis et pro illis, infero mihi, in nomine Domini." *VA* 1.34, p. 565.

60. "O vere felicem puerum, de quo recenter nato tam solicita est mater gratia, ut non solum nutriat eum lactis dulcedine, sed etiam myrrhatum vinum propinet ei ad bibendum; dum alligat eum in cunis infantiae suae tam pugentis fascia funiculi, et cultro tam acutissimo carnalem in eo circumcidit lasciviam." *VA* 1.10, p. 560.

61. Bynum, *Fragmentation and Redemption*, chap. 3; and Leo Steinberg, *The Sexuality of Christ in Renaissance Art and in Modern Oblivion*, 2nd ed. (Chicago, 1996).

62. Herbert of Clairvaux, *De miraculis*, 1.3, *PL* 185:1278–79. For studies of nocturnal emissions and the way they created "anxious acknowledgment of gender turmoils," see Elliott, "Pollution, Illusion, and Masculine Disarray," 1–23; and C. Leyser, "Masculinity in Flux: Nocturnal Emission and the Limits of Celibacy in the Early Middle Ages," in *Masculinity in Medieval Europe*, ed. Hadley, 103–21.

63. "Nec apparuit in loco dicto aliquod vestigium genitalium nisi sola planities plana, clara et munda, reverberans oculos intuentium claritate nimia." *Cronica Villariensis monasterii*, in *Gesta Episcoporum Abbatum Ducum Aliorumque Principium Saec. XIII*, ed. G. Waitz, Monumenta Germaniae Historica. Scriptores (hereafter MGH SS) (Hannover, 1880) 25:202.

64. Brian Patrick McGuire, "The Cistercians and the Transformation of Monastic Friendships," *Analecta Cisterciensia* 37 (1981): 38.

65. See especially Bynum, *Holy Feast and Holy Fast*.

66. For example, Caroline Bynum has argued that the imagery of role reversal appealed more to men than women because the gradations of male status created a situation in which men might need a periodic release from their social position (*Holy Feast and Holy Fast*, 286). But such an argument does not consider what sort of release low-status men might need. For the suggestion that we consider factors such as class and race in complicating gendered analyses, see Elizabeth Spelman, *Inessential Woman: Problems of Exclusion in Feminist Thought* (Boston, 1988). For debates over binary sex/gender distinctions, see the works cited in note 4. If, as Swanson argues in "Angels Incarnate," the clergy comprised a "third sex," should we then consider the lay brothers a fourth?

67. The compilation was then reorganized sometime before 1459. For a discussion of the two recensions of this text, see Roisin, *L'hagiographie cistercienne*, 23–26, and Moreau, *L'abbaye Villers*, xviii–xxiv.

68. *Gesta sanctorum Villariensium* in MGH SS 25:234.

69. Bruges, Bibliothêque Municipale MS 425, fol. 98ra. Peter's *vita*, while included in the *Gesta*, was not included in the MGH edition.

70. *Vita beatae Christinae mirabilis Trudonopoli, Acta sanctorum*, June 5, 637–60; and *Vita Marie Oiginiacensis, Acta sanctorum*, June 5, 542–72.

71. Bynum, *Holy Feast and Holy Fast*, 113–49.

72. Roisin, *L'hagiographie cistercienne*, 96. See also Ernest W. McDonnell, *The Beguines and Beghards in Medieval Culture* (New Brunswick, NJ, 1954).

73. As well as the works cited in note 2, see Richard Kieckhefer, *Unquiet Souls: Fourteenth-Century Saints and Their Religious Milieu* (Chicago, 1984). Kieckhefer, who studied both male and female saints, concluded that their asceticism may reflect their attempt to pursue monastic ideals without withdrawing from society.

74. For warnings about this, see Richard Kieckhefer, "Holiness and the Culture of Devotion," in *Images of Sainthood*, ed. Kosinski and Szell, 305; and Amy Hollywood's critique of *Holy Feast and Holy Fast* in *Soul as Virgin Wife*, 27–39.

75. John Coakley, "Friars as Confidants of Holy Women in Medieval Dominican Hagiography," in *Images of Sainthood*, ed. Kosinski and Szell, 245; and the essays in *Gendered Voices*, ed. Mooney.

76. For the lay brother revolts, see James Donnelly, *The Decline of the Medieval Cistercian Laybrotherhood* (New York, 1949).

77. VA 1.15, 1.22, pp. 561, 562; *Gestis sanctorum Villariensium, MGH SS* 25:234. See also McGuire, "Self-Denial and Self-Assertion," 254.

78. For the identification of Goswin as the author of this life, see Roisin, *L'hagiographie cistercienne*, 54–59. There are both thirteenth- and early-fourteenth-century editions of

the *vita*. Most of it was edited by Chrysostomus Henriquez in *Quinque prudentes virgines* (Antwerp, 1630), 199–297; the prologue and other previously unedited passages appear in the *Catalogus codicum hagiographicorum bibliothecae regiae Bruxellensis* (Brussels, 1889), 2:222–26. Martinus Cawley discusses the problems with Henriquez's edition in Cawley, "Ida of Nivelles: Cistercian Nun," in *Hidden Springs: Cistercian Monastic Women*, ed. John A. Nichols and Lillian Thomas Shank (n.p., 1995), 1:305–21.

79. *Vita beatae Idae,* in *Quinque prudentes virgines,* 173, 207–08, 221–24, 273–76, 280. For passages with similar wording that helped Roisin identify Goswin as the author of the *Vita beatae Idae,* see *L'hagiographie cistercienne,* 56–59. The prologue suggests that many of Ida's friends and witnesses to her miracles were still alive when the author wrote; see Roisin, ibid., 59.

80. *Vita beatae Idae,* in *Quinque prudentes virgines,* 281–85.

81. *Vita beatae Idae,* in *Quinque prudentes virgines,* 223, 247, 252. See the essays by Barbara Newman, John Coakley, and Dyan Elliott in *Gendered Voices,* ed. Mooney, for arguments that this nuptial language also could be the addition of the hagiographer.

82. "transiret ad dormitorium spirituale, in quo a sensibus corporeis alienata inter sponsi sui brachia quiete felicissima sopiretur." *Vita beatae Idae,* in *Quinque prudentes virgines,* 274; see also 212, 281.

83. *Vita beatae Idae,* in *Quinque prudentes virgines,* 252.

84. *VA* 2.9, p. 567; *Vita beatae Idae,* in *Quinque prudentes virgines,* 256–58.

85. "sic eius anima sanctae Trinitati glutino ardentissimi amoris impressa erat, ita ut spiritus eius unus cum Domino spiritus efficeretur." *Vita beatae Idae,* in *Quinque prudentes virgines,* 271. Martinus Cawley stresses the non-verbal and non-literate spirituality of Ida of Nivelles: "Ida of Nivelles," 309, 313. But the examples he uses to demonstrate this also show that Ida had access to books even if she wasn't fully literate.

86. McGuire, "Cistercians and the Transformation of Monastic Friendship," 29–35.

87. For the continued importance of the Song of Songs for Cistercian nuns, see Hamburger, *Rothschild Canticles.*

88. McGuire, "Cistercians and the Transformation of Monastic Friendship," 51.

89. For the literacy of late medieval nuns, see David N. Bell, *What Nuns Read: Books and Libraries in Medieval English Nunneries* (Kalamazoo, 1995); and Hamburger, *Rothschild Canticles,* 3–7.

90. See Bynum, *Holy Feast and Holy Fast,* 115–23. These *vitae* include those of Alice of Shaarbeek (d. 1250), *Acta sanctorum,* June 2, 476–83; Beatrice of Nazareth (d. 1268), *The Life of Beatrice of Nazareth, 1200–1268,* ed. and trans. Roger De Ganck (Kalamazoo, 1991); Ida of Lewis (d. ca. 1273), *Acta sanctorum,* October 13, 100–124; Ida of Leuven (d. 1290?), *Acta sanctorum,* April 2, 156–89; and Elisabeth of Spaalbeek (d. 1304), *Catalogus codicum hagiographicorum bibliothecae regiae Bruxellensis,* 1:362–78.

91. *The Life of Beatrice of Nazareth,* x. Compare book one, chapter 5 of Beatrice's life (36–39) to *VA* 1.11–24, pp. 560–62. In his study of Beatrice, De Ganck identifies Beatrice's biographer as a Cistercian, *Beatrice of Nazareth in her Context* (Kalamazoo, 1991), 7; but in the introduction to her *vita,* he is less certain: *The Life of Beatrice of Nazareth,* xxii–xxv. Amy Hollywood has carefully compared the hagiographer's descriptions of Beatrice's behavior to the passages in the *vita* that reproduce Beatrice's own language. She demonstrates how

this author took Beatrice's internal experiences and made them visible on Beatrice's body. Whereas De Ganck believes that Beatrice may have consciously modeled her behavior on that of Arnulf, Hollywood takes this repetition as more evidence that Beatrice's hagiographer had manufactured her self-mortification: if she herself had undertaken such practices, why would the hagiographer copy the descriptions of someone else? *Soul as Virgin Wife,* 29–34.

92. *Vita Idae Lewensis, Acta sanctorum,* October 13, 112. De Ganck, *Beatrice of Nazareth in Her Context,* 7, identified the biographer as a Cistercian from Villers.

93. "non muliebriter aut ignave, sed forti virilique constantia propulsaret," and "per virilem proterviam." *Vita Idae Lovaniensi, Acta sanctorum,* April 2, 159. For other examples, see Bynum, *Holy Feast and Holy Fast,* 318–19, n. 68.

7

"Because the Other Is a Poor Woman She Shall Be Called His Wench": Gender, Sexuality, and Social Status in Late Medieval England

Ruth Mazo Karras

In Geoffrey Chaucer's Manciple's Tale, the teller questions the linguistic distinction between different types of sexually deviant women:

> Ther nys no difference, trewely,
> Betwixe a wyf that is of heigh degree,
> If of hir body dishonest she bee,
> And a povre wenche, oother than this—
> If so be they werke bothe amys—
> But that the gentle, in estaat above,
> She shal be cleped his lady, as in love;
> And, for that oother is a povre womman,
> She shal be cleped his wenche or his lemman.
> And, God it woot, myn owene deere brother,
> Men leyn that oon as lowe as lith that oother.[1]

Chaucer here presents both an essentialist and a socially contingent view of gender and sexuality. The speaker recognizes that medieval society habitually labels women's behavior differently depending on the social class to which they belong. The aristocracy had a vocabulary of romantic love that could be applied to extramarital or non-marital relationships.[2] To Chaucer's gentle or upper-bourgeois readers, on the other hand, a poor woman who enters into a sexual relationship is described in derogatory terms, although not the most derogatory available.[3]

Chaucer, however, has his character point out here that in another sense the different terminology—in effect, the different registers of language—does not really matter. A loose woman is a loose woman. The phrase "Men lay the one as low as lies the other," with its masculine subject and its sexual imagery, implies that all women are fundamentally the same—specifically, sex objects. Chaucer's insight goes deeper, however, for it also includes a recognition of the hypocrisy of society. If aristocrats are not held as culpable, it is because of society's peculiar attitudes and linguistic practices, and not because of any real moral difference.

These lines from The Manciple's Tale raise a fundamental question for historians of medieval sexualities. Is it possible to speak of a feminine sexuality, or of a single set of standards for women's behavior? Or did standards and attitudes differ according to social status or class?[4] Were the discourses—law and pastoral literature, for example—that attempted to control women's sexuality aimed at behavior that was deemed appropriate for one social group and inappropriate for another? Many medieval discourses refer to an essentialized "woman" and hold that it is possible to understand a generalized feminine nature.[5] When this assumption was translated into behavior and attitudes toward actual individual women, however, social position or class difference strongly affected how misogynist conceptions of feminine sexuality were applied.[6]

Despite the normative teaching of the church, women's experiences of sexuality and sexual behavior obviously varied a great deal by social position, and the fact that the Manciple recognized two different sets of names for what he considered to be the same thing is an indication of this variation. This article examines social difference in feminine sexuality by looking at how prostitution and rape were regarded in medieval England.[7] I will examine the legal regulation of prostitution, the impact of that regulation on women who were not prostitutes, other forms of sexual exploitation of low-status women (including rape), and the way women's sexual behavior was viewed by their male peers. Most of the sources are court records (which, of course, entail their own problems of interpretation), but literary evidence helps illuminate the cultural attitudes that informed the courts' actions.

This article deals with the way a male-dominated society understood women's sexuality, and deals with heterosexual activity only. It is likely that women of different social statuses entered into same-sex relationships differently. As Judith Bennett has suggested, women who never married and lived together can be considered "lesbian-like" whether or not we have evidence of sexual relations between them.[8] Certainly working women had different choices about refusing marriage—a "lesbian-like" behavior—than aristocratic women did. However, the bulk of discussion in medieval sources about women's sexual behavior deals with their heterosexual behavior. The men who wrote the texts, whether legal or literary, discussed here were concerned with the women's availability (or not) to men and with the legitimacy of children they might bear.

The issue posed here—is it possible to speak of "a" feminine sexuality, or did standards and attitudes differ by social status?—is not either/or, but both/and. Despite a set of dominant discourses that described all women as sexual and all sexuality as sinful, medieval society in fact had different expectations for different women. I have argued elsewhere that the construction of prostitution through legislation, legal practice, and literature was aimed at the control of feminine sexuality generally. By recognizing the existence of commercial prostitutes, yet delineating a category of "whore" that did not necessarily require financial exchange, a variety of discourses worked together to conflate any sexually deviant woman with a prostitute.[9] Yet, though the thrust of medieval thought agreed with Chaucer's Manciple that the two were the same in their basic feminine (sinful and sexual) nature, an aristocratic lady who had an affair outside of marriage was obviously not the same, in terms of her life experience or her subjective sexuality, as a streetwalker.

For other periods, particularly the nineteenth century, historians have focused on the variation by class in sexual norms. Middle-class regulators, for example, attempting to control the lower classes, focused on the sexual behavior of working-class women. They deployed the label of "prostitute" to control these women's independence and mobility. Linda Mahood writes in her study of Edinburgh:

> ...working-class sexuality was increasingly the object of middle-class scrutiny and attempts at colonization. The contemporary discourses and apparatuses did not address the working class directly, however, but apppeared to divide the population up on other grounds, by singling out specific objectionable sexual characters and certain behaviours. What are apparently non-class-based characters emerge. However, on closer examination we find that these characters were mobilized in class- and gender-specific ways. It is significant that it was, by and large, working-class women whose behaviors were scrutinized and stigmatized.[10]

In the Middle Ages, the bourgeoisie did not control the dominant discourses in the same way. True, in late medieval towns there was a developing upper stratum, which was afraid of the social disorder that the poorer people might cause; this is one reason for the prominence of the rhetoric of social order in legislation about prostitution.[11] The women whose behavior was regulated most directly did in fact tend to be the poorer women. But in the Middle Ages the aristocracy were also an important social force, and there was in addition the discourse of moral theology that emanated not so much from any particular level of society as from a long tradition.

The urban regulation of prostitution supports both the idea of differing treatment of social groups and the idea of a universalizing discourse on feminine sexuality. The regulation affected poorer women most directly, but by applying one standard of behavior to women generally, towns threatened any sexually deviant woman with classification as a whore. This, of course, is not unique to the Middle Ages: even in contemporary society the regulation of prostitution reinforces all women's dependence on men. The regulation of prostitution, though it may have been directed mainly against one group of women, functioned—and may have been deliberately intended by legislating authorities to function—as a vehicle for the control of all. But in practice it was poor women whose behavior was regulated as prostitution, both because regulation was designed and implemented in part to control the behavior of the lower levels of society generally and because the poorest women were the ones most likely to take up the not especially attractive working conditions implied in the provision of sex for money.

Sumptuary legislation indicates that a main problem towns perceived with prostitution had to do with women claiming a social standing beyond that ascribed to them. In London an ordinance of the late thirteenth century provided:

> that no woman of the town shall henceforth go to market, or in the street, or outside her dwelling, with a furred hood, whether of lamb or rabbit, on pain of forfeiting the hood to the use of the sheriffs, except ladies who wear furred capes, the hoods of which bear what fur they wish. And because brewsters, nurses, other servants, and women of evil life adorn themselves and wear hoods furred with fur or miniver in the manner of ladies of good birth [bones dames]. . . .[12]

Here the legislation lumps prostitutes (or women of suspect sexual morals generally) with urban working women. The purpose of this regulation is not so much to distinguish prostitutes from chaste women but to distinguish different levels in the social hierarchy. This was, in fact, the general purpose of sumptuary legislation in many parts of Europe.[13] But in the case of prostitutes other reasons also became important: distinguishing them in order to advertise their availability, to prevent the harassment of respectable women who might be mistaken for prostitutes, to prevent the contamination of those respectable women, or even to keep the expenses of the bourgeois household down by prohibiting certain kinds of expensive adornment to the chaste.[14]

This combination of motives for sumptuary legislation—marking both social standing and sexual deviancy—became important in the later legislation from London. The Liber Albus, a customary from the early fourteenth century, did not give a reason for its prohibition on prostitutes' wearing furred hoods or gowns, but an ordinance of 1351 provided that no "common wanton woman" (commune fole femme) should wear fur or other noble lining, because they "have recently from time to time taken up the fashion of being dressed and adorned in the manner and in the dress of good and noble ladies and damsels of the realm, against reason." They were to wear unlined striped hoods so that everyone "could have knowledge of what condition they are."[15] Clearly the legislation was intended to keep such women in their place, whether that place was a social class position or a position on the margins of society based on sexual behavior.

Women who were actually what we would call prostitutes, engaged in sex for money (and this can often only be determined when they were working in the officially sanctioned brothels that existed in many parts of Europe) tended, as one would expect, to come from groups of low social status.[16] Perhaps more relevant than working prostitutes, however, is the greater number of women whom the justice system called "whores" but who may not have been engaged in commercial sex. Here, too, it seems likely that the conflation of extramarital sexual behavior with prostitution was more pronounced for urban workers or the poor than the bourgeoisie or aristocracy.

The courts do not get very specific about the social backgrounds of women accused of being "whores" *(meretrices)*, or of repeated offenses of fornication or adultery with a number of different men. Nevertheless, while any woman who engaged in sex outside of marriage fell within the purview of legal regulation, poorer women were more likely in practice to bear the brunt of enforcement.

Certain occupations were seen as particularly suspect of sexual deviance, for example, laundress or washerwoman. London citizens who wished to keep bathhouses had to give sureties that they would not permit laundresses to enter: it was assumed that they would be there for sexual purposes. Similarly brothelkeepers in the legal stewhouses of Southwark were limited in the number of laundresses they could have, again probably because there was a danger of unofficial prostitution taking place alongside the sanctioned trade.[17] Court records reveal laundresses and accused whores lodging together; they came from the same social milieu.[18] Courtesy books warned against the dangers to a noble house's honor of having too many women servants in the household, especially laundresses.[19] This sort of warning is particularly telling, because it implies that within the aristocratic establishment it was not elite but subordinate women who were seen as the bringers of sexual disorder.[20]

Laundresses were perhaps the clearest example of a group suspected of sexual immorality based simply upon occupation. They had free access to houses (including those of celibate men), had knowledge of intimate details of status and behavior, and were associated with filth. But all female domestic servants were potentially sexually available to their employers or men of their employers' milieu in much the same way and were seen as disruptive because of this. Women who came to the city in search of domestic work might end up working as prostitutes— because of deception by wicked bawds, they claimed, although it is possible that some entered the sex trade because of financial necessity, fully aware of what they were doing.[21] Even those who did find domestic or other work might find themselves prostituted by their employers.[22]

Female servants were generally considered sexually available to their employers even if the latter did not prostitute them to others. The records of *ex officio* prosecutions in any late medieval church court reveal frequent accusations of men having sex with their female servants. In many cases, of course, this may have been consensual, at least insofar as a woman who chooses to form a liaison with her employer in order to improve her financial position or guarantee herself a job can be said to be acting as a free agent. In other cases, though, it clearly was coerced, whether by physical force or by threats of economic ruin. Whether or not coerced, this sexual behavior differed substantially from that expected of elite women, and the women servants were often blamed for it, both in court and in the writings of moralists.

Just as the regulation of prostitution indicates standards differentially applied, the legal treatment of rape also reveals different expectations of sexual behavior at different social levels. The records of late medieval London indicate that it was especially young women in domestic service who were considered fair game for rape. The reasons for this may have been largely practical: rape was a difficult crime to prove and convict in any case, but this would have been especially so for young women without family or resources (and many of these young women in service came from outside the town). Thus men looking for sex felt that there were certain women they could rape with impunity.

In fact, any woman seen walking in the street after curfew—presumably poorer women, or servants who had errands to run—was a potential sexual partner. When John Britby was arrested in 1394 for having sex with another man, John Rykener, he testified that he had approached the latter, "thinking he was a woman, asking him as he would a woman if he could commit a libidinous act with her."[23] Any woman found in the streets of the City of London on an evening was assumed to be sexually available. In the case of the transvestite Rykener, this assumption was well founded. In other cases, the assumption led to rape. In 1440 a "young girl" (*iuvencula,* a term often used for women depicted in the extant documents as vulnerable or gullible) named Margaret testified that "she went to a gentleman of my lord of Gloucester called Caxton to bring a bag there, and the said Caxton kissed her and lay on top of her on the bed and repeatedly violated her...."[24] The fact that the man was not prosecuted for rape (a woman who was accused of arranging the encounter was sentenced to the pillory for bawdry) is an indication of the level of sexual availability assumed in late medieval society, at least when the man was of high rank and the woman was not.

The problem of underreporting complicates the use of judicial evidence for the incidence of rape at different social levels. It is precisely those women who were the most vulnerable—the poor, the servants raped by aristocrats—who were the least likely to have reported it, because they knew how slim were the chances of conviction. Thus, rape of poor or dependent women is likely to have been even more common than the sources indicate. Of course, according to scholars who have studied rape in medieval France, the rape even of a well-off widow, when committed by clients of a powerful man, could also go very lightly punished, and such rapes may sometimes have been a prelude to forced marriage.[25] Rape could also be used as a tool of social control, a way for groups of men to punish women who had done something they thought was inappropriate: priests' partners, servants who had sex with their masters, wives separated from their husbands.[26] Women had several incentives not to report such rapes: not only might the chances of conviction be slim but publicizing the crime would create a stain upon the woman's honor.

Most cases of rape by individuals (as opposed to gangs) in the Middle Ages seem not to have been deliberate attempts at social control or at the demonstration of masculine power over women, but rather served these functions as by-products of an assumed, unquestioned gender and status privilege. Thus rape was directed especially against women of low social status. To the man the rape was not violence but sex; the consent of the woman, at least one whose family was not important, simply did not matter one way or the other.[27] Echoes of this attitude may still be seen today.[28]

A rape case from fourteenth-century London provides a good example of the pervasive attitude stemming from social privilege. Joan Seler, the

eleven-year-old daughter of a saddler, claimed that she was raped by Reymund de Limoges, a foreign merchant, who saw her outside her house,
grabbed her by the arm and dragged her to his dwelling. Reymund was
eventually acquitted on technical legal grounds.[29] If one assumes that
the accusation was a true one, the question arises of Reymund's psychology. Perhaps we might call him a pedophile, but an eleven-year-old
would not be considered a child as would a girl of the same age today;
girls were able to marry legally at twelve and occasionally married younger.
John Marshall Carter suggests that this was, in modern psychological
terms, an "anger rape," because of the violence involved.[30] However, the
language of violence is highly formulaic. "Force and arms" had to be alleged to bring the matter into the court. "Vilely and cruelly handled her
limbs" is vague; Barbara Hanawalt suggests that this referred to injuries
"that are often encountered when an adult male has forced intercourse
with a young girl."[31] The only reference to physical violence that mentions specific injury to a specific part of the girl's body is to the penetration itself. With no evidence of pain for the sake of inflicting pain, the
most likely scenario seems to be that the rapist saw the young woman,
desired her, didn't care whether or not she desired him, and based on
their relative social standing (a member of a family of a not particularly
prosperous craftsman, versus a wealthy merchant) thought he could get
away with rape. In the course of events this turned out to be a fair assessment of the situation.

This assumption of privilege that makes the will or consent of the
lower-status woman simply irrelevant is clearly reflected in descriptions
of rape in literature, from Andreas Capellanus's recommendation on
how to deal with a peasant woman onwards.[32] The Old French *pastourelle*
is a genre in which one basic plot line involves the rape of a shepherdess
by a knight. The texts assume that the woman is there for the taking. As
Kathryn Gravdal writes, "The pastourelle genre mediates class conflict
by displacing it onto a sexual axis where its violence can be directed at
the figure of the woman."[33] The consent of the woman is not always irrelevant here: in many of the poems the woman ends up enjoying the
rape, even asking the knight to return. Only in about eighteen percent of
the poems in the genre does the knight rape the shepherdess; in the others she freely consents. This norm of consent would have created expectations that justified the rape in the other poems. The poems work to

naturalize the sexual access aristocratic men had to women of lower social standing.

The heterosexual behavior of men, in literature and in practice, varied according to the social status of the women (and men) involved.[34] It is more difficult to determine how poorer men and women felt about elite male sexual privilege. In a community where poor, unattached women did sometimes work as prostitutes on a casual basis in order to make ends meet, this behavior might have been accepted by those around them, and this acceptance might have helped make it possible for men to assume that such women were generally available for sex.

It seems more likely, however, that even lower levels of society accepted the church's sexual norms and therefore treated women who did not meet those standards with lack of respect. In other words, women of lower social standing were in a double bind: the expectations of their behavior in practice were quite different from those for elite women, but they could still be criticized for not adhering to the same standards as elite women. The degree of respect prostitutes received, or did not receive, from the communities around them provides an illustration. Prostitutes did not compose a separate subculture, especially since many worked as prostitutes only occasionally or were labeled as such when they were not involved in commercial sex. Nor were they effectively limited to a particular district: legal brothels were in one particular area of each town, and towns attempted to restrict clandestine prostitution to one part of town as well, but this was often not effective. These women lived among and interacted with the rest of the townspeople. Nevertheless the stigma placed upon the prostitute did affect her relations with her contemporaries and was not just a legal fiction. The attitude of the authorities, religious and secular, towards prostitution cannot be taken as reflective of the attitude of society in general, but it did have a deep effect on it. Though not necessarily shunned or ostracized, prostitutes were never considered quite respectable.

Prostitutes embodied the specifically lower-status version of the "woman as disorder" topos. They were accused of causing disorder in their neighborhoods, and the specifics of these accusations go beyond the formulaic "to the nuisance of her neighbors." Angelo Taylor's stewhouse in the London suburb of East Smithfield was accused of causing "many quarrels, beatings, and hues and cries at night." Several "malefactors and disturbers of the peace" who were harbored at Petronilla Bednot's stew "about midnight, on several nights, when the neighbors living there-abouts were in their beds, came with sticks to their windows and beat on them maliciously and said to the neighbors, 'you who are in there, come out and be beaten!'"[35] Like inner-city residents today who resent having their neighborhoods relegated to drug dealing, residents did not appreciate the disturbances prostitution caused. Thus, whatever they thought of the prostitutes' sexual morals, they suffered from the effects of commercial sex.[36]

Some people showed their lack of acceptance of independent feminine sexual behavior by taking direct action against brothels in their neighborhoods. In 1305 the Prior of Holy Trinity in Aldgate Ward, London, was accused of trespass in the house of his neighbor; he responded that because it had been presented at the Wardmote that prostitutes lived in the house, and the owner had not removed them, "the beadle gathered the neighbors, including the Prior and others, and removed the doors and windows." The Prior won his case. The Vicar of St. Sepulchre claimed that the doors of the butcher William Cock in Cock's lane were torn down for identical reasons.[37] This was not spontaneous action by the neighbors of the brothel, but rather was instigated by an ecclesiastical institution in each case. Nevertheless, the neighbors were willing participants.

Prostitutes who operated independently rather than in brothels, or women who engaged in commercial sex only occasionally, may have been less offensive to the community. They interacted with other women, even giving them information about potential marriage partners. In 1515 Robert Harding of London testified that Katherine Worsley, who had been accused of whoredom, "reported to divers women of the said parish that certain young men which were in contemplation of marriage with them had not what men should have to please them and that she knew it for a truth, by reason whereof the said men were refused by the said women, to their great hurt." Harding was afraid that Worsley "should have made like report of him to the said rich widow whom he wooed, by reason whereof the said widow should have in like manner refused him."[38] The fact that Worsley had been accused of whoredom does not mean that she was a prostitute; the point is that a woman who had the reputation of a whore could engage in gossip with respectable women.

Prostitutes were on rare occasions—in cases of male impotence—respected enough to serve in an official capacity in the church courts. This was not ostensibly by virtue of the fact that they were prostitutes (for purposes of the depositions they had to claim to be respectable matrons of the town) but for York, the one place from which these depositions survive, some of the women involved have been identified as prostitutes based on other records.[39] In one case, a witness testified that she "exposed her naked breasts, and with her hands warmed at the said fire, she held and rubbed the penis and testicles of the said John. And she embraced and frequently kissed the same John . . . the whole time aforesaid the said penis was scarcely three inches long, . . . remaining without any increase or decrease." The witness and her companions cursed the man "for presuming to marry a young woman, defrauding her if he could not serve and please her better than that." In another case, however, the women testified that the man's penis was "large enough for any woman living in this world."[40] The facts that these women had to swear that they were respectable and of good character and that their oaths were not challenged did not reflect the way prostitutes were regarded in general; these oaths were formal, to fulfill a requirement of the canon law. The fact that they could be regarded as expert witnesses at all accords them some degree of respect, but we must note that they served as experts only in sexual cases, in which their assumed lack of shame made them the best choice. In other cases having been accused of sexual misbehavior would seriously impeach the credibility of a woman's testimony.

Yet a number of women who were clearly practicing prostitutes repeatedly escaped conviction by finding respected women to act as compurgators in the church courts. This was the case with Isabella Wakefield and Margaret Clay, of York, both of whom had long careers in the sex trade.[41] It is impossible for us now to pronounce on the guilt or innocence of parties in medieval court cases, for women may have been accused based on gossip and then rightly succeeded in purging themselves. However, when the same person was presented year after year for offenses involving commercial sex, we may assume that she was a practitioner and that her successful purgation reflected local networks of influence rather than her lack of culpability.

Though prostitutes were not ostracized from their communities, they were certainly degraded, so that accusations of whoredom would be an effective weapon against women who were resented for other reasons. This might be the case with Maud Sheppster of London, accused in 1423: she "holds open shop and retails, and is not a freewoman [admitted to citizenship and free trade in the city]; also she is a strumpet to more than one and a bawd also."[42] Perhaps she had multiple sex partners and perhaps not; whatever the truth of the accusation it probably would not have been brought had there been no concern over her commercial activities. The case of Joan Grubbe in 1311 in the town of Ramsey might be similar: she was charged with "being a thief of geese and hens and stealing her neighbors' geese, hens and dregs, to the value of 10d., and for being nothing more than a common whore."[43]

These accusations of deviant sexual behavior came directly or indirectly from the people around them, whether from peers or those of higher status wanting to enforce moral standards. The church courts brought the prosecutions *ex officio,* but this was based on information gleaned from deliberate informing and from local gossip networks.[44] In effect, then, what the church courts were enforcing was community standards of morality, although these standards were heavily influenced by the teaching of the church itself. In addition to church courts, people also ended up in manorial courts because of sexual offenses, again because of the concerns of their neighbors and peers.[45] When people defamed each other, this also indicates community standards; in late-fifteenth-century London, for example, women were defamed of sexual offenses far more often than men, and data from other jurisdictions, some from earlier in the century, confirm the much greater number of sexual defamations against women.[46] While it is not possible to distinguish the relative social standing of accuser and accused, and so there may be some element here of the bourgeoisie complaining about the sexual behavior of the poor, many of those who defamed each other were people who had mutual friends or lived and worked in proximity. It is clear that norms of sexual behavior were coming from within a given social group, not entirely imposed from outside.

Marriage practices among the poor tend to confirm that their notions of sexual morality were not that different from the mainstream teaching of the church. Thus, in this area, the poor seem to have accepted the dominant discourse. Less educated people may have entered into unions more informally than canon law dictated, but Michael Sheehan has argued that by the fourteenth century the church was regularizing marriage among the poor by recognizing informal relationships as clandestine marriages, illicit but indissoluble. They were thus treated in practical terms as marriages, whether or not the poor initally regarded them as such, and this would have affected how people came to view them. L. R. Poos found in his study of late medieval Essex that the popular culture of marriage generally regarded vows, clandestine or otherwise, as permanent.[47]

Just because groups at various levels of society had the same view of marriage, however, does not mean that they regarded in the same way women who transgressed against marriage. Poorer women might have run a higher risk of abandonment and destitution and would be more likely to turn to prostitution; they might also be more likely to be labeled as whores if they transgressed against their marriage vows. Yet accusations of whoredom were not limited to the poor, and other women ran similar risks. The clear recognition that commercial prostitutes were women of the lower classes, that is, below the level of the gentry or merchant class (leaving aside the issue of courtesans, for which there is little evidence for England), and that women of the lower classes can be expected to be whores did not mean that other women could not be accused. It is impossible to discern from the records exactly what was the social status of most women involved.[48]

Accusations of sexual misbehavior against aristocratic women, of course, existed. They tended not, however, to speak in terms of prostitution and whoredom. Accusations of adultery could be deployed in all sorts of circumstances, to sexualize what were really struggles over property.[49] The importance of adultery in the aristocratic context was somewhat different from that of the poor. In both cases it had to do with masculine control over women as, in effect, men's property, but for the aristocracy the genealogical result was paramount. It was lineage, not the women's behavior, that mattered. Thus with the accusations of adultery traded between the Lancastrian and Yorkist sides in the Wars of the Roses, what mattered was not that the women were adulteresses but that their sons were bastards, and the rumors were phrased accordingly. The phrasing is not likely to have resulted from a fear of retaliation if one accused the queen—after all, calling her son a bastard was making the same accusation—or a squeamishness of language, but rather the overwhelming importance of the genealogical connection. Dominic Mancini, for example, reported that Richard of Gloucester persuaded priests to say that Edward IV "was conceived in adultery and in every way was unlike the late Duke of York, whose son he was said to be." He said nothing explicit about the moral character of Cecily Neville, Edward's (and Richard's) mother. Indeed, Mancini claimed that in anger at Edward's clandestine marriage to Elizabeth Wydeville, Duchess Cecily herself claimed that Edward was a child of adultery.[50] When Richard claimed the throne he did so on the grounds that the sons of Edward IV were bastards: according to various accounts, he claimed that their father had been precontracted to another woman and that Queen Elizabeth, who had been married to another man, had been "rather ravished than married" by the king.[51] No statement was made about the queen being a whore, despite the fact that in common parlance a woman who believed she was married to a man, but was not, could be called "his whore."[52] Jane Shore, the alleged mistress of the Marquess of Dorset and/or Lord Hastings, on the other hand, was not an aristocrat, although caught up in the intrigue of Richard III's usurpation, and she could be called "unshampfull and myschevous."[53]

In other discourses, too, there are several registers of language at work, one for those of good birth and another for those below, to describe what is essentially the same behavior. In the Digby *Play of Mary Magdalene*, for example, the Magdalen is depicted as being from a wealthy and noble background. Even while searching for a lover, she takes care to distinguish herself from a lower class of women. When a man in a tavern professes his love for her, she replies, "Why, syr, wene ʒe þat I were a kelle?" ("Why, sir, do you think that I am a loose woman?")[54] Yet she immediately thereafter accepts him as a lover. Her objection is not to the behavior, but to the language; she is a paramour, not a slut.

One purpose of this book is to complicate gender as a category of analysis by focusing on differences among women and men. In the realm of sexuality, were poor women different from their better-off sisters? Medieval society, as we have seen, gave a double answer. The teaching of the church on women's sexuality was largely essentialist: all women were sinful unless they managed to repress their innate lustful urges.[55] To an extent, as we have seen, all levels of medieval society accepted this essentialist teaching. Communities enforced moral norms on their own members, neighbors on their own neighbors or acquaintances. The sexual practices of women of different classes, however, differed by necessity and economic situation, and thus the enforcement of social norms upon them differed as well. From the point of view of the religious discourses that accorded women a negative subjectivity and the secular ones that treated them as objects, women were fundamentally the same. In practical terms, however, poor women's experience was quite different than that of elite women, as were attitudes about them. The tension expressed by Chaucer's Manciple, between women's differences and their similarities, was a pervasive feature of medieval constructions of gender. The different treatment of groups of women belied the essentializing tendencies of medieval views of "women."

Notes

1. "There is no difference, truly, / Between a wife that is of high degree, / If of her body dishonest she be, / And a poor wench, other than this— / If it so happens that they both do amiss— / But that the gentlewoman, in estate above, / She shall be called his lady, as in love; / And, because the other is a poor woman, / She shall be called his wench or his leman. / And, God knows, my own dear brother, / Men lay the one as low as lies the other." Larry D. Benson, gen. ed., *The Riverside Chaucer*, 3rd ed. (Boston, 1987), 284–85, lines 212–22; my translation.

2. See, for example, the tracts on love found in a manuscript made in 1500 for Prince Arthur: Leslie C. Brook, ed., *Two Late Medieval Love Treatises: Heloise's "Art d'Amour" and a Collection of "Demandes d'Amour", Medium Ævum* Monographs 16 (Oxford, 1993); these are examples of the type of materials on love available to the late medieval aristocracy.

3. On Chaucer's readership, see Paul Strohm, *Social Chaucer* (Cambridge, MA, 1989), 47–83.

4. Many historians consider the concept of "class" problematic when applied to the Middle Ages. It is certainly true that the lines of social demarcation were quite different from those that exist today, or that existed when Karl Marx wrote. The same could be said of gender, however, and no one questions that gender is a relevant concept for the Middle Ages. The idea of class, conceived of as broad social groupings rather than as strictly defined and self-conscious categories of proletariat and bourgeoisie, can help illuminate the Middle Ages because it can indicate ways in which studies of other periods may be relevant and applicable. Nevertheless, in order to avoid waving red flags, I shall try to use terms like "social status" or "social position," which I consider roughly synonymous.

5. R. Howard Bloch, *Medieval Misogyny and the Invention of Western Romantic Love* (Chicago, 1991), 5.

6. Sharon Farmer, "Manual Labor, Begging, and Conflicting Gender Expectations in Thirteenth-Century Paris," this volume, argues that sexuality was more of a concern for servants, male and female, than for elite matrons.

7. Arguments about how rape is not about sex but rather about power are not relevant here, even apart from the impossibility of separating the two. Even though in analyzing the behavior we might well want to apply modern categories, we are here analyzing not behavior but the categories themselves in use in the Middle Ages. Medieval society regarded rape as sex as well as violence.

8. Judith Bennett, "'Lesbian-Like' and the Social History of Lesbianisms," *Journal of the History of Sexuality* 9 (2000): 1–24, at 23–24. The present article was completed before Judith Bennett first shared a draft of her article with me in 1998. Had the chronology been reversed, my article may well have been conceptualized rather differently.

9. Ruth Mazo Karras, *Common Women: Prostitution and Sexuality in Medieval England* (New York, 1996).

10. Linda Mahood, *The Magdalenes: Prostitution in the Nineteenth Century* (London, 1990), 3. Cf. Judith R. Walkowitz, *Prostitution and Victorian Society: Women, Class, and the State* (New York, 1980), 192–213; John D'Emilio and Estelle B. Freedman, *Intimate Matters: A History of Sexuality in America* (New York, 1988), esp. 183–86, 194–200.

11. Karras, *Common Women*, 31.

12. Corporation of London Records Office, Letter-Book A, fol. 130v. My translation; that of Reginald R. Sharpe, *Calendar of Letter-Books Preserved among the Archives of the Corporation of the City of London at the Guildhall*, vol. A (London, 1899), 220, translates "femmes de fole vie" as "women of disreputable character" and "bones dames" as "reputable women."

13. Frances Elizabeth Baldwin, *Sumptuary Legislation and Personal Regulation in England*, Johns Hopkins University Studies in Historical and Political Science, Series 44, 1 (Baltimore, MD, 1926). But cf. Diane Owen Hughes, "Sumptuary Law and Social Relations in Renaissance Italy," in *Disputes and Settlements: Law and Human Relations in the West*, ed. John Bossy (Cambridge, 1983), 69–99.

14. James Brundage, "Sumptuary Laws and Prostitution in Late Medieval Italy," *Journal of Medieval History* 13 (1987): 343–55.

15. *Liber Albus*, ed. H. T. Riley, vol. 1 of *Munimenta Gildhallae Londoniensis* (London, 1859), 283; translation available in H. T. Riley, trans., *Liber Albus: The White Book of the City of London* (London, 1861), 247. Corporation of London Records Office, Letter-Book F, fol. 208r; translation available in H. T. Riley, *Memorials of London and London Life in the Thirteenth, Fourteenth, and Fifteenth Centuries* (London, 1868), 267.

16. The data are generally better for regions other than England. Jacques Rossiaud, *Medieval Prostitution*, trans. Lydia G. Cochrane (Oxford, 1988), 32, characterizes the prostitutes at Dijon between 1440 and 1540 as follows: "Daughters of artisans or workingmen, wives of masters or servants, only one out of five came from the more affluent milieux." Richard Trexler provides data for Florence on geographical, though not social, origins, indicating that most prostitutes were not native to the town and may be assumed to be marginal to the community: "La prostitution florentine au xve siècle: patronages et clienteles," *Annales: Économies sociétés civilisations* 36 (1981), 985–88.

17. Corporation of London Records Office, Letter-Book K, fols. 54r and 64r; Ruth Mazo Karras, "The Regulation of Brothels in Later Medieval England," *Signs: A Journal of Women in Culture and Society* 14 (1989): 428. See Karras, *Common Women*, 54–55, for further discussion of laundresses.

18. Corporation of London Records Office, Coroner's Roll F, m. 7; Reginald R. Sharpe, ed., *Calendar of Coroners Rolls of the City of London A.D. 1300–1378* (London, 1913), 197–98.

19. Kate Mertes, *The English Noble Household 1250–1600: Good Governance and Politic Rule* (Oxford, 1988), 57.

20. Cf. Farmer, "Manual Labor."

21. For examples of women who claimed they were forced into prostitution, see London, Public Record Office, C/48/191 (Chancery petition, 1473x1475); Corporation of London Records Office, Letter-Book N, fol. 47v, and Repertory Book 3, fols. 157v–158r (1517); Repertory Book 3, fol. 102r. For further discussion of these and other cases see Karras, *Common Women*, 57–60.

22. Corporation of London Records Office, Letter-Book H, fol. 194v (1385), trans. in Riley, *Memorials*, 484; Letter-Book K, fol. 11v; Corporation of London Records Office, Journal of Court of Common Council 2, fol. 19r; London, Guildhall Library, MS 9064/8, fol. 254v.

23. Corporation of London Records Office, Plea and Memoranda Roll A34, m. 2; trans. David Lorenzo Boyd and Ruth Mazo Karras, "The Interrogation of a Male Transvestite Prostitute in Fourteenth-Century London," *GLQ* 1 (1994): 463.

24. Corporation of London Records Office, Journal 3, fol. 71v.

25. Walter Prevenier, "Violence against Women in a Medieval Metropolis: Paris around 1400," in *Law, Custom, and the Social Fabric in Medieval Europe: Essays in Honor of Bryce Lyon*, ed. Bernard S. Bachrach and David Nicholas, Studies in Medieval Culture 28 (Kalamazoo, 1990), 263–84.

26. Rossiaud, *Medieval Prostitution*, 11–29.

27. From this point one could argue as easily that "all sex was rape" as that "no sex was rape," and indeed some have made this point about the modern period.

28. In surveys, male undergraduates report that they have had sex with an unwilling woman by the use of physical force, which meets the legal definition of rape, but deny that they have ever committed rape (and the women who are victims of such assaults do not call it rape). Mary P. Koss, "Hidden Rape: Sexual Aggression and Victimization in a National Sample of Students in Higher Education," in *Violence in Dating Relationships: Emerging Social Issues*, ed. Maureen Pirog-Good and Jan E. Stets (New York, 1989), 145–68. In several causes célèbres the victim has been a woman of a different social class (a "townie" at an Ivy League school) or race; it is not clear how this affects the men's perceptions of their actions.

29. Helen M. Cam, ed., *The Eyre of London, 14 Edward II, A.D. 1321*, Selden Society 85–86 (London, 1968), 1:87–92. This case is discussed in much greater detail by Barbara Hanawalt, *Of Good and Ill Repute: Gender and Social Control in Medieval England* (New York, 1998), 124–41.

30. John Marshall Carter, *Rape in Medieval England: An Historical and Sociological Study* (Lanham, MD, 1985), 146–47.

31. Hanawalt, *Of Good and Ill Repute*, 129.

32. Andreas Capellanus, *De Amore libri tres*, ed. E. Trojel, 2nd ed. (Munich, 1964), 1:11, 236.

33. Kathryn Gravdal, *Ravishing Maidens: Writing Rape in Medieval French Literature and Law* (Philadelphia, 1991), 105–06. This discussion of the *pastourelle* is drawn from

Gravdal, 104–21. She has a good deal more to say about the *pastourelle* in literary terms than is summarized here.

34. This might well also be true of homosexual behavior, which is not covered in this article. See Michael Rocke, *Forbidden Friendships: Homosexuality and Male Culture in Renaissance Florence* (New York, 1996), 134–47.

35. London, Public Record Office, SC2/191/56, m. 2, m. 2d.

36. Cf. Bronislaw Geremek, *The Margins of Society in Late Medieval Paris*, trans. Jean Birrell (London, 1987), 211–41, esp. 213–14, on Paris.

37. Corporation of London Records Office, Plea and Memoranda Roll A11, m. 5.

38. Corporation of London Records Office, Repertory Book 3, fol. 40r. The history of this case is scattered through fols. 33r–42v, with its conclusion at 49v–50r. Apparently Worsley had been presented as a whore in the wardmote on the testimony of three men, she sued them for defamation in the church court, and they complained to the Court of Aldermen. The Court finally determined that each side should apologize and make a formal release to the other. The defamation case is not found in the extant church court records.

39. P. J. P. Goldberg, "Women in Fifteenth-Century Town Life," in *Towns and Townspeople in the Fifteenth Century*, ed. John A. F. Thompson (Gloucester, 1988), 119, has identified some of the women who so testified as prostitutes (see, e.g., York, Borthwick Institute of Historical Research, D/C AB 1, fol. 84r and 85v, and York Minster Library H2/1, fol. 4v, where Joan Lawrence, one of the witnesses in York, Borthwick Institute of Historical Research, CP.F.111, was accused of multiple adultery and fornication).

40. York, Borthwick Institute of Historical Research, CP.F.111 and CP.F.175. The first of these is translated in R. H. Helmholz, *Marriage Litigation in Medieval England* (London, 1974), 89.

41. Karras, *Common Women*, 66–68.

42. Corporation of London Records Office, Plea and Memoranda Roll A51, m. 2.

43. Edwin Brezette DeWindt, ed., *The Court Rolls of Ramsey, Hepmangrove and Bury, 1268–1600* (Toronto, 1990), fiche 1, 165.

44. L. R. Poos, "Sex, Lies, and the Church Courts of Pre-Reformation England," *Journal of Interdisciplinary History* 25 (1995), 585–607.

45. Margery K. McIntosh, "Finding Language for Misconduct: Jurors in Fifteenth-Century Local Courts," in *Bodies and Disciplines: Intersections of Literature and History in Fifteenth-Century England*, ed. Barbara Hanawalt and David Wallace (Minneapolis, 1996), 87–122.

46. Ruth Mazo Karras, "Two Models, Two Standards: Moral Teaching and Sexual Mores," in *Bodies and Disciplines*, ed. Hanawalt and Wallace, 131–32 and n. 56; see also Richard Wunderli, *London Church Courts and Society on the Eve of the Reformation* (Cambridge, MA, 1981), 76 and 78, and Poos, "Sex, Lies, and the Church Courts," 594–600.

47. Michael M. Sheehan, "Theory and Practice: Marriage of the Unfree and Poor in Medieval Society," *Mediaeval Studies* 50 (1988): 484–87; L. R. Poos, *A Rural Society After the Black Death: Essex, 1350–1525* (Cambridge, 1991), 135–40.

48. There are, for example, very few wills of prostitutes that would give some indication as to wealth and hence social status. Karras, *Common Women*, 97.

49. Paul Strohm, *Hochon's Arrow: The Social Imagination of Fourteenth-Century Texts* (Princeton, NJ, 1992), 121–44.

50. Dominic Mancini, *The Usurpation of Richard III*, trans. C. A. J. Armstrong, 2nd ed. (Oxford, 1969), 94–95, 60–63.

51. Ingulf, *Chronicle of the Abbey of Croyland*, trans. H. T. Riley (London, 1854), 489; Mancini, *Usurpation of Richard III*, 96–97. See Alison Hanham, *Richard III and His Early Historians 1483–1535* (Oxford, 1975), 113, for the relation among these allegations.

52. E.g., York, Borthwick Institute of Historical Research, CP.F.99 (a marriage case in which witnesses testified that Henry Helwys had reproached Alice Newton with being "his whore and not his wife" because he had previously contracted with another).

53. "De proclamationibus faciendis pro morum reformatione," 1483, in Thomas Rymer, *Foedera, Conventiones, Literae, et cujuscunque generis acta publica*, vol. 12 (London, 1727), 204.

54. Donald C. Baker, John L. Murphy, and Louis B. Hall, eds., *The Late Medieval Religious Plays of Bodleian MS Digby 133 and E Museo 160*, Early English Text Society 283 (Oxford, 1982), 41, line 520. The editors translate the word "kelle" as "prostitute" (251), but they have derived this meaning entirely from context. They note that it means "clearly a 'loose woman'"; I find no warrant to get any more specific than that and translate it as "prostitute." See Sherman Kuhn, ed., *Middle English Dictionary* (Ann Arbor, MI, 1956), s.v. "kelis." The clear implication is that she does not want to be taken for someone of low status.

55. Sharon Farmer argues in "'It Is Not Good that [Wo]man Should Be Alone': Elite Discussions of Single Women in High Medieval Paris," in *Singlewomen in the European Past, 1250–1800*, ed. Judith M. Bennett and Amy Froide (Philadelphia, 1999), that Humbert of Romans, for example, associates lust especially with lower-class women. However, much of the later medieval exemplum literature does not make this distinction. See, e.g, Ruth Mazo Karras, "Misogyny and the Medieval Exemplum: Gendered Sin in John of Bromyard's *Summa Praedicantium*," *Traditio* 47 (1992): 233–57.

8

RE-ORIENTING DESIRE:
WRITING ON GENDER TROUBLE IN
FOURTEENTH-CENTURY EGYPT

MICHAEL UEBEL

When, over ten years ago now, the AIDS crisis was labeled "an epidemic of signification,"[1] critical attention was drawn to the fantasy spectacle of disease as the absolute borderline between health and unhealth, subjectivity and nonsubjectivity. Queer lifestyles were so blatantly put on display for the scrutiny of straight spectators that, as one commentator remarked, "when they come to write the history of AIDS, socio-ethnologists will have to decide whether the 'practitioners' of homosexuality or its heterosexual 'onlookers' have been more spectacular in their extravagance."[2] For at stake in this decision concerning how to handle history is the spectacular way that certain sexual practices are constructed as *extravagant*, a word, Jonathan Dollimore reminds us, that immediately signals perversity and deviance from the norm.[3] Posing the question of history here as a split between homosexual practice and heterosexual inspection assumes that the specter of deviance haunting both extravagant acts is itself the cause of introspection. Deviance, we assume, somehow inhabits the core of identity. In the case of the heterosexual spectator, the difference or deviance that engages introspection functions as the defensive tactic of disavowed, or failed, introspection. What the heterosexual subject cannot tolerate is the acknowledgment that its very constitution crucially depends on the enjoyment of the deviant spectacle. This is because, as this essay will suggest, any construction of selfhood based on the spectacle of extravagant differences in sexuality is so fully reciprocated as to be open to its own radical undoing. In, or as, this very failure, the contemplative subject of extravagance constitutes itself in a scene of "gender trouble."[4]

This essay considers how fourteenth-century Egypt, in the hands of western crusade apologists, became a scene of "gender trouble," a fantasy space wherein religious and racial differences were mapped onto sex and gender differences. In this way, the heterosexual-homosexual binary that the apologists constructed was interdependent with the effort to justify a Christian-Muslim political opposition. Demonizing the homosexual Saracen, the male Christian crusader fantasied scenes of desire called into being by the very otherness over against which he asserted himself.

Otherness, I argue, causes desire, precisely because it is the nature of intersubjective fantasy to search for the origins and effects of a desire that originates from elsewhere, from outside the self. Anti-homosexual discourses, we will see, have the effect of modeling desire as a return to or recuperation of the self, a possible antidote to the centrifugality of desire. What ensues, however, is a kind of gender and identity trouble that dramatically poses the problem of inveterately multiform desire. Each of the following three sections takes up the problem of desire and the possibility of recuperation and consolidation of self-identity.

Orientalist Desire and the Fantasy of Recovery

In writing on the East, surely the most familiar term given to the process whereby the theorist fashions herself through the otherness she observes, and inevitably comes to recognize as cause of her desire, is Edward Said's "orientalism." Said's powerful discussion of how western knowledges have shaped and unshaped the Orient, turning it into a theater onto which are projected fantasies of cultural dominance and domestication, has, arguably, lost little of its critical force over the last twenty years.[5] Certainly, for those working in medieval studies, it was Said who crucially opened up—and continues to enable—critical analysis of those gestures of power and knowledge that deny the other autonomy. Across disciplines, "orientalism" has come to designate that process of silencing the other's voice whereby the irrevocable assumption is made that others are incapable of describing themselves. Annihilating the power of self-description, according to Said, can only eventuate in squelching empirical reality, forcing reality to yield to the relentless "battery of desires, repressions, investments, and projections"[6] that comprise western fantasies of the East. What is at stake here, we must note, is nothing less than the authenticity of lived reality, or, more exactly, identifying who is authorized to determine what is authentic and what is not.[7]

If the question of such authority is to be settled, it is so around the issue of libidinal investment: the point at which imaginary attachment to a particular mode of behavior or to a special cultural object empowers one to identify and claim the authentic—the "real thing"—over against, say, the perverse or pathological. Heterosexuals, for example, can fantasmically justify their lifestyle as being unproblematically true, and thus authentic, precisely because they imagine finding everywhere around them—in the Bible, in the media, in institutions such as marriage, family, and law—its ideological confirmation.[8] Yet this kind of heterosexual confidence is grossly tautological since it is the nature of ideology to inherit and inhabit the form of the imaginary, in fact, to embody all sorts of imagined, often conflicting and overlapping, identifications. My present investigation of desire and homosexuality in medieval Egypt will attend to the libidinal imaginary of two fourteenth-century crusade apologies. The question before us concerns the problem of libidinal investment: how does the intersubjective imaginary content of desire (the mingled forms of coincidental desires and ideological fantasms) propel the late crusade project? I will be interested in the ways in which the medieval Arabic Orient is actively reauthenticated, through the logic of perversion, as a set of western representational codes and protocols.[9] Here another question obtrudes: is there a way in which occidental discourse, by imputing to the other all kinds of perversity, comes to pervert systematically its own epistemological foundations? And further: what are the implications for historicism of epistemological self-perversion?

To begin to answer, however, is to rethink Said's account of western fantasy and epistemology in the hope that sensitivity to the psychic issues underpinning the invention of culture is not sacrificed. Texts such as William of Adam's crusade apology, *De modo Sarracenos extirpandi* (On the means of rooting out the Saracens) and Marino Sanudo's *Liber*

secretorum fidelium crucis super terrae sanctae recuperatione et conservatione
(Book of the secrets of the true cross concerning the recovery and salvation of the Holy Land) add a crucial psychic dimension to the phenomenon of orientalism by making graphic an aspect of the Orient's "exotic"
allure that Said for the most part elides: namely, its homoerotic promise.
As we will see, William and Marino figure homosexuality in order to
arouse the moral disgust of their readers toward oriental perversities more
generally. Of course, in this, William's and Marino's polemics are not
unique. In the West, since about the late tenth century on, sexual perversity, particularly sodomitical practice, was taken to be the most repellent
aspect of Muslim society, and thus it became persistently emblematic of
an entire culture.[10] Curiously, though, Said stops short of elaborating
the full implications of orientalist sexuality: "Why the Orient seems still
to suggest not only fecundity but sexual promise (and threat) . . . is not
the province of my analysis here, alas, despite its frequently noted appearance."[11] Yet, within the experience of medieval occidental culture,
the Orient's "sexual promise (and threat)" to which Said alludes are already inescapably tied to the desire and dread underwriting an encounter
with male homosexuality.[12] The Arab other represents radical difference,
an at once attractive and threatening sexual *possibility*. It is this possibility of homosexual encounter, as Joseph A. Boone has argued in a compelling reading of modernist travel narratives concerning the Arabic
Orient, that "underwrites and at times even explains the historical appeal of orientalism as an occidental mode of male perception, appropri-
ation, and control."[13] Indeed, the project of orientalism seems, from the
point of its inception, a deeply masculinist one, a frenzied manifestation
of the doubled forces of tyranny and fascination, intolerance and yearning.

The fantasy of recovering the Holy Land is itself a masculinist response to the perceived threat of homosexual invasion. One of the *Ur*-
documents of the crusades, a forged letter from Alexius I Comnenus to
Count Robert of Flanders circulating before 1098, tells of the many sexual atrocities supposedly committed by the advancing infidels. The letter's catalogue of Muslim abuses builds to the *nefarium peccatum* (abominable sin) of sodomy:

> But what next? We move on to worse things. Men of every age
> and rank—that is, boys, adolescents, young men, old men, no-
> bles, servants, and, what is worse and more wicked, clerics and

monks, and even, alas and for shame! something which from
the beginning of time has never been spoken or heard of, bish-
ops—have been degraded by the sin of sodomy. They have already killed one bishop with this abominable sin.[14]

The death of a bishop by sodomy quite obviously makes for great propaganda.[15] As a fantasmic threat to all strata of men, oriental sodomy could
be seen as a special kind of weapon, one inimical to both masculinity
and Christianity. Guibert of Nogent's citation and elaboration of the letter accentuate what is most threatening about infidel desire—its refusal
of women as sexual objects:

> And while they do not spare the feminine sex—which neverthe-
> less might be excused by virtue of its agreement with nature—
> they go on to the masculine, with [even] animality and the laws
> of humanity broken. From which point, that impudence, which
> raged against the ordinary and the worst [of men], spread, so
> that it is to be cursed by each and, in the greatness of its shame-
> ful crime, [is] almost intolerable to hearing: he says that they
> killed a certain bishop by means of sodomitical abuse. And how
> might this appetite *[libido]*—headlong and standing out com-
> pletely from all other madnesses, which, always fleeing counsel
> and modesty, is driven by a perpetual impetus, and by however
> much it is more frequently extinguished, by that much repeat-
> edly is its flame more briskly kindled—temper itself toward hu-
> man affairs, which is dirty with sexual minglings unheard of for
> brute animals and forbidden to Christian sight? And although
> it is allowed the wretches, in their own opinion, to have many
> women, this is accounted little by them unless dignity is also
> sullied in the pigsty of such filth with men.[16]

Guibert's invective makes it clear that sodomitical desire not only trans-
gresses the limits of human culture, but that, precisely because it lacks a
fixed, culturally sanctioned object (woman), it is endlessly mobile, ob-
scene, and contaminative. Such uncontainable and self-renewing desire,
in other words, lacks a gravitational center and, through its centrifugality,
poses a special threat to the very idea of desire as object-oriented. Libido
emerges as multiple in both object and aim. The spectacle of such poly-

morphous desire, which should remain "forbidden to Christian sight," signifies nothing less than what must be overlooked if recovery of the center and goal of all Christian endeavor—the Holy Land—is ever to take place. But what becomes clear is that, while such desire might be overlooked, labeled over, and effectively sanitized with classificatory language, it cannot be overcome or erased. Indeed, it returns to haunt the very discourses determined to eradicate it. As we will see, the crusade project, as a fantasy of retrieval, contains self-destructive residues of its crucial admission that desire is inveterately multiform. It is as if Guy Hocquenghem's claim for homosexuality's place in capitalist culture should give us pause to rethink medieval culture's fascination with perverse desire: "Every effort to isolate, explain, reduce the contaminated homosexual simply helps to place him at the centre of waking dreams."[17]

MEDIEVALIST DESIRES AND THE FANTASY OF RECOVERY

> Erudition becomes the refuge of many a failed Oedipus.
> —Paul Zumthor, *Speaking of the Middle Ages*

There is another, closely related, "waking dream" we must momentarily pause over: the medievalist's own fantasmic investment in retrieval. In his *Parlez du moyen âge,* a trenchant reading of the institutional and philosophical status of French medievalism, Paul Zumthor locates desire at the heart of literary historical inquiry. "Every relationship we maintain with a text," Zumthor observes, "involves some latent eroticism.... Thus, the personal factor in our studies is defined primarily within the order of desire." "My 'truth,'" he continues, "implicates *me* at the same time as *my* object—though we must not, at any moment, mistake ourselves; that trust is only a place of transition: between me and an Other, made believable, despite absence, by my discourse; placed in me and in you to whom I speak while remaining irrevocably hidden."[18] For Zumthor a delicate act of trust, conceptualizing historical alterity, follows, first, from the acknowledgment of the unavoidable, silent distance across which "truth" is projected, and, second, from a reading of that distance as structured by a matrix of desires, not the least of which is the personal wish to speak, the desire to make known. Retrieval of the past, then, necessitates a willingness to inhabit the transitional and fantasmic space of our own, sometimes inexpressible, desires. On Zumthor's formulation, reading alterity must involve acute attention to inner relays of desire, understood *subjectively*, in terms of the needs, wants, anxieties, and satisfactions experienced by—and represented in the image of—the reader and her object.

It is around the centrality of desire as found in the critical discourse of alterity that we might provisionally describe the interpretative strategy of historicizing under the sign of enjoyment. In medieval studies, the most well-known formulation of alterity is Hans Robert Jauss's, in an article and collection of essays both entitled "The Alterity and Modernity of Medieval Literature" (1979; 1977). Recall that here Jauss outlines a three-step hermeneutic that begins with private aesthetic pleasure (in what Zumthor calls "the order of desire"), works through the "surprising otherness" of the object by reconstructing the medieval reader's "horizon of expectations," and finds its telos in building a "bridge" between contemporary reader and text, in which is discerned the "model character" of medieval literary production.[19] The hermeneutic facilitates "the pleasurable discovery of the other." It is important to note that this quest for knowledge of the other, motivated by desire for pleasure, produces the eroticism Zumthor locates at the heart of the historical recuperative enterprise.[20] But it is also a quest for the self in, and in place of, the other—a process that may be no less passionate. The meaning of medieval texts, Jauss writes, is only "obtained by a *reflective* passage through its alterity."[21] The image of specularity here underscores the notion that the modern self is found in the reflection of the historical other. The scholar passes through a kind of jubilant mirror stage[22] in which she "discover[s] the modernity of medieval literature in its alterity"[23] as part of the ultimate project of recovering the so-called lost *Welt-Modell*, or world-model. She necessarily travels in a circuit: into the past on the way to the future.

In at least one crucial way, Jauss's hermeneutic eludes Said's critique of "orientalist" appropriations of alterity. Both theorists view alterity as the matrix of alien forces that provides a determinative influence upon subjectivity, either by means of a constructed "world-model" or of a narcissistic delimitation on meaning. Jauss's three steps privilege the modern self by asserting a vital continuity between the historical other and the modern reader, a "fusion" allowing for the rehabilitation of modernity and, it is hoped, for the renewal of medieval studies. While Said might very well warn against such bridge building as inescapably narcissistic, even intolerantly imperial, he nevertheless, like Jauss, tends to see alterity as designating the historical and ideological field *through* which selfhood is fashioned.[24] It is alterity that constantly repositions the self in relation to larger social forces such as political and epistemological codes, at the same time that it reorients the self to the field of desire. So whereas Jauss's aesthetics of alterity positions readers in relation to historically specific generic codes and an inclusive "world-model," Said's orientalism places the western orientalist in relation to the taxonomic imagination of imperialism. Both theories rely, then, on seeing subjectivity as unavoidably conditioned by its place in, or relation to, a web of categorical constructions. Yet what constitutes subjectivity is purely a feature of the moment in which the subject is framed. Thus medieval literary genres *appear* to work just like the orientalist's encyclopedia: both mark out the ways in which individual experience is put in the service of ideology. To recognize, however, how this actually takes place is to reflect upon the complex, often momentary, libidinal investments inherent in and sublimated through the historicist enterprise.

There is, I believe, a way, within historicist projects such as medievalism, of talking about highly charged kinds of otherness that, like the scholar's refound past, are inscribed with subjective states of desire and enjoyment. Louise Fradenburg's recent work on "enjoying the Middle Ages" is a brilliant intervention into what she sees as a tendency within medievalism (and beyond) to ignore the deep relation between practices of knowledge and the logics of passion, *jouissance,* and oblativity.[25] Rhetorics of need and productivity, she argues, occlude pleasure and desire, breeding suspicion of the pleasures inherent in identification with otherness. In place of utility and the myth of ascesis as indices of value within historicism, Fradenburg substitutes the Lacanian notion of ethical relationality, "our responsibilization of ourselves in relation to others, [which] is not an effect of the sacrifice of a putatively more fundamental desire for the comforts of sameness, but is itself a way of structuring desire—enabled by the form of desire *as* the desire of the other."[26] Radiating both spatially and temporally, desire, qua desire of the other, opens up the subject to history in its radical contingency and possibility. Indeed, as Lacan indicates, the other, in its mirroring function, structures the temporal process of subjectivization around a fundamental misrecognition of what is imagined as originary and intrinsic, namely, the image of the other.[27] The drama of the nascent subject is, in some sense, that of an original desire to retrieve the other already within.

I will pick up only this Lacanian thread of Fradenburg's richly textured argument in order to underscore the transferential dynamics of historicity.[28] History, she reminds us, is an "erogenous zone," and as such, I would emphasize, it is subject to the same stimulations, repressions, and reterritorializations as its somatic counterpart. In fact it is hard to imagine history apart from that of body-space,[29] especially that of our own sensitive erogenous zones. The kind of historicism Fradenburg calls for (and indeed practices), and to which I am (re)calling us, manages, however, to elude the transferential trap that arises when historicism attempts to formulate identity.[30] Mark Bracher, for instance, has recently identified in current historicisms what he believes to be a crippling transferential relation to the "Great Other," Lacan's term for the authoritative person or institution who is "presumed to know" the secret of desire and enjoyment. For Bracher, any historicism necessitates engaging with one's own desires, but *only as they exist in an external, represented form.* In studying the other's desire, we sacrifice attention to our own, and thus, he contends, fail to expose the other's deficiency, "the Other's failure to constitute an absolute, transcendental ground for being or truth and hence for one's own identity and jouissance."[31]

I am suggesting that in fact the historicist passion for retrieval constitutes a primary way to shake off and oppose the sacrificial demands of the Great Other. The affective mode of retrieval addresses itself to a series of individual issues such as the authority and anxieties of the self, the possibilities and repressions of erotic agency, and the genres of pleasure and pain. It historicizes private desire by focusing on the ways in which *jouissance* conditions signification and sensation (to become, in Lacan's pun, *joui-sens*). The practice of retrieval offers, in short, the possibility of recasting historicism in terms of the psychoanalytic process, by recognizing that unconscious desires have their historical analogues. Since, in the process of retrieval, emphasizing contextual determinants of meaning always risks effacing subjective desires, fantasies, anxieties, and repressions, we must attend all the more closely to the way some historical structures of "social logic" *have indeed effaced* the events of personal logic. It is not then a matter of excavating personal events from the debris of social forms, but a matter of making the analogies that will allow us to link, say, private desiring with communal mythmaking. If Bracher's general intuition is right, that historicizing too often channels desire away from the subject, then becoming the "failed Oedipus" Zumthor postulates as a condition of learning may be exactly what is required to restore the power to confer utopic attraction or redemptive ideality upon the historical other.

The obvious task, then, is to read desire across the historical matrix, looking for those historical focal points wherein it is possible to scrutinize transitions between past and present libidinal and epistemological investments. The reading I will construct of William of Adam's *De modo Sarracenos extirpandi* and Marino Sanudo's *Liber secretorum fidelium crucis* harmonizes with Jonathan Dollimore's attempt to recover what he calls "the lost histories of perversion,"[32] or culturally central expressions and classifications of what is marginal, illegitimate, negative, perverse. Dollimore's project, like mine, does not concern recovery of "repressed" elements in the form of some originary plenitude, but rather is liberatory, or utopic, in another, more radical sense. Lost histories of perversion dramatize the intimate linkage of personal pathology and political activity by reanimating dissident desires, desires that emerge, dialectically, within the dominant social order.[33] Once we recognize, through the retrieval work of historicism, the intense proximity of otherness to self-identity, the other, as cause of desire, shields us from the temptations of a narcissism aimed at conserving libido at the cost of "displacing it into the image of a seamless (timeless) unity—the ego as substantial self-identity enduring through all change."[34] However, as I hint above, this refusal to disavow the proximity of alterity carries with it certain epistemological risk. As the object of analysis shifts from otherness per se to the psychic operations—the defensive splitting, fetishism, and phobia—that work to defend and consolidate self-identity, the very systems of knowledge used to produce a safe, seamless self begin to come undone. They crumble into what Foucault calls multiple "systems of the transgressive," separate fields of *savoir* wherein deviations from the norm "coincide neither with the illegal nor the criminal, neither with the revolutionary, the monstrous nor the abnormal, not even with the sum total of all of these deviant forms; but each of these terms designates at least an angle."[35] Becoming symbolically untethered, deviance stresses its own epistemological moorings and its classificatory straitjackets.

EGYPTIAN DESIRE AND THE
FANTASY OF RETRIEVAL

Western accounts of Islam in the Middle Ages—a field of texts including crusade chronicles, *itineraria*, translations and commentaries, *miribilia*-lists, massive polemic and propaganda—display shifting attitudes, multiple angles, toward the "perverse" Muslim other, perverse because at once unknown and threatening. According to the ambivalent logic of fetishism, Islam was imagined as barring the way to enjoyment of the Holy Land, as arresting retrieval of the "umbilicus terrae," source of Christian sustenance,[36] *at the same time* it kept alive the desire for recovery. The persistence of this way of imagining Islam, and even Islam's antidote (Prester John's Indian utopia[37]), testifies to its deeply perverse function.[38] It was *necessary* to believe that the source of happiness was blocked, not in order to intensify desire, but so that it was possible to defend against the notion that without such blockage the object of desire was directly attainable.[39] Throughout the Middle Ages, direct access to the Holy Land would be endlessly deferred, this much is clear from travel narratives and *miribilia*-texts such as the *Letter of Prester John* (ca. 1150) alone.[40] For the medieval western imaginary, Islam must represent a perennial gray area, blocking access to the desired object by ensuring and extending its instability as a fully apprehended object.[41]

Grasping the refractory other often involved a process of reduction whereby unsettling alterity was converted to orderly similarity. Eulogius and Paul Alvarus, the first in the West (ca. 850) to develop a coherent vision of the Muslim enemy, fantasmically framed Arab alterity in the familiar and inevitable terms of Christian apocalypse.[42] According to R. W. Southern, Islam epitomized alterity in the Middle Ages: "the existence of Islam was the most far-reaching problem in medieval Christendom," a danger that was at once "unpredictable and immeasurable."[43] Yet the salient image of Islam throughout the Middle Ages was that of an explosively carnal and sadistic religion. Writers around the time of the first and second crusades, such as William of Malmesbury, Guibert of Nogent, Alain of Lille, and Peter the Venerable, put forward moral and historical arguments that set in place a mighty two-pronged polemic against Islam, described by Norman Daniel as responses to the intertwined images of immorality and force. This willingness to conflate violence, power, and sexuality indelibly marks western polemical writings.

So, for example, contentions such as the following were commonplace: Muhammed is a false prophet, murderer, and sodomite, whose power depends on deception and is proliferated both by violence and permission to his followers for the sexual perversities in which he himself indulges. Islam, it was maintained, set out to destroy Christendom with the two-edged sword of sexual license and aggression.[44]

A weapon and phallus in one, that sword found its incarnation in the aggressive, sodomitical Arab. The vice of sodomy, it was asserted, is not only tolerated in Muslim society, but actively encouraged and openly practiced. The image of aggressive homosexual desire in fact has its origins in anti-Islamic literature, for example, the well-known tenth-century legend of St. Pelagius as told by Hrotsvit of Gandersheim. In this legend, the alleged homosexual desire of the Muslim other, embedded in religious discourse in order to emphasize both the alterity of the rival religion and the power and necessity of Christian martyrdom, becomes the figure for a deeper anxiety: the pollution of one faith by another, across bodily boundaries. In refusing the physical advances of the caliph, Pelagius is reminded that, within Muslim law, he is guilty of blasphemy. When an attempt is made to kiss Pelagius a second time, the caliph receives a punch to the nose "such that immediately blood flowing from the resulting wound polluted his beard and even drenched his clothes."[45] The king ends up wearing the violent signs of his disrespect for the sanctity of boundaries, corporeal and religious. In one way, the punch dramatizes the inability of the caliph to contain his bodily flows, the signifiers of his unarrestable desire to possess the attractive Pelagius. Aggressive infidel same-sex desire is seen as particularly repugnant since it represents the antithesis of ideal Christian charity and chastity. Indeed, after the fateful punch that causes Pelagius to be catapulted over the city walls, Hrotsvit's narrative turns to issues of bodily integrity as they bear on the problem of Christian greed (the fishermen who collect and restore Pelagius's body only because they can sell it to the church) and chastity (the testing of corporeal integrity when Pelagius's body becomes a holy relic). Infidel desire was figured as both an insult to and test for Christian innocence.

The sexual abuse of Christian innocents figures prominently in the early-fourteenth-century propaganda tracts of William of Adam and Marino Sanudo. William, born in France according to the *Scriptores ordinis Praedicatorum*[46] (other authors claim he was born in Antivari, Albania[47]), was one of six Dominican missionaries sent to Persia by Pope John XXII. On the first of June, 1323, William succeeded one of his fellow Dominicans as Archbishop of Soltanieh, a town near the Caspian Sea in northern Iran. William died in 1329. Not much else is known of him. Dating his polemical tract is difficult; most likely it was written in Europe before 1318, the year he was dispatched to the hinterland. More, however, is known about Marino Sanudo, a scion of Venetian high nobility.[48] Born in Venice around 1270, Marino lived for about two years (1285–86) in Acre before he was to become an active businessman. After his attachment to the court of Palermo in 1300, Marino spent the next four years in Rome, where he served as the protégé of Richard of Siena, then Cardinal of St. Eustace, before the Roman curia was moved to Avignon in 1305. The following year, and until 1309, Marino worked on a short proposal to the pontifical curia in the name of recuperating the Holy Land. Called *Conditiones Terrae Sanctae,* this treatise would eventually become the first book of the tripartite *Liber secretorum fidelium crucis,* finally presented to John XXII on 24 September 1321. In 1323, Marino presented a copy to Charles IV of France. The papal commission appointed to examine proposals for recovering the Holy Land, though evidently impressed with Marino's plan, ended up shelving it along with similar tracts.[49]

At the time William and Marino were writing, Europe had all but lost its taste for crusading, which seemed to offer little advantage, mundane or spiritual. After the fall of Acre in 1291, and after the last Latin kingdom was decimated, commercial enterprises supplanted crusading interests. Norman Daniel notes that "merchant communities took the place of crusading feudatories; or, more exactly, the merchant communities and the groups of mercenary soldiers found a new relation with the Arab world, as tolerated aliens."[50] Despite papal prohibitions, exorbitant taxes, and boycotts, the trade in luxury goods and slaves flourished.[51] Both William and Marino emphasized the necessity of putting an end to such trade, a commerce established for the most part by treaty between European and Arab communities.[52] Acknowledging the futility of all-out war, thirteenth-century crusade plans called for new kinds of economic warfare designed to cripple Egypt's economy by means of naval blockading and trade embargoes. As the main transit country for commerce with the East, Egypt, it was imagined, could only be crippled if the country's imports, as well as exports, were interrupted.[53] For William and Marino, goods flowing into Egypt presented the most urgent problems, not only because most of these goods were European, and thus it would be hard to overcome the opposition of Christian merchants, but because the goods had to be shown to have special military uses.[54] William and Marino thus focused their attention on the slaves being shipped to Egypt. Whereas by the thirteenth century a slave had become a luxury in western Europe,[55] slavery in the Arab world, particularly Mamluk Egypt, was commonplace. Slaves were sought as harem inmates, servants, agricultural laborers, and, chiefly, as recruits for the Mamluk army. William believed that if Egypt could be forced to rely on its own non-military population, enervated as it was by excessive vice,[56] then its fall would be swift and decisive.

William thus opens his tract with a scathing invective against the Christian merchants who pander to the homosexual lust of the Saracens. By means of these "ministros inferni, falsos christianos" ("false Christians, servants of the devil"), Egypt is supplied with its most precious commodity—boys who, it is claimed, will reinvigorate a debilitated land "that devours and consumes its own inhabitants" through practices of abortion.[57] This fantasy of regeneration occupies William and Marino, whose sexual panic is filtered through both a larithmic and a moral calculus. "Speaking to itself in the delirium of its repressed others,"[58] the fantasy of replenishment contains the logical seeds of its own destruction by calling attention to a sexual practice that is not generative. Yet perhaps in this very contradiction the secret of homophobic fantasy resides: a fantasy that is not so much a matter of projecting onto the other some unacknowledged or disavowable aspects of the self, but rather of organizing and orienting identity before a fantasmic other who never ceases to make demands. Chief among these demands is the open-ended question of the very nature of the other's impinging desire.[59] What do Saracens really want from Christians? And why do Christians seem to provide so readily exactly what this other desires? Why do Saracen desires always appear potentially satisfied, while Christian desires go unsatisfied? Posing these questions alone provides a structured response to threatening homosexual desire. These questions, in other words, unearth the meaning of a complex social event such as the reputed homosexually abusive slave trade, at the same time that they provide formulae according to which Christian desire can be (properly) conducted and thought.

William's and Marino's treatises are, I am suggesting, attempts to solve such riddles through the elaborate staging of desire.[60] In order to

provide an answer to the enigma of the other's desires, a flash point
must be articulated, a point at which desire is catalyzed and contested.
William and Marino find this flash point in the slaves who become the
objects of oriental desire.[61] The fantasmic approach to demonized sexuality, to the homosexual desire for attractively commodified slave boys
employed as catamites, renders visible sodomitical practice, in ways that
partially displace sodomy onto other kinds of deviation and threat. Let
us consider William's depiction of effeminate men in the mise en scène
of homoerotic commodification:

> In the Saracen sect any sexual act at all is not only not forbid-
> den, but permitted and praised. So, in addition to innumerable
> prostitutes, who are among them, there are a great number of
> effeminate men who shave their beards, paint their own faces,
> put on women's clothes, wear bracelets on their arms and feet
> and gold twisted collars around their necks, just as women do,
> and adorn their chests with jewels. Thus selling themselves into
> sin, they weaken and expose their bodies: men with men doing
> that which is disgraceful (unsightly), they receive in themselves
> the recompense of their sin and error.[62] Therefore the Saracens,
> oblivious to human dignity, are shamelessly attracted to those
> effeminates, and live with them just as with us a husband and
> wife cohabitate publicly. Furthermore—and this is a sin above
> all sins—our own catholics, enemies of justice, are turning to-
> ward this sin among the Saracens, by knowingly assenting to it
> and preparing the way to and incentive for this sin. And when
> they are able to find some boy, Christian or tartar, suitable in
> body, as he is dispatched for sale, no supplication is for them
> too dear for the sake of those whom, more apt to total sinful-
> ness of this sort, they seek. After they buy them, like a statue,
> they are dressed in silk and covered in gold, their bodies and
> faces are washed often in baths and other washings. And they
> are fed sumptuous meals and delicate beverages to make them
> plumper, pinker, and more voluptuous, and thus they appear
> more alluring and apt to satisfy the full lust of the Saracens.
> And when the libidinous, vile, and abominable men, the Sara-
> cens, corrupters of human nature, see the boys, they immedi-

ately burn with lust for them and, like mad dogs, race to buy the boys for themselves so that they can have their evil way with them.[63]

At one level, William's objection to the slave trade expresses multiple fears and anxieties displaced onto the cross-dressed bodies of the "effeminate youths" and the lusty Arabs who allegedly corrupt them.[64] There is, foremost, the unavoidable context for William's portrait of Saracen perversion, namely, a non-sexual fear of Saracen violence and power. A trade embargo imposed on the enemy, as William and Marino urge, would in fact reduce Mamluk power, which is largely foreign and military; but Muslim military strength had already proved itself almost invulnerable. The sack of Alexandria in 1365, for instance, shows that real damage could be done to Egypt without weakening it enough to make Christian conquest possible. A recuperation treatise such as *De modo Sarracenos extirpandi*, I would suggest, is thus the product of a moment of crisis in western Christendom. Facing the hopelessness of a military crusade, the failure of economic boycotts and restrictions, and the threat of the recently converted Mongols, William activates an enduring mythology in order to displace crisis onto the Egyptian other. The non-sexual fear of force is easily displaced onto the sodomite, an "effeminate" transgressor whose deviance is intimately connected to another kind of transgression, Arab military conquest.[65] Oliver of Paderborn, for instance, in his *Historia* of the Fifth Crusade (1217–22), a crusade directed against Egypt, describes the Saracen threat as combining "terror mundanus" and "voluptas carnalis."[66]

A second kind of displaced anxiety is apparent from the way in which religious transgression is associated with reputed homosexual perversion. The equation of heterodoxy and sexual deviance has a long history, far too long to trace here,[67] yet suffice it to say that the link between sodomy and heresy was used, increasingly in the thirteenth and fourteenth centuries, by the forces of the Inquisition to root out nonconformers.[68] (Indeed, the religious order to which William belonged was invested with the administration of the Inquisition.) The standard argument can be made that the nonconformity perceived here as internal deviance is refigured as foreign threat. William in this sense acts as a kind of Inquisitor of the imaginary, actively policing the symbolic border between what is normal and abnormal, dignified and shameless, ascetic and immoderate. The boundary between the ideal of Christian asceticism and chastity and the infidel's uncurbed and easily satisfied desires marks, then, more than a clash of religious ideologies. The incommensurability of the two suggests rather a polemic at the heart of western medieval self-identity, that is, the ubiquitous conflict between ascetic imperative and the countervailing forces of desire itself.

At another level, however, William's fantasy of the preparation and commerce of catamites dressed in silks, ornamented, washed, and fed with "sumptuous meals and delicate beverages to make them plumper, pinker, and more voluptuous" conveys something of the radically intersubjective nature of oriental sex fantasies. The crucial question here is, for whose gaze is the spectacle of the washed and succulent boys being offered? We note that the visual objectifications taking place here are multilayered. The boys, themselves objects of a double Saracen and Christian gaze, are transformed, through verbal play, into their own digestible objects. The washing of the boys replicates the "washing" of the delicacies they consume: *lautis cibariis,* literally "washed foods," or figuratively "sumptuous or elegant foods." Boys are figured as the edible objects of "mad" Saracen sexual hunger, but only after the boys are figured as consumers themselves. William would seem to be offering a spectacle of satisfied consumption, within another spectacle of satisfied consumption, in order to draw attention here to the contagious nature of homosexual desire. The scene of homosexual desires, folded into a narrative of hunger and satisfaction, puts in motion an intersubjective libidinal fantasy wherein the object of this fantasy is precisely, and only, what Saracens, fascinated by the boys, see in all Christians. In the contagious coincidence of Saracen and Christian desire, the boys do not function as the fantasmic point at which desires intersect, but rather that potential that the Saracens "see" in Christians. What is fantasized is fascination itself, or better, fascination in the self. Put another way, what is staged is the desire that makes the self fascinating.

A crucial feature of this intersubjective fantasy is William's emphasis on the speed and ease with which Saracens indulge their carnality. Egypt is imagined as an arena of infinite, yet ultimately fulfilled, desire, a land where desire yields to pure enjoyment. What, in some sense, has been excluded by Christian ascetic imperative returns not as William's own desire but as that which, within the libidinal economy of recuperative crusade, functions as a key component of identity consolidation, that is, enjoyment itself as a way of organizing identity. By coming to terms with Saracen desire, medieval Christianity can more easily map its own.[69] At first approach, such a map seems simple: William orients us to the zones of sexual perversion by merging several binaries. Not surprisingly, the opposition masculine/homosexual conflates two other violently hierarchical pairings, masculine/feminine and hetero-/homosexual. And so it follows that misogyny intersects with homophobia, both gestures of exclusion based upon fear of otherness as proximate or same.

But in a second approach, the map appears more complicated. Materialized in specific gender and sex practices, enjoyment, and the identificatory fantasies upon which it is predicated, underwrites the most basic attitudes toward alterity. As Slavoj Žižek's compelling reading of racism and nationalism suggests, alterity is a special condition of enjoyment, in which, from the perspective of the self-same, the other manifests the desire to steal enjoyment away and/or an unlimited "access to some secret, perverse enjoyment."[70] Alterity disturbs because it confronts the self-same with ways of organizing enjoyment that pervert or exceed one's own ways of enjoying. Arab wealth, for example, was a preoccupation of churchmen—like Gerard of Strasborg, Frederick I's ambassador to Saladin, and Ricoldo of Montecroce—who, increasingly in the late Middle Ages, wondered if the richest parts of the world were not entirely in infidel possession.[71]

Around the problem of perversion, anxieties caused by enjoyment find their clearest articulation in these anti-Muslim discourses. The perverse enjoyments of the Muslims represented for Christians the traumatic expression of their own felt responsibilities. The responsibility felt by William and Marino to recuperate the Holy Land constitutes what Blanchot has called an "extreme of *subissement*" [subjection]: "it is," Blanchot continues, "that for which I must answer when I am without any answer and without any self save a borrowed, a simulated self, or the 'stand-in' for identity."[72] Responsibility for the Christian slave trade and for its contribution to homosexual culture was felt as a kind of "innocent guilt," a troubled answer that must, at all costs, be provided to the questioning, demanding other who is at once trading partner and enemy.

Responding to the incessant demands of the other carries with it the full ambiguity of libidinal fantasmatics: assertions of masculinity and heteronormativity must give way to, or turn into, their opposites if the crusading ideology is to hold up. So, for example, in his *De praedicatione sanctae crucis contra Saracenos* (1266–68), an instruction manual for preachers of the crusade, Humbert of Romans enumerates Saracen vice (polygamy, adultery, and sodomy) while proceeding to denigrate the manliness of Christians, who, like palfreys, only parade about ostentatiously, never fighting but preferring to spend their time in the stable, gorging food.[73] A common theme in crusade propaganda,[74] the effeminacy of Christian men serves to provide just the "mandatory proxy" (Blanchot) required to sustain invective against the Muslims. For without impugning the masculinity of Saracens and Christians alike, the anti-homosexual discourse lacks its most determinant feature: the fantasy that enjoyment is only ever about enjoying a self-image, but a very specific one, the imago of our desire that is a *desire for us* (a desire that belongs to us, rather than is thrust upon us). Undermining masculinity with charges of homosexuality has the effect of reflecting all desires, Narcissus-like, back to the male subject such that it *appears* desires are irrevocably the male subject's own. In such a fantasmic scenario, the foreclosure of enjoyment thus becomes a crucial feature of Christian masculine identity.

Yet, I am suggesting, what has always been at stake in crusade projects is recuperating the right to enjoyment. In setting up differences between Saracens and Christians, recuperation texts call attention simultaneously to different reified forms of enjoyment and to the radical contingency of gender identity. For gender identity functions only as a fantasmic guide to enjoyment. In this essay, I have been concerned with the fantasy dimensions of this right to enjoyment, a right intimately tied to responsibilities to and for the other's desire. If desire can only ever be the other's desire, then anti-homosexual discourses in particular are subject, through a kind of mirroring effect, to the disruptions of the very homoerotic desires whose existence they wish to cancel. By openly acknowledging the multiform and centrifugal nature of all desire, thereby risking their own ideological security, they illustrate well the fantasmic structure of desire as an attempted mapping of the subject's own enjoyments. It is here, in this fantasmic structure, that we are re-oriented (rather than returned) to our own desires.

Notes

I would like to acknowledge my debt, as ever, to my brilliant colleagues Debra Morris and D. Vance Smith. For critical and editorial suggestions, I wish to thank the editors of this book, Sharon Farmer and Carol Pasternack.

1. See Paula A. Treichler, "AIDS, Homophobia, and Biomedical Discourse: An Epidemic of Signification," *Cultural Studies* 1 (1987): 263–305.

2. Jacques Leibowitch, *A Strange Virus of Unknown Origin*, trans. Richard Howard (New York, 1985), 3; quoted in Treichler, "AIDS."

3. See Jonathan Dollimore's reading of *Othello* in his *Sexual Dissidence: Augustine to Wilde, Freud to Foucault* (Oxford, 1991), 148–65.

4. Thanks to Vance Smith, whose advice regarding the shape and formulations of this paragraph was of great help.

5. This is not to ignore important critiques of Said's project, including Robert Young, *White Mythologies: Writing History and the West* (New York, 1990), 119–40; James Clifford, "On *Orientalism*," in his *The Predicament of Culture: Twentieth-Century Ethnography, Literature, and Art* (Cambridge, MA, 1988), 255–76; and Aijaz Ahmad, "*Orientalism* and After: Ambivalence and Metropolitan Location in the Work of Edward Said," in his *In Theory: Classes, Nations, Literatures* (New York, 1992), 159–219.

6. Edward W. Said, *Orientalism* (New York, 1978), 8.

7. As Said writes, Orientalist "texts create not only knowledge but also the very reality they appear to describe" (*Orientalism*, 94).

8. The terms "imaginary" and "fantasmic" are meant to signal the not always successful desire to correspond to the demands of the "Great Other." I am not, here, describing desire in the registry of subjectivity known as the imaginary, but desire in relation to the Symbolic Other. On the Symbolic Other, see Mark Bracher, *Lacan, Discourse, and Social Change: A Psychoanalytic Cultural Criticism* (Ithaca, NY, 1993), 22–31.

9. On what I am calling the "perversion" of oriental culture, see especially Malek Alloula's reproduction and description of postcards of Algerian women, produced and sent by the French in the first quarter of this century, that reflect the deep imbrication of colonialism and sexuality. The harem became an obsessive image of untrammeled eroticism and transgression, promoting "a universe of generalized perversion and of the absolute limitlessness of pleasure." Malek Alloula, *The Colonial Harem*, trans. Myrna Godzich and Wlad Godzich (Minneapolis, 1986), 95.

10. See Rana Kabbani, *Europe's Myths of Orient: Devise and Rule* (London, 1986). See also my "Unthinking the Monster: Twelfth-Century Responses to Saracen Alterity," in *Monster Theory: Reading Culture*, ed. Jeffrey Jerome Cohen (Minneapolis, 1996), 264–91, where I treat Muslim otherness in terms of both its perverse disruption and monstrous construction of the limits of the Christian universe.

11. Said, *Orientalism*, 188. Curious is the effect of that "alas."

12. A fine example of the promise and threat that homosexual practices evoke is Hrotsvit of Gandersheim's version of the passion of St. Pelagius (third quarter of the tenth century), which I discuss briefly below, where male homosexual desire, though largely

erased through condemnation, reappears in sublimated forms. For a good discussion of
the "hesitations" in the Pelagius story, see Mark D. Jordan, *The Invention of Sodomy in
Christian Theology* (Chicago, 1997), 10–28. The attribution of deviant sexualities, particularly the *peccatum contra naturam* ("crime against nature"), to Islam is of course commonplace throughout the Middle Ages. A thorough overview is still Norman Daniel, *Islam and
the West: The Making of an Image* (Edinburgh, 1969), esp. his chapter on "The Place of
Self-Indulgence in the Attack on Islam," 135–61. The discussion of Muslim sodomy in
John Boswell, *Christianity, Social Tolerance, and Homosexuality: Gay People in Western Europe from the Beginning of the Christian Era to the Fourteenth Century* (Chicago, 1980), 278–
84, is a locus classicus. For a general treatment of the concept and culture of medieval
homosexuality, see Warren Johansson and William A. Percy, "Homosexuality," in *Handbook
of Medieval Sexuality*, ed. Vern L. Bullough and James A. Brundage (New York, 1996), 155–
89. For the place of homosexuality and boy-love in early Islamic culture, see Marc Daniel,
"Arab Civilization and Male Love," trans. Winston Leyland, in *Reclaiming Sodom*, ed.
Jonathan Goldberg (New York, 1994), 59–65.

13. Joseph Boone, "Vacation Cruises; or, The Homoerotics of Orientalism," *PMLA*
110 (1995): 90.

14. "Sed quid adhuc? Veniamus ad deteriora. Totius aetatis et ordinis viros, id est
pueros, adolescentes, juvenes, senes, nobiles, servos, et, quod pejus et impudentius est,
clericos et monachos, et heu proh dolor! et quod ab initio non dictum neque auditum est,
episcopos Sodomitico peccato deludunt, et etiam unum episcopum sub hoc nefario peccato jam crepuerunt" (*Patrologia cursus completus, series graeca*, ed. J.-P. Migne [Paris, 1857–
66], 131:565). I have consulted the translation of the letter in Boswell, *Christianity, Social
Tolerance, and Homosexuality*, Appendix Two, 367–69.

15. The letter, surviving in at least three manuscripts of the early twelfth century, was
incorporated into the histories of Robert the Monk, Guibert of Nogent, and William of Tyre.
Norman Daniel remarks that its different versions "are variations on a pornographic theme,"
part of a "hysteria" in which the distance between "the acts they [the Christians] condemned"
and "the acts they committed" was short enough that medieval Europeans were led to "an
acceptance that the acts concerned are *possible*" (italics mine); Norman Daniel, *The Arabs and
Mediaeval Europe* (London, 1975), 124. This sense of the "possible" seems to me crucial,
and this essay is an attempt to articulate it in terms of identity, otherness, and solidarity.

16. *Patrologia cursus completus, series latina* (hereafter *PL*), ed. J.-P. Migne, 221 vols.
(Paris, 1841–66), 156:694; the passage quoted here is from Steven F. Kruger's very fine
translation of Guibert's labyrinthine prose, "Medieval Christian (Dis)identifications: Muslims and Jews in Guibert of Nogent," *New Literary History* 28 (1997): 185–203. See Kruger's
article for a fine reading of Christian (dis)identificatory processes concerning the bodily
condition and practices of the other.

17. Guy Hocquenghem, *Homosexual Desire*, trans. Daniella Dangoor (Durham, NC,
1993), 52.

18. Paul Zumthor, *Speaking of the Middle Ages*, trans. Sarah White (Lincoln, NB,
1986), 22.

19. See Hans Robert Jauss, "The Alterity and Modernity of Medieval Literature,"
trans. Timothy Bahti, *New Literary History* 10 (1979): 181–227; also, his *Alterität und Moder-
nität der mittelalterlichen Literatur* (Munich, 1977).

20. Jauss sublimates the erotic pleasure as a form of intellection: the reader is to exercise an "aesthetic 'bill of rights' of a pleasurable understanding and an understanding pleasure" ("Alterity and Modernity," 183).

21. Ibid., 198.

22. What Jauss calls "passing through the surprise of otherness" (ibid., 182) bears striking affinities to the Lacanian notion of the mirror stage. The mirror stage is the genetic moment of the ego wherein a child, between the ages of six and eighteen months, anticipates, in the form of an imaginary unification, its own bodily defragmentation through identifying with the imago of a counterpart. This identification is described by Lacan as "the triumphant assumption of the image, with the accompanying jubilant mimicry and the playful complacency with which the specular identification is controlled"; see "Propos sur la causalité psychique," *L'évolution psychiatrique* 12 (1947), 34. See also Jacques Lacan, "The Mirror Stage as Formative of the Function of the I as Revealed in Psychoanalytic Experience," in *Écrits: A Selection*, trans. Alan Sheridan (New York, 1977), 1–7.

23. Jauss, "Propos sur la causalité psychique."

24. Said argues that western medieval constructions of the oriental self as other were dependent upon the creation of ideologically charged literatures, or what he terms "typical encapsulations." These included "the journey, the history, the fable, the stereotype, the polemical confrontation" (Said, *Orientalism*, 58).

25. Louise Fradenburg, "'So That We May Speak of Them': Enjoying the Middle Ages," *New Literary History* 28 (1997): 205–30.

26. Ibid., 216.

27. See ibid., 228 n. 31; Lacan, "The Mirror Stage," 4.

28. Dominick LaCapra has posed the question of the relation of historicism and psychoanalysis in terms of transference, though in ways different from my own. See his "History and Psychoanalysis," in *The Trial(s) of Psychoanalysis*, ed. Françoise Meltzer (Chicago, 1988), 9–38. Another reading of the linkage of history and psychoanalysis is Michael S. Roth, *Psycho-Analysis as History: Negation and Freedom in Freud* (Ithaca, NY, 1987). Roth understands Freud's work in terms of its development of a theory of history, a theory predicated upon its commitment to transference as a way of negating the past and opening new possibilities of acknowledging history through freedom; see esp. 99–133.

29. Cf. Michel Foucault, "Nietzsche, Genealogy, History," in *Language, Counter-Memory, Practice: Selected Essays and Interviews by Michel Foucault*, ed. Donald F. Bouchard, trans. Bouchard and Sherry Simon (Ithaca, NY, 1977), 148: "The body manifests the stigmata of past experience and also gives rise to desires, failings, and errors. These elements may join in a body where they achieve a sudden expression, but as often, their encounter is an engagement in which they efface each other, where the body becomes the pretext of their insurmountable conflict.... [Genealogy's] task is to expose a body totally imprinted by history and the process of history's destruction of the body."

30. I refer the reader to Mark Bracher's Editor's column, "Always Psychoanalyze! Historicism and the Psychoanalysis of Culture and Society," *Journal for the Psychoanalysis of Culture and Society* 2 (1997): 1–16, to which I am indebted for my thinking about the narcissistic dangers of historicism and the possibilities of "recovery" within both historicism and psychoanalysis. What Bracher fails to see, as he attempts to distinguish the historical enterprise from the psychoanalytic one and argue for the abandonment of the former, is

that not all historicism "tends to avoid and even prevent" (7) examination of the "exti-macy," or alien *jouissance* within, that comprises the repressed substance of desire for and hatred of the other. See, for example, Louise Fradenburg's work; in addition to the article already cited, see her *City, Marriage, Tournament: Arts of Rule in Late Medieval Scotland* (Madison, WI, 1991) and editor's Introduction to *Premodern Sexualities*, ed. Louise Fradenburg and Carla Freccero (New York, 1996).

31. Bracher, "Always Psychoanalyze!" 12.

32. Dollimore, *Sexual Dissidence*, 27.

33. See ibid., 228–30.

34. Peter Canning, "Transcendental Narcissism Meets Multiplicity (Lacan: Deleuze)," in *Thinking Bodies*, ed. Juliet Flower MacCannell and Laura Zakarin (Stanford, CA, 1994), 199.

35. Michel Foucault, "Les déviations religieuses et la savoir médical," in *Hérésies et sociétés dans l'Europe pre-industrielle, XIe–XVIIIe siècles*, ed. Jacques Le Goff (Paris, 1968), 19.

36. See my discussion in "Unthinking the Monster," 269–71.

37. While the scholarly consensus is that Prester John's kingdom is a utopic space, the argument, to the best of my knowledge, has not been made that such a utopia forms a crucial compensatory response to Christian loss of the Holy Land. The *Letter of Prester John* begins to circulate right after the failure of the second crusade, and represents new ways of thinking about loss and the possibility of recovery (this is an argument I will make in a forthcoming article). On Prester John as utopia, see Leonardo Olschki, "Der Brief des Presbyters Johannes," *Historische Zeitschrift* 144 (1931): 1–14; Karl Helleiner, "Prester John's Letter: A Mediaeval Utopia," *The Phoenix* 13 (1959): 47–57; and Martin Gosman, "La royaume du Prêtre Jean: l'interpretation du bonheur," in *L'idée de bonheur au moyen âge: actes du Colloque d'Amiens de mars 1984* (Göppingen, 1990), 213–23. The two best extended studies of the *Letter of Prester John* are Vsevolod Slessarev, *Prester John: The Letter and the Legend* (Minneapolis, 1959), and Gioia Zaganelli, *La Lettera del Prete Gianni* (Parma, 1990).

38. On the linkage of perverse structures of knowledge to utopian thinking, see Joel Whitebook, *Perversion and Utopia: A Study in Psychoanalysis and Critical Theory* (Cambridge, MA, 1995).

39. The logic here, according to Žižek's formulation, is that of the "masochistic theater" of courtly love. Žižek reads back onto the libidinal economy of courtly love a masochistic matrix in which impediments to desire—e.g., the knight's tasks given to him by the lady—function to support a fantasy not of possession but of deferral. Fantasies are only ever kept alive by defending against the desire that carries the subject into self-shattering *jouissance*. Desire is thus maintained in its dissatisfaction. See Slavoj Žižek, "Courtly Love, or Woman as Thing," in *The Metastases of Enjoyment: Six Essays on Woman and Causality* (New York, 1994), 89–112.

40. Much of this deferral, I would argue, has to do with the utopic nature of medieval travel narratives, where a projection of space onto time occurs such that travel narratives are structured according to discontinuities, interruptions, and accidents. The rhythm of the medieval travel narrative can be compared to both masochism and fetishism: a search for lost origins whose fantasmic vitality depends upon dilation and deferral. On the imbrication of masochism and fetishism, and their relation to deferral, see Gilles Deleuze and Leopold von Sacher-Masoch, *Masochism: Coldness and Cruelty/Venus in Furs* (New

York, 1991), 9–138. On space and time in medieval travel narratives, see Paul Zumthor, "The Medieval Travel Narrative," *New Literary History* 25 (1994): 809–24.

41. Islam, as fetish, constitutes an attempt to make sense of a world that appears constantly in flux. Accordingly, the object itself (Islam) must remain in a condition of plasticity (cf. the notion of the "transitional object"). On this problem, from the point of view of psychoanalysis, see Phyllis Greenacre, "The Transitional Object and the Fetish: With Special Reference to the Role of Illusion," in her *Emotional Growth* (New York, 1971), 1:335–52; also, D. W. Winnicott, *Playing and Reality* (New York, 1971). Given its historical status as a liminal point between East and West, Egypt, as we will see, is ideally suited to function in the western imaginary as zone of intermediacy and transition. This is a point taken up in a different context by Antonia Lant. See her "The Curse of the Pharoah; or, How Cinema Contracted Egyptomania," *October* 59 (1992): 86–112.

42. Alvarus's *Indiculus luminosus* (ca. 854), an interpretation of the Book of Daniel in terms of the rise of Islam as the fourth and final kingdom, is in *PL* 121:397–566. Other writings of the Cordovan martyrs can be found in *PL* 115:705–870.

43. R. W. Southern, *Western Views of Islam in the Middle Ages* (Cambridge, MA, 1962), 3–4. Edward Said also discusses Islam in terms of its effects as "a lasting trauma" (59) for medieval Europe. See Said, *Orientalism*, 58–72.

44. This is a composite of the views of writers such as Guibert of Nogent, Gerald of Wales, Walter of Compiègne, and Thomas Aquinas.

45. "Sanguis ut absque mora stillans de vulnere facto barbam foedavit necnon vestes madefecit." Text from "Pelagius," in *Hrotsvithae Opera*, ed. Helene Homeyer (Munich, 1970), lines 274–75.

46. Jacques Quetif, *Scriptores ordinis Praedicatorum* (Paris, 1910–34), 1:537.

47. See Guillelmus Adae, *De modo Sarracenos extirpandi*, vol. 2 of *Recueil des historiens des croisades Arméniens* (Paris, 1841–1906), 522 n. All quotations are from this edition, and translations are mine.

48. See Marinus Sanutus, *Liber secretorum fidelium crucis super Terrae Sanctae recuperatione et conservatione* (1611; reprint, Hanau, 1972). Biographical information comes from Joshua Prawer's "Foreword," v–xiv.

49. The Pontiff gave Marino a sizable gratuity and rich vestments in return for his work. In addition to the *Liber secretorum*, Marino wrote a number of letters to different political luminaries to promote his idea for an Egyptian crusade. Ten letters, written between 1330 and 1334 are found in Friedrich Kunstmann, "Studien über Marino Sanudo den Älteren mit einem Anhang seiner ungedruckten Briefe," *Königliche Bayerische Akademie der Wissenschaften. Abhandlungen, Phil.-Historische Classe* 7 (1853): 697–819. Five letters and three memos, written between 1334 and 1337, are collected in Leon Dorez and L. de la Roncière, "Lettres inédites et mémoires de Marino Sanudo l'Ancien, 1334–1337," *Bibliotheque de l'Ecole des Chartes* 56 (1895): 21–44. See also Aldo Cerlini, "Nuove lettere di Marino Sanudo il Vecchio," *La Bibliofilia* 42 (1940): 321–59.

50. Daniel, *The Arabs and Mediaeval Europe*, 218.

51. On the products traded, see the commercial account of the fourteenth-century Florentine Francesco Balducci Pegolotti, *La pratica della mercatura*, ed. Allen Evans (Cambridge, MA, 1936).

52. See Wilhelm von Heyd, *Histoire du commerce du Levant au moyen-âge*, 2 vols. (Leipzig, 1885–86), and Louis de Mas Latrie, *Traités de paix et de commerce et documents divers concernant les relations des chrétiens avec les Arabes de l'Afrique septentrionale au Moyen Âge*, 2 vols. (New York, 1964).

53. A Venetian businessman such as Marino was certainly aware that interrupting all commercial intercourse with Egypt could have disastrous consequences for the European trade economy. His commitment to the crusade led him to seek alternative commerce partners and trade routes. He proposed, for example, expanding the trade route from India, and advocated finding elsewhere in Christian lands the same products then imported from Egypt.

54. Merchandise sent to Egypt such as timber, iron and other metals, and pitch for shipbuilding had obvious military uses. For Marino and William, however, slaves were the linchpin to the anti-Egyptian crusade because slave trafficking was at once an economic, military, and moral issue.

55. While persisting in southern Europe after the thirteenth century, clearly defined slave populations virtually disappeared from northern Europe. Within a century of the Domesday survey, slavery died out entirely in England. On this, see David A. E. Pelteret, *Slavery in Early Mediaeval England: From the Reign of Alfred until the Twelfth Century* (Rochester, NY, 1995). On slavery in Scandinavia, see Ruth Mazo Karras, *Slavery and Society in Medieval Scandinavia* (New Haven, CT, 1988), and, in Iceland, Marlis Wilde-Stockmeyer, *Sklaverei auf Island: Untersuchungen zu rechtlich-sozialen Situation und literarische Darstellung der Sklaven im skandinavischen Mittelalter* (Heidelberg, 1978). On medieval slavery and traffic in slave children, see Charles Verlinden, *Péninsule ibérique-France* (Brugge, 1955), and Verlinden, *Italie, Colonies Italiennes du Levant, Levant latin, Empire Byzantin* (Ghent, 1977), vols. 1 and 2 of his *L'Esclavage dans l'Europe médiévale*. Children constitute, according to John Boswell, a significant percentage (about one-third) of the slave trade in the later Middle Ages, especially in southern Europe, where, Boswell claims, slavery "became more common...than it had been at any time after the fall of Rome" (405–06). See John Boswell, *Kindness to Strangers: The Abandonment of Children in Western Europe from Late Antiquity to the Renaissance* (New York, 1988), esp. 405–08. On the (still current) sexual abuse of servile children, see 407 n. 29.

56. "Gens eciam Egipciaca, utpote carnali luxui dedita, minus est apta ad actus milicie exercendos" (*De modo*, 524).

57. "Dampnosa est christianitati hec negociacio, quia Egiptus terra est que suos habitores devorat et consumit, quia non dabunt radices altas viperarum genimina abortiva" (*De modo*, 524).

58. Peter Stallybrass and Allon White, *The Politics and Poetics of Transgression* (Ithaca, NY, 1986), 200.

59. My argument should be recognizable as bearing resemblance to the Lacanian notion that "desire is the desire of the other," a notion that Žižek puts to splendid, if repeated, use in his readings of the logic of racism. See, for instance, Slavoj Žižek, *Tarrying with the Negative: Kant, Hegel, and the Critique of Ideology* (Durham, NC, 1993), 225–27; Žižek, *The Sublime Object of Ideology* (New York, 1989), 114–16, 125–28; and Žižek, *The Plague of Fantasies* (New York, 1997), 9. Perhaps we could say that the orientalist figure of

the Arab is precisely "the sublime object of ideology," that fetish that materializes the cause of Christian non-satisfaction of desire (cf. *Plague of Fantasies*, 76).

60. The figuration of Egypt as a visual space, open to the introjection of western gazes, is wonderfully elaborated upon in the context of late-nineteenth-century tourism and exhibitions by Timothy Mitchell. See his *Colonising Egypt* (Cambridge, 1988).

61. Another polemicist who finds commodified slave boys an ideological flash point is William's and Marino's contemporary, Jacopo da Verona, whose *Liber peregrinationis* describes the same homosexual attraction for boys who were bought as slaves for the Sultan's army. The sultan is said to practice such crimes "excrabile et publice." See Jacopo da Verona, *Liber peregrinationis*, ed. Ugo Monneret de Villard (Rome, 1950), IX–X. Marino himself refers to the slave trade in youths as a military advantage for the Sultan, and refers to their sexual abuse; see Marinus Sanutus, *Liber secretorum*, 27.

62. Paraphrase of Vulgate Romans 1:27.

63. "Apud sectam Sarracenorum actus quicumque venereus non solum est improhibitus, sed licitus et laudatus. Unde, preter meretrices innumerabiles, que apud eos sunt, homines effeminati sunt plurimi, qui barbam radunt, faciem propriam pingunt, habitum muliebrem assumunt, armillas portant ad brachia et ad pedes, et ad collum torques aureos, ut mulieres; et ad pectus monilia circumponunt, et sic sub peccato venumdati contumeliis afficiunt sua corpora et exponunt, et masculi in masculum turpitudinem operantes, mercedem iniquitatis et erroris recipiunt in seipsis. Sarraceni ergo, humane dignitatis obliti, se ad illos effeminatos impudenter inclinant, vel cum eisdem habitant, sicut hic inter nos publice habitant vir et uxor; sed et adhuc quid iniquitatis super inquitatem addunt nostri catholici, inimici justicie, hoc vicium inesse Sarracenis animadvertunt, sciunt et consenciunt, et viam et incentivum preparant ad hoc scelus. Et cum aliquem puerum aptum corpore invenire possunt, christianum vel tartarum, ut premittitur, ad vendendum, nullum precium est eis carum dandum pro hiis quos vident ad hujusmodi complendam nequiciam aptiores. Quos, postquam emerunt, ut statuam, ornant sericis et aureis indumentis, corpus eorum et facies lavant sepius balneis et aliis lavamentis, et eos pascunt lautis cibariis et potibus delicatis. Et hoc faciunt ut pinguiores et rubicundiores et delicaciores, et per consequens magis apti et allectivi ad Sarracenorum complendam libidinem videantur. Quos ut vident libidinosi, scelerosi et nefandi homines, Sarraceni videlicet, humane nature perversores, statim in eorum concupiscenciam exardesccunt, sed, ut canes insani, ad istos pueros, diaboli laqueos, sibi emendos festinant currere, ut possint cum eis suam impudiciciam exercere" (*De modo*, 524–25).

64. William's use of cross-dressing as a signifier of gender transgression is clearly a trope, yet, given the literary and historical evidence attesting to transvestism and cross-gender behavior as institutionalized forms in the Muslim Middle East, from Islam's inception to the present, it seems likely that William is not entirely fabricating these customs. On the cross-dressing traditions of the Caliphal court of ninth-century Baghdad, see Everett K. Rowson, "Gender Irregularity as Entertainment," this volume.

65. This displacement is simultaneously a reinforcement of the anti-Muslim military project itself. That is, homosexuality does not threaten the libidinal economy of the crusading army, its phallic and patriarchal armor, but rather strengthens the homosocial bonds whose success depends in great part upon how actively homosexuality is disavowed

and silenced. On the libidinal structure of the two great "artificial groups," the army and the church, see Sigmund Freud, *Group Psychology and the Analysis of the Ego*, in *The Standard Edition of the Complete Psychological Works of Sigmund Freud*, ed. and trans. James Strachey (London, 1955), 18:65–143.

66. See Oliver of Paderborn, *The Capture of Damietta*, trans. Joseph J. Gavigan, in *Christian Society and the Crusades, 1198–1229: Sources in Translation*, ed. Edward Peters (Philadelphia, 1971), 49–139.

67. The locus classicus is Peter Damian's *Liber Gomorrhianus*, written between 1048 and 1054. For the English text, see Peter Damian, *Book of Gomorrah: An Eleventh Century Treatise against Clerical Homosexual Practices*, trans. Pierre J. Payer (Waterloo, Ont., 1982). For a general discussion of heresy and sexual deviance, see Vern L. Bullough, *Sexual Variance in Society and History* (New York, 1976), 390–97. The imbrication of heresy and deviance outlived the Middle Ages: e.g., Edward Coke's *Laws* assigns sodomy to the tripartite category, "Sorcerers, Sodomers and Hereticks": Edward Coke, *The Third Part of the Institutes of the Laws of England* (London, 1644), 36.

68. The most spectacular case linking sodomy and heresy is probably the trial of the Knights Templar. And, as Jeffrey Richards cites, in the first political trial (1310–11) to involve demon worship Pope Boniface VIII was charged in addition with heresy and sodomy. "The use of deviancy charges to dispose of enemies was [by the fourteenth century] a regular part of medieval politics," Richards notes (144). See Jeffrey Richards, *Sex, Dissidence, and Damnation: Minority Groups in the Middle Ages* (New York, 1991).

69. The emphasis in anti-Muslim writing on Saracen enjoyment is profound, and an indication of its necessity as a guide to Christian enjoyment. See, for example, Petrus Alphonsi's *Dialogus*, *PL* 157:597–608, where he discusses the *lex larga* of the Saracens and earthly and heavenly enjoyments permitted to its followers.

70. Slavoj Žižek, "Eastern Europe's Republics of Gilead," *New Left Review* 183 (1990): 54.

71. For Gerard's statements, second-hand, see Arnold of Lübeck, *Chronicon Slavorum*, ed. J. M. Lappenberg in Monumenta Germaniae Historica, Scriptores (Hannover, 1868), 21:235–41. See also Ricoldo of Montecroce, *Itinerarius* [sic], in *Peregrinatores medii aevi quatuor*, ed. J. C. M. Laurent (Leipzig, 1864), esp. chaps. 21 to 29. A spurious correspondence of the early fourteenth century between the sultan and Pope Clement V also plays up the wealth of the Arabs, in boasts designed to show that all desires are satisfied, except the desire for more Christian blood. See Wilhelm Wattenbach, ed., "Correspondance fausse du Sultan," in *Archives de l'Orient latin*, ed. Comte Riant (Paris, 1881), 1:299–300.

72. Maurice Blanchot, *The Writing of the Disaster*, trans. Ann Smock (Lincoln, NB, 1986), 22.

73. Humbert of Romans, *De praedicatione sanctae crucis contra Saracenos* (Nuremburg, [1495?]), 24–27, 41–45. Humbert continues the beast imagery, likening such men to Flemish cows, fish, and tame roosters. There are eighteen manuscripts, none extant before 1400, however. On this treatise, see A. Lecoy de la Marche, "La Prédiction de la croisade au troizième siècle," *Revue des questions historiques* 48 (1890): 5–28; Fritz Heintke, *Humbert von Romans, der fünfte Ordensmeister der Dominikaner* (Berlin, 1933), 103–7; Palmer Throop, *Criticism of the Crusade: A Study of Public Opinion and Crusade Propaganda* (Amsterdam, 1940), 151–62; Valmar Cramer, "Humbert von Romans Traktat über die Kreuzpredigt,"

Das heilige Land 79 (1935): 132–53, and vol. 80 (1936): 11–23, 43–60, 77–98; and Edward Tracy Brett, *Humbert of Romans: His Life and Views of Thirteenth-Century Society* (Toronto, 1984), 167–75.

74. See, for example, Jacques de Vitry's sharp assault on the masculinity of the de-latinized Latins in the Holy Land, in the *Historia Hierosolimitana*, in *Gesta Dei per Francos, siue Orientalivm expeditionvm, et regni Francorvm hierosolimitani historia a variis, sed illius aeui scriptoribus, litteris commendata . . .* , ed. Jacques Bongars (Hanover, 1611), 1085 ff. and 1097.

PART III

INDIVIDUAL CHOICES,
STRATEGIES OF RESISTANCE

9

Manual Labor, Begging, and Conflicting Gender Expectations in Thirteenth-Century Paris

Sharon Farmer

One of the paradigms that influenced the ways in which thirteenth-century clerics viewed men's and women's roles was the description in Genesis 3:16–19 of the punishments that God imposed on Adam and Eve:

> To the woman he said, "I will greatly increase your hardship and your pregnancies: in pain you shall bring forth children, and you shall be under the control of your husband, and he shall rule over you." And to Adam he said, "...cursed is the ground that you work: in toil you shall eat of it all the days of your life. Thorns and thistles it shall bring forth for you, and you shall eat the crops of the earth. By the sweat of your face you shall eat bread until you return to the ground from which you were taken...."[1]

My own reading of this text is that it associates both man and woman with physicality and bodily pain. Adam and Eve's curses focused on the physical matter from which each was created—Adam from earth and Eve from the human body. Moreover, manual labor and reproductive labor are both bodily engagements with the physical realm; as a result of the Fall neither form of labor can bring forth fruit without bodily toil and pain. Interpreted in this way, the Genesis passage does not support a simplistic assertion that in western culture woman is identified with body and physicality and man is associated with soul and immateriality.[2] In the Genesis passage both Adam and Eve are deeply identified with body and physicality. The operating distinction points more to a division of labors—productive and reproductive—and thus, by implication, to a division of realms—public and domestic.

What I want to do in this article is to examine the ways in which thirteenth-century Parisian clerics and lay people interpreted and experienced this cultural construct of gendered labors and gendered realms. I want to suggest, moreover, that two categories of difference complicated the ways in which this construct was both appropriated and transformed. Those differences included not only differences of social status, but also the distinction between necessary and voluntary—or penitential—labor.

COMPLICATIONS OF SOCIAL STATUS

Dominican and Franciscan theologians of the mid-thirteenth century viewed productive "labor" as an important aspect of masculinity, but they made distinctions among male "labors" in accordance with differences of social or clerical status. Thus, they excused themselves from the necessity of engaging in the physical realm of manual labor, arguing that their own productive labors were more important than this demeaning necessity. For instance, the Franciscan Master General Bonaventure (d. 1274) divided male "work" into three categories: inferior or corporal work (that which was necessary for preparing food, clothing, etc.); exterior or civil work (that of governors, soldiers, merchants, and servants); and, most important of all, spiritual work (that of preachers and priests). In response to the attacks of Parisian secular clerics—who criticized the mendicant orders because their members were not required to engage in manual labor—Bonaventure argued that the "labor of wisdom" was better than corporal work.[3]

In some discursive contexts thirteenth-century theologians compressed all women into a single reproductive function. Such was the case with the discussion by the Dominican Thomas Aquinas (d. 1274) concerning why God created woman:

> it was necessary for woman to be made, as the Scripture says, as a helper to man not, indeed, as a helpmate in other works, as some say, since man can be more efficiently helped by another man in other works; but as a helper in the work of generation.[4]

Occasionally, however, clerical elites made important distinctions among women according to their social status. Thus, several thirteenth-century clerics indicated that while elite lay women's responsibilities lay in the domestic realm, they were not as tied to the physical realm as were women of lower status. For instance, in recounting the various temptations to which bourgeois women were most likely to succumb the Dominican Master General Humbert of Romans (d. 1277) said nothing about adultery, although that sin predominated in his discussions of peasant and servant women.[5] Moreover, the Franciscan Gilbert of Tournai (d. 1284) wrote that the principal responsibility of a "wife" (by which he meant an "elite wife") was to draw on her intellectual and moral capacities in order to govern her household: she should "educate" the children, "humble" male servants, "correct" female servants, and "guard" the house.[6] With respect to her servants—both male and female—one of the matron's principal duties was to ensure that they refrained from lascivious behavior and remained chaste.

Gilbert's suggestion that the matron must control the sexuality of both her male and her female servants points to a widespread assumption that lower-status men and women were lascivious, vulgar, and tied to their bodies. That assumption frequently manifested itself in artistic representations of peasants.[7] Humbert of Romans said nothing about sexuality in his discussion of hired laborers, but he did mention another vulgar characteristic, drunkenness, that he never mentioned in his discussions of elite men. Humbert also stressed that many hired laborers were "exceedingly" ignorant of things pertaining to salvation.[8]

Like the Genesis passage, these discussions by some of the leading churchmen and authors of the thirteenth century, all of whom trained in Paris, call into question generalizations about a tendency in medieval culture for men to be associated as a generic category with the intellectual or spiritual realm and women to be associated as a generic category with the physical realm.[9] These texts by thirteenth-century clerics emphasized that differences of social status, rather than gender, marked the dividing line between those who were more associated with the intellectual realm and those who were more associated with the physical realm. However, while these discussions complicated the Genesis paradigm by dividing both productive and reproductive labor into levels that were more and less associated with physical and intellectual endeavors, the binary associating men with productive labor in the public realm and women with reproductive labor in the domestic realm nevertheless remained intact.

But did the Genesis paradigm always prevail—did medieval clerics and lay people always associate men with productive labor and the public realm and women with reproductive labor and the domestic realm? The answer, I suggest, is a qualified no. I approach that answer by unravelling the discourses and experiences that shaped a single story about a thirteenth-century lower-status Parisian woman whose physical incapacity compelled her both to beg, apparently because she could not work, and to work, because she wanted to get better. The story comes from the *Miracles of Saint Louis,* which was written by a Franciscan named Guillaume de St.-Pathus around the year 1303:

> In the year of our Lord 1276, in the winter, a great malady took Jehanne of Serris [a village in the diocese of Paris from which Jehanne had emigrated to Paris], the wife of Jehan the Carpenter.... This malady seized her in such a way that, whereas before she had been healthy and robust in all her limbs, now she could not walk, stand, or use her feet and legs. It took her during the night, between the feast of the Purification [February 2] and the beginning of Lent. She went to bed healthy and robust on a Tuesday evening . . . and when she awoke she found herself so weak and ill in her thighs, legs and feet that she could not use those members. . . . She was like that in her house for a month. . . .
>
> And since she was thus afflicted in her house, and she was poor and had no one to help her, and since her husband did not want to do that which was necessary for her, she was carried to the Hôtel Dieu of Paris, where she lay paralyzed and sick, for a long time, until just after the feast of Sts. Peter and Paul [June 29]. And afterwards the sisters of the Hôtel Dieu decided to

make crutches for her. . . . and when . . . she was taken out of her bed and the sisters assisted her, she went with great effort to the altar of St. Leonard which is in that hospital. . . . And when she went on crutches she placed her right foot firmly on the ground, but she could not control the left foot at all, and so she dragged it behind her.

And as soon as she was able to move about she wanted to go home to her husband and children . . . so she started to return to her house on crutches, but she could not make it, and so her husband carried her all the way. . . . And it happened after that that her husband did not want to find that which was necessary for her, and so with great difficulty she went on crutches to the church of St.-Merry in Paris to seek alms.

And when Jehanne heard that many miracles were occurring at the tomb of St. Louis and that sick people were cured there, she . . . had hope that she would be cured there by the merits of the blessed St. Louis. And since she wanted to live by her own means when she went to the tomb, she spun some yarn until she gained three sous, which she carried with her. And on a Sunday morning she took up the route to St.-Denis [a distance of about five miles], on her crutches, and one of her daughters accompanied her, barefooted and in a wool chemise. She went with great difficulty, and vespers were already ringing when she arrived. She was at the tomb each day for four days, then she was cured, and she offered a candle as long as she was tall.

. . . And afterwards she limped a bit . . . but she was healthy and robust . . . and she took care of her needs just like any other healthy woman.[10]

I am especially drawn to three moments in this narrative: the moment when Guillaume seems to blame Jehanne's husband for putting her in the public hospital; the moment when Guillaume again seems to blame the husband for the fact that Jehanne has to beg; and the moment when Jehanne decides that she will pay for her pilgrimage not with the money that she gains by begging for alms but with money that she earns with her own hands, by spinning.

These moments in Jehanne of Serris's story are illustrative of two largely unrelated discourses that thirteenth-century clerics developed about the role of manual labor in a woman's life. On the one hand, when discussing daily survival—necessary labor—clerics viewed the activities of lower-status men and women through the Genesis paradigm, and thus they tended to ignore the fact that many married women worked, assuming instead that labor and supporting the family were part of the masculine sphere. On the other hand, in discussing women's penitential behavior, clerics impressed upon women the idea that they should engage in manual labor largely because begging was a tainted activity, especially if the person who begged was both involuntarily poor and a woman.

In addition to providing a window into two different clerical discourses about women's work, Jehanne's story, along with the other sources for St. Louis's miracles, suggests that poor and laboring men and women sometimes held views about women's work and women's begging that differed from those of the clerical elites. At other times, however, the St. Louis sources indicate that the behavior and self-perceptions of poor women, including Jehanne, were shaped by elite discourses.

In this, and in many of his other miracle stories, Guillaume de St.-Pathus depicted the daily lives of the poor with meticulous detail. Indeed, I have argued elsewhere that Guillaume's narratives give us more detail about poor people's strategies for surviving long-term disability than any other source yet to be exploited by a medieval historian.[11] Guillaume de St.-Pathus got close to the ground, so to speak, in his miracle stories because he based his narratives on the written record of the ecclesiastical inquest that was held in St.-Denis in 1282–1283 in order to determine whether or not miracles were taking place at the tomb of King Louis IX, who had died in 1270. Around three hundred thirty individuals who claimed to have witnessed sixty-three different miracles made statements before the panel holding the inquest. Many of those witnesses were poor people from Paris or St.-Denis. Unfortunately, most of the record of the inquest does not survive. What remains are Guillaume de St.-Pathus's summaries and a fragment of the original Latin record of the inquest, which contains the redacted testimonies of twenty-one witnesses from Paris and St.-Denis, concerning three different miracles.[12]

Guillaume's stories reveal aspects of the lives of the thirteenth-century poor that we otherwise could not learn, and a comparison of his retellings with the surviving fragments of the original inquest indicates that he remained quite faithful to his source: while abridging the information, he managed to incorporate aspects of the narratives of multiple witnesses, and he never inserted new material. Nevertheless, his narratives are not transparent windows into the lives of the poor. It is important to note, first, that Guillaume spent most of his career as a mendicant friar serving as spiritual advisor to the family of King Louis IX and that he wrote the *Life and Miracles of Saint Louis* at the request of Louis's daughter Blanche.[13] As I indicate below, Guillaume's retellings are mediated—through selective silences and word choices—by his own prejudices and assumptions and presumably by those of his intended audience as well. Moreover, the questions that were posed at the original inquest and the ways in which the answers were recorded were mediated by the prejudices, purposes, and assumptions of the clerics who were responsible for the inquest. Finally, the information that the clerics on the panel managed to collect was mediated by the memories, purposes, and prejudices of the witnesses. In this last case, however, the clerics were able to discourage deliberate distortions and to compensate for faulty memories by interviewing multiple witnesses.

WOMEN'S NECESSARY LABOR

In the story about Jehanne of Serris, Guillaume's own mediations and those of the panel of clerics upon whose inquest he relied are most evident in the silences and interjections concerning necessary productive labor. While Guillaume identifies Jehanne's husband as a carpenter, he never tells us whether or not Jehanne worked before she became ill and after she recovered. However, the fact that Jehanne begged once she returned to her household, despite the pain that she endured in order to reach her parish church, suggests that her household could not survive on the income-producing work of her husband alone. It seems that Jehanne's begging was a necessary "labor," one that contributed to the survival of the household, and it is thus reasonable to assume that before she became ill Jehanne contributed to the survival of the household by generating income in some other way. In a household that constituted a single occupational unit of production, in which a husband and wife worked together at a single craft, Jehanne's economic contribution to her family's survival would have been valued but not easily measured. It is certainly possible that a husband and wife worked together in the carpentry craft; however, statistics from the Parisian tax assessments indicate that women were significantly underrepresented in this craft.[14] It seems more likely that Jehanne's begging compensated for the loss of income that she gained independently, perhaps by laboring in the home (spinning, carding, processing victuals), perhaps by hiring herself out (as a laundress, for instance).[15]

Guillaume also implies that Jehanne's unfortunate situation, once she became ill, was in part the result of her husband's refusal to live up to his role as provider. Thus, Guillaume tells us, "since ... she was poor and had no one to help her, and since her husband did not *want* to do that which was necessary for her" Jehanne was taken to the Hôtel Dieu of Paris; and again, after she had returned from the hospital to her home, she started begging at her parish church because "her husband did not *want* to find that which was necessary for her."[16] But was Jehan the carpenter really as negligent as Guillaume suggested? Certainly, he was attentive enough to carry his wife home from the hospital, and it was probably he who carried her there in the first place. And what alternatives were available to him if he wanted to keep his wife out of the hospital and, later, off of the streets? Could a laborer afford to take time off from work to care for his wife during her illness? If he was one of the many laborers whose salary did not suffice to support a family, was it not a caring gesture to place his wife in the hospital, where she could at least be assured of receiving daily meals? Once she returned home, what means did he have other than his wife's begging to supplement an apparently inadequate income?

In his representations—and apparent misrepresentations—of the earning capacities and responsibilities of Jehanne and her husband, Guillaume, like other clerical authors of the thirteenth century, seems to have viewed men's and women's necessary labor through a lens that was colored by the third chapter of Genesis. This association of men with work and women with reproduction and sexuality provided preachers and moralists with a grid for categorizing men and women: in most collections of *ad status* sermons—sermons for people from various social strata—men were classified by social status or profession, while women were classified by sexual status, as virgins, wives, and widows. Even Humbert of Romans, who classified women according to social status, profession, and age group, actually viewed women through the lens of sexual status: as Carla Casagrande has pointed out, his "noble," "bourgeois," and "peasant" women were really "wives of" nobles, bourgeois, and peasants. Moreover the only legitimate working women whom he discussed were servants—working singlewomen who were encompassed within the household.[17]

This division of men's and women's realms into the realm of productive labor and the realm of reproductive labor even mediated the way in which information about men and women was recorded both in secular and ecclesiastical records. For instance, in the Parisian tax assessments from the late thirteenth and early fourteenth centuries—which listed only heads of households that generated some kind of income—women were much more likely than were men to be identified in relational terms (as "the wife," "the widow," or "the servant" of so-and-so). By 1300, most men and women were identified by their profession or by a combination of their surname and their profession; however, men were identified in this way more often than were women.[18] Moreover, most of the women who were listed in the tax assessments were either widows or unmarried: the work of married women is nearly invisible in these records.[19]

The panel of clerics who held the inquest into St. Louis's miracles followed a pattern of gendering that resembles that of the Parisian tax assessments. At the beginning of each interview the panel apparently asked each witness a series of questions that established the identity of that witness. The surviving fragment of the inquest indicates that all of the twenty-one witnesses whose testimonies survive were asked to state their names, where they were born, where they currently lived, how long they had lived there, and how old they were. Only when the witness was a woman, however, did the scribes record the identity of the witness's spouse: marital status was part of the sexual sphere and thus essential to identifying a woman but not a man. Work, by contrast, was part of a man's identity, although not always an essential part: as part of the initial identifying information the scribes recorded the occupation of nine of the fourteen male witnesses whose testimonies survive.[20] By contrast, in the initial sections for the seven female witnesses whose testimonies survive the scribes indicated neither whether the women worked nor in what capacity.[21] In a number of cases, both male and female, we learn later in the interview what the witness did for a living but not because the interviewers asked for that information.

In his summaries of the material from the original inquest, Guillaume de St.-Pathus went even further than the inquisitors and scribes, filtering out information that the scribes at the inquest had recorded concerning women's work. Luce of Rémilly, a woman who was believed to have been cured of blindness at Louis's tomb, is a case in point. The surviving fragment of the original inquest includes the testimony of eight witnesses to Luce's cure. Four of those witnesses cited the facts that Luce now worked in petty sales and that she could discern one coin from another as evidence that she had been completely cured of her blindness. Guillaume, by contrast, only mentioned that Luce could now identify coins.[22]

We do not know the degree to which Guillaume filtered out the evidence about women's work in most of the other sixty-four narratives. Nevertheless, the statistics are striking: somewhere in Guillaume's narrative we learn what over one-half (thirteen out of twenty-four) of the married men did for a living. By contrast, we learn nothing about the work of twenty-three of the twenty-four married women—neither if they worked nor in what capacity. In the case of the twenty-fourth woman, we learn that she spun because she made a vow that if her daughter was cured by St. Louis she would stop spinning on Saturdays, unless she was compelled to do so by extreme poverty.[23] We learn more about the occupations of single people, both male and female, but again the information is biased in favor of the men: Guillaume tells us what ten of the thirteen single laymen did for a living, and what seven of the thirteen single laywomen did.[24]

If we turn from what clerics thought (or did not think) about the necessary labor of women, and especially married women, to what the women themselves thought, we get a very different picture. At the end of each interview with a witness to a miracle, the clerics conducting the St. Louis inquest asked the witness what he or she was worth. Those who owned real property told the clerics what that property was worth. Those who did not own real property answered that they "had nothing" and that they were sustained by their own labor or that of another. All of the seven women whose testimonies survive were married. Two of the seven had real property, valued at over sixty and over two hundred livres.[25] One of the remaining five answered that she lived on the labor of her husband, who was a dyer.[26] The other four answered that they lived on their own labor and that of their husbands.[27]

At first glance it appears that, like their clerical brothers, men from the laboring poor did not wish to acknowledge that married women worked. All eight of the unpropertied laymen whose interviews survive stated that they lived on their own labor, mentioning nothing about the work of their wives. Two of the eight men also indicated that they supported their families with their own labor. One of those seems to have contradicted his wife in making this claim, since she indicated that she lived on her own labor *and* that of her husband.[28]

While these answers might suggest that some laboring men internalized the clerical myth about the male breadwinner, it is not necessary to read them in this way. Rather, differences between the men's and women's answers reflected the economic realities of the High and later Middle Ages: men from the urban laboring classes tended to earn more than what was required to support themselves but not enough to support an entire family. Women, by contrast, frequently earned less than what was required to support an individual.[29] Thus, when men answered that they lived by their own labor, and women that they lived by their own labor and that of their husbands, their answers accurately described their situations.

Working men and women thus experienced women's work as important and necessary to the household economy. But they also experienced that work as secondary in importance and as an activity that married women often incorporated into or worked around their domestic responsibilities. Thus, in the miracles of St. Louis, mothers spent more time than did fathers awaiting the cures of their children in St.-Denis. Five mothers stayed at St.-Denis for between nine and sixteen days, and a sixth stayed a full month. Several of these probably gave up working for the entire period of their stay. Some may not have been working wives. And some, such as Yfamia, who spun to enhance the family income, may have taken their work with them to St.-Denis.[30] Working people, then, recognized that both married men and married women worked, but they were also more inclined to associate women with domestic responsibilities. There were still male and female realms, but those realms sometimes overlapped; there were no clear lines of demarcation. Men and women like Jehanne of Serris and her husband experienced women's work as a necessary part of the household economy. While they realized that men earned more and that women mixed productive labor with reproductive labor, they also understood that their households depended upon the laboring contribution of every adult even if that adult had to beg to bring in her share of income.

Clerical elites, by contrast, tended to perpetuate a vision of exclusive and separate realms—a productive realm inhabited by men, and a reproductive realm inhabited by women. That vision was so powerful for the clerics that they often ignored, or even erased, the evidence that the wives of laboring men also worked. As a result, it remains extremely difficult for historians to calculate the numbers of working women in the medieval urban economy.

DISABILITY, BEGGING, AND WOMEN'S PENITENTIAL LABOR

On first consideration, it might seem implausible that Jehanne of Serris, who had been unable to walk a few blocks from the Hôtel Dieu of Paris to her home in the parish of St.-Merry, could then make a pilgrimage on crutches to the town of St.-Denis, a trip of about five miles. And it might seem equally contradictory that a woman who had to beg for her living would suddenly decide to earn some travel money by spinning yarn. But the desire for a cure could energize a person to make extraordinary changes in his or her behavior.

Jehanne's pilgrimage and her work with her own hands constituted penitential acts.[31] Jehanne may have been strongly motivated to perform such penitential acts (apparently, in the case of the pilgrimage, with much assistance from her daughter) because clerics of the thirteenth century taught that in some cases disease and disability were punishments from God for specific sins that afflicted individuals had committed.[32] In other cases, however, clerics taught that disease and disability were gifts from God, which gave afflicted individuals the opportunity to begin to pay off their debt to God for their sins, thereby diminishing the amount of time that they would have to spend in purgatory after their deaths. Bodily suffering, the clerics also taught, was a gift because it prevented the afflicted from committing more sins.[33]

In any case, disease and disability, like death, were reminders of the fallen nature of humanity; thus they were linked, in a general way, to the need for redemption from sin. Moreover, Jehanne probably learned from her parish priest that in asking God to make her body whole she needed to approach him with a soul that was as spotless as possible. Thus, like many of the other pilgrims who went to St. Louis's tomb, Jehanne probably made confession to her parish priest before embarking on her pilgrimage.[34]

While disability itself was not necessarily interpreted as a sign of divine disfavor towards the afflicted individual, those among the involuntary poor and afflicted who begged did tend to be regarded with suspicion. This may help to explain why Jehanne chose to earn the money for her pilgrimage by working with her hands rather than by begging. But why would Jehanne believe this? After all, she clearly fit the thirteenth-century category of the deserving poor: those who sought alms because they were incapable of supporting themselves by working.[35] Moreover, as the spirituality of the mendicant orders made clear, begging could also be considered penitential behavior. One problem that Jehanne faced was that there was a big difference between voluntary and involuntary begging: the involuntary poor, most especially those who begged, always fell under a cloud of suspicion. A second problem was that of gender: clerics did not want women to share in the activity of voluntary—or penitential—begging.

The central problem with the poor who did not choose to be poor, most especially with those who begged, was desire: the poor were consumed with desire for that which they did not have. As Thomas Aquinas, the dominant Dominican theologian of the mid-thirteenth century, put it, "spiritual danger comes from poverty when it is not voluntary, because a man falls into many sins through the desire to get rich, which torments those who are involuntarily poor."[36] Similarly, the fourth-century church father Jerome had asserted, in a passage that both Aquinas and Bonaventure cited, that it was better to give alms to the voluntary rather than to the involuntary poor, "among whose rags and bodily filth burning desire has domain."[37] Along similar lines, the early-thirteenth-century moralist Thomas of Chobham maintained that many beggars who truly needed to beg were nevertheless guilty of the sin of envy. Others may have started out needing to beg, but they then hoarded the alms that they collected, thereby committing the sin of avarice.[38]

Clerical elites also tended to assume that the life of the beggar was easier than the life of the simple laborer. Thus, they maintained, beggars among the involuntary poor tended to slide into the sin of sloth, or laziness. One story that originated in the twelfth century concerned two lazy disabled beggars who tried to escape miraculous cures for their disabilities because they wanted to preserve their leisurely way of life rather than having to go to work. This story was widely disseminated in the thirteenth century, in Jacob of Voragine's *Golden Legend* and in copies of the *ad status* sermons of the early-thirteenth-century cleric Jacques de Vitry.[39] More negative still were the assertions by the late-twelfth-century Parisian theologian Peter the Chanter, and by his student Thomas of Chobham, who wrote a widely disseminated manual for confessors, that many beggars faked their disabilities and illnesses in order to avoid work and to enhance their incomes.[40]

The stigma of begging was even greater when the beggar was a woman, for it exposed her to sexual danger and called her sexual modesty into question. Thus, while some clerics lauded and others criticized men's voluntary begging—begging for penitential purposes—they consistently argued that women should not voluntarily beg for penitential purposes.[41] St. Elizabeth of Hungary wanted to live by begging, but her confessor, Conrad of Marburg, forbade it. She took up spinning instead.[42] Margaret of Ypres begged until her advisors convinced her not to.[43] Clare of Assisi wanted to imitate the mendicant poverty of St. Francis, but she was compelled to live out her life of poverty as a cloistered nun rather than as a mendicant who could beg in the streets. She and her fellow nuns at the convent of San Damiano in Assisi supported themselves by working—Clare, by spinning and doing needlework.[44]

According to Jacques de Vitry, manual labor was central to the penitential spirituality of the Beguine Mary of Oignies, with whom Jacques had a close personal relationship. Indeed, in the preface to his *Life of Mary of Oignies,* Jacques highlighted manual labor—earning "a sparse meal with their hands"—as a central aspect of the voluntary poverty of the Beguine movement in the Low Countries.[45] In his description of early Franciscans in Italy, Jacques wrote of the differing activities of the men and women: the men "go into the cities and villages during the day, so that they convert others, giving themselves to active work"; the women, by contrast, "live near the cities in various hospices. They accept nothing, but live from the work of their hands."[46]

Jacques's association of manual labor with penitential behavior was natural enough: it was, after all, the punishment that God had imposed on Adam. Indeed, manual labor played a central role in the penitential life of Benedictine monks, and the Genesis text describing Adam's punishment was part of the standard liturgy for public penance, which was performed at the beginning of Lent.[47] What I find surprising is that clerics would avoid discussing manual labor as a necessary daily activity for women who were members of the involuntarily laboring poor, but would then turn around and tell women that they should engage in penitential labor. I would even go so far as to assert that clerics like Jacques de Vitry associated penitential labor *especially* with women, since they gave men more free rein to engage in either penitential begging or penitential labor. Robert Grosseteste, the bishop of Lincoln (1235–53) who was closely associated with the Franciscans even drew on the example of female Beguines in order to promote manual labor as a form of voluntary poverty that was superior to begging, even for men.[48]

Jacques de Vitry was so committed to promoting manual labor for religious women that he devoted almost half of a sermon for Benedictine nuns to the topic. In addition to arguing that manual labor was a good aid in fighting temptations and sloth, that it was an excellent instrument of penance, and that it gave one the means to help the poor, Jacques stressed that it was especially important for religious women because it made them financially independent. Nuns who shunned manual labor, he argued, sometimes left their cloisters to seek gifts from relatives, and thus they encountered "many enemies of chastity and corruptors of modesty."[49] As was the case with Robert Grosseteste, Jacques de Vitry seems to have associated penitential manual labor especially with women: he wrote nothing concerning manual labor in his four model sermons for Benedictine and Cistercian monks.[50]

Like Jacques de Vitry, the foundation charter of the Beguinage of St. Elizabeth of Gand also stressed manual labor as a central aspect of the Beguine's way of life, and it represented manual labor as a way of protecting religious women's chastity. According to the charter, the countesses of Flanders and Hainault saw many poor women of their area who had to go begging or support themselves by other shameful means. They founded the Beguinage so that such women could "support and clothe themselves by suitable work, without shaming themselves or their friends."[51]

Jacques de Vitry's sermon to Benedictine nuns and the foundation charter of St. Elizabeth of Gand highlight one of the central reasons for male clerics' promotion of penitential manual labor for religious women: they viewed this "productive labor" as a means that would enable religious women to remain off the streets and, in the case of cloistered nuns, within the domestic sphere of the convent. Strict cloistering was not an issue for religious men, and thus it was not necessary to focus attention on penitential manual labor for religious men. The paradox, here, is that religious women's manual labor was associated not with the public but with the private realm.

A second explanation for male clerics' tendency to associate religious women especially with penitential manual labor had to do with their perceptions of women's capacities: even the best among women could not rise as high in the spiritual and intellectual realms as could the best men. As Bonaventure and Jacques de Vitry put it in their discussions of male labor, those men who should engage in manual labor were the "simple" ones, or the "robust poor," who were not capable of fulfilling the responsibilities of higher forms of labor, such as performing the sacraments and preaching.[52] All women—including women religious—were considered unfit for fulfilling the highest spiritual labors, and thus it was appropriate to encourage all religious women to engage in penitential manual labor, while exempting some religious men from that activity.

In a powerful meditation on his own experience of crippling disability, anthropologist Robert Murphy observed that while white men of his own professional stratum began to distance themselves from him after he became disabled, undergraduates, women, and black men began to treat him as one of their own, or at least as a non-threatening person of equal or less-than-equal status.[53] Murphy's observation suggests that the social position of the observer plays a central role in determining his or her response to disabled and, by extension, to other stigmatized individuals. Thus, in addition to analyzing the texts of thirteenth-century clerics, we need to ask what cultural meanings non-elites constructed for stigmatized individuals and stigmatized activities. In the medieval context, stigma was sometimes attached to disability alone, but it occurred much more frequently when poverty and involuntary begging were also involved. Thus, we need to examine non-elite responses to disability, involuntary begging, and the disabled poor. We also need to ask what non-elites thought about penitential labor as opposed to penitential begging.

As I suggested above, it is difficult to determine the exact meaning that Jehanne of Serris assigned to her own disability. There is no reason to assume that she saw her affliction as a specific punishment for sins that she committed. However, in the case of Nicole of Rubercy, Guillaume de St.-Pathus's narrative does give us reason to believe that Nicole associated her affliction—probably the effect of a stroke—with her own sins. Thus we are told that when she reached St. Louis's tomb Nicole expressed her faith that Louis "was so powerful that no matter how much of a sinner she was he could deliver her from the affliction that had imprisoned her for so long."[54]

Jehanne of Serris's choice to work with her hands in preparation for her pilgrimage suggests that she viewed manual labor as a preferable activity to begging. Perhaps Jehanne chose to work with her hands because her manual labor could be perceived as voluntary rather than involuntary, and thus it could be interpreted as a more effective penitential and supplicatory activity. It is possible, however, that she had internalized the clerical message that involuntary begging was morally suspect. At least one other pilgrim to Louis's tomb, the mother of a crippled girl, believed that "God would be more favorable to them" if they lived by their own labor while they waited at Louis IX's tomb for a cure, and thus she did not want alms to be given to her daughter.[55]

Evidence from the corpus of sources for St. Louis's miracles also suggests that poor people, like clerical elites, sometimes suspected beggars of faking their disabilities. The clerics who held the inquest into Louis's miracles asked the witnesses who had known a person who was allegedly cured by St. Louis if that person could have faked his or her condition. In the surviving fragment of the inquest, all of the witnesses who were asked that question answered no. Moreover, three of the witnesses who had known Luce of Rémilly, the blind woman, pointed to the fact that she had never begged while she was blind as proof that she had not faked her condition.[56] The underlying assumption, here, was that the only rationale for faking a disability was to gain more alms as a beggar.

While working poor people shared some of the clerics' negative attitudes towards the activity of begging, and some afflicted individuals like Nicole of Rubercy apparently saw their disabilities as punishments for sins, the working poor generally tended towards greater generosity and empathy in their responses to individual disabled beggars than did clerical elites. Moreover, unlike clerical elites, the working poor did not view disability as a condition that some lazy individuals might choose in order to avoid the necessity of working.

We learn from the St. Louis sources that a number of working poor people went out of their way to care for poor men and women who had to beg because of their disabilities. Ace the Smith, for instance, gave shelter to Amelot of Chambly, whose body was bent in two with what seems to have been spinal tuberculosis. On days when the ground was too muddy for Amelot to go out begging, Ace provided food for Amelot as well.[57] Laboring men and women like Ace the Smith apparently realized that they themselves might some day become victims to similar misfortunes.

The original inquest concerning Amelot of Chambly indicates that the working poor also recognized that the begging of the disabled was a form of labor. One of Amelot's neighbors, a smith named Robert of Cantarage, declared that it was absurd to think that she could have feigned her malady, "given the great labor and difficulty" that was required of her in order to move about,[58] which she needed to do in order to beg. Similarly, witnesses to the cure of Guillot of Caux, a young man who had begged while he was crippled, highlighted the extreme suffering associated with disability. One of the witnesses declared that "he would not want to have [that disability] for all the kingdom of France."[59]

Did poor people think that women's begging compromised their feminine virtue? It might seem that Jehanne of Serris thought so, given her decision to earn the money for her pilgrimage by spinning. Nevertheless, we need to remember that she also begged during her illness, and that the working distinction between her begging and her manual labor involved both the difference between necessary and penitential labor and that between involuntary and voluntary acts. The fact that Jehanne's husband accepted her necessary begging, as did the husband of Amile of St.-Mathieu, suggests that these women were not seen as compromising their sexual virtue when they went out begging.[60] Economic necessity bred a different attitude towards women's begging than did clerical speculation. In any case, moreover, the fact that these women begged at the door of their parish churches would have eased any worries that their husbands had, since their begging activities took place within sight of neighbors who knew them.

The story of Avice of Berneville, a sixty-year-old woman living in Paris, suggests that unattached women, at least those who were older, could also maintain their virtuous reputations despite the necessity of begging. Avice was cured of a crippling malady in her foot after she had suffered, and begged for her living, for three years. We learn from Guillaume de St.-Pathus's narrative that after her cure her reputation was that of "a good woman," who wore a hairshirt, disciplined her flesh, and fasted.[61]

Given clerical discussions about involuntary begging, their opposition to women's voluntary begging, and their discussions of women's penitential manual labor, and given the ways in which they would have conveyed the conventions of supplicatory pilgrimage to women like Jehanne of Serris, I have no difficulty believing that Jehanne acted in the way that Guillaume de St.-Pathus describes, and that Guillaume saw no contradictions in the narration of her story. Although Jehanne was both painfully crippled and compelled to beg for her living, she made a pilgrimage on crutches to St.-Denis and she paid for that trip by selling a bit of yarn that she had produced with her own hands. Thirteenth-century society was willing to support a disabled woman like Jehanne through formal and informal charitable channels, such as the Hôtel Dieu of Paris and almsgiving in the streets, but its clerical elites also taught Jehanne—in the pulpit, in the confessional, and perhaps in the hospital—that begging was a doubly questionable activity for a lower-status woman.[62] While the working and non-working poor harbored differing views about women's begging, Jehanne chose to conform her behavior to the teachings of the clerics when she embarked on a supplicatory pilgrimage. Those clerics suggested that if she desired divine assistance in the form of a miraculous cure, Jehanne should do penance for whatever sins she had committed and she should choose manual labor, rather than begging, as her penitential activity.

Once she was cured of her ailment, Jehanne would rejoin the ranks of the working poor, but the very elites who encouraged her to do penitential labor while she was sick would remain silent about her need to do manual labor once she was well. For the involuntarily working poor, clerical elites constructed gendered spheres: a sphere of productive labor for men and a sphere of reproductive labor for women. Those spheres conformed neither to the realities of life in the streets of thirteenth-century Paris nor to the gendered roles that clerics constructed for men and women who engaged in penitential activities.

What I have suggested, then, is that several categories of difference complicated the ways in which the third chapter of Genesis functioned in thirteenth-century Paris as a paradigm for men's and women's roles.

First, when clerical elites were the viewers, there was the difference of social status. Clerical authors sometimes elevated the productive and reproductive labors of elite men and women, associating both with the intellectual rather than the material realm. By contrast, they associated the productive and reproductive labors of lower-status men and women with the material realm, and they portrayed both lower-status men and lower-status women as lascivious.

Second, when clerical elites were the viewers, there was the difference of involuntary and voluntary poverty. In their representations of the necessary labors of the involuntarily working poor, clerical elites remained so wedded to the Genesis paradigm that they ignored, or even erased, the productive labor of women, and especially of married women. By contrast, in their discussions of the penitential activities of the voluntary poor, clerical elites placed manual labor in a binary with begging, and they associated women especially with penitential manual labor.

Finally, there was the difference of the viewers themselves. Unlike clerical elites, lower-status men and women experienced on a daily basis the necessity of women's contribution to the household income. They may have wished that things were otherwise, but they certainly were not blinded to women's productive labors and to the necessity of women's begging. Nevertheless, clerical ideologies did at times affect their views, or at least their behavior. Thus, even Jehanne of Serris, who had to beg in order to survive, conformed her behavior to the message that begging was a tainted activity and that God was more likely to answer her petitions if she paid for a supplicatory pilgrimage with money that she earned with her own hands rather than by begging.

The uses and transformations of the Genesis paradigm, and the intersections of that paradigm with distinctions between the physical and intellectual realms, indicate that there was no simple binary system at work in the formation of high medieval gender categories. The difference of social status was sometimes more important than gender differences in drawing the line between the physical and intellectual realms. Social status complicated, without completely undermining, the ways in which the Genesis paradigm worked to draw distinctions between male and female realms. Finally, the purposes behind a woman's engagement with manual labor, which the Genesis paradigm associated with men, determined the degree to which clerical elites accepted, or even perceived, the woman's laboring activity.

NOTES

1. My translation from the Vulgate: "Mulieri quoque dixit: Multiplicabo aerumna tuas, et conceptus tuos: in dolore paries filios, et sub viri potestate eris, et ipse dominabitur tui. Adae vero dixit...maledicta terra in opere tuo: in laboribus comedes ex ea cunctis diebus vitae tuae. Spinas et tribulos germinabit tibi, et comedes herbam terrae. In sudore vultus tui vesceris pane, donec revertaris in terram de qua sumptus es...."

2. See below at note 9 for references to medievalists who have emphasized this distinction. For a critique of scholars who emphasize this distinction in studies of ancient Greek philosophers, see Elizabeth Spelman, *Inessential Woman: Problems of Exclusion in Feminist Thought* (Boston, 1988), chaps. 1 and 2.

3. Bonaventure, "Quaestiones disputatae de perfectione evangelica," Quaest. 2, art. 3, Conclusion, and Bonaventure (attributed), "Expositio super regulam Fratrum minorum," chap. 5, no. 3, *Doctoris Seraphici S. Bonaventurae Opera Omnia,* ed. College of St. Bonaventure (Quaracchi, 1891), 5:161, 8:420. For a general discussion of Bonaventure's views on manual labor, see Christian Wenin, "Saint Bonaventure et le travail manuel," in *Le travail au moyen âge, une approche interdisciplinaire,* ed. Jacqueline Hamesse and Colette Muraille-Samara (Louvain-la-Neuve, 1990), 141–55. On the critique of the mendicant orders by the Parisian secular clergy, see D. L. Douie, *The Conflict Between the Seculars and the Mendicants at the University of Paris in the Thirteenth Century,* Aquinas Society of London, Aquinas Paper 23 (London, 1954); Ernest W. McDonnell, *The Beguines and Beghards in Medieval Culture* (New Brunswick, NJ, 1954), 456–73; and Penn R. Szittya, *The Antifraternal Tradition in Medieval Literature* (Princeton, NJ, 1986), chap. 1.

4. Thomas Aquinas, *Summa Theologica,* 1.92, First Article, ed. Fathers of the English Dominican Province (London, 1914), trans. Elizabeth Clark and Herbert Richardson, in *Women and Religion: A Feminist Sourcebook of Christian Thought* (New York, 1977), 86.

5. Humbert of Romans, "Sermo xcvi ad mulieres burgenses divites," "Sermo xcviii ad famulas divitum," "Sermo xcix ad mulieres pauperes in villulis," *Prediche alle donne del secolo xiii,* ed. Carla Casagrande (Milan, 1978), 47–48, 50–53. Humbert's advice concerning sermon material for various groups in society was highly influential. See Edward Tracy Brett, *Humbert of Romans: His Life and Views of Thirteenth-Century Society* (Toronto, 1984); and D. D'Avray and M. Tausche, "Marriage Sermons in *ad status* Collections of the Central Middle Ages," *Archives d'histoire doctrinale et littéraire du moyen âge* 47 (1980): 71–119.

6. Gilbert of Tournai, "Ad coniugatas, Sermo tertius," in *Prediche alle donne,* ed. Casagrande, 93–97. Like other moralists, Gilbert grounded his description of wifely duties in the biblical text concerning Sarah, the wife of Tobias: Tobias 10:12–13 (this passage is in the Vulgate but not in Protestant translations of the Bible). Gilbert may have been influenced by Aristotelian writings as well. See Silvana Vecchio, "The Good Wife," trans. Clarissa Botsford, in *A History of Women in the West, vol. 2: Silences of the Middle Ages,* ed. Christiane Klapisch-Zuber (Cambridge, MA, 1992), 105–35. On the influence of Aristotle in fourteenth-century discussions of wives see Mireille Vincent-Cassy, "Quand les femmes deviennent paresseuses," in *Femmes, mariages, lignages, xiie–xive siècles: Mélanges offerts à Georges Duby* (Brussells, 1992), 439.

7. Jonathan Alexander, "*Labeur* and *Paresse:* Ideological Representations of Medieval Peasant Labor," *The Art Bulletin* 72 (1990): 439.

8. Humbert of Romans, *De eruditione religiosorum praedicatorum*, 2.1.88, "Ad operarios conductivos," *Maxima bibliotheca veterum Patrum et antiquorum scriptorum ecclesiasticorum*, ed. Marguerin de la Bigne (Lyon, 1677), 25:500.

9. A number of scholars, including myself, have argued that in the Middle Ages women, in general, were more associated with physicality and body than were men. See, for instance, Caroline Walker Bynum, *Holy Feast and Holy Fast: The Religious Significance of Food to Medieval Women* (Berkeley, 1987), 260 ff.; Bynum, *Fragmentation and Redemption: Essays on Gender and the Human Body in Medieval Religion* (New York, 1991), 200 ff.; Barbara Newman, "Flaws in the Golden Bowl: Gender and Spiritual Formation in the Twelfth Century," in her *From Virile Woman to WomanChrist: Studies in Medieval Religion and Literature* (Philadelphia, 1995), 22 ff.; Sharon Farmer, "Softening the Hearts of Men: Women, Embodiment and Persuasion in the Thirteenth Century," in *Embodied Love: Sensuality and Relationship as Feminist Values*, ed. Paula Cooey, Sharon A. Farmer, and Mary Ellen Ross (San Francisco, 1987), 118–19; Farmer, "Feminine Folly, Burgher Calculation and Anti-Communal Rhetoric in Thirteenth-Century Tours," *Studies in Iconography* 17 (1996): 143–76.

10. "En l'an de Nostre Seigneur mil II^c sessante et seze en yver prist une grief maladie Jehenne de Sarris de la dyocese de Paris, femme Jehan le Chapentier.... Et cele maladie la prist einsi que ele ne pooit aler ne soi sostenir ne soi aidier des piez ne des jambes. Et la prist la dite maladie en une nuit entre la Purificacion et Quaresme prenant, tout soit ce que ele entrast en son lit sainne et hetiee en un jour de mardi au soir...quant ele s'esveilla, ele se trouva si afebloiee et malade es cuisses et es jambes et es piez que ele ne se pooit de ses membres aidier.... Et einsi fu ele par l'espace d'un mois en sa meson....

"Et com ele fust einsi malade en sa meson et fust povre ne n'eust qui li aidast, et son mari ne li vosist amenistrer ce qui li failloit, ele fu portee a la meson Dieu de Paris, la ou ele jut lonc tens nonpuissant et malade jusques aprés la feste saint Pere et saint Pol. Et en aprés les sereurs de la meson Dieu se conseillierent entre eles que l'en li feist unes potences.... Et quant... ele fu mise hors du lit et les dames li aidierent, ele ala a grant poine jusques a l'autel de saint Liennart qui est en cele meesme meson.... Et en alant ele metoit le pié destre a terre, mes le senestre n'i pooit ele metre en nule maniere, ainçois le trainoit aprés soi.

"Et puis que ele se pooit movoir ele desirroit estre a sa meson avecques son mari et avecques ses enfanz...Lors emprist ele la voie a potences de revenir a sa meson, mes ele ne pooit aler. De quoi son mari la portoit ausi comme par toute la voie.... Et avint aprés que son mari ne li voloit pas trouver ce que il li couvenoit, et por ce ele aloit a grant poine a potences a l'eglise Saint Merri de Paris querre des aumones.

"Et quant la dite Jehenne oÿ que mout de miracles estoient fez au tombel saint Loÿs et que les malades estoient ilecques gueriz, ele...avoit esperance que ele porroit ilecques estre guerie par les merites du benoiet saint Loÿs. De quoi cele Jehenne qui voloit venir au dit tombel et vivre du sien propre, fila tant que ele gaaigna trois sous que ele porta. Et en un jour de dyemenche au matin ele emprist la voie a Saint Denis a potences, et l'acompaigna une seue fille nus piez et en langes, et vint au dit tombel a grant force, et sonnoient vespres quant ele fu ilecques. Et fu ilec chascun jour par quatre jours aprés le dit tombel ainçois que ele fust guerie, et offri une chandele de sa longueur. . . .

"Et aprés ces choses tozjors, tout fust ce que ele clochast un petitet . . . Et fu saine et hetiee . . . et fist sa besoigne ausi comme une autre femme saine": Guillaume de Saint-Pathus, Confesseur de la reine Marguerite, Les miracles de St. Louis, ed. Percival B. Fay (Paris, 1913), 131–34. Translation is my own. Guillaume recounted sixty-five miracles in all. Thirty-four of those concerned people from Paris and St.-Denis, which was just outside of Paris. On the date of Guillaume's work, see Louis Carolus-Barré, Le procès de canonisation de St. Louis (1272–1297), Essai de reconstitution (Rome, 1994), 24.

11. Sharon Farmer, "Down and Out and Female in Thirteenth-Century Paris," American Historical Review 103 (1998): 345–72.

12. H. Delaborde, "Fragments de l'enquête faite à Saint-Denis en 1282 en vue de la canonisation de St. Louis," Mémoires de la Societé de l'Histoire de Paris et de l'Ile de France 23 (1896): 1–71. For a general discussion of Louis's canonization process, and the sources, see Carolus-Barré, Le procès. Two of the sixty-five miracles were investigated separately from the St.-Denis inquest: Delaborde, "Fragments," 4.

13. Carolus-Barré, Le procès, 24.

14. Janice Archer, "Working Women in Thirteenth-Century Paris," (Ph.D. diss., University of Arizona, 1995), 211–12, 108–10. Women made up 13.8% of the total number of assessees in the 1297–1300 tax assessments, but only 3.1% of the carpenters.

15. For an excellent discussion of historians' tendency to exaggerate the degree to which the members of medieval households were engaged in only one occupation, see Heather Swanson, "The Illusion of Economic Structure: Craft Guilds in Late Medieval English Towns," Past and Present no. 121 (1988): 29–48. For an excellent discussion of women's makeshift economic activities as essential to household survival, see Olwen Hufton, "Women and the Family Economy in Eighteenth-Century France," French Historical Studies 9 (1975): 1–22. The fragments of the St. Louis inquest provide examples of wives living in Paris and St.-Denis who worked selling petty merchandise, spinning, and doing laundry: Delaborde, "Fragments," 49, 52, 58, 62, 66, 70.

16. "Et com ele . . . fust povre ne n'eust qui li aidast, et son mari ne li vosist amenistrer ce qui li failloit," "son mari ne li voloit pas trouver ce que il li couvenoit, et por ce" (Guillaume de Saint-Pathus, Les miracles, 131, 132).

17. Carla Casagrande, "The Protected Woman," in A History of Women in the West II, ed. Klapisch-Zuber, 70–104. Women's "work" is mentioned in one of Gilbert of Tournai's sermons to married women, but he means by that the wife's role in the domestic sphere: "Ad coniugatus, Sermo tertius," 96. Casagrande, "The Protected Woman," mentions a number of moralists who advocated domestic work for women. However, with the exception of the secular author Philippe de Novarre, they post-dated the thirteenth century. Mireille Vincent-Cassy has argued that in the fourteenth and fifteenth centuries moralists became preoccupied with the idea that elite women were especially prone to the sin of idleness. Prescriptions for manual labor were intended to ward off idleness, and its consequence—adultery: "Quand les femmes deviennent paresseuses."

18. In 1292 40% and in 1300 31% of the women in the tax assessment were identified in relational terms, while only 10% and 5.5% of the men were so identified in those

years. In 1300 92.8% of the men were identified by the craft or trade that they practiced, while 78.5% of the women were so identified: Caroline Bourlet, "L'anthroponymie à Paris à la fin du xiiième siècle d'après les rôles de la taille du règne de Philippe le Bel," in *Genèse médiévale de l'anthroponymie moderne*, ed. Monique Bourin and Pascal Chareille, vol. 2, bk. 2 (Tours, 1992), 16, 23. On similar patterns in Florentine tax lists see Isabelle Chabot, "La reconnaissance du travail des femmes dans la Florence du bas Moyen Age: contexte idéologique et réalité," in *La donna nell'economia secc. xiii–xviii*, ed. Simonetta Cavaciocchi (Florence, [1990?]), 565 ff.

19. Archer, "Working Women," 103–08.

20. Male witnesses whose work is named in the initial part of the redaction of the interview: 5–1, 5–3, 5–4, 5–5, 5–6, 5–7, 41–1, 41–2, 51–5. Other male witnesses: 5–2, 41–3, 51–3, 51–6, 51–8. See Delaborde, "Fragments," 19, 21, 24, 27, 29, 31, 33, 39, 42, 44, 59, 62, 64, 69. I am counting "literatus" (5–1) as a professional identification.

21. Delaborde, "Fragments," witnesses 41–4, 41–5, 41–6, 51–1 (the initial part of the interview is missing), 51–2, 51–4, 51–7; pp. 46, 50, 52, 54, 56, 61, 67.

22. Delaborde, "Fragments," 58, 62, 67, 70; Guillaume de Saint-Pathus, *Les miracles,* 158.

23. Guillaume de Saint-Pathus, *Les miracles.* Married men whose work is identified: miracles 3, 6, 10, 25, 28, 31, 33, 36, 42, 46, 48, 49, 64. Married men whose work is not identified: miracles 1, 11, 16, 19, 22, 23, 41, 51, 52, 53, 65. Married women: same miracles as married men. Married woman who spun: miracle 41. I am counting only the beneficiaries of the miracles, or the fathers of the beneficiaries. Since my goal here is to determine Guillaume's gender bias, I have used all sixty-five miracle narratives for this statistic, and not just the stories that deal with Paris and St.-Denis.

24. Guillaume de Saint-Pathus, *Les miracles.* Single men whose occupations are identified: miracles 7, 8, 9, 13, 14, 15, 20, 24, 45, 63. Single men whose work is not identified: miracles 17, 18, 40. The marital status of the men in miracles 60 and 61 is not clear. The work of both is identified. Single women whose work is identified: miracles 2, 4 (this woman later married, we only know what she did before marriage), 39, 44, 55, 58, 59. Single women whose work is not identified: miracles 5, 32, 35, 37, 43, 57. It is unclear if the mother in miracle 54 is married, widowed, or single, so I have not counted her. Her work is not identified. I am counting only the beneficiaries of the miracles and their parents.

25. Delaborde, "Fragments," 62, 69.

26. Delaborde, "Fragments," 54.

27. Delaborde, "Fragments," 50 (there is a gap after "dicit quod nichil nisi quod lucratur de labore suo . . ."; presumably the text continued, "et de labore viri sui"), 52, 56, 59.

28. Delaborde, "Fragments," 21, 26 (he also has a house), 33, 42 (he says he supports his wife and three daughters, while his wife [p. 50] says she lives on her own labor [and presumably that of her husband—there is a gap in the text]), 44 (he says he supports himself and his family), 61, 67, 71.

29. Bronislaw Geremek, *Le salariat parisien au xiiie–xve siècles,* trans. from the Polish by Anna Posner and Christiane Klapisch-Zuber (Paris, 1982), 89–91.

30. Guillaume de Saint-Pathus, *Les miracles.* Mothers who stayed at the tomb: miracles 6, 11, 16, 23, 41, and 49. In miracle 41 the father accompanied the mother to St.-Denis, but

then returned to Paris. In four other miracles (10, 53, 54, 56) the mother alone took the child to the tomb. In three additional miracles (22, 31, 36) both parents took the child; and in two (26/27 and 47) the father alone took the child, but did not stay at the tomb for more than one day. Yfamia, the mother who spun, is in miracle 41: Delabord, "Fragments," 49.

31. On walking as "la forme élémentaire et primordiale de la pénitence," see Raymonde Foreville, "Les 'Miracula S. Thomae Cantuariensis,'" in *Assistance et assisté jusqu'a 1610, Actes du 97ᵉ Congrès National des Sociétés Savantes* (Paris, 1979), 452; citing E.-R. Labande, "Eléments d'une enquête sur les conditions de déplacement du pèlerin aux xᵉ et xiᵉ siècles," in *Pellegrinaggi e culto dei santi in Europa fino alla prima crociata*, Convegni del Centro di studi sulla spiritualità medievale v (Todi, 1963).

32. Jerome Kroll and Bernard Bachrach, "Sin and the Etiology of Disease in Pre-Crusade Europe," *Journal of the History of Medicine and Allied Sciences* 41 (1986): 395–414.

33. See, for instance, Humbert of Romans, *De eruditione*, 2.1.92, "Ad infirmos in hospitalibus" (*Maxima*, 25:502).

34. Miri Rubin, *Charity and Community in Medieval Cambridge* (Cambridge, 1987), 148–51. In the St. Louis corpus, confession is explicitly linked to the pilgrimage in miracles 5, 7, 11, 20, 28, 39, 43, 45, 48, 51, 58: Delaborde, "Fragments," 32; Guillaume de Saint-Pathus, *Les miracles*, 26, 35 (pilgrim confesses while staying in St.-Denis), 69, 87, 123, 135, 138–39, 145, 156, 178.

35. See Brian Tierney, "The Decretists and the 'Deserving Poor,'" *Comparative Studies in Society and History* 1 (1958–59): 360–73.

36. Thomas Aquinas, *Summa theologiae*, 2a2ae, quaest. 186, art. 3, resp. ad 2, ed. and trans. Blackfriars (Oxford, 1973), 47:108–11.

37. Jerome, "Against Vigilantius," 14, *The Principal Works of St. Jerome*, trans. W. H. Freemantle, The Nicene and Post-Nicene Fathers 6 (Grand Rapids, MI, 1954), 422; Thomas Aquinas, "Contra impugnantes dei cultum et religionem," chap. 7, *Sancti Thomae Aquinatis Doctoris Angelici Ordinis Praedicatorum Opera Omnia*, 25 vols. (Parma, 1852–73), 15:43; Bonaventure, "Apologia pauperum," chap. 12, in *Doctoris Seraphici S. Bonaventurae Opera Omnia*, ed. College of St. Bonaventure, 8:329.

38. Thomas of Chobham, *Summa de arte praedicandi*, chap. 3, lines 1053–57, ed. Franco Morenzoni, Corpus christianorum, continuatio mediaevalis 82 (Turnhout, 1988), 88.

39. Gustave Cohen, "Le thème de l'aveugle et du paralytique dans la littérature française," in *Mélanges offerts à Émile Picot par ses amis et ses élèves* (Paris, 1913; reprint, Geneva, 1969), 2:393–404; Thomas Frederick Crane, *The Exempla or Illustrative Stories from the Sermones Vulgares of Jacques de Vitry* (London, 1890; reprint, New York, 1971), 52; Jacobus de Voragine, *Legenda aurea*, ed. Th. Graesse (Dresden, 1846), 750.

40. Peter the Chanter, "Verbum abbreviatum," in *Patrologia cursus completus, series latina*, ed. J.-P. Migne, 221 vols. (Paris, 1841–66), 205:152–53 (hereafter referred to as *PL*); Thomas of Chobham, *Summa confessorum*, ed. F. Broomfield, Analecta Mediaevalia Namurcensia 25 (Louvain, 1968), 297; Thomas of Chobham, *Summa de arte praedicandi*, chap. 3, lines 1050–53 (p. 88).

41. On the controversy surrounding voluntary male mendicancy see McDonnell, *The Beguines*, 456–73. On male prohibitions against and critiques of female mendicancy see ibid., 146, 463; Jean-Claude Schmitt, *Mort d'une hérésie: L'Église et les clercs face aux*

béguines et aux béghards du Rhin supérieur du xive au xve siècle (Paris, 1978), 56–59; Brenda Bolton, "Vitae Matrum," in *Medieval Women*, ed. Derek Baker (Oxford, 1978), 262; Jo Ann Kay McNamara, *Sisters in Arms: Catholic Nuns Through Two Millennia* (Cambridge, MA, 1996), 250–51; Amy M. Hollywood, *The Soul as Virgin Wife: Mechthild of Magdeburg, Marguerite Porete, and Meister Eckhart* (Notre Dame, 1995), 42–44.

42. Letter of Conrad of Marburg, ed. Albert Huyskens, *Quellenstudien zur Geschichte der hl. Elizabeth Langräfin von Thüringen* (Marburg, 1908), 158; Testimony of Elizabeth's servant Irmengardis, ibid., 130.

43. Thomas de Cantimpré, *The Life of Margaret of Ypres*, trans. Margot H. King (Toronto, 1990), 57.

44. John Moorman, *A History of the Franciscan Order from Its Origins to the Year 1517* (Oxford, 1968), 32–39, 207.

45. Jacques de Vitry, *The Life of Marie d'Oignies*, prologue, trans. Margot H. King (Saskatoon, 1986), 3; on Mary's manual labor, 39.

46. *Lettres de Jacques de Vitry*, 1.116–22, ed. R. B. C. Huygens (Leiden, 1960), 75; trans. Regis J. Armstrong, *Clare of Assisi: Early Documents* (New York, 1988), 246.

47. The Rule of St. Benedict, chap. 48, *RB 1980: The Rule of St. Benedict in Latin and English with Notes and Thematic Index*, ed. Timothy Fry, abridged edition (Collegeville, MN, 1981), 96; Burchard of Worms, *Liber decretorum*, 19.26, *PL* 140:984; Reimbaldus Leodiensis, *Stromata, seu de uoto reddendo et de paenitentia non iteranda*, 82, *Reimbaldi Leodiensis Opera Omnia*, ed. C. De Clercq, Corpus christianorum, continuatio mediaevalis 4 (Turnhout, 1966), 110.

48. Thomas of Eccleston, *Tractatus de adventu Fratrum Minorum in angliam*, ed. A. G. Little (Manchester, 1951), 99.

49. "Nonnulle etiam ut a parentibus uel consanguineis aliqua extorquent, dum de claustro sicut Dina euagando exeunt, multos hostes castitatis et pudicitie corruptores reperiunt et inimici monialis domestici eius": Jacques de Vitry, "Sermo xxvii, ad moniales nigras," ed. Jean Longère, "Quatre sermons *ad religiosas* de Jacques de Vitry," in *Les religieuses en France au xiiie siècle*, ed. Michel Parisse (Nancy, 1985), 251; on all of the advantages of manual labor, 249–52. Humbert of Romans made similar comments about the dangers encountered by nuns who left the cloister in order to seek necessities: Brett, *Humbert of Romans*, 193. On late-twelfth-century precedents for this association of "want and wickedness" in clerics' attitudes towards nuns, see Bruce Venarde, *Women's Monasticism and Medieval Society: Nunneries in France and England, 890–1215* (Ithaca, NY, 1997), 168.

50. Paris, Bibliothèque Nationale, MS lat. 3284, fols. 56v-67v.

51. *Cartulaire du Beguinage de Sainte-Elisabeth à Gand*, ed. Jean Béthune (Bruges, 1883), trans. Emily Amt, *Women's Lives in Medieval Europe: A Sourcebook* (New York, 1993), 264.

52. Jacques de Vitry, "Sermo xxxv ad Fratres Minores," *Analecta novissima spicilegii Solesmensis Altera continuatio*, ed. J. P. Pitra (reprint, Farnborough, 1967), 2:400–402; Bonaventure, "Quaestiones disputatae," Quaest. 2, art. 3, Conclusion (*Doctoris Seraphici S. Bonaventurae Opera Omnia*, 5:161): "inter membra Christi sunt quaedam maxime idonea ad operationes corporales et minime ad spirituales . . . hinc est quod illis pauperibus validis, qui ad opera corporalia maxime sunt idonei et minime ad spiritualia . . . eis est opus manuale in *praecepto*."

53. Robert Murphy, "Encounters: The Body Silent in America," in *Disability and Culture*, ed. Benedicte Ingstad and Susan Reynolds Whyte (Berkeley, 1995), 140–58. See the essays in this volume and in *The Disability Studies Reader*, ed. Lennard J. Davis (New York, 1997) for a general introduction to the cultural construction of disability, and the intersections of disabilities with gender constructions.

54. Guillaume de Saint-Pathus, *Les miracles*, 123.

55. "Nolebant quod daretur ei elemosina, pro eo quod, sibi videbatur quod, si de suo labore hic [Louis's tomb] viveret cum filia sua predicta, magis esset propitius sibi Deus" (Delaborde, "Fragments," 49).

56. Delaborde, "Fragments," 57, 62, 66.

57. Delaborde, "Fragments," 31–32.

58. "Dicit quod assurdum et inhumanum est quod, cum tanto labore et difficultate [several words missing from document] sic incessisset" (Delaborde, "Fragments," 25).

59. "Il ne la vodroit avoir pour tout le roiaume de France" (Guillaume de Saint-Pathus, *Les miracles*, 59).

60. Amile of St.-Mathieu is in Guillaume de Saint-Pathus, *Les miracles*, miracle 52.

61. Guillaume de Saint-Pathus, *Les miracles*, 107.

62. On confession and pilgrimage, see note 34 above.

10

FEMALE HOMOEROTIC DISCOURSE AND RELIGION IN MEDIEVAL GERMANIC CULTURE

ULRIKE WIETHAUS

Love has the days, And I, the nights and the madness of love.
—Hadewijch, Poems in Stanzas

As the editors of *Gender and Difference in the Middle Ages* point out, medieval constructions of gender were more complex, contradictory, and unstable than has been assumed in much of traditional scholarship. The current surge of interest in medieval homosexuality adds a much-needed depth dimension; unfortunately, however, it still suffers from a certain lopsidedness: scholarship on homoerotic discourse and behavior in medieval western Europe has produced significantly fewer studies of women than of men. This discrepancy is usually explained as being due to (1) a scarcity of available sources, (2) the absence of a satisfactory conceptual framework to interpret existing data, and (3) a methodological tendency to subsume female homoerotic activity under the rubric of male homoeroticism.[1] I will begin by addressing these three issues as they pertain to western European, especially German-speaking, medieval culture and thus create a context for the second part of this essay, a close reading of the works of a woman writer who was prominent in the formation of

Christian bridal mysticism, the Beguine Hadewijch of Brabant (fl. first half of thirteenth century.).

I suggest that, especially in the religious realm, the current perception of a lack of source materials is influenced by our search for descriptions of aesthetics and relations that fit contemporary models of homoeroticism. As recent work on the twelfth-century Benedictine abbess Hildegard of Bingen and the fourteenth-century laywoman Margery Kempe demonstrates, however, our reading practices must expand to accommodate a conceptual framework capable of capturing and decoding the "otherness" of medieval female homoerotic (sub)cultures.[2] In the context of the complex textual landscape of medieval religious writing, the issue here is precisely the power of medieval literary genres to delimit, encode, and police the transmission of knowledge and concomitant social practices. Religious genres are not only purely compositional drills in rhetoric or devotional exercises in piety, but reenact social conflicts and demarcate relations of power as they represent the specific communities that engendered them.[3] In a heterosexist patriarchal social system, who can speak/write what about female same-sex attraction is thus determined by a subject's social and economic status, her gender, and her (in)ability and (limited) choice to master, to employ, to usurp, to subvert the laws of speech and textual genres. To use James C. Scott's terminology, it is not only skill that determines the use of public and hidden transcripts, but first and foremost social location and one's investment in maintaining existing power relations.[4] I propose that since ecclesiastical elites publicly disapproved of sexual difference of any kind, non-conforming female subcultures, like other subaltern groups, developed alternative, carefully coded types of discourse and social practices to express both homoerotic desire and resistance to heterosexist politics of domination.

Hildegard of Bingen's reflections on homoeroticism are a case in point. Conflict-ridden as they are, they include both submission to the public transcripts of the ecclesiastical elite and resistance to its ideological stance. When writing, on the one hand, within the parameters of a theologico-visionary genre (my term), Hildegard, like Hadewijch a member of the elite class, repeated the condemnatory rhetoric found in other elite theological texts. On the other hand, her liturgical songs and personal letters constituted genres aimed at a gender-inclusive or even exclusively female audience. Given this change in social context and the genres' greater flexibility to express individual creative impulses, songs and letters permitted Hildegard to express same-sex attachment and to develop a homoerotic liturgical aesthetics.[5] She could thus both advocate a vision of social order based on heterosexist homogeneity (as expressed in the theological visions) and give voice to an intimate community of difference, the small circle of her monastery, where she lived surrounded by women (as articulated in her letters and liturgical songs composed for her nuns).[6]

To highlight the background of patriarchal literary genres against which some religious women developed their aesthetics of homoerotic attraction, I will begin the essay with a brief survey of the ways in which elite male discourse framed and regulated the cultural and social trans-mission of knowledge about female homoeroticism. Of course, any genre allows for degrees of subversion of its rules, but as I hope to demonstrate below, it appears that within a medieval religious context, only genres practiced predominantly by women and composed for other women could foster positively inscribed explorations of female homoerotic dif-ference. To what extent these textual productions reflect the practices of communities of women less privileged, less educated, and less religiously inclined than Hadewijch and Hildegard is almost impossible to recon-struct. All sources used in this essay reflect only a small spectrum of medieval society, that of literate female and male elites.

Following the survey of male writings on female homoeroticism be-low, I will contextualize Hadewijch's homoerotic religious aesthetics within the parameters of linguistic idiom and geographical place by presenting some evidence of same-sex attachments from German-speaking religious women's communities. My argument is that given the potential for ex-periencing and safely articulating female same-sex attraction in these exclusively female communities as well as the material and economic possibility for the cultural production of imaginative and playful spiritual texts and performances, it is likely that at least some women did venture into creating homoerotic aesthetics and practices. I suggest that Hadewijch attempted precisely this in some of her devotional writings. Much like Margery Kempe perfected her performance of polysemous devotional "sobs and sighs" and Hildegard pursued her innovative liturgical com-positions, clad in the "flesh of her voice," Hadewijch developed thick layers of spiritual metaphors and tantalizing descriptions of homoerotic discourse. Through these metaphors and descriptions, Hadewijch created multiple and fluid gendered positions that challenge our notions of gendered binaries. No doubt, mystical discourse with its emphasis on metaphorical speech as *conditio sine qua non* offered a privileged site for such explorations, whether in Christian mysticism or in mystical traditions of other religions (see, for example, the works of the medieval Muslim mystic Rumi).

A caveat, however: in none of these cases do we know to what degree the author's homoerotic sensibility translated into sexual acts, or even what would and would not constitute such acts as homoerotic/homosexual from her point of view. For these three authors/performers, erotic desire for woman/women focused most explicitly on imaginary spiritual figures legitimized by dominant cultural discourse: the Virgin Mary (as in the case of Hildegard and Margery) and Lady Love, or Minne, a symbol of divine ecstatic love (for Hadewijch). Explored with passion and fervor, the realm of soul, spirit, and metaphor shielded the women from condemnatory social censure and yet permitted them to affirm in writing and performance what secular and religious institutions encoded in negative terms only. For Hadewijch, the world of metaphor moved dangerously close to material reality and destabilized any expectations of fixed gender identities. In her texts, Minne/Lady Love/Divine Ecstatic Love appears to have eventually transmutated into Hadewijch's alter ego. At times, it is impossible to determine whether Hadewijch spoke about her passionate attraction to another woman, or whether Minne wooed the soul in the spiritual realm.[7] Sometimes, Hadewijch seemed to imply that Minne and Christ were one. In the dynamics of bridal mysticism, Hadewijch's female soul thus engaged in courting another woman under the guise of heterosexual pursuits. As in the case of Margery Kempe's worship of the Virgin Mary, the figure of Christ turned into Hadewijch's go-between in the female-male-female courtly drama.[8]

We know very little about Hadewijch the author. The sophistication of her writings betrays a highly educated, literate, and therefore most likely well-to-do person. All of Hadewijch's works appear to be pedagogical in intent and communicate esoteric insight into the nature of God and spiritual transformation.[9] Hadewijch left us fourteen visions, thirty-one letters, most of which were written to a group of female students, forty-five Poems in Stanzas (the *Strophische Gedichten*) formally indebted to secular love lyrics, and sixteen Poems in Couplets (the *Mengeldichten*). Although the works were composed in the first half of the thirteenth century, the earliest manuscripts available date from the fourteenth century. Her writings, especially the letters, appear to have been widely excerpted and circulated among religious houses in the Low Countries and Northern Germany. Hadewijch influenced in particular the late medieval *Devotio moderna* movement. The Augustinian priest and mystical author Jan van Ruusbroec (1293–1381) appropriated verbatim some of Hadewijch's teachings. He also left us a eulogy that stressed her rare insight and subtlety.[10] The wide distribution of her texts suggests that she enjoyed authority and fame as a spiritual teacher and a writer and that her own community was well connected to other religious centers of her time.

DISCOURSE OF DOMINATION: ECCLESIASTICAL AND SECULAR SOURCES ON MEDIEVAL WOMEN'S HOMOEROTICISM

The sources at our disposal are quite diverse in style, comprising theological writings, canonical and synodal statements, penitentials, and law codes.[11] Despite some noteworthy surface differences, all texts are consistently condemnatory. Unsurprisingly perhaps, ecclesiastics could not tolerate their own exclusion from female same-sex acts nor could they bear the female use of mechanical representations of male body parts. Female same-sex acts were thus reimagined with a potent male presence: either God or Satan looked on *in loco viris*.[12] In the penitentials and law books, female use of an artificial penis was punished more heavily than any other female homoerotic activity. Apart from such shared intentions and anxieties, each public transcript generated a distinct image of female same-sex activity. It is vaguest in the language of the councils, described here as un-gendered "sin," equally applicable to men and women, and with neither gender's activities singled out. In the discourse of law codes and theology, homoeroticism was constructed as a symmetrically gendered activity, with male and female genders named explicitly, yet the sex act was left unspecified. It remained unmentioned in secular literature. In the discourse of penitentials and inquisitorial texts, finally, homoerotic activity became framed as asymmetrically gendered (female as inferior to male), sex-act specific (particulars were provided), physiologically concrete rather than abstract, and detailed. It is a testimony to the social staying power of these patriarchal speech genres and the institutions they represent that they have remained more intelligible, more amenable to contemporary reading habits than the genres of resistance developed by women's homoerotic (sub)cultures.

In theological discourse, writers invented the rather vague and catch-all concept of sodomy, which was defined as both male and female sin.[13] Following Paul, theologians approached both male and female homosexuality and homoeroticism primarily as a religious problem, defined as human distortion of divine order.[14] Only a few theologians, however, concerned themselves explicitly with female homosexual behavior. Following Romans 1:26, female homosexual activity was turned into a subcategory of sins *contra naturam* that also included bestiality and other sex acts precluding procreation (masturbation, male homoerotic activity, etc.). Carolingian archbishop Hincmar of Reims (ninth century) castigated women's "devilish manipulations" with "certain instruments."[15] Peter Abelard (twelfth century), infamous for his own transgressive heterosexual behavior, declared female same-sex acts sinful because female genitalia were divinely prepared for the "use of men," not other women.[16] Albertus Magnus (thirteenth century) deserves the dubious recognition of being the first theologian who labeled female (and male) homosexual activity the worst of all sins and, drawing on his medical background, suggested its highly contagious nature.[17] Thomas Aquinas followed the views of his teacher Albertus Magnus and placed female and male homosexual activity in the same category.[18] The central theological argument that homosexual activity was a sin *contra naturam,* that is, violating God's established order, eventually found its way into definitions of heresy and witchcraft. In Middle High German, the Latin word *catharus* (Cathar) gave birth to the noun *Ketzer* (heretic). Both the noun and the verb *ketzern* eventually denoted anal intercourse.[19] In Germany, the identification of heresy as homosexual activity can be documented in a law code as early as 1276, to be punished by death by fire.[20]

Whereas for theologians, female homosexuality (when mentioned) generally belonged to the same category as male homosexuality, the authors of penitential literature differentiated between the two: women were punished more leniently than men, and widows and girls received less punishment for homosexual activities than married women. The earliest texts referring to women are the penitentials by Theodore (ca. 670) and Bede (before 734). Transgressing male prerogatives—in this instance the use of an artificial penis—was defined as more of a sin than female homoerotic acts as such.[21]

Medieval canonical statements declared homosexual activity as worthy of excommunication. The Third and Fourth Lateran Councils (1179 and 1215) condemned homosexual activity in general terms as *incontinentia contra naturam,* punishable by excommunication and suspension from ecclesiastical office; no difference was made between male and female acts.[22]

In German laws, the earliest mention of male homosexuality can be found in the *Schwabenspiegel,* composed in the thirteenth century. Here, the activity itself was not deemed worthy of punishment by death, but falsely accusing others of it was.[23] Thirteenth-century German-speaking countries witnessed at least two executions of men by burning: one in Augsburg in 1276 for homosexual acts defined as heresy, one in Ghent in 1292 as punishment for pederasty.[24] The first European law explicitly decreeing the burning of women condemned of homosexual relations originated in Orleans around 1260.[25] In 1477, the city court of Speyer executed Katherina Hetzeldorfer for seducing other women, by drowning her in the Rhine river.[26] In 1507, German law decreed death by fire for both female and male homosexual activity, a practice that would remain in force until the eighteenth century.[27] In a catalogue of questions used by German inquisitors, composed in 1558, lesbian activity became associated with witchcraft, a view illustrated in chilling drawings by Hans Baldung Grien (1475–1545).[28]

In contrast, secular authors were more reticent on the topic than their ecclesiastical brothers or colleagues in the legal profession. In German literature, male homosexual acts are mentioned rarely, female acts never.[29] According to one analysis, male homosexual activity generally tended to be described as a crisis in masculine identity formation, a negatively inscribed aberration from the norm. German courtly novels brim with tantalizing information about intense same-sex friendships and interaction among women, and even go so far as to offer visions of harmonious utopian places inhabited exclusively by women.[30]

We may conclude that wherever the closest physical contact (i.e., sinful sexual behavior) and most direct and immediate punishment of women became a possibility for celibate authors, male rhetoric turned the most voyeuristic, sex-specific, and detailed. The male formation of a secular rhetoric on female homoeroticism, whether in law or in literature, developed more hesitantly than in religious discourse. Does this indicate that there was a greater lack of interest in and tolerance of female (and male) same-sex attraction outside the church than within it? Do we need to conclude therefore that ecclesiastical elites within the church must shoulder the greatest responsibility for the rise in homophobia and the virulent disdain for sexual difference in western Europe? It is noteworthy that sex-act specific and physiologically concrete and detailed accounts of German trials of lesbians appear many centuries after the appearance of such language in penitential discourse. The punishments are lethal: the 1477 trial of Katherina Hetzeldorfer led to her drowning; the trial of 1721 ended in the beheading of 27-year-old Katherina Margaretha Linck. Her court records are filled with explicit descriptions of female genitals and sex acts between Katherina and her lover/wife Margaretha Mühlhahn.[31]

If genres employed toward the social control of female sexuality and the eradication of sexual difference applied the strategies of physical explicitness, voyeurism, and the invocation of "divine order" and "natural" law, what discursive tools were chosen by female religious authors to assert and articulate sexual difference and a location at the margins of the church?

FEMALE RELIGIOUS AUTHORS AND THE CONSTRUCTION OF SAME-SEX AFFECTION

In the rare female-authored medieval discourse on *physical* same-sex attraction, emphasis appears to have been placed on kissing and caressing, but not on genital activity. Depictions of strong emotional attraction seem to have been the norm but only rarely expressed an appreciation of physical attributes. Given that explicit descriptions of female-female genital activity characterized heterosexist discourse with the intention to penalize and to control female sexual difference, there is little reason to assume that religious women would tend to appropriate such discursive praxis for themselves. One might argue that the religious ideal of celibacy served as another determent for religious women writers. Unlike today, however, medieval religious discourse, especially in the realm of spirituality, thrived on often explicit hetero-erotic imagery. For example, women mystics such as the Austrian Beguine Agnes Blannbekin (d. 1315) revelled in

√ descriptions of rapturously swallowing Christ's foreskin.[32] Hadewijch left us one of the most erotic descriptions of fusion with the human Christ that include references to the body (see discussion below).

A few medieval women authors commented on (male) sodomy and reiterated some of the male views referred to above, thus aligning themselves closely with the patriarchal elites whose status was invested in the dissemination and persuasiveness of such views. For these women, class solidarity seems to have outweighed identification with one's gender group. In the tenth century, Hrotsvit of Gandersheim described male homosexual desire in her play on the contemporary adolescent martyr St. Pelagius. In her narrative, Pelagius, imprisoned by the Muslims, refuses the advances of the Caliph, a man "corrupted by Sodomitic vices."[33] In the drama, unbelief, male homosexuality, and the threat of Islamic culture are tightly linked.[34] In the twelfth century, Hildegard of Bingen defined sodomy within the parameters of theological discourse as *maxima blasphemia.* In the *Liber divinorum operum,* she explained sodomy as the work of the diabolical snake; in *Scivias,* homosexual acts subvert the divinely ordained gendered sexual behavior assigned to men and women.[35] Mechthild of Magdeburg, a thirteenth-century Beguine, never mentioned female homosexual activity explicitly, but referred to sodomy in general in her dramatic vision of the city of hell, where the "sin of Sodom" represents one of its cornerstones. Situated in the lowest depth of the smoldering city, Lucifer inhales sodomites into his belly only to spit them out again when coughing. Although we might expect some references to genitals or the anus, it is those who are stingy that Lucifer devours, digests, and eventually defecates. Interestingly, his "dreadful kisses" are bestowed on hypocrites posing as saints.

Female same-sex attraction is expressed in two, possibly three, rhymed love letters written, so it seems, by anonymous nuns. They are part of a twelfth-century manuscript found in the male monastery of Tegernsee.[36] Both in form and content, these letters follow male traditions within the genre of Latin love lyrics, lamenting the absence of the beloved. Given women's stricter enclosure within a monastery, it is not clear how literal the topos of a lover's absence was intended to be. Unlike other women's texts but similar to male-authored letters, the poems contain vague references to physical attributes of the sorely missed lover as well as hints of physical intimacy.[37] The letters boldly depart from the literary norm by changing the sender's sex from male to female. In my view, the explicit mixture of literal and metaphorical possibilities of interpretation does not necessarily mean that the poems describe actual relationships, as it has been repeatedly suggested, although this interpretation cannot be excluded. What the poems do suggest very clearly and unambiguously constitutes a significant corrective to heterosexist genres: at least some authors, whether female or even perhaps male (can we exclude the possibility that a male author took on a female author's persona in order to play with the limits of this genre?) had the intellectual and emotional ability to conceive of female same-sex attraction in positive and nonpunitive terms.

Religious women writers thus wrote about same-sex attraction in genres that suited their particular needs. Some could be disseminated most effectively among female audiences. These genres comprise letters, visionary writings, and devotional texts. I have discussed Hildegard's epistolary oeuvre as a document of passionate same-sex friendship and possibly homoerotic attraction elsewhere;[38] Hadewijch's letters, poems, and visionary writings will be analyzed below. The social and material context for these writings was always an exclusively female, elite, and literate environment, whether a monastery or beguinage. The texts reveal to us a spectrum of women's relationships, some of them fostering exclusivity in affection. We find male suspicion of such attachment as early as 423, when Augustine of Hippo reminded his sister about her proper behavior as a nun:

> The love which you bear one another ought not to be carnal, but spiritual: for those things which are practiced by immodest women, even with other females, in shameful jesting and playing, ought not to be done even by married women or by girls who are about to marry, much less by widows or chaste virgins dedicated by a holy vow to be handmaidens of Christ.[39]

It appears to be a recurring pattern in this milieu that one woman was chosen as confidante and special companion; her notable attributes were faithfulness, that is, complete reliability, and the wish to remain in close physical proximity to her friend. When and how faithfulness turned into playfulness and joyful jesting, we do not know: all we can do is to note

an exclusively female climate of affection, loyalty, and intense attachment that *could* allow for the homoeroticism expressed by Hildegard
and Hadewijch and eloquently described eight centuries later by contemporary lesbian nuns. Eroticism in this context has equally blurred boundaries as the notion of a "climate" of mutual affection: in contrast to the
concept of sodomy that denotes specific male sex acts, it tries to reflect
the *range* of medieval women's testimonies to their same-sex attraction,
from an appreciation of physical attributes and activities to emotional and
spiritual components of their desires.[40] The Dominican mystic Margaretha
Ebner (d. 1351), best known for her correspondence with her spiritual director Heinrich of Nördlingen, left us a description of close emotional
bonding in a climate conducive of same-sex affection:

> I had a sister, whom God had given me for consolation. By divine
> design she served me joyfully throughout the years and protected
> me from all things that could disturb me. When, in my illness,
> I was sometimes unkind to her while she served me, she did
> not hold that against me. This sister became very ill by God's
> design. Then we were both sick and in suffering and patiently
> endured much pain. Because of that I was greatly distressed
> out of concern for my sister. I slept little every night due to sor-
> row, and still I desired to see her even in her suffering up to my
> own death.... I would gladly have died for her.... I was with
> her all the time until she died.... When I saw her lying on the
> bier I found it hard to bear.[41]

Margaretha secretly desired to kiss a large crucifix mounted high up
on a wall, but, as she wrote, "only one sister knew about my desire; otherwise no one else."[42] God asked her to pray for numerous sisters, and a
strong bond developed between herself and one of the women prayed
for. Margaretha described their attachment and its religious implications
as follows:

> She trusted me completely. It happened that she became sick
> and miserable. I never looked at her without experiencing true
> joy; this my Lord Jesus Christ knows well. Whenever I left the
> table, I had the custom of bringing her whatever I saw that would
> please her. I always went to her as if she were God Himself.[43]

In the daily life of a female monastery, in the ordinary transactions between religious women, a radical theology was lived that was declared anathema in male theological discourse: God is a woman, and she is cared for intimately, materially, physically.

Other examples of women's friendships are movingly depicted in Book Five of Gertrud of Helfta's *Legatus Divinae Pietatis;* the affection of the nuns for each other becomes most poignant at the point of death. Gertrud recounted how the painfully dying Mechthild of Hackeborn (d. 1299) comforted her distraught friends:

> She consoled the sisters with loving kindness and said, 'Do not cry and do not be sad because of me, my loved ones. Your despair affects me so deeply that if my beloved Lover [Christ] would will it, I would rather live with such pain so that I may continue to be your solace.'[44]

As these examples make clear, literate men's and women's conceptual maps of female same-sex attraction differed dramatically. In comparison, two points stand out clearly. First, women did not employ the abstract categories and explicit and/or detailed references to female genitals and/or sexual activities of patriarchal discourses of domination when describing same-sex attraction; when such categories formed part of a discourse mastered by a woman writer, she would also accept and reproduce the inherent damnation of sexual difference. Hrotsvit, Hildegard, and Mechthild commented on sodomy as theological abstraction and condemned it; the anonymous authors of the Tegernsee described female physiology according to the rhetorical laws of love lyrics, thus rehearsing the male gaze.[45] Second, female authors conceptualized female same-sex attraction in the context of intense attachments to a specific female friend; no abstract theory was formed to analyze and describe the friendship; the possibility of an erotic dimension remained unnamed, although the relationship evolved in the realm of the physical, in the realm of the body, and was shaped by experiences related to food, sleep, illness, death, worship, and work.

In the final section of this essay, I will demonstrate how Hadewijch invented an exception to both ecclesiastical and female monastic frameworks. She developed the language of close female friendship further to include (1) a category of abstraction (her interpretation of bridal mysticism), and (2) explicit eroticism couched in spiritual imagery. Life in a tightly knit female religious subculture and her recognized status as a teacher and an educated, literate, and most likely wealthy person provided the social location for her remarkable achievement. Hadewijch's strong affections for at least one of her younger disciples might also point to a distinctive medieval type of female homoeroticism: the age-differentiated female mentor-student relationship.[46] We find possible references to such dyads in other texts as well. One of the Tegernsee letters refers to the sender's *pectuscula,* "little breasts," another to the addressee in the company of a *conventus iuvencularum* a convent of young "little girls," assuming that at least one partner was quite young and sexually attractive.[47] Hildegard of Bingen's beloved companion and aide Richardis was much younger than herself. The abbess Benedetta Carlini engaged in same-sex behavior with the younger nun Bartolomea.[48] Was it simply the association of female youthfulness with sexual attractiveness that formed the background to these admittedly fragmentary stories, or does it represent a well-established historical pattern that permitted at least some medieval women to explore intense same-sex attraction within the socially accepted parameters of age-differentiated relationships?

"SEDUCTION IS THE CUSTOM OF HER SCHOOL" (POEMS IN COUPLETS, 13:30): HOMOEROTIC DYNAMICS IN HADEWIJCH'S WORK

The genre of devotional literature, still unaffected by the increase in institutionalized abstract thinking propagated by scholastic theology and, much later, by the iconoclasm of the Reformation era, could accommodate a variety of spiritual systems. I propose that the symbolically flexible model of bridal mysticism permitted Hadewijch to develop a subtle narrative theology of same-sex affection with a strong homoerotic bent. It offered Hadewijch the same opportunities for a discourse of resistance as the social practice of female mourning did for Margery Kempe or the genre of liturgical songs provided for Hildegard. In Hadewijch's mystical writings, the imaginary bigendered figure of Minne plays a three-fold role: as a spiritual guide, she models esoteric same-sex student-mentor relations; as a symbol of love, she becomes a foil on which to project a

specific form of female desire for another woman; as an idealized alter
ego, she can speak Hadewijch's own desire.[49]

Hadewijch is usually approached as a proponent of bridal mysticism,
in which a male Christ is imagined as bridegroom and the female soul
as bride. This interpretative emphasis places her squarely and safely in a
heterosexual matrix, but it only captures a partial truth. For example, the
first part of Hadewijch's famous Eucharistic vision of fusion with the
human Christ seems to leave no doubt about its inherent erotic heterosexuality. Hadewijch wrote:

> With that he came in the form and clothing of a man, as he was
> on the day when he gave us his body for the first time; looking
> like a human being and a man, wonderful, and beautiful, and
> with a glorious face, he came to me as humbly as anyone who
> wholly belongs to another. . . . After that he came himself to me,
> took me entirely in his arms, and pressed me to him; and all
> my members felt his in full felicity, in accordance with the desire
> of my heart and my humanity. So I was outwardly satisfied and
> fully transported.[50]

What is especially noteworthy about this passage is the essential equality
between the two lovers as well as the scene's tenderness and harmony.
As such, it already posed a challenge to medieval concepts of "divinely
ordained" gender inequity. And yet, such pre-lapsarian bliss and lack of
domination led to even more dramatic dismantling of gender expectations.
As the vision unfolds, the heterosexual imprinting of the scene quickly
dissolves into gender ambiguity. In feeling one with Christ, Hadewijch
absorbs his gender. She can no longer distinguish him within her, her
within him. On the most profound ontological level, gender proved to
be dramatically unstable, an insight that Hadewijch applied to her definition of de-gendered mutual love:

> Also then, for a short while, I had the strength to bear this; but
> soon, after a short time, I lost that manly beauty outwardly in
> the sight of his form. I saw him completely come to naught and
> so fade and all at once dissolve that I could no longer distinguish
> him within me. Then it was to me as if we were one without
> difference. . . . So can the Beloved, with the loved one, each wholly

receive the other in all full satisfaction of the sight, the hearing, and the passing away of the one in the other.[51]

Acknowledging the gender instability of Hadewijch's religious aesthetics, her descriptions of encounters with the female allegory of divine love, Lady Minne, raise numerous questions. What shall we make of the fact that Minne is mentioned more frequently than both Christ and God together? That erotic encounters with Minne far outnumber descriptions of fusion with Christ? Why are the Poems in Stanzas and Poems in Couplets dedicated almost exclusively to Minne, not to God or Christ? I suggest that the figure of Minne allowed Hadewijch to speak of female homoerotic desire and then to disguise it safely under the cloak of her ambiguous and unstable gender identity. In a few instances in her text, Minne as person is identified with Christ, a rhetorical conflation not consistently used by other female proponents of bridal mysticism. It feminizes Christ as much as it masculinizes Minne.[52] Minne is both feminine and masculine, yet her masculinity is only referred to in the abstract as a pale reflection of God's gender. "May God be to you vast and eternal Minne" (Letter 14); "Minne . . . is God himself by nature" (Letter 19); "May God be God for you in truth, in which he is God and Minne at once" (Letter 23); "In God, because he is our Minne / As Far As I know Minne" (Poems in Couplets 12); "What is actual Minne? It is the divine power that must have priority" (Vision 11); ". . . so it was with other revelations in great number . . . with the understanding of Minne, how he is our Minne in himself, and outside himself he is Minne in us . . ." (Vision 14).[53]

In a way, all of Hadewijch's teachings can be approached as esoteric commentary on the Gospel of John with its mythic promise of rebirth/ transformation as child of God/Love, which is in itself a feminine image.[54] The human task is to move from a literal/material understanding of reality to a spiritual/mystical one.

In truth I tell you, no one can enter the kingdom of God without being born from water and spirit. Flesh can give birth to flesh; it is spirit that gives birth to spirit. You ought not to be astonished, then, when I tell you that you must be born over again.[55]

If the soul chooses Minne as her teacher, it is Minne's responsibility to engineer that existential shift. Minne's impact on human nature is transformative and unitive. In an intriguing image, Hadewijch compared a human being to the dark moon that receives its light from Minne, the sun. Fusion between light and darkness creates wholeness. Hadewijch wrote:

> The souls engulfed in God who are thus lost in him are illuminated on one side by the light of Minne, as the moon receives its light from the sun.... this simple light then catches their darker half, so that the two halves of the soul become one; and then there is full light.[56]

Hadewijch taught a spiritual hermeneutics of paradox, of which the madness of Minne is the supreme paradigm:

> The madness of Minne
> Is a rich fief;
> Anyone who recognized this
> Would not ask Minne for anything else:
> It can unite opposites
> And reverse the paradox.
> I am declaring the truth about this:
> The madness of Minne makes bitter what was sweet,
> It makes the stranger a kinsman,
> And it makes the smallest the proudest.[57]

Any attempt at systematic spiritual devotion is misguided; as in other esoteric religious systems, the path to spiritual perfection is no path:

> He who wishes to taste veritable Minne
> Whether by random quest or sure attainment,
> Must keep to neither path nor way....
> Beyond all the ways men can think of,
> That strong steed of Minne bears him....
> I leave rhyme: what mind can say eludes me.[58]

I argue that it is precisely this central mystical insight into the limits of rational discourse and of analytic, binary consciousness that freed Hadewijch to abandon the heterosexual matrix with its rigid gender

dualism and to create a playful and sensuous "queer" mysticism.[59] Light
and darkness belong together; a paradox contains greater truth than
Aristotelian logic; the mystical path is no path: these spiritual principles
elucidate and confirm the destabilizing hermeneutics that Hadewijch
applied to heterosexual normativity. Minne is feminine, but not like patriarchal women, as we shall see below. Minne is also masculine, but not
fully so. Minne is neither one nor the other, yet is both: "To lose one's
way in her is to touch her close at hand; / To die of hunger for her is to
feed and taste."[60]

Moving out of fixed heterosexual binaries takes place not just intel-
lectually and theologically, but also emotionally and, at least on an imaginary level, physically. Hadewijch thus deconstructed the double bind
inherent in celibate monasticism that forbade all sexual activity and demanded exclusive and intense interaction with members of the same sex
yet did not permit a full exploration of same-sex bonding.[61] For Hadewijch,
heteroerotic and homoerotic religious aesthetics can coexist outside patriarchal dualism, at least in the performance of writing; whether or how
much the realm of the mystical was lived in the world of concrete inter-
personal encounters, we do not know.

DRINKING LOVE'S KISSES

Hadewijch, in Poems in Stanzas 43, calls herself the "Love/ress of Love,"
consciously choosing a grammatically female form to denote a same-sex
erotic relationship to Minne.[62] References to sensual encounters and experiences of fusion between Minne and herself occur numerous times:
"... sometimes the sweet nature of Minne blinds me to such a degree
that when I can taste and feel her it is enough for me; and sometimes I
feel so rich in her presence that I myself acknowledge that she contents
me";[63] "lightning is the light of Minne ... in order to show who Minne is
and how she can receive and give—in the sweetness of clasping, in the
fond embrace, in the sweet kiss, and in the heartfelt experience when
Minne actually speaks, 'I am the one who holds you in my embrace!'"[64]
Her students in turn are encouraged to lose themselves, to melt in Minne:
"For if you abandon yourself to Minne, you will soon attain full growth."[65]
"Minne, your name is poured out, / And since it overflows with a flood
of wonder, / The young maidens are melted away in you / And love with

violent longing, above counsel."[66] Desire and longing fuel both female lovers. "Never was so cruel a desert created / As Minne can make in her land! / For she impels us to long desiringly for her / And to taste her without knowing her being."[67] Note the stunning absence of any reference to male gender in the tender and sensuous verses of Poem 20 of Poems in Stanzas:

> When Minne thus draws the soul in resemblance to her,
> And the loving soul shows love to Minne
> I know not how, for it remains unspoken
> And also past understanding;
> For no comparison is adequate for this—
> How Minne can embrace the loving soul. . . .
> All who love must be moved to pity
> That Minne lets me moan thus
> And cry so often: "Woe is me!"
> In what season and when
> Will Minne reach out to me
> And say: "Let your grief cease?
> I will cherish you;
> I am what I was in times past;
> Now fall into my arms,
> And taste my rich teaching!"[68]

Another female allegory, Pleasure, is imagined to engage in sweet caresses with Minne: "Pleasure would certainly close her eyes / And gladly enjoy what she possesses. . . . / Pleasure would gladly have a safe place / Where she may consort with her Beloved in sweet repose."[69]

Gender instability occurs only rarely in descriptions of Minne's student. She is imagined as grammatically male, for example, in the following quotation, where she performs a gender-specific activity ("noble service"): "But before Minne thus bursts her dikes and before she ravishes man *(mensche)* out of himself and so touches him with herself that he is one spirit and one being with her and in her, he must offer her noble service and the life of exile."[70] The gender instability of Christ's humanity, depicted in Hadewijch's Eucharistic vision quoted above, serves as a dramatic valorization of female-female fusion in Poems in Couplets 16. Here, union with Christ is imagined as unrequited male desire and thus not fully consummated. In the following verses, note the unexpected lack of desire for Christ and the separation among humans (Hadewijch's group of female students?) that it engenders:

> Minne's most intimate union
> Is through eating, tasting, and seeing interiorly.
> He [Christ] eats us; we think we eat him,
> And we do eat him, of this we can be certain.
> But because he remains so undevoured,
> And so untouched, and so undesired,
> Each of us remains uneaten by him
> And separated so far from each other.[71]

In the same poem, this lack of mutuality is contrasted with union with Minne. Hadewijch wrote:

> When the loved one receives from her Beloved
> The kisses that truly pertain to Minne . . .
> Minne drinks in these kisses and tastes them to the end.
> As soon as Minne thus touches the soul,
> she eats her flesh and drinks her blood.
> Minne that thus dissolves the loved soul
> Sweetly leads them both to the indivisible kiss.[72]

As I noted earlier, Hadewijch moved her spiritual characters dangerously close to the world of earthly delights. The realm of divine and human emotion are mixed, one mirrors the other. The theological vision of Margarete Ebner's female friend as Christ is pushed to its sensual limits when Hadewijch described her view of human friendship as an example of her feelings for God: "for it is the custom of friends between themselves to hide little and reveal much, what is most experienced is the close feeling of one another, when they relish, devour, drink, and swallow up each other."[73] Friendship and sexual encounters, erotic and affectionate gestures resemble each other closely, as we can see in her description of the behavior of lovers as "interchanges of Minne that lovers receive from each other—in the embrace, in the kiss, in union, in knowledge, in receiving, in giving, in humility, in mutual greeting, and in gracious welcome—and that the Beloved can hide so little from his loved one."[74]

"ALAS! WHEN MINNE IS SO SWEET, WHY DO YOU NOT FALL DEEP INTO HER?"[75]

Other scholars have suggested Hadewijch's homoeroticism on the basis of Letter 25, addressed to two of her female students, one of whom is named Emma.[76] Writing about a woman named Sara, she complained about Sara's neglect of her and stressed that no one mattered more to her than she. Her affection for Sara is again mentioned in Letter 29. Hadewijch proclaimed to the anonymous recipient of the letter, "I am close to you in heart, and trusted; and for me, you—after Sara—are the dearest person alive."[77] In Letter 25, personal comments about experiences of love are placed next to religious evocations of Minne:

> Greet Sara also in my behalf, whether I am anything to her or nothing. Could I fully be all that in my love I wish to be for her, I would gladly do so; and I shall do so fully, however she may treat me. . . . Now that she has other occupations . . . she lets me suffer. . . . And you, Emma, and yourself—who can obtain more from me than any other person now living can, except Sara— are equally dear to me. But both of you turn too little to Minne, who has so fearfully subdued me in the commotion of unappeased Minne. . . . Minne is all![78]

Such confluence of human mentor-student love and religious language appears in other sections of Hadewijch's work as well. In Letter 23, Hadewijch warned her student about being pulled away to another group jealous of their mutual attachment:

> They would gladly draw you away from us and attach you to themselves; their hearts suffer from our exceptional fidelity. . . . Do everything with reliance on Minne. Live in the same fervor as we; and let us live in sweet Minne. Live for God; let his life be yours, and let yours be ours.[79]

Not only in this letter, but also in Vision 14 is her love for her student tightly linked to her love for God. It is impossible to say which love was felt more ardently. Desire, spirituality, pedagogical persona, body, spirit, and soul flow together in this subtly crafted confession to her student:

> And because I loved you so greatly, and neither could nor can
> forget you in any hour; and because I felt this death and your
> nonfulfillment in Minne so closely with you, in stormy desire of
> God—that I was closer to God than you, pained me the more.[80]

The language of religious emotions allowed Hadewijch to speak about
female same-sex love without speaking it; to remain both in and out of
the closet; to let love for God be love for women, and vice versa. Such
"double-speak" and rich layering of meaning is cunningly applied to the
role of pedagogue as well. Like Hadewijch, Minne is a teacher;[81] she
leads others to her school daily to teach the art of combat[82] and to explain
her own nature, which is as paradoxical as her gender, as Hadewijch
implies in her assertion, "In high Minne's school / Is learned the madness of Minne; / For it causes delirium / In a person formerly of good
understanding."[83] And not surprisingly, experiences of teaching, touching,
and seducing become fused. In Poem 13 of Poems in Couplets, Hadewijch
described Minne's pedagogy as a list of sensual, erotic paradoxes:

> What is sweetest in Minne is her tempestuousness
> Her deepest abyss is her most beautiful form;
> To lose one's way in her is to touch her close at hand;
> To die of hunger for her is to feed and taste . . .
> To languish for her sake is to be in good health; . . .
> Seduction is the custom of her school;
> Encounters with her are cruel storms; . . .
> Her promises are all seductions;
> Her adornments are all undressing. . . .
> I will belong to her, whatever she may be,
> Gracious or merciless;
> to me it is all one![84]

Perhaps the most open and yet (therefore?) the most ambiguous declaration of Hadewijch's homoerotic aesthetics is expressed in Poem 15 of
the Poems in Couplets. In this stormy assertion of passion and mystical
union, the addressees keep shifting their identity; it is never quite clear
whom Hadewijch talks to—is it Minne, "Sweet Repose," Most Beloved
Lord, "Sweet Nature," My Beloved, or her female student, the "O dearly
loved maiden"? In the end, it seems, Minne, herself, her beloved, and

the Divine all become one, interchangeable, a frenzied vision of what could be possible if the realm of the secular and the realm of the mystical would become one. Hadewijch wrote:

> I greet what I love
> With my heart's blood.
> My senses wither
> In the madness of Minne....
> O dearly loved maiden
> That I say so many things to you
> Comes to me from fresh fidelity,
> Under the deep touch of Minne....
> I suffer, I strive after the height,
> I suckle with my blood...
> I tremble, I cling, I give....
> Beloved, if I love a beloved,
> Be you, Minne, my Beloved;
> You gave yourself as Minne for your loved one's sake,...
> O Minne, for Minne's sake, grant that I,
> Having become Minne, may know Minne wholly as Minne![85]

And thus, Hadewijch could speak her truth without speaking it, creating and developing a radical because woman-identified Christian theology of sexual/spiritual difference, safely escaping the ever tightening net of ecclesiastical repression. Through her remarkably sophisticated efforts, Hadewijch sheds light on a subculture of medieval authors who created a distinctly female homoerotic discourse, a discourse of subversion and resistance steeped in non-literary practice and supported—perhaps not exclusively—by religious same-sex communities. With the rhetorical tools of a long-standing tradition of mystical speech, Hadewijch was able to fashion alternative nomenclatures of female desire and its satisfaction; to destabilize the patriarchal gender binary until it collapsed into the language of female homoerotic seduction; to valorize the feminine, conceptualized in the fluid dynamics between teacher, student, and Minne, to such a degree that its definition moved beyond patriarchal limitation into the unspeakable, the mystical, the undefinable, the radically transgressive: "O Minne, for Minne's sake, grant that I, / Having become Minne, may know Minne wholly as Minne." The fact that her literary achievements were accomplished within the ideological framework of Christianity raises substantial questions as to the "Otherness" of medieval culture, especially medieval mysticism.

NOTES

I express my gratitude to Gary Ljungquist for many challenging conversations that helped me develop my approach to the subject; to Laurie Finke, Jane Chance, Elizabeth Grosz, Regine Prenzel-Guthrie, Duncan Lewis, and in particular the editors of this volume for critical and incisive feedback on the work in progress. Special thanks to Christina Yu and the staff at the Z. Smith Reynolds Library for their relentless productions of minor miracles when it came to the task of locating materials at the last minute.

1. The *Medieval Feminist Newsletter* devoted the Spring 1992 issue to this problem. See also Diane Wolfthal's reflections in her essay "An Art Historical Response to 'Gay Studies and Feminism: A Medievalist's Perspective,'" *Medieval Feminist Newsletter* no. 14 (1992): 16–19. All monograph surveys on medieval homosexuality discuss female homo-eroticism only in passing without trying to analyze in any substantial fashion whatever data is available. The only notable exception for Germany is the survey of lesbian history by Monika Barz, Herta Leistner, and Ute Wild, *Hättest Du gedacht, daß wir so viele sind? Lesbische Frauen in der Kirche*, 2nd ed. (Stuttgart, 1993). John Boswell's one-liner is symptomatic for the current situation: "There is, unfortunately, little written on female homoeroticism in Europe in antiquity or during the Middle Ages" (*Same-Sex Unions in Premodern Europe* [New York, 1994], xxix). Bernadette Brooten offers a trenchant critique of Boswell's treatment (or lack thereof) of women in *Love between Women: Early Christian Responses to Female Homoeroticism* (Chicago, 1996), 10–13. In his recent study of theological concepts of sodomy, Mark Jordan recognizes the deep structural reliance on misogyny in theological texts, but does not concern himself with an analysis that extends beyond one paragraph: Jordan, *The Invention of Sodomy in Christian Theology* (Chicago, 1997), 169. It appears that the hard-won achievements of feminist scholarship tend to evaporate when it comes to the topic of medieval queer studies, creating a "conceptual ghetto" for feminist queer studies and producing a distorted "body" of knowledge; I have borrowed the apt term "conceptual ghetto" from Laura S. Brown, "New Voices, New Visions: Toward a Lesbian/Gay Paradigm for Psychology," in *The Culture and Psychology Reader*, ed. Nancy Rule Goldberger and Jody Bennet Vernoff (New York, 1995), 560.

2. Bruce Wood Holsinger, "The Flesh of the Voice: Embodiment and the Homo-erotics of Devotion in the Music of Hildegard of Bingen (1098–1179)," *Signs: Journal of Women in Culture and Society* 19, no. 1 (Summer 1993): 92–126; Kathy Lavezzo, "Sobs and Sighs between Women: The Homoerotics of Compassion in *The Book of Margery Kempe*," in *Premodern Sexualities*, ed. Louise Fradenburg and Carla Freccero (New York, 1996), 175–99.

3. See M. M. Bakhtin, "The Problem of Speech Genres," in *Speech Genres and Other Late Essays*, ed. Caryl Emerson and Michael Holquist (Austin, 1986), 60–103; James C. Scott, *Domination and the Arts of Resistance* (New Haven, CT, 1990). I wish to thank Laurie

Finke for pointing me to Bakhtin and Scott to articulate more clearly how medieval women's homoerotic writings could be approached as subversive texts composed in oppressive cultural climates. In the remainder of the essay, I employ Scott's helpful distinction between "public transcripts," written, performed, and disseminated by social elites to maintain their grip on subaltern groups, and "hidden transcripts," ingeniously devised and circulated by less powerful groups to resist domination.

4. Scott, *Domination*.

5. To make this point regarding liturgical songs, Holsinger focused in particular on Hildegard's *Ave, generosa* and *O viridissima virga*. I have discussed Hildegard's same-sex friendships in "In Search of Medieval Women's Friendships: Hildegard of Bingen's Letters to Her Female Contemporaries," in *Maps of Flesh and Light: The Religious Experience of Medieval Women Mystics*, ed. Wiethaus (Syracuse, NY, 1992), 93–112.

6. The question arises whether she was aware of the tensions implicit in such maneuvering. Maria Lugones has explored the politics, methodologies, and possibilities of such rhetorical shape-shifting for latina writers: "Purity, Impurity, and Separation," *Signs: Journal of Women in Culture and Society* 19, no. 2 (Winter 1994): 458–79. Arts of resistance, as she calls them, include among other strategies, "code-switching, categorial blurring and confusion, . . . multiple naming" (478).

7. The role of Minne in Hadewijch's writings has puzzled numerous interpreters. For recent approaches, see Elizabeth Alvilda Petroff, "Gender, Knowledge and Power in Hadewijch's *Strophische Gedichten*," in her *Body and Soul: Essays on Medieval Women and Mysticism* (Oxford, 1994), 182–203; and Barbara Newman, "*La mystique courtoise:* Thirteenth-Century Beguines and the Art of Love," in her *From Virile Woman to WomanChrist: Studies in Medieval Religion and Literature* (Philadelphia, 1995). As Otfrid Ehrismann has recently pointed out, the meaning of the term Minne before the fifteenth century was extremely fluid and covered a wide range of secular and religious meanings: Hadewijch to my knowledge is the only female author who pushes the concept towards homoerotic aesthetics. Ehrismann, *Ehre und Mut, Aventiure und Minne. Höfische Wortgeschichten aus dem Mittelalter* (Munich, 1995). Unfortunately, I have received Mary Suydam's insightful analysis of Hadewijch's unusual use of pronouns for the allegorical figures of Minne and Soul only after this study was completed. Suydam offers an analysis of the text of the *Mengeldichten* and comes to the conclusion that Hadewijch intentionally and playfully destabilized a gendered understanding of the Divine that sabotages both homoerotic and heterosexual readings. My own work explores the possibilities a homoerotic reading might offer in understanding Hadewijch's work. Either way, both approaches underscore Hadewijch's rejection of androcentric interpretations of the Divine and mystical faith experiences. See Mary Suydam, "'Ever in Unrest': Translating Hadewijch of Antwerp's *Mengeldichten*," *Women's Studies* 28 (1999): 157–84.

8. Kathy Lavezzo has employed this hermeneutical strategy of reading against the common homosocial male-female-male triad by positing a female-male-female triad in her reading of Margery Kempe, an interpretative stance learned from Terry Castle: Lavezzo "Sobs and Sighs between Women," 178.

9. I have analysed Hadewijch as pedagogue in "Learning as Experiencing. Hadewijch's Model of Spiritual Growth," in *Faith Seeking Understanding: Learning and the Catholic*

Tradition, ed. George C. Berthold (Manchester, 1991), 89–107; see also Frank Willaert, "Hadewijch und ihr Kreis in den 'Visionen,'" in *Abendländische Mystik im Mittelalter. Symposion Kloster Engelberg 1984,* ed. Kurt Ruh (Stuttgart, 1986), 368–88.

10. Jan van Ruusbroec's comments are reprinted in Esther Heszler, "Stufen der Minne bei Hadewijch," in *Frauenmystik im Mittelalter,* ed. Peter Dinzelbacher and Dieter R. Bauer (Ostfildern bei Stuttgart, 1985), 99–100. A survey of the history of manuscript transmissions can be found in Ria Vanderauwera, "The Brabant Mystic Hadewijch," in *Medieval Women Writers,* ed. Katharina Wilson (Athens, GA, 1984), 186–204.

11. For overviews, see Part II in Boswell, *Christianity, Social Tolerance, and Homosexuality: Gay People in Western Europe from the Beginning of the Christian Era to the Fourteenth Century* (Chicago, 1980); Brigitte Spreitzer, *Die stumme Sünde: Homosexualität im Mittelalter* (Göppingen, 1988); Jeffrey Richards, *Sex, Dissidence, and Damnation: Minority Groups in the Middle Ages* (New York, 1991), chap. 7; Vern L. Bullough, "The Sin Against Nature and Homosexuality," in *Sexual Practices and the Medieval Church,* ed. Bullough and James Brundage (Buffalo, NY, 1982), 55–72; Derrick Sherwin Bailey, *Homosexuality and the Western Christian Tradition* (London, 1975); James A. Brundage, *Law, Sex, and Christian Society in Medieval Europe* (Chicago, 1987); Jacqueline Murray, "Twice Marginal and Twice Invisible: Lesbians in the Middle Ages," in *Handbook of Medieval Sexuality,* ed. Vern L. Bullough and James A. Brundage (New York, 1996), 191–222. Murray covers much the same ground as the following survey on male medieval sources, but include more sources outside of Germanic cultures; she also comments on the problem of female sources. For feminist historiographical reflections on the challenge to reconstruct a history of women's same-sex (sub)cultures, see Brooten, *Love between Women,* and Margit Göttert, "'Chloe liebte Olivia...' Frauenbeziehungen als Gegenstand historischer Forschung," in *Frauengeschichte: Gesucht—Gefunden? Auskünfte zum Stand der historischen Frauenforschung,* ed. Beate Fieseler and Birgit Schulze (Cologne, 1991), 92–111.

12. On witchcraft, see the insightful discussion in Spreitzer, *Die stumme Sünde,* 59–77.

13. For the most recent discussion of medieval theology and homosexual behaviors, see Jordan, *Invention of Sodomy.* Regretfully, Jordan does not analyze female homoeroticism as a separate category.

14. Romans 1:26 states, "In consequence, I say, God has given them up to shameful passions. Their women have exchanged natural intercourse for unnatural, and their men in turn, giving up natural relations with women, burn with lust for one another": *New English Bible* (Oxford, 1970). See Brooten, *Love between Women,* for an outstanding discussion of Paul's view and its repercussions in Early Christian thought.

15. On Hincmar's views, see Boswell, *Christianity, Social Tolerance, and Homosexuality;* Boswell quotes the crucial passage on p. 204.

16. On Peter Abelard's peculiar exclusion of male homosexual behavior in his discussion of "natural" vs. "unnatural" uses of genitalia in his *Expositio in Epistolam Pauli ad Romanos I, Patrologia cursus completus, series latina,* ed. J.-P. Migne, 221 vols. (Paris, 1841–66), 178:806, see Boswell, *Christianity, Social Tolerance, and Homosexuality,* 312–13 n. 40.

17. On Albertus Magnus, see Spreitzer, *Die stumme Sünde,* 36–39, 137–46. Jordan, *Invention of Sodomy,* chap. 6. Helen Rodnite Lemay found one medical reference to female homosexual activity in William of Saliceto's treatise, which described a penis-like female

genital protrusion he named ragadia, with which some women would engage in homo-sexual intercourse: Helen Rodnite Lemay, "Human Sexuality in Twelfth- through Fifteenth-Century Scientific Writings," in *Sexual Practices and the Medieval Church,* ed. Bullough and Brundage, 196. The idea of contagion spilled over into other genres as well. For Bernardino of Siena's preaching on sodomy and contagion, for example, see Michael Rocke, *Forbidden Friendships: Homosexuality and Male Culture in Renaissance Florence* (New York, 1996), chap. 1.

18. On Thomas Aquinas, see Spreitzer, *Die stumme Sünde,* 39–45, 146–53; Jordan, *Invention of Sodomy,* chap. 7.

19. See Spreitzer, *Die stumme Sünde,* 57–59; Rudolf His, *Das Strafrecht des deutschen Mittelalters* (1920; reprint, Aalen, 1964), 2:166–68.

20. For the execution in Augsburg, see Spreitzer, *Die stumme Sünde,* 57 n. 262, and His, *Das Strafrecht,* 167 n. 5.

21. The German bishop Burchard of Worms (d. 1025), more lenient than many other authors of penitential literature, stressed that the use of an artificial penis demanded special penance. Spreitzer labels his remarks pornographic: *Die stumme Sünde,* 29–31. For a more sympathetic reading, see Boswell, *Christianity, Social Tolerance, and Homosexuality,* 205–06.

22. On canon law, see Spreitzer, *Die stumme Sünde,* 23–25.

23. On the *Schwabenspiegel,* see Spreitzer, *Die stumme Sünde,* 20 ff.

24. On the execution in Ghent, see His, *Das Strafrecht,* 168; Crompton, "The Myth of Lesbian Impunity: Capital Laws from 1270 to 1791," in *Historical Perspectives on Homosexuality,* ed. Salvatore J. Licata and Robert P. Petersen (New York, 1981), 11–27.

25. See Barz, Leistner, and Wild, *Hättest Du gedacht,* 190. Crompton, "The Myth of Lesbian Impunity," 13, quotes the full text.

26. See Theodor Hartster, *Das Strafrecht der freien Reichsstadt Speier* (partial reprint of vol. 61, Altwasser, 1906), 184–85.

27. See Spreitzer, *Die stumme Sünde,* 21; the law is documented as article 141 of the *Constitutio criminalis Bambergensis,* authored by Johann von Schwarzenberg.

28. The images are reproduced and discussed in Spreitzer, *Die stumme Sünde,* book cover and 59–77.

29. See Spreitzer, *Die stumme Sünde,* 77–105. In contrast, see the French romance of Princess Ide, discussed in Crompton, "The Myth of Lesbian Impunity," 13. In order to save her from execution by fire because of her lesbian love affair, the Virgin Mary transforms Ide into a man: *The Boke of Duke Huon of Bordeau,* ed. Sidney Lee, trans. Lord Berners, Early English Text Society, Series 2, vol. 40 (London, 1882).

30. For a theoretical interpretation of late medieval male anxiety regarding male homosexual activity, see Richard C. Trexler, *Sex and Conquest: Gendered Violence, Political Order, and the European Conquest of the Americas* (Ithaca, NY, 1995). On women's relation-ships, see Petra Giloy-Hirtz, "Frauen unter sich. Weibliche Beziehungsmuster im höf-ischen Roman," in *Personenbeziehungen in der mittelalterlichen Literatur,* ed. Helmut Brall, Barbara Haupt, and Urban Küsters (Cologne, 1994), 61–89. Giloy-Hirtz interprets female same-sex utopian societies as "peculiar marginal phenomena," but notes how Christine de Pizan successfully employs the topos in her proto-feminist work *Le livre de la Cité des Dames* (composed 1404/05): "Frauen unter sich," 77–80.

31. Brigitte Eriksson, trans., "A Lesbian Execution in Germany, 1721: The Trial Records," in *Historical Perspectives on Homosexuality*, ed. Salvatore J. Licata and Robert Petersen, *Journal of Homosexuality* 6 (1981): 27–41. Among Katharina's intriguing comments on her "crimes" is her defiant affirmation that "even if she were done away with, others like her would remain," 34.

32. On Agnes, see Peter Dinzelbacher, "Die *Vita et Revelationes* der Wiener Begine Agnes Blannbekin (d. 1315) in Rahmen der Viten-und Offenbarungsliteratur ihrer Zeit," in *Frauenmystik im Mittelalter*, ed. Dinzelbacher and Bauer, 152–78.

33. Hrotsvit of Gandersheim, *Hrotsvithae Opera*, ed. Helene Homeyer (Munich, 1970). See discussion in Jordan, *Invention of Sodomy*, 18–22.

34. On the Christian association of homosexuality with Arab people and the construction of Mohammed as sodomite, see Susan Schibanoff, "Mohammed, Courtly Love, and the Myth of Western Heterosexuality," *Medieval Feminist Newsletter* no. 16 (1993): 27–32; Boswell, *Christianity, Social Tolerance, and Homosexuality*, 194–200; David F. Greenberg, *The Construction of Homosexuality* (Chicago, 1988), 172–83; Michael Uebel, "Re-Orienting Desire: Writing on Gender Trouble in Fourteenth-Century Egypt," in this volume.

35. Hildegard of Bingen, *Liber divinorum operum simplicis hominis*, Pars II, visio V; quoted by Spreitzer, *Die stumme Sünde*, 134–35. For the context of Hildegard's teachings on sexuality, see Barbara Newman, *Sister of Wisdom: St. Hildegard's Theology of the Feminine* (Berkeley, 1987), chap. 4. Holsinger and Murray discuss the *Scivias* text, "The Flesh of the Voice" and "Twice Marginal and Twice Invisible."

36. Anonymous, "Love Letters," Latin and English translation in *Medieval Latin and the Rise of European Love-Lyric*, ed. Peter Dronke (Oxford, 1966), 2:478–81.

37. The erotic references to the body are "your only one . . . who . . . loves you with soul and body" ("unicam tuam . . . que anima et corpore te diligit"), letter VI; "when I remember the kisses you gave, and with what words of joy you caressed my little breasts" ("dum recordor que dedisti oscula, et quam iocundis verbis refrigerasti pectuscula"), letter VII, quoted in Dronke, *Medieval Latin and the Rise of European Love-Lyric*, 478–81. For a sensitive description of the context of monastic women engaged in writing Latin love poetry in the eleventh and twelfth centuries, see Peter Dronke, *Women Writers of the Middle Ages* (Cambridge, 1984), chap. 4.

38. See note 5. As a biblical model for her feelings for Richardis, Hildegard chose the relationship between Paul and Timothy, a metaphor I have found nowhere else in women's writings.

39. Quoted in Judith C. Brown, *Immodest Acts: The Life of a Lesbian Nun in Renaissance Italy* (Oxford, 1986), 8. The quote is contextualized in Brooten, *Love between Women*, 350–55.

40. Judith Brown recounts the homoerotic story of abbess Benedetta Carlini (d. 1661) and her sexual relations with the younger nun Bartolomea, *Immodest Acts*; a much later homoerotic relationship between a spiritual teacher and her student is possible in the case of Rebecca Jackson (1795–1871), African-American Shaker eldress, and her student Rebecca Perot. See *Gifts of Power: The Writings of Rebecca Jackson, Black Visionary, Shaker Eldress*, ed. Jean McMahon Humez (Amherst, MA, 1981).

41. "Nu het ich ain swester, die mir got geben het ze trost ze libe und ze sel und die grosse triu gen mir het. Siu dient mir in fräuden und in götlichen fürsacz diu jar alliu und

behuot mich vor allen den dingen, diu mich betrüeben mohten. Und so ich von kranchait wegen etweene ungüetlich tet zuo irem dienst, daz liezz siu mich niht entgelten. Nun geschach daz von der ordenung gotes, daz diu in grozze crankheit viel. Do warn wir bede krank und ellend und heten vil ellendes. Dar zuo het ich grozzen unmuot umb min swester und was alle neht, daz ich lützel geschlief vor rehtem laid, und het die begird, daz ich daz ellend gern wolt haben, daz ich sie also krank solt gehebt haun biz an minen tot.... da wer ich vil gern für sie tot.... also was ich do bi ir alle zit, biz daz sin endet.... Und wenn ich sie sach uf der baur ligen, daz maht wol geliden von dem lust den ich het zuo minem ellend"; "Offenbarungen," in *Margarete Ebner und Heinrich von Nördlingen: Ein Beitrag zur Geschichte der deutschen Mystik*, ed. Philipp Strauch (1882; reprint, Freiburg, 1966), 10–12. Translations from Margarete Ebner, *Major Works*, trans. and ed. Leonard Hinsley (New York, 1993), 90–91. It is possible that this sister might have been a lay sister. For a contrast between Margarete's affection and the harsh treatment of lay brothers by thirteenth-century Cistercians, see Martha G. Newman's contribution in this volume. On women's friendships among fourteenth-century Dominican nuns in Germany, see Rosemary Hale, "For Counsel and Comfort: The Depiction of Friendship in Fourteenth-Century German Convent Literature," in *Word and Spirit* (Still River, MA, 1989), 11, 93–103.

42 Margarete Ebner, *Major Works*, 96.

43. "...diu het grossen trost zuo mir. nu geschach, daz siu siech und ellend wart, und waiz daz min herre Jhesus Cristus wol, daz ich sie aune reht fröde nimer an gesahe. Nu het ich gewonhait, wenn ich von dem tisch gienk, daz ich ir denne braht, waz ich sah daz ir fuogt, und in der mainnunge alle zit über sie gienk, as ob ez got selber wer" (*Margarete Ebner und Heinrich von Nördlingen*, 39). This particular sister is a *laiswöster*, a lay sister. Margaretha, however, wrote about many other intense same-sex attachments to choir nuns as well. For a biblical basis for this theology of identification, see Luke 9:46–48; Matthew 10:40.

44. Gertrude of Helfta, *Gesandter der göttlichen Liebe (Legatus Divinae Pietatis)*, trans. Johanna Lanczkowski (Darmstadt, 1989), Book V.6, 425, English translation mine.

45. The only exception I could find is a remarkable poem celebrating female genitals by a female Welsh author, Gwerful Mechain (d. ca. 1500). Carolyne Larrington suggests that Gwerful composed the poem as a response to Dafydd ap Gwilym's poem to his penis. She calls the vulva, among other things, a "warm quim, clear excellence, / tender and fat, bright fervent broken circle / ...it is silk, / little seam, curtain on a fine bright cunt... / lovely bush, God save it." Quoted in Carolyne Larrington, ed., *Women and Writing in Medieval Europe: A Sourcebook* (London, 1995), 71–72.

46. In a cross-cultural study of male homosexual behaviors, four social categories seem to occur most frequently: age-specific (sexual activity takes place between older and younger partners); gender-oriented (one same-sex becomes "feminized"); professional (e.g., as temple prostitution); and egalitarian/"gay": Stephen O. Murray, *Latin American Male Homosexualities* (Albuquerque, NM, 1995), 4 ff. These categories may overlap and coexist in any given culture. No societies except Northern Atlantic cultures, however, seem to equate male with female homosexual activity. Greenberg devoted a section of his historical survey to "The German Heritage," *The Construction of Homosexuality*, 242–55. It is intriguing to think that we may one day discover distinct medieval patterns of female same-sex (sub)cultures.

47. Letters VII and V in *Medieval Latin and the Rise of European Love Lyric,* ed. Dronke, 78–80. In the Rule of Donatus of Besançon (d. 624), a variation of the Rule of St. Benedict for women, Rule 32 states, "none take the hand of another or call one another 'little girl.' It is forbidden that any take the hand of another for affection whether they stand or walk or sit together. She who does so, will be improved with twelve blows. And any who is called 'little girl' or who call one another 'little girl,' forty blows if they so transgress." Another seventh-century Rule for a woman's community, possibly by Waldebert of Luxueil, demands that sleeping arrangements are carefully monitored to forestall sexual contact among young nuns: ". . . we think that young girls should never lie down together lest in some adversity of the flesh their warmth carries them off to sin" (rule 14, "How they should always sleep in the schola"). Both Rules are translated by Jo Ann McNamara and John Halborg, in Jo Ann McNamara, *The Ordeal of Community* (Toronto, 1993). How much had changed between the seventh and the twelfth century?

48. Age-differentiated relationships appear to have been the norm for much of male homoerotic activity during the Middle Ages. For a sophisticated study of such relationships in late medieval Florence, see Rocke, *Forbidden Friendships.* For a French example of age-differentiated female same-sex desire, see Kathleen M. Blumreich, "Lesbian Desire in the Old French *Roman de Silence,*" *Arthuriana* 7 (1997): 47–62. See also Greenberg, "The German Heritage," 242–68, for male medieval age and gender patterns; Murray, *Latin American Male Homosexualities,* 16–19, for the historic model as a whole. Murray discusses the lack of studies among women regarding these four categories, but suggests some cross-cultural evidence for age-stratified, gender-stratified, and egalitarian female same-sex eroticism (6–7). For a cross-cultural survey of religious roles and homoeroticism, see Randy P. Conner, *Blossom of Bone: Reclaiming the Connections between Homoeroticism and the Sacred* (San Francisco, 1993). In African, Afro-Brazilian, West Pacific, Northern American, and Siberian cultures, religion often allowed for a profession-specific expression of homosexual activity, whether as shamans, temple prostitutes, dancers, or musicians. Since the Middle Ages, it has been a common stereotype in western culture that Catholic priesthood attracts homosexual men in particular, and that monasticism attracted both lesbians and gay men. See Eugen Drewermann, *Kleriker: Psychogramm eines Ideals* (Munich, 1991), 580–603. E. Ann Matter offered cautionary methodological reflections on Benedetta and Bartolomea's case in her essay "Discourse of Desire: Sexuality and Christian Women's Visionary Narratives," *Journal of Homosexuality* 18 (1989/90): 119–31. Yet even a socially acceptable niche for religious/monastic female same-sex attraction might not have been without its own vicissitudes. Jeffrey Weeks has articulated the ambivalent nature of socially acknowledged homoerotic roles, at least for western society: "Such a role has two effects: it helps to provide a clear-cut threshold between permissible and impermissable behavior; and secondly, it helps to segregate those labeled as deviant from others, and thus contains and limits their behavior patterns. In the same way, a homosexual subculture, which is the correlative of the development of a specialized role, provides both access to the socially outlawed need (sex) and contains the deviant" (Jeffrey Weeks, "The Construction of Homosexuality," in *Queer Theory/Sociology,* ed. Steven Seidman [Cambridge, MA, 1996], 41–64). My argument is that age-stratified patterns of friendship (and here I expand the model used in my essay on Hildegard of Bingen's friendships, Wiethaus, "In Search of Medieval

Women's Friendships") were possibly a "soft" category rather than a hard and clear-cut role that protected women's homoerotic expressions since it denoted first and foremost non-erotic behaviors, but was possibly flexible enough to accommodate homoerotic desire.

49. Other interpreters of Hadewijch's allegory of Minne, most recently Elizabeth Alvilda Petroff and Barbara Newman, have noted the "queerness" of Minne's actions and the instability of Hadewijch's gender categories, but both scholars remained fully in a heterosexual interpretive matrix. Petroff, "Gender, Knowledge and Power, 182–203; Newman, "*La mystique courtoise,*" 137–68. For recent surveys of Hadewijch's theology that represent less conflictual approaches, see Saskia Murk Jansen, *The Measure of Mystic Thought: A Study of Hadewijch's "Mengeldichten"* (Göttingen, 1991), and John Giles Milhaven, *Hadewijch and Her Sisters: Other Ways of Loving and Knowing* (Albany, NY, 1993). My thesis is based on the a priori assumptions that (1) Hadewijch's literary and autobiographical voice, her roles as a mystagogue, author, and devotee of Minne, as well as the realm of the "real" (whatever that may be) and the "imaginary" cannot be neatly separated, but reveal each other in the brokenness/wovenness of the planes of text and voice, and that (2) all four genres of her oeuvre illuminate each other and should be read dialogically and synchronically.

50. "Daer mede quam hi in die ghedane des cleeds / ende des mands dat hi was op dien dach / doen hi ons sinen lichame iersten gaf, also ghedane mensche / ende man / Soete ende scoene / ende uerweent ghelaet tonende, / ende also onderdanechleke te mi comende / Alse een die eens anders al es. / . . . Daer na quam hi selue te mi, ende nam mi alte male in sine arme / ende dwanc mi ane heme; / ende alle die lede die ic hadde gheuoelden der siere in alle hare ghenoeghen / na miere herten begherten na miere menscheit. / Doe werdic ghenoeghet van buten in allen vollen sade" (Vision 7:64–80). For this and all following quotations from the primary sources, I use J. van Mierlo's critical editions of Hadewijch's works and the beautiful translations by Mother Columba Hart, which are not always completely literal, but are accurate in capturing Hadewijch's poetic spirit as much as is possible in a translation: Mierlo, *De Visioenen van Hadewych. Hadewijch: Strophische Gedichten. Brieven. Mengeldichten,* 6 vols. (Louvain, 1924–52); Hart, *Hadewijch: The Complete Works* (New York, 1980). Citations provide the number of the item and section or line numbers.

51. "Ende oec haddic doe ene corte wile cracht dat te draghene. Maer saen in corter vren verloesic dien sconen man van buten in siene in vormen, / ende ic sachene al te niete werdene Ende alsoe sere verdoiende werden / ende al smelten in een, / Soe dat icken buten mi niet en conste bekinnen / noch vernemen, / Ende binnen mi niet besceden. / Mi was op die vre ochte wi een waren sonder differencie. / . . . Also lief met lieue ontfaen mach in aller voller ghenoechten / van siene / ende van hoerne, van veruarne deen inden anderen" (Vision 7). Note that in the concluding comment, Hadewijch uses the more colloquial and intimate term "lief" rather than "minne," a term that she consistently applied to her human relationships (Vision 7:64–80).

52. In the work of Mechtild of Magdeburg (Hadewijch's closest contemporary woman writer on bridal mysticism), Minne is comparatively unerotic, gender categories are never ambiguous, and Minne is predominantly visualized as force rather than as fully developed person. For example, in an allegorical vision of the soul as bride, Mechthild wrote: "The bride has four virgins [with her]. One is Minne; she guides the bride; she is dressed in

ULRIKE WIETHAUS

chastity and crowned with high esteem" (My translation. "Die brut hat vier jungfrowen. Die eine ist minne, die leittet die brut, die ist gekleidet mit der kuschekeit und ist gekronet mit der wirdekeit": *Das fließende Licht der Gottheit*, 1:46, 8–9, ed. by Hans Neumann and Gisela Vollmann-Profe [Munich, 1990], 33). See also Margot Schmidt, "'die spilende minnevlut'. Der Eros als Sein und Kraft in der Trinität bei Mechthild von Magdeburg," in *Mystik in Geschichte und Gegenwart*, ed. Schmidt and Helmut Riedlinger (Stuttgart/Bad Cannstatt, 1986), 4:71–133. See also Marianne Heimbach-Steins, "Trinität-Minne-Prophetie. Grundstrukturen theologischen Denkens im Werk Mechthilds von Magdeburg," in *Denkmodelle von Frauen im Mittelalter*, ed. Beatrice Acklin Zimmermann (Freiburg/Switzerland, 1994), 83–107. On interpretations of Minne in Hadewijch's oeuvre that bracket the question of gender, see Heszler, "Stufen der Minne bei Hadewicjh," 99–123.

53. "God si v grote ende ewelike Minne" (Letter 14:1); "want wi nemen Minne die God selue bi naturen es" (Letter 19:31); "God si v inder waerheit, Daer hi god ende Minne met een es" (Letter 23:1); "In gode, die es onse minne, / Also verre alsic minne bekinne" (Poems in Couplets 12:1–2); "Wats minne selue? Dats godlike moghentheit die moet vore gaen" (Vision 11:174); "...ende alsoe van anderen reuelatien menechfout /...ende verstannesse der minne; hoe hi onse minne in hem seluen es / ende vte hem seluen minne in ons..." (Vision 14:133–41).

54. John 1:10–14.

55. John 2:5–7.

56. "Die verswolghene zielen die aldus in hem verloren sijn die ontfaen in Minnen hare ziele half, Alsoe de mane haer licht ontfeet vander zonnen...soe veet dat enighe licht dat ander ane, Ende soe werden die twee halue zielen een; ende soe eest tijt" (Letter 19:62–64, 67–68).

57. "Oereswoet van minnen / Dats een rike leen; / Ende die dat woude kinnen / Hine eyscede hare el negheen: / Die tiersten waren twee / Die doetse wesen een. / Dies ic die waerheit toghe: / Si maect dat soete es soer / Ende den vremden nagheboer, / Ende si brenct den nederen hoghe" (Poems in Stanzas 28:4). The literal translation of lines 35 and 36 is, "Those who [first] were two / She can make one." Hart's translation captures the essence of these lines and the rest of the poem, which contains a long list of paradoxical transformations caused by the force of Minne (*Complete Works*, 206).

58. "Die rechter Minnen wilt smaken, eest in dolen eest in gheraken, Hine sal houden pade noch weghe.... Buten allen weghe van mneschen sinnen, Dreghet hem dat starcke ors van Minnen...Je late den rijn: hiers vte den sen" (Letter 19:11–13, 17–18, 26).

59. Sue-Ellen Case attempted another aesthetics of queer mysticism in her reading of St. John of the Cross: "Tracking the Vampire," *Differences: A Journal of Feminist Cultural Studies* 3 (1991): 1–20. On queer spirituality in Richard Crawshaw, see Richard Rambuss, "Pleasure and Devotion: The Body of Jesus and Seventeenth-Century Religious Lyric," in *Queering the Renaissance*, ed. Jonathan Goldberg (Durham, NC, 1994), 253–79. For a thoughtful criticism of the limits of queer theory in medieval studies, see Allen J. Frantzen, "Between the Lines: Queer Theory, the History of Homosexuality, and Anglo-Saxon Penitentials," *Journal of Medieval and Early Modern Studies* 26, no. 2 (Spring 1996): 255–97.

60. "Jn haer verdolen dats na gheraken; / Om haer verhongeren dats voeden ende smaken" (Poems in Couplets 13:3–4).

61. The double bind is described in Spreitzer, *Die stumme Sünde*, 35. See also Drewermann, *Kleriker*.

62. The verse in Poems in Stanzas 43:4 addresses Minne as follows: "And how with love you love your loved ones. / That I, your Minne / loveress, may glory with them / For I, your Minne / loveress, have never gloried / As now do they who taste you" ("Hoe ghi met minnen mint u lief; / Dat ic mi, minnen, met hen verhieve; / Want ic mi, minne, so nie en verhief / Alsi nu doen die uwes ghesmaken").

63. "Ende bi vren maect mi der minnen suete nature Soe blent met hare te ghesmakene Ende te gheuoelne, dat mi ghenoeghet" (Letter 11:43–45).

64. "Blixeme dat es licht van Minnen . . . om hare te toenne wie si es, Ende hoe si can nemen ende gheuen in soetheiden van omuane, Jn lieuer behelsinghen, Jn soeten cussene Ende in ouerherteleken gheuoelne, Dat selue sprect: Jc beent die di gheuanen hebbe" (Letter 30:155; 157–61).

65. "Want wildi v ter Minnen verlaten, soe suldi saen volwassen" (Letter 6:45–46).

66. "Dies, minne, u name es uutgheghoten, / Ende met wonders vloede al overgaet, / So sijn die opwassende dorevloten / Ende minnen in woede boven raet" (Poems in Stanzas 42:5).

67. Poems in Stanzas 22:5.

68. "Alse minne dus effenne haer lieve weghet, / Ende minne der minnen met minnen pleghet, / Ic en weet hoe, het blivet ongheseghet / Ende oec onverstaen, / Want dies ghelike ghene en leghet / Hoe minne can lieve bevaen / Hen allen die minnen moet ontfarmen / Dat mi minne aldus laet carmen / Ende so dicke roepen: 'wacharmen' / Welken tijt ende wanneer / Sal mi minne bescarmen / Ende segghen: 'dijns rouwen si keer. / Ic sal di warmen / Ic ben dat ic was wilen eer? Nu fallen in minen armen / Ende ghesmake mijn rike gheleer'" (Poems in Stanzas 20:11–12).

69. "Ghenuechte loke wel die oghen / Ende plaghe gherne dies si hevet / . . . Ghenoechte name gerne toeverlaet / Te pleghenne haers liefs in sueter rasten" (Poems in Stanzas 25:5, 6).

70. "Mer eer Minne dus ouerbrake waert Ende eer si den mensche soe sere vte hem seluen nemt, Ende soe na met hare seluen gherijnt dat hi een gheest Ende een wesen si met hare in hare, soe sal hare de minsche bieden scoenen dienst ende ellendich leuen" (Letter 6:361–66).

71. "Dat dat ware die naeste der minnen / Dore eten, dore smaken, dore sie van binnen. / Hi et ons ende wij wanen hem eten. / Oec eten wine, dat moghen wij weten. / Maer omme dathi lijft so onuerteert, / Ende so ongheren ende so onbegheert, / Daeromme blijft elc ongheeten / Ende so verre buten andere gheseten" (Poems in Couplets, 16:37–44).

72. "Daer lief van lieue sal ontfaen / Selc cussen als wel ghetaemt der minnen. / . . . Si doresughetse ende doresmaket. / Alse minne die lieue dus gheraket, / Si et hare vleesch, si drinct hare bloet. / Die minne diese dus verdoet / Verleidet suetelike hen beiden / Jn enen cussen sonder sceiden" (Poems in Couplets, 16:114–22).

73. "Alsoe alse vriende pleghen deen den anderen luttel te helene ende vele te toenne, datmen alre meest heuet in na gheuoelne elc anders, Ende in doer smakene, Ende in doer etene, Ende in doer drinckene, Ende in verswelghene elc anderen" (Letter 11:22–27). For a comparison, see Aelred of Rievaulx's (1110–67) remarkable text on male spiritual friendship,

De spiritali amicitia, Corpus christianorum, continuatio medievalis 1 (Turnhout, 1971), 287–350. Aelred's homoeroticism has been discussed with great sensitivity by Brian Patrick McGuire, *Brother and Lover: Aelred of Rievaulx* (New York, 1994). I will compare Hadewijch's homoerotics to that of male authors in my forthcoming book on sex roles in medieval mysticism.

74. "Van allen oefeninghen van Minnen, die lief van lieue sal ontfaen Jn helsene, Jn cussene, Jn enicheiden, Jn bekinnissen, Jn nemene, Jn gheuene, Jn oetmoedicheiden, Jn onderlinghe groeten, Jn ghenadeghen ontfane, Ende dat lieue soe luttel helen mach" (Letter 27:22–27).

75. "O wi, soe suete soe Minne es, waer omme en valdiere niet diep inne?" (Letter 5:30–31).

76. See E. Ann Matter, "My Sister, My Spouse: Woman-Identified Women in Medieval Christianity," in *Weaving the Visions: New Patterns in Feminist Spirituality,* ed. Judith Plaskow and Carol Christ (San Francisco, 1989), 51–63; Barz, Leistner, and Wild, *Hättest Du gedacht,* chap. 5.

77. "Dat ic v na ben van herten ende bekint Ende de liefste mensche die leuet na saren" (Letter 29:15–17).

78. "Groet mi oec saren metten seluen yet ende niet, dac ic ben. Dat ic hare al dat vol wesen conste, daer si in hemint es, dat dade ic hare gherne, Ende ic saelt haere oec voldoen, hoe si mi aldus doet.... Nu alse si andere onlede heuet ende ghedueren mach ende ghedoghen mijns herten leet, soe laete mi dolen.... Ende ghi die meer van mi gheleisten moghet dan yeman die nu leuet sonder sare, Emme ende ghi, die sijt mi al eens. Oec keerdi v beide te luttel ter Minnen die mi soe vreseleke omuaen heuet inberoeringhen van onghecoster Minnen.... De Minnne es al" (Letter 25:1–5, 10–12, 16–20, 39).

79. "Si souden v gerne van ons trecken met hen. Haren herten es wee om onse sonderlinghe trouwe.... Doet alle dinc op der Minnen sach, Ende leuet in enighen vlite met ons, ende laet ons inder soeter Minnen leuen. Leuet gode ende hi v ende ghi ons" (Letter 23:23–29).

80. "Ende dat ic di soe sere minde ende ne ghene vre dijns vergheten en conste noch en can, / dat ic dier doet / ende dijnre onghenaden van minnen soe na te di gheuelde in verstormtheiden te gode dat mi te meer was te gode met di, / dat saerde mi te meer" (Vision 14:57–63).

81. Poems 23, 27, 36 of Poems in Stanzas.

82. Poem 11, Poems in Stanzas.

83. "In hogher minnen scolen/ Leert men orewoet. / Want si brenghet dien in dolen / Die hem wel verstoet" (Poems in Stanzas 28:6).

84. "Dat suetste van minnen sijn hare storme; / Haer diepste afgront es haer scoenste vorme; / Jn haer verdolen dats na gheraken; / Om haer verhongeren dats voeden ende smaken / ... Hare seertse wonden es al ghenesen; / ... Verleidinghe es wijse van harer scolen; / Hare hanteren sijn storme wreet; / ... Hare gheloeften sijn al verleiden; / Hare chierheiden sijn al oncleiden; / ... Jc wille hare wesen al datse si; / Si goet, si fel: al eens eest mi" (Poems in Stanzas 13:1–5, 30–31, 49–50).

85. "Ic groete dat ic minne / Met miere herten bloet. / Mi dorren mine sinne / Jnder minnen oerwoet. / ... Ay, hertelike ioffrouwe, / Dat ic so vele te v spreke / Dat doet mi

nuwe trouwe / Van dieper minnen treke. / . . . Jc doge, ic poghe omt hoghe, / Jc soghe met minne bloede; / . . . Jc beue, ic cleue, / ic gheue, / . . . Ay, lief, hebbic lief en lief, / Sidi lief mijn lief, / Die lief gauet omme lief, / Daer lief lief mede verhief. / Ay, minne, ware ic minne / Ende met minnen minne v minne! / Ay, minne, om minne gheuet dat minne / Die minne al mine volkinne" (Poems in Couplets 15:1–4, 21–25, 37–39, 41, 45–52).

11

Nonviolent Christianity and the Strangeness of Female Power in Geoffrey Chaucer's Man of Law's Tale

Elizabeth Robertson

The work of the fourteenth-century English poet Geoffrey Chaucer has long been viewed as a rich compendium of late medieval English culture. Because Chaucer's work is more inclusive (although clearly not all-inclusive) of many societal elements than that of his contemporaries, it, not surprisingly, calls attention to a variety of categories of difference. Given the multiplicity of character types and social conditions in Chaucer's work, a study of difference in its several Chaucerian manifestations can have implications for a larger investigation (as this present volume embraces) regarding difference in the whole of late medieval culture.

Recent Chaucer criticism amply demonstrates Chaucer's engagement with categories of difference. Major books by critics such as Lee Patterson and Paul Strohm have explored the importance of class—or, to use a term more suited to the Middle Ages, social status—to an understanding of Chaucer's work.[1] These critics argue that because of his peculiarly liminal position as an "esquire en service" (that is, one who earned his position in the aristocracy through work rather than inheritance), and because he mingled, both by marriage and by profession, with royalty, Chaucer was particularly attuned to the implications of at least one category of difference, social status.[2] Another major group of critics, including Carolyn Dinshaw and Elaine Tuttle Hansen, has investigated Chaucer's complex engagement with gender issues.[3] With the exception of Jill Mann, most feminist studies conclude that Chaucer subscribes to essentialist notions of women as submissive helpmates victimized by their husbands and lords. More recently, critics have called attention to Chaucer's representation of ethnic difference in two of his tales: The Squire's Tale, a romance of flying horses, magic rings, and speaking birds, for its "orientalism," and The Man of Law's Tale for its portrayal of the Islamic other as stereotypically monstrous, violent, and unnatural.[4] Critics have recognized not only the importance of "race," "class," and "gender" as critical categories that map difference, but also the complexity of ideas produced when these categories interact with one another.[5] Current interest in the trinity—race, class, and gender—has, however, tended to mask what this paper argues is an equally deep source of radical otherness, at least to Chaucer, and perhaps more generally in the period: religion. Chaucer's representation of religion has of course been a subject of discussion from the beginning of Chaucer criticism, but it has yet to be considered as another category of difference for Chaucer. Indeed, it is generally assumed that Chaucer, while critical of the corruptions of the institution of the church, if religious at all, embraces a blandly orthodox vision of Christianity.

Most of these critics tend to argue that Chaucer is both conventional and politically conservative in his representations of difference: that is, he upholds the prevailing, usually misogynistic, politically repressive, religiously conservative, and religiously intolerant views commonly held by members of the aristocracy. If we consider Chaucer's engagement with not one, but several, categories of difference as they interact with each other in one representative tale, The Man of Law's Tale, we will come to see that Chaucer's work challenges essentialized categories of difference. Thus, religion and gender work together to create the radical otherness of The Man of Law's Tale. Visionary literature, such as that of Chaucer, by revealing the structures that form society for good and for ill, and by expanding our sense of the possibilities of individual agency within these structures, can challenge accepted hierarchies of difference. In this literary work, we shall see how intersections of categories of difference can enhance such visionary dismantlings of oppressive social formations.

Since The Man of Law's Tale, may not be familiar to an audience composed not only of Chaucerians but also of those interested in Byzantine, Islamic, or Judaic cultures, let me summarize the tale's plot briefly here. One of Chaucer's pilgrims, known as the Man of Law, on the road to Canterbury and engaged in a tale-telling contest proposed by the host of the Tabard Inn, tells an impassioned tale of a woman, Constance, who suffers for her Christian faith. The tale begins with an account of travelers to Rome who, hearing of the perfection of the emperor's daughter, Constance, return home to Syria where their report of their travels inspires their Sultan to relinquish his religion, Islam, in exchange for her hand in marriage. The Sultan's mother foils this plan and at the wedding feast incites the crowd to kill her son and those who have denied their faith. She then puts Constance into a rudderless boat in which she floats aimlessly until she lands upon the shore of Northumberland. There, taken in by an admiring constable and his wife, Constance, proceeds to inspire the pagans she meets to embrace the Christian faith. Meanwhile, in Northumberland, a young knight, foiled in his desire to possess Constance, kills the constable's wife and frames Constance, who is saved from false condemnation by the miraculous appearance of a hand of God in the court. The king of Northumberland, Alla, moved by Constance's innocence and beauty, marries her. Again a non-Christian mother-in-law, here Alla's mother, Donegild, in Alla's absence, plots to overthrow Constance by proclaiming Alla and Constance's newborn child a monster and setting Constance adrift in a rudderless boat. Yet again Constance floats aimlessly until she comes to Rome with her son, Maurice. Meanwhile, her father receives the news of the Syrian bloodbath and enacts a brutal revenge upon the Islamic mother-in-law. In Rome, Alla arrives, recognizes first his son and then Constance, and they are reunited. She is then reunited with her father. Alla dies; Constance lives for some time and her son Maurice eventually becomes emperor of Rome. The Man of Law punctuates his story with apostrophes proclaiming the wondrous nature of Constance's steady faith and heaven-sent salvation.

It is only by considering the ways in which Chaucer interweaves and complicates categories of difference in this tale that we can come to appreciate that, to Chaucer, both gender and religion are deliberate constructs rather than essential, static categories. The Man of Law's Tale appears to be first about Islam and then about suffering women, but closer inspection—especially to the tale's imagery—demonstrates that Islam is, in part, a mere foil for an equally strong challenge to convention—apostolic Christianity as it is embedded in a version of the feminine. In his representation of Constance as linked to the history of the conversion of Britain as well as to Christianity's early history—apostolic Christianity as revealed in the Gospels—Chaucer presents a form of non-violent Christianity that is simultaneously less coercive, less hierarchical, and more communal than the institutionalized form of Roman Christianity operating in the fourteenth-century English Church. As the tale unfolds, the expectations raised by the work's evocation of categories of religious difference and social status are displaced by a different, though related, set of ideas brought out by Chaucer's intertwining of medieval concepts and practices concerning women with his concept of apostolic Christianity. The fears and desires that are produced by religious difference, and brought into being through the social mobility of aristocratic women on the marriage market, are intensified by the different set of emotions evoked by a constructed "feminine" other. Certain particular ideas about the feminine current in the period—its association with water, motherhood, the semiotic (vs. reason), submissiveness, and abjection—serve Chaucer in positing his ideal of apostolic Christianity. Chaucer utilizes and transforms the medical and theological conventions of fluidity, subjection, and abjection commonly ascribed to feminine others in late medieval England by absorbing into this construction the exotic magnetism associated with ethnic religious others and the mobility that occurs historically among aristocratic women on the marriage market. Through metonymy the augmented feminine lends itself to Chaucer's representation of apostolic Christianity.

Let me clarify at this early point in the essay that much of the provocative power of The Man of Law's Tale results from the subtlety and variousness of the versions of the feminine represented here. Equally, Constance's responses to religious others do not fall neatly into binary oppositions: for example, Islam vs. Christianity, paganism vs. Islam or Christianity. In the following paragraphs it is, as it were, the genius of Constance in reacting to oppression more precisely, and more realistically, than the conventional binaries will allow that I will be at pains to delineate.

Chaucer initially utilizes the category of religious difference to establish ideas of strangeness, simultaneous attraction and repulsion (the "orientalist" desire described by Edward Said), and the tendency of religious and ethnic others to inspire violence, and then draws on contemporary concepts and practices about women to articulate an unpredictable and utopian vision of women as politically and spiritually effectual.[6] By complicating gender through evoking concepts associated with religious others and through linking gender with a particular form of Christianity, Chaucer is able to transcend the restrictive category of feminine identity (as encapsulated most clearly in Aristotelian medical theory as it intersects with Christian theology). Cast in a rudderless boat in the formless ocean, yet capable of positively affecting the lives of others, Constance resists the strictures of the ideology into which the dominant culture would like to place her. Through its association with the category of religious difference, gender becomes reconfigured as a category of power and mystery, despite its origins in apparent powerlessness. While this idea draws on well-established and conservative articulations of Marian spirituality, Chaucer radicalizes this vision by presenting Marian spirituality embodied in a woman who is sexual and firmly established in the secular world. Chaucer's use of stereotypes of both religious and feminine others to construct his visionary ideals of Christianity illuminates the historical contingency rather than the essential nature of all these categories.

The opening sequence of the tale apparently sets Christianity and Islam in opposition to one another in stereotypical ways. However, Chaucer concretizes this opposition in the body of a woman, thus adding another category of difference, gender, to religious difference. By interweaving categories of difference Chaucer complicates the colonialist impulses that normally govern the meeting of East and West. Constance's otherness, as we shall see, criticizes imperialistic and colonizing impulses, whether Christian or Islam. A number of critics have observed that The Man of Law's Tale begins with a stereotypical and perhaps racist representation of Islamic people.[7] In an important recent essay, Susan Schibanoff has described the motivations for the late medieval hatred of Islam, motivations that she points out stem not only from Islam's difference from, but also its similarity to, Christianity. Not least among the challenges posed by Islam was the monotheism it shared with Christianity. The Islamic people portrayed at the opening of the tale are particularly threatening because their religion and Christianity might be equally powerful. The Islamic Sultan and his mother are stereotypically portrayed as respectively naive and duplicitous, and the mother's followers are represented as exotic, cruel, and unnatural. The Sultan's

monstrous mother incites the Muslims to barbarism, and their brutal
behavior predictably motivates the imperialist genocide enacted by the
heroine, Constance's, father at the tale's conclusion. Clearly the tale asserts stereotypes marking religious and ethnic difference in its portrait
of the cunning and barbarous Islamic mother-in-law who resists the imposition of Christianity on her culture and of the sweeping power of the
Roman Christian war machine that flattens the Islamic community in
revenge for its treatment of the Christian ambassadors.

As the tale progresses, another monstrous mother-in-law, as well as
additional cruel characters, torment Constance, but they are not ethnic
others. The valence of the ethnic and religious caricature of the Islamic
mother-in-law is thus called into question by the fact that Chaucer portrays a pagan British mother-in-law, Donegild, in the same way. What
Donegild shares with the Islamic mother-in-law is not a different ethnicity, but rather a different religion, for both women oppose Constance
only because she believes in a different religion than their own. Ethnic
difference as a category here, as elsewhere in the period, is therefore
complicated, if not defined by, religious affiliation. Schibanoff points
out that medieval ideology distinguished pagans from those of the Islamic faith because, "As 'outlaws' rather than 'inlaws' non-believers—
pagans or infidels—posed the lesser threat to Christianity. Clearly defined as Other, non-Christians occupied a stable, unambiguous position."[8]
In this tale, however, pagans and those of the Islamic faith are seen as
interchangeable. Furthermore, when Constance looks back on her experience, she is disturbed not so much by her contact with foreign peoples
as by her contact with other religions. She begs her father, "Sende me
namoore unto noon hethenesse."[9] She applies "hethenesse" equally to
her experiences in Syria and to her experiences in pagan England.[10]

If we add gender to our analysis of the representation of Islam of the
opening sequence, a more complicated picture of the work's representation of difference emerges. Schibanoff also makes this observation, but
her analysis leads to a very different conclusion than mine for she argues
that the construction of religious others in the tale reinforces its sexism.
In discussing Constance's apparent passivity, Schibanoff argues,

> Not only does Constance's behavior provide a model of female
> submission, but it helps the Man of Law reach a more fun-
> damental goal in his tale: to establish and maintain woman's

difference from (inferiority to) man, her otherness. The Man of
Law's overriding aim . . . is to preserve and enhance such difference—between women and men, East and West, Islam and
Christianity, ultimately between western patriarchal culture and
the Other.[11]

The tale does indeed use stereotypes of the religious other to reinforce
the otherness of Constance, but in my view Constance's otherness, rather
than being a mark of her inferiority, sets her apart as superior to that of
any non-Christian in the tale, eastern or western, and furthermore is en-
twined inextricably with her religion.

Despite the fact that he uses cultural stereotypes in his representations of Islam, Chaucer complicates his literary inheritance concerning
otherness; while, on the one hand, he stereotypically demonstrates Roman
Christianity's imperialist conquest of the Islamic other, on the other
hand, he also depicts Islam's colonizing impulses vis a vis Constance.
Constance is portrayed from the point of view of Islamic observers as a
stranger, the foreign other. Syrian merchants see her first, and their description of her initiates the plot. As Schibanoff argues, in contrast to its
sources, the tale here expresses the commonalities between the Syrians
and the Romans, even though a momentary anxiety occurs when "the
sultan's councilors doubt that a Christian emperor would allow his
daughter to marry under 'Mahoun's' law, 'By cause that ther was swich
diversitee / Bitwene hir bothe lawes' (220–21)"; as Schibanoff argues,
this diversity is easily overcome.[12] Following the impulses of a number
of late medieval theologians, Chaucer represents Islam as close to Christianity; as Schibanoff points out, the Sultan's councilors use reason to
convince the Sultan to convert, a representation in keeping with medieval
theological respect for the rationality of Islam. In the tale this respect is
indicated in the councilor's description of Islam as a "sweete" law (223)
compared to the narrator's "deere" law of Christianity (237).[13]

The underlying danger of similitude emphasized in these opening
sequences extends to the text's representation of the imperialist impulses
shared equally by East and West. Like Christians motivated by the desire
to conquer and possess foreign lands, the Sultan desires to possess this
exotic other, Constance: "this Sowdan hath caught so greet plesance / To
han hir figure in his remembrance, / That al his lust and al his bisy
cure / Was for to love hire" (186–89). If he cannot "han Custance with-

inne a litel space, / He nas but deed" (208–09). His lust for this ideal-ized image pushes him to the point of relinquishing his own religion. Here Chaucer paints a portrait of possessive desire that blinds and ob-scures values in a way that is analogous to the violent impulse of the Christian conqueror desirous to overcome the heathen other. The other in this case is not a person of color, however, but Constance—a woman of a different faith and, from the point of view of the Syrians, of a differ-ent ethnicity. The preeminent other in this opening sequence, then, is arguably not the Islamic mother-in-law, but Constance. Thus, Chaucer here uses the trope of difference to emphasize, first, Christianity's power and, second, its strangeness, for it is not only Constance's experiences in a foreign land that are at issue here, but also her experiences as a for-eigner bringing with her a foreign religion into a familiar land.

Chaucer represents the Islamic other as dangerously the same not only in its monotheism, but also in an imperialist impulse awakened by storytelling itself. These opening stanzas entwine medieval orientalism with a subtle elucidation of the potentially dangerous effects of "tid-ynges" (181: reported accounts of things seen). The poem opens with a description of a company of merchants in Syria "that wyde-where senten hir spicerye, / Clothes of gold, and satyns riche of hewe" (136–37). These merchants who trade in spices and luxury goods, their "chaffare" (138), also trade in stories, for they return to Syria with tales: "whan they cam from any strange place, / He wolde, of his benigne curteisye, / Make hem good chiere, and bisily espye / Tidynges of sondry regnes, for to leere / The wondres that they myght seene or heere" (178–82). In this passage the usual orientalist expectations are reversed in that the Syrian Sultan desires to know more about the exotic West, rather than being the object of its curious desire.

These opening passages tell us that desire for the other is inspired not only by Constance's image but also significantly by the report or "tidynges" of her, that is, by the outsized image of her coming not from a single human source but from "sondry regnes" (181), from the exotic collective authority culled from many realms. Chaucer distinguishes the person from the collective image of her. The merchants first hear a re-port of the "renoun / Of...dame Custance" (150–51). After hearing of her virtues, then they see her. Upon their return, their report of Constance inspires the Sultan to desire "to han hir figure in his remembrance" (187); "telling" inspires a colonialist desire to see and possess the image in his mind. "Tidynges" not only evoke a desire to possess, but also are strong enough to inspire conversion. Chaucer here represents storytelling as both powerful and dangerous. Given the fact that the larger work within which The Man of Law's Tale appears is itself a series of told stories, perhaps Chaucer is here drawing our attention to the power of writing itself, suggesting that an encounter with writing can be considered an encounter with a category of difference. Writing can therefore be understood to inspire the fears, resistances, desires, and transformations that are commonly evoked by other categories of difference or encounters with the strange.

In this case, stories ultimately have the power to convert. The Sultan's motivation for conversion is a worldly one, but unbeknownst to the Sultan, an image inspires an act of faith that has the potential, from a Christian point of view, to be salvific. The Syrian Sultan feels the need for salvation as he asks his councilors to "Saveth my lyf... / To geten hire that hath my lyf in cure" (229–30). Although on one level he simply uses a secular courtly convention by describing his beloved as a cure to lovesickness, the Sultan's unconscious reference to salvation also suggests at another level the salvific potential offered by the Christian Constance. The Sultan little realizes that, from a Christian point of view, Constance's requirement that he convert before marrying might literally save his life. In some senses, the Sultan is on the "right" road to Christianity because he has already responded with an act of faith, faith in the reported image of Constance.

This incident highlights the veracity and reliability of reports of things unseen and the nature of the colonialist imagination that is to act upon secondhand reports. The interplay between report, image, and desire here anticipates the interest of The Man of Law's Tale in secondhand reports, narrative, argument, and rhetoric, all set in opposition to the much more effective and powerful image itself; and, as we shall see, these oppositions are played out through the interplay of gender and Christianity that fully emerges in the second half of the work. The tale becomes increasingly interested in the power of the image in Christian pedagogy; and here what is said of Constance—what her image can convey by report—is linked to God: "And al this voys was sooth, as God is trewe"(169) the narrator asserts, affirming other people's assessment of her virtue. The veracity of Constance's reputation is here compared to the truth of God, a comparison that both increases her exotic desirability and reinforces the "oriental" qualities of God. As is said in the *Ancrene Wisse*, the hope offered by Jesus "is a swete spice."[14] Dealing in spices, the merchants inadvertently stumble upon the agent of the "true" Christian God. Thus, in the opening lines of the tale, playing with the colonialist ideas inspired by categories of difference, Chaucer establishes and complicates a variety of categories of difference including ethnicity, religion, gender, and writing itself in order to establish the "difference" of Constance who will emerge in the tale as an embodiment of a particular form of Christianity, one that inspires both violence and desire.

Constance's role in this opening sequence is bound up with her social status, a subject that has rarely been considered in studies of Constance. In an important essay, Sheila Delany, one of the few readers of the tale to consider social status and gender, argues that Constance's passivity is set as a counter model to the revolutionary behavior of the participants of the English Rising of 1381.[15] However, Delany discusses conflict between social groups by analogy rather than by considering the ways in which social status operates literally in the tale; that is, Delany fails to consider the particular strengths and weaknesses afforded to Constance as a member of the aristocracy. As an aristocratic woman, Constance is particularly mobile on the marriage circuit since it was more common for women of upper rather than lower social status to become objects of exchange in foreign marriage markets. Despite medieval Christianity's doctrinal belief in the importance of female consent in marriage, secular practice, especially among the aristocracy, rarely solicited such consent, and in this representation, Constance is no exception. Stressing her identity as a commodity while commenting on her lack of voice in her marriage, the narrator concludes, "Wommen are born to thraldom and penance" (286). Constance is not simply a religious heroine; she is a religious heroine who disseminates, along with the seeds of Christianity, the genes of her father, emperor of Rome. Her roles as agent of conversion and as aristocratic mother are inseparable in this story, and both her strength as a mother and the powerlessness she experiences because of her marriageability become crucial to the tale's unfolding.

If we turn our attention away from the Islamic other and from issues of social status and toward the otherness of Constance, we will develop a more complex understanding of the tale's representation of categories of difference. Critics have had trouble talking about Constance, so

much so that A. S. G. Edwards argues that there seems to be a conspir-
acy to avoid discussing Constance herself.[16] The habit of turning away
from Constance is true not only of criticism that concludes the work is
more about the teller than the tale, but also of criticism that praises the
tale for its celebration of Christian values. V. A. Kolve, for example, and
those who agree with him (e.g., C. David Benson and Eugene Clasby),
talk about Constance as an agent of the dissemination of Christianity,
one who joins a long history of men and women who have suffered for
the promulgation of the Christian faith.[17] Yet most commentators on
the religious issue overlook the fact that Constance, besides being a suffering Christian, is also a suffering woman. The interpretive significance of Constance's gender is virtually ignored.

Instead of attending carefully to Constance, critics tend to measure
Constance's power in terms of that exhibited by the other women in the
tale, the violent mothers-in-law. In their condemnation of what they see
as Chaucer's endorsement of female submissiveness in the figure of
Constance, Delany, Dinshaw, and Schibanoff all conclude that Chaucer
reinforces his views by presenting women who do exhibit power as monstrous. The narrator criticizes both women for their mannishness (the
Islamic mother-in-law is called a "virago" [359] and Donegild unwomanly
[782]). Critical understandings of the mothers-in-law tend to assume,
however, that in these passages Chaucer criticizes women; I would like
to offer an alternative reading by arguing that in his representations of
the mothers-in-law Chaucer criticizes not women, but rather a certain
kind of masculinity present in either men or women, one that uses
power for its own selfish purposes. Chaucer's description of the Islamic
mother-in-law as a "feyned womman" (362) and later of Donegild as
"mannysh" (782) thus signals Chaucer's recognition that gender is constructed and variable. He criticizes not only the fact that women attempt
to seize power, but also the kind of masculine power in which they are
invested, one marked by violence, deception, and cruelty. Such violent,
tyrannical, "male" power seems suspect even when wielded by the Christian heroes of the tale. For example, as an agent of conversion, Constance's rudderless boat sailing between the powerful war machines bent
on revenge (lines 946–59) is far more effective than that army that brings
not conversion but mass destruction.[18] And Constance, although powerless in some senses, brings a powerful ruler, Alla, to his knees. While it
is undoubtedly true that Chaucer here criticizes women who exhibit mas-

culine power, might not Chaucer be drawing our attention to the negative consequences of male-identified violence and proposing instead non-violent religion? For her part, Constance never advocates violence even when it seems justified. Alla commands the death of the false knight, but Constance "hadde of his deeth greet routhe" (689).

Chaucer seems aware of the social construction not only of femininity, but of masculinity as well. While violence is associated with the masculine, it is not *essential* to masculinity as formulated by Chaucer. Indeed, with the exception of his own act of vengeance, Alla seems to be "feminized" and contrasted with the mannish mothers-in-law. He is, for example, inspired to excessive, perhaps "feminine" tears: "Alla kyng hath swich compassioun / As gentil herte is fulfild of pitee, / That from his eyen ran the water doun" (659–61). By his "feminine" feeling, as David Benson has noted, he is brought to his knees in awe of Constance's faith.[19]

Rather than focus on the mothers-in-law as antitypes reinforcing Constance's weakness, then, I would argue that the mothers-in-law offer a model that reinforces Constance's difference—a difference that exhibits a power of its own. However, those who have studied the representation of gender in the tale do not grant Constance any power. Dinshaw, for example, in her brilliant analysis of the narrator's problems with female power in his portrait of the incestuous mothers-in-law, concludes that Constance is a nothing, "an essential blankness that will be inscribed by men."[20] Jill Mann, whose reading comes closest to mine, nonetheless fails to see the peculiarly feminine, if not feminist, aspects of Constance's power.[21] Delany, in her argument that Chaucer uses this tale as an allegory of contemporary class issues, concludes that Constance is merely passive. Schibanoff, in the most recent assessment of gender in the tale, similarly dismisses Constance as a reinscription of medieval ideals of the submissive female.[22]

In contrast to many feminist critics, my view is that Constance holds power, but unlike the view of Constance's power held by Christian apologists, I see Constance's power as problematic because of her gender. It is difficult to talk about the power Constance holds because she does not participate in systems we know, although her power, as Kolve, Benson, and Clasby demonstrate, emanates from her Christianity. Distinct from other kinds of Christian power, and in spite of her status as a daughter of an emperor, Constance's faith is buttressed neither by institutional religion nor by the state. Having suppressed her aristocratic origins,

Constance converts others without the violence associated with imperialist, hegemonic Christianity. Her Christian power, when combined with gender, finally becomes radically other; its force resides in its otherness and it operates from the margins. If we consider the tale's representation of otherness as a locus of both repulsion and desire, it is Constance who is the central and productive "other" of the tale. Like ethnic others, Constance, the embodiment of a foreign religion in foreign lands, is the site of such desire (all who see her want to possess her) and repulsion (many who see her want to hurt her). Her otherness as a woman combined with her otherness as a religious minority (a Christian in an Islamic country, then in a pagan country) is central to the tale's representation of apostolic Christianity as a potentially dangerous, "elvish," unknowable force.

Although most critics agree that Constance has no agency in the tale, Chaucer's representation of Constance's apparently passive submissiveness is more complex than it first seems. Constance's relationship to action is obscure. She inspires extreme and often irrational violence in others, but she herself is neither an instigator nor a perpetrator of that violence. She triumphs over others, but she chooses neither to suffer nor to triumph. Rather than being obedient, Constance seems outside of law. The primal image of her in a rudderless boat in the sea reinforces her unknowable, anarchic power. Whether or not Constance can be called active or passive therefore seems indeterminate.

Indeed, Chaucer seems intent on obscuring her agency. Critics often bolster their assessment of Constance as passive by pointing to the fact that Chaucer changed his sources to diminish Constance's involvement in action. Chaucer's revisions to his sources do not erase her agency, but rather problematize it. In Trivet's and Gower's earlier versions of the story, for example, Constance purposely places the would-be rapist at the edge of the boat and then prays for aid from God. In Chaucer's version, on the other hand, Mary comes to her aid unasked, and Constance's involvement in the overthrow of the rapist is ambiguous. Chaucer tells us "For with her struglyng wel and myghtily / The theef fil over bord al sodeynly" (921–22). The language is double here: it gives the reader the opportunity to attribute the fall both to God and to Constance's struggle. Later in the work, Chaucer treats the incident when her son Maurice goes to meet her father in a way that veils Constance's active participation in the event. The sources tell us she sends Maurice to Alla. Chaucer's narrator obscures Constance's agency. We are told first only that she might have sent the boy and second that it was at least at her command that the boy stares at his father: "Som men wolde seyn at requeste of Custance / This senatour hath led this child to feeste; / I may nat tellen every circumstance— / Be as be may, ther was he at the leeste. / But sooth is this, that at his moodres heeste / Biforn Alla, durynge the metes space, / The child stood, lookynge in the kynges face" (1009–15).

Constance's power and effectiveness are revealed not through her actions so much as through her face. As the work progresses, her face becomes the site of signification for others. The tale's repeated use of the imagery of sight underscores the importance not just of seeing that face but of understanding it properly. The story is set in motion, as we have noted above, by the reported sight of Constance. As the story unfolds, characters observe Constance, some for good and some for ill, and seeing her incites desire in them. When Constance first sets foot in Northumberland, her example, indeed simply the sight of her, inspires pity, devotion, service, and love despite her obscure origins: "She was so diligent, withouten slouthe, / To serve and plesen everich in that place / That alle hir loven that looken in hir face" (530–32). In a passage of sweet irony, Constance urges Hermengyld to give a blind Briton back his sight in the name of Christ. Although we never know whether or not the Briton's sight is restored, Constance's power is revealed in this scene around issues of sight. As the tale puts it, the constable is "abasshed of that sight" (568), and only after observing the same does he ask to hear Christ's lay, "And so ferforth she gan oure lay declare / That she the Constable, er that it was eve / Converteth" (572–74). Alla is moved to believe in Constance's innocence "whan he saugh so benigne a creature" (615). Others defend her "for they han seyn hire evere so vertuous" (624). The senator praises Constance by saying "Ne saugh I nevere as she" (1025); Satan, on the other hand, "saugh" (583) all her perfection and then incited the knight to kill Hermengyld. The would-be rapist is part of a crowd that "gauren" on her ship (912). To judge Constance's power solely in terms of her activity or passivity overlooks the ways other kinds of power are revealed in the tale. As we see in these events, Constance's inner being is conveyed not by how she herself acts, but rather by her effect on others.

Constance is initially praised as a "mirour of alle curteisye" (166), that is, as someone or some idealized object of desire who merely reflects, a point that to Dinshaw suggests Constance's non-existence in the text. But mirrors in the Middle Ages were understood as more than mere reflectors and Constance's face does more than reflect, for it generates power, the power to convince Alla of her probable innocence and, more importantly, the power to convert. Dinshaw argues that the thrice-repeated image of Constance's pale corpse-like face is further evidence of her nothingness. But the image of her deathly pale face can serve other functions. First, it enhances Constance's abject unknowability in that paleness signifies her ghostliness, a kind of marginality that places her on the border between life and death. Donegild furthers the impression of Constance's otherworldliness. She objects to her son's marriage to so peculiar a person, "Hir thoughte a despit that he sholde take / So strange a creature unto his make" (699–700), and in her invented letter hopes to capitalize on that difference by associating Constance with other forms of strangeness, namely the supernatural. She labels Constance an elf, an appellation that suggests her affiliation with the world of spirits as much as with the world of humans: "The mooder was an elf, by aventure / Ycomen, by charmes or by sorcerie" (754–55). Although we know this is a slanderous fiction, the attribution articulates the potential fear her difference can inspire in others.

The ambiguity of Constance's nature is further enhanced by the oft-noted generic confusion of the work, for she is at once a romance heroine deeply involved in the secular world and a saint, at once asexual and sexualized as a wife and mother. Indeed the narrator responds to the confusion inspired by her secular saintliness in his passage about Alla and Constance's intercourse on their wedding night: "They goon to bedde, as it was skile and right; / For thogh that wyves be ful hooly thynges, / They moste take in pacience at nyght, / Swiche manere necessaries as been plesynges / To folk that han ywedded hem with rynges, / And leye a lite hir hoolynesse aside, / As for the tyme—it may no bet betide" (708–14). Critics have often commented upon the odd combination of prudishness and prurience of this passage, but Chaucer is also arguably drawing our attention here to the problems of secular sanctity. Constance is not Mary; she is neither asexual nor "alone of all her sex." Thus, she offers a model of power that is all the more threatening to the hegemony.

The narrator's description of Constance's arrival in Northumberland further emphasizes her mystery. When she lands at Northumberland the constable finds first "the tresor that she broghte" (515), surely a sign that might convey her identity. The narrator does not reveal the nature of this treasure. Its status as treasure might enhance the constable's open reception of Constance. But we do not know whether treasure signifies a monetary or a symbolic value, or both. If monetary, the constable might conclude that Constance is an aristocrat whose recovery might offer him future reward. The treasure might only be symbolic; for example, it might simply be a wooden cross. Perhaps it is both monetary and symbolic; for example, a gold cross. Like us, the constable is unable to discern her meaning from the treasure that travels with her. Surely, however, the unknowable treasure reinforces her intriguing attractiveness.

The constable must then rely on conversation to determine Constance's identity. Constance, however, proves to be even linguistically strange, that is, she speaks a corrupt language, not even that of the people whose land she has entered. Nonetheless, she is understood. As is characteristic of her, her strangeness does not prevent her from communicating even across languages: "In hir langage mercy she bisoghte, / ... A maner Latyn corrupt was hir speche, / But algates therby was she understonde" (516–20). As an agent of conversion, Constance is translatable, despite her foreignness. Her universal linguistic power is perhaps again hinted at rather indirectly when the false knight swears upon "A Britoun book, written with Evaungiles" (666) in that Constance is protected in this scene by the sudden appearance of a British form of the Gospels. At the time of the conversion of Britain, where might such a text have come from? Is this a version of the Gospels written in British hands or a translation of the Gospels into British? Given the controversy concerning English Bibles in Chaucer's own day, the presence of this "underground" Bible reinforces Constance's mysterious power.[23] At least like the Bible, Constance's speech can universally be understood.

Constance conveys meaning not only by words, but by gesture, for her first act is to kneel and pray that the constable kill her. Constance is aware of the long history of danger induced by the arrival of a foreigner on native shores. By articulating abjection, however, Constance disarms the constable's fear of her difference. It is not gesture alone that makes Constance understandable, for besides kneeling down, she continues to speak to the constable in her strange language, further and deliberately obscuring her origins: "She seyde she was so mazed in the see / That she forgat hir mynde, by hir trouthe" (526–27). In Chaucer's sources, Constance must hide her family origins, fearful of the pursuit of her incestuous father. Chaucer's elimination of the fear of incest serves to reinforce Constance's obscure motivations and origins. An acknowledgment of her father as emperor of Rome, through an announcement of her aristocratic affiliations, would immediately categorize her and limit her. In Chaucer's version, Constance's obscurity thus reinforces her mysterious association with God.

Why should Chaucer here, as elsewhere in *The Canterbury Tales*, choose to embody Christianity in a woman? And why does he in this tale use one kind of other (a woman) to convert a different other (the non-Christian)? Women's historical experience of Christianity is complex, as Caroline Bynum has so ably demonstrated, and Christianity seems to have afforded women a range of power.[24] Jerome, for example, praised women who entered the convent for being able to abandon their femininity. Other theologians and Christian commentators, however, as I have discussed elsewhere, argue the opposite, that women can never escape their inherent sinfulness and bodiliness despite their devoutness.[25] These contrary views seem to originate in two different strands of Christianity, one that condemned women as followers of Eve, and the other that praised their potential to be like Mary. Indeed, the figure of Mary allows for the development of a powerful legitimation of female identity, for Mary's marriage to Joseph inspires the development of the theological doctrine of the autonomy of women in marriage, a doctrine that had profound influences on secular as well as religious female power in the late Middle Ages. As members of the fourth estate, women are both integral to medieval culture's functioning and excluded from its power structure, yet they manage to exert influence despite or perhaps through their marginality. As commodities on the marriage market aristocratic women are objectified, yet their assent in marriage is encouraged within Christian ideology and ecclesiastical court practice. In The Man of Law's Tale, Chaucer uses Constance's secular marginality and ambiguous status within Christianity to construct a kind of Christianity that is itself also marginal.

That women are marginal within medieval secular society is suggested both in the prologue and the tale. The prologue, with its long list of Chaucerian stories of classical women abandoned by men, reminds the reader of the ways in which secular patriarchy repeatedly betrays women. The tale itself reinforces the idea of the culture's objectication of women in its representation of Constance's treatment by most, although not all, of the men she encounters in her travels. Those women who are able to exert power within secular culture seem only to be able to do so by forfeiting their gender, that is, by becoming mannish. In this tale, the marginal position is the only place where women can maintain their integrity. While it may appear from some perspectives to be weakness, marginality in some ways grants power. In a review of Cixous, Verna Conley explains how Cixous describes marginality as a "position of... maximum maneuverability... a 'feminine border' in which outmoded male logic ceases to speak."[26] And who has more mobility in this tale than Constance? In her border position as a Christian in a pagan land she does succeed in overthrowing an outmoded logic. Marginality, then, can enhance rather than weaken Christianity's power.

Constance's gender contributes to Chaucer's delineation of Christianity in yet another way. In his portrait of Constance, Chaucer may well be invoking a historical woman who also effected a major conversion without violence: Bertha, the Frankish bride who facilitated the conversion of Anglo-Saxon England, thus restoring the earlier forms of Christianity present among Roman Britons.[27] Her marriage to Æthelberht took place on the condition that she be allowed to bring her priests with her. She brought with her a Frankish bishop named Liudhard, and Christian observances took place in the king's household almost nine years before Augustine's mission. Bertha did not demand that Æthelberht convert, nor did he convert until some years after Augustine's landing in Britain in 597, but that conversion ultimately changed the face of Britain. We do not know if Chaucer was aware that Bertha was memorialized at Canterbury in the font dedicated to her in the church of St. Augustine, but at the very least he may have known of Bertha's role in British national Christianity. Female and religious power were thus closely intertwined in Britain's history from its beginnings. This focus on the role gender plays in Britain's religious history further delineates the superior otherness of Constance's religion as one that emerges and flourishes specifically in Britain; and as Schibanoff points out, that British form of Christianity becomes authorized in the tale by its ultimate links to Rome through Maurice, Constance's son, who eventually becomes the new emperor of Rome.

The tale demonstrates the effectiveness and power of non-violent, non-coercive conversion. Most of the men in the tale, Constance's father and his ambassadors, are far less successful in their forceful attempts at conversion than is Constance in her non-violent teaching. In this work, conversion is a mystery rarely achieved by force. Christianity is associated with violence, the violent revenge Constance's father takes for the killing of the Christian ambassadors, for example, or the punitive hand that appears from heaven, but this violence is not primarily in the service of conversion nor is it perpetrated by Constance. While the miraculous hand does effect conversion, its occurrence is motivated by a need to protect Constance. Conversion seems to be inspired by observation of an example and seems to be a matter of time and choice. Constance's image is far more forceful than even a fleet of ships.

It would be a mistake to dismiss these qualities as conventional. The non-violent ideal Chaucer advocates here is by no means a complacent one. Christian power is disturbing in the tale. It inspires extreme violence in others, including murder and attempted rape, and its operation depends on the suffering of an innocent woman. Chaucer embodies these unsettling qualities in an apparently helpless woman who is also a mother, therefore enhancing their shock value. And just as Constance's timeless devotion to faith continually disrupts the various forms of secular corruption she encounters, so the tale distrusts and disrupts the reader's assumptions about the nature of power itself. In this tale Christianity's power finally resides in what its characters perceive to be its otherness, a power that operates from the margins in the body of a woman.

This textual construction of a marginal form of Christianity reflects apostolic Christianity's marginal status in the fourteenth century when, as Kolve argues, institutionalized religion had moved far from the original tenets of the Christian faith. The apostolic Christianity described in The Man of Law's Tale is most definitely in the world (Constance is not a nun or a saint) but not of this world. In keeping with early apostolic Christianity, her religion is communal and non-hierarchical and ties are formed horizontally, rather than vertically in a structure of ascending power. She, Hermengyld, and Hermengyld's husband, the constable, form horizontal bonds that even affect their sleeping arrangements so that Hermengyld and Constance share a bed. Conversion to her religion is effected through prayer and the expounding of the new law rather than by coercion, although violence occurs around her and sometimes to those who try to interfere with her. Thus, the hand that appears from heaven to smite the false accusing knight, although followed by the conversion of those who witnessed the event, is preceded by Alla's inclination towards Constance because of her appearance, an inclination that causes him to inquire further into her case. As opposed to the Christianity represented by her father, Constance's religious ideal is a force of personal transformation rather than an institutional power. In this personalized and non-hierarchical form of religion, Chaucer here recalls the religion practiced by Christ and the apostles in the Gospels.

The Christianity represented here disturbs not so much in itself—indeed, the images of Constance praying in Northumberland are peaceful—but rather because of the difficulty of conversion and because of the violence it inspires in others. It is Christianity's alien quality—a category of difference—that is frightening to others. It also provides a model for the acceptance of the strange. For example, when Alla learns that his child is purportedly a monster, rather than reject that child, he welcomes him as a product of God's will. Constance herself accepts difficulty because of her faith. Christianity thus provides access to understanding of what is inscrutable and often painful.

Apostolic Christianity, then, and conversion to it propel the convert not only into strangeness but into the realm of the abject. The abject, as Kristeva has shown, is at once attractive and repellent, and those modern readers who have been repelled by Constance's hyperbolic submission have failed to recognize the psychological power of this abject realm.[28] This form of religion can invite the convert to turn away from the limited realm of the symbolic and towards the realm of the Kristevan preverbal semiotic. In the tale, living out the Christian life involves risk. Constance, for example, encourages Hermengyld to display her faith despite fear of reprisal, and it is this point, rather than the potentially miraculous restoral of sight, that is emphasized in the scene of the blind Briton. Indeed, the outcome of this miracle is curiously absent in Chaucer's version of the story. Although the blind Briton asks for the restoration of his sight in Christ's name, whether or not Hermengyld succeeds in effecting that result is unknown. Chaucer's version of this incident emphasizes the risk a public declaration of faith incurs.

Christianity is conveyed in this tale through silent comparison rather than through argument or through causal developments. Thus innocence is juxtaposed to violence, although violence is not caused by innocence. Conversion occurs in the presence of violence as in the judgment scene, but is not the result of a miracle. Miracles are juxtaposed with explanations of doctrine, and conversion, with the exception of the judgment scene, takes place over time.

The mystery of Christian power as embodied in Constance is reinforced by the work's insistence on the primacy of the image over the word, the repudiation of verbal for iconic force. Consider, for example, the fact that the written word twice fails to achieve its purpose in the story in the letters of the messenger; indeed these letters reinforce how susceptible the written word is to distortion and manipulation. The image, although ineffable, does not distort meaning. As Kolve has demonstrated, images of Constance dominate her story—images that evoke other well-known images. For example, as she leaves Syria, Constance prays to the cross and it is the image of her, helpless, that dominates here. She is repeatedly associated with both Mary and Christ and thus with innocence and excessive pain and suffering. Images comparing her to Mary evoke our pity; for example, as she leaves Northumberland with her small child, she stands on the shore and prays, recalling images of Mary's suffering, "hir litel child lay wepyng in hir arm, / And knelynge, pitously to hym she seyde" (834–35). Furthermore, as Kolve so thoroughly demonstrated, the poem is permeated with images of Constance floating rudderless in the "salte see." The narrative produces a series of tableaus and images that are overdetermined and offer more meaning than the narrative can make sense of. Chaucer teases our imaginations with heavily loaded and ultimately obscure imagery. For example, what do we make of the image of the bloody knife placed between Hermengyld and Constance when they are in bed together—a knife that evokes Mark's sword in the story of Tristan and Isolde? Or, as mentioned earlier, how do we interpret the image of a British Bible in a pagan court? These images finally are evocative rather than decodable.

With Kolve, I agree that Chaucer's portrait of Constance invokes a body of familiar images, primarily Marian images, and that these images have pedagogical power and range in their ability to convey complex doctrinal issues to both literate and non-literate audiences. But where Kolve (and others who have studied the Christian pedagogical power of medieval imagery such as Eamon Duffy and Margaret Miles) reads such images as serving a univalent orthodoxy, I believe Chaucer's use of this store of familiar religious imagery produces neither complacency nor a sense of the familiar.[29] Rather, Chaucer teases and challenges us by calling up familiar associations in his descriptions of Constance, only to defamiliarize these associations by emphasizing her departure from the stereotype. Images of Constance make us uncomfortable precisely because she, Constance, is not Mary or a saint, despite her similarities to both, but rather a secular heroine, a commodity on the aristocratic marriage market, and the producer of an heir who will become powerful to both church and state. Her secular status forces us to realize the difficulties of bringing a certain kind of religious idealism into practice in the midst of a variety of conflicting hegemonic ideologies.

The Christian images evoked by Constance are not in my view the images of the familiar and the comfortable that Kolve argues they are and that they might be in other medieval contexts. Kolve seems to have overlooked some of the discomfort that these images seem designed to produce not only in themselves but in the violent and irrational responses they inspire in others from lust to envy to desire for God. Constance's image inspires both the rapist and the false accusing knight to lust after her. The firmness of Constance's commitment incites their sexual desire. Constance further incites the excessive desires for power and for control of the mothers-in-law. Thus, while the experience of Christianity may offer security and a haven from pain, occupying that space by no means induces complacency, for it stirs violent reactions in others.

The dominant image of the tale is of Constance floating in a rudderless boat. Kolve has shown how pervasive this image is in his discussion of the ship of the church and/or the ship of the soul floating in the sinful sea.[30] Kolve has overlooked, however, how evocative this image is as a specifically gendered one. Luce Irigaray has powerfully explored the ways in which the image of water has particular resonance for women, evoking other cultural ideas of women as fluid, lacking in boundaries, and uncontainable.[31] Within the context of medieval ideology, fluidity is especially associated with women, who, according to Aristotelian medical views of women, were seen as containing excess fluid. Chaucer seems to draw on these cultural constructions of gender to reinforce his concept of the timeless uncontainability of his form of Christianity.

Constance's association with imagery that has the power to convert without violence is in opposition to the far less persuasive language of both the narrator and the men like him in the story who repeatedly try, but fail, to know the causes and nature of things. Like Dinshaw, I would argue that the law of men is under scrutiny in this tale. But unlike Dinshaw, I would argue that the different law of a woman, the "law" represented by

Constance through imagery, comments on and resists the "law of men." The narrator himself comments upon the insufficiency of men's wits to predict the future: "mennes wittes ben so dulle / That no wight kan wel rede it atte fulle" (202–03). Christ's work, the Man of Law reminds us, "ful derk is / To mannes wit" (481–82), but to woman's wit, that is, from the perspective of Constance's knowledge, appears to be less obscure. The narrator ridicules the Syrian's inadequate attempts to know things, but Chaucer lets the reader know that he is, and that we should be, skeptical of the Man of Law's attempts to know and understand; that is, the Man of Law's rhetorical interpolations, which provide lists of classical and biblical precedents for Constance's life, are seen by some critics as so excessive as to point to Chaucer's satire of the religious life; to others they are seen as simply dull, a sign of Chaucer's lack of interest in his subject.[32] Chaucer may indeed be satirizing the Man of Law's rhetoric, but that alone does not mean that he is also satirizing Constance. The Man of Law continually tries—and fails—to authorize and appropriate Constance's experience, a religious experience that is finally inexplicable in words. Ultimately Constance's experience goes beyond the wit of the men she encounters in her tale or even that of the narrator who tries to contain her with his legalistic epistemology. To put this argument in Kristevan terms, Constance embodies the semiotic realm, an embodiment reinforced by her gender and her representation as a mother, and this semiotic realm can be approached but not contained by the symbolic realm articulated by the Man of Law. The Man of Law's rhetoric is shown to be inadequate to the understanding of the ineffable, which Chaucer assigns in this tale to Christianity and Constance.

Constance presents a challenge to conventional time schemes. Constance is difficult to know in part because she inhabits a different temporal reality from the Man of Law, and even from those she encounters in the tale, for Constance lives in the realm of liturgical time. That we should attend carefully to the meaning of time is signaled in the introduction to the tale, where the host warns the pilgrim not to waste time: "Leseth no tyme, as ferforth as ye may. / Lordynges, the tyme wasteth nyght and day" (19–20). The link between time and gender represented in the tale is anticipated in the introduction by the host's comparison of lost time to the breaking of a woman's hymen: "'But los of tyme shendeth us,' quod he. / It wol nat come agayn, withouten drede, / Namoore than wole Malkynes maydenhede, / Whan she hath lost it in hir wan-townesse" (28–31)—a passage whose significance in terms of men's law has been illuminated by Dinshaw. Tale telling is seen as profitable when it does not waste time. The Man of Law, describing his storytelling as required by law, and agreeing to the host's request, says "ich assente; / ... / Biheste is dette, and I wole holde fayn / Al my biheste, I kan no bettre sayn, / For swich lawe as a man yeveth another wight, / He sholde hym-selven usen it, by right" (39–44), and then promises to tell a tale in prose. Of course the story that follows is not in prose but in rhyme royal, a metrical pattern that complicates the timing of the presentation of the story. The Man of Law tells a history, one very self-consciously committed to linear time, but Constance's story defies such linearity, for hers is a story of repetition and circularity, one that begins and ends in the same place, Rome, at the home of her father. This kind of double time scheme, one that encompasses both linear and liturgical time, is common in medieval works, but Constance's gender enhances her association with liturgical time, because as a woman she is associated with birth and regeneration, repetition and cycles. These attributes contribute to the definition of what Kristeva calls "monumental" or "women's time."[33] That time intersects with the world of "cursive" time occupied by the Man of Law, but finally transcends it.

Chaucer further complicates his notion of Christianity by drawing on conflicting attitudes towards the female body, and especially towards the female reproductive body, attitudes that pervade late medieval secular and Christian ideology and practice. These conflicts are illustrated in the complex representation of motherhood in the tale. In the portraits of the overly possessive and self-serving mothers-in-law, one form of motherhood is condemned. The portrait of Constance, on the one hand, celebrates a Marian motherhood that, despite its passivity and piteousness, is powerful both in itself and in the access it affords to a higher power through intercession. In this model, patriarchal fathers disappear, the marriage market is disrupted, and only God the father is relevant, a condition that both contains and emancipates Constance.

On the other hand, the portrait of Constance also valorizes aristocratic secular motherhood for its ability to guarantee patrilineal descent. As the tale comes to a close, the mother herself becomes less significant in the story as her child, Maurice, emerges into adulthood and takes on his assigned role as leader of the church and state. Yet, Constance's face remains reflected in her son's visage, a reminder of the female contribution to that patrimony and of the force of the female other that late medieval secular marriage practices and hegemonic Christianity can neither fully acknowledge nor erase. When Maurice is first seen "lookynge in the kynges face" (1015), the boy's image evokes the emperor's memories: "Now was this child as lyk unto Custance / As possible is a creature to be. / This Alla hath the face in remembrance / Of Dame Custance" (1030–33). "Whan Alla saugh his wyf" he weeps, he knew her at first sight, and she swoons "in his owene sighte" (1051; 1058). Constance's father similarly remembers her as he "looked bisily / Upon this child, and on his doghter thoghte" (1095–96). But the narrator soon turns us away from his "story," to the story of Constance: "This child Maurice was sithen Emperour / Maad by the Pope, and lyved cristenly; / To Cristes chirche he dide greet honour. / But I lete al his storie passen by; / Of Custance is my tale specially" (1121–25). Despite its patriarchal frame, Constance, rather than patriarchal lineage, is the primary focus of the tale.

Constance is thus associated with ineffability, timelessness, repetition, circularity, generation, fluidity, obscured agency, and mediation. Many of these qualities, while not necessarily gender determined, are gender linked. According to medieval physiology, they are seen as essential to women. Commentaries on Genesis circulating in the Middle Ages stress that as a consequence of the Fall women are prone to suffering. Chaucer seems to question such essentialism in his exposure of a brutal marriage economy that reduces women to voiceless agents, in his condemnation of the "mannishness" of the mothers-in-law, and in his celebration of the "womanishness" of a man, Alla. The Man of Law's rhetoric, on the other hand, defines a world that is bound by time, certain knowledge, intrusiveness, containment, boundaries, and control of the female body (through incest, marriage contracts, and the like).

Constance's ineffability, her "elvishness," resides not so much in her gender as in her ability to convert, to turn people from one system of belief to another without exerting any force. It is perhaps significant that the other use of the word elf in The Canterbury Tales appears in the Thopas/Melibee link where the host describes Chaucer: "He semeth elvyssh by his contenaunce" (Prologue to Sir Thopas, line 703). One of Chaucer-the-narrator's key features is his unknowability, but perhaps his "elvishness" is not so much in his appearance as in what he does, that is, in his poetry, writing that also converts without violence. In The Man of Law's Tale, Chaucer seems to privilege the power of the image—specifically the Christian image—to convert. That Chaucer's poetics is also at issue in this tale is suggested by the prologue with its concern with profitable use of time, its list of Chaucer's works, and its praise of stories as riches that counter poverty. Just as the Syrians obtained access to Constance through the stories of merchants, so the Man of Law heard this story from merchants. Stories and Constance are thus both valuable commodities of exchange—and like women on the marriage market, subject to distortion and corruption (e.g., incest).

To conclude, The Man of Law's Tale intertwines categories of difference, especially those of gender and religion, in complex ways in order to articulate the ineffability of a non-institutionalized early form of Christianity that proselytizes through example and communal exchange, that is powerful as much through its mystery as through its exertion of force, and that is cyclical and repetitious as much as it is teleological. Constance succeeds in converting those around her to this form of Christianity through her example, that is, through what others observe in her. By embodying conversion in a female rather than a male body, Chaucer is able to construct a form of Christianity that is marginal; that is, he is able to separate spirituality from its contemporary institutionalization. Since what is true to the spiritual is a belief in the other, Constance's gender as a marker of marginalized difference is crucial to Chaucer's exploration of the nature of the spiritual. To return, Constance-like, to where we began, our introduction to Constance explains how she becomes a commodity to the Syrian merchants, one among the other riches of their trade, rich satins, cloths of gold, and spices. She is an exotic other coveted in the West as well as the East as any spice would be. If we consider the etymology of the word "spice" her affinity to this particular commodity becomes even more readily apparent, for the word spice originates from the Latin *species*, look or appearance.[34] Like the spices used perhaps most significantly to embalm the dead, Constance is the spice that can overcome death, and through contemplation of her image, the viewer turns away from the deadly pale realm of mortality and towards a transcendent realm. Perhaps it is in his valorization of imagery that we can locate one form of Chaucer's religiosity for here he seems to celebrate at least one aspect of poetry—imagery—for its power of conversion and its salvific power.[35] The Man of Law's Tale, then, like Constance's face, takes us beyond the familiar and beyond the limitations of conventional expectations of the possibilities for female agency in late medieval England, into the empowering realm of the strange.

NOTES

I would like to thank Mark Amsler, Dana Cuff, Bruce Holsinger, Gerda Norvig, Wahid Omar, Karen Palmer, Elihu Pearlman, Jeffrey Robinson, Karen Robertson, Dana Symons, and the editors for their help with this essay. I am also grateful to A. S. G. Edwards for his help with an earlier draft of this essay.

1. Paul Strohm, *Social Chaucer* (Cambridge, MA, 1989), and Lee Patterson, *Chaucer and the Subject of History* (Madison, WI, 1991).

2. On this topic see the groundbreaking work of Paul Strohm in his *Social Chaucer.*

3. Carolyn Dinshaw, *Chaucer's Sexual Poetics* (Madison, WI, 1989), and Elaine Tuttle Hansen, *Chaucer and the Fictions of Gender* (Berkeley, 1992).

4. The Squire's Tale has been the subject of a number of talks on the category of race in Chaucer at the International Congress on Medieval Studies at Kalamazoo in recent years; The Man of Law's Tale was first commented upon in terms of issues of race and ethnicity by Glory Dharmaraj in "Multicultural Subjectivity in Reading Chaucer's 'Man of Law's Tale,'" in *Medieval Feminist Newsletter* no. 16 (1993): 4–8, and more recently and comprehensively by Susan Schibanoff in "Worlds Apart: Orientalism, Antifeminism and Heresy in Chaucer's *Man of Law's Tale,*" *Exemplaria* 8, no. 1 (Spring 1996): 59–96.

5. The call to bring together the categories of "race," "class," and "gender" was first sounded by African-American feminists in such essays as Hazel Carby's "White Woman Listen: Black Feminists and the Boundaries of Sisterhood," which first appeared in *The Empire Strikes Back: Race and Racism in 70s Britain* (Birmingham, 1982), 212–35, and then again in her *Cultures of Babylon: Black Britain and African America* (New York, 1999), 67–92. For an important essay that considers how the categories of "race" and "gender" complicate one another, see Gayatri Spivak, "French Feminism in an International Frame," in her book *In Other Worlds* (New York, 1988), 134–53. Patricia Parker and Margo Hendricks were among the first to historicize the study of these categories in their *Women, "Race," and Writing in the Early Modern Period* (New York and London, 1994). For a specific study of the difficulties the critic faces in bringing the three categories together in a study of a literary text see Margaret Ferguson, "Juggling the Categories of Race, Class, and Gender in Aphra Behn's *Oroonoko,*" *Women's Studies* 19 (1991): 159–81, reprinted in the Parker and Hendricks volume. For a recent excellent study of the necessity for historical specificity in the analysis of "race," see David Nirenberg, *Communities of Violence: Persecution of Minorities in the Middle Ages* (Princeton, 1996). For an excellent study of medieval ideas of skin color and justified violence, see Bruce Holsinger, "The Color of Salvation: Desire, Death and the Second Crusade in Bernard of Clairvaux's *Sermons on the Song of Songs,*" in *The Tongue of the Fathers: Gender and Ideology in Twelfth-Century Latin,* ed. David Townsend and Andrew Taylor (Philadelphia, 1998).

6. Edward W. Said, *Orientalism* (New York, 1978).

7. Because the category of race as we understand it today had not yet consolidated as a formation in fourteenth-century England, it is difficult to locate exactly what race or racism means in a medieval context, especially given the fact that there was no equivalent term for race or racism in medieval European languages. The terms for race do not enter the English language until after 1500. In the earlier English uses of the term it seemed to refer generally to tribes or groups of descendants rather than groups defined by shared physical characteristics. Several critics have observed that in the Middle Ages differences between peoples tend to be marked not as color differences but as religious differences; indeed, I would argue that the dark-light binarism of religious difference becomes one of the central components of the consolidating understanding of race in this period. Thus, we have to recognize the historical contingency and fluidity of the term. As Henry Louis Gates has commented, race "has become a trope of ultimate, irreducible difference between cultures, linguistic groups, or practitioners of specific belief systems, who more often than not have fundamentally opposed economic interests." See Henry Louis Gates, "Writing, 'Race,' and the Difference it Makes," in his *Loose Canons: Notes on the Culture Wars* (New York, 1992). For a discussion of the intersection of constructs of race and Islam in particular in the Middle Ages see Israel Burshatin, "The Moor in the Text: Metaphor, Emblem and Silence," in *Race, Writing and Difference*, ed. Henry Louis Gates, Jr. (Chicago, 1985), 117–37. For a useful summary of the controversies about the origins and development of the term race, see Nicholas Hudson, "From 'Nation' to 'Race': The Origin of Racial Classification in Eighteenth-Century Thought," *Eighteenth-Century Studies* 29, no. 3 (Spring 1996): 247–64.

8. Schibanoff, "World's Apart," 65.

9. Larry Benson, gen. ed., *The Riverside Chaucer* (Boston, 1987), The Man of Law's Tale, line 1113. All quotations from the tale are taken from this edition and all further line references will be cited within parentheses in the body of my text.

10. Schibanoff argues that late medieval texts "troped the familiarity of Islam . . . not to mute the threat of the new religion to Europe, but to intensify it, to increase rather than reduce the 'pressure' it created upon the occidental mind . . . the pressure posed by the heretic as proximate Other [here the heretic is those who embrace Islam] had to be released," "World's Apart," 70; Schibanoff, following Jonathan Dollimore (*Sexual Dissidence: Augustine to Wilde, Freud to Foucault* [Oxford, 1991]), makes an extremely important case here about the dangers of similitude. One might argue that the Islamic people in The Man of Law's Tale are all the more dangerous in their similarity to the pagans. It is also true that all of the Islamic accusers of Constance are destroyed, whereas only some of the pagans are. Most of the pagans are redeemable because of their potential convertability. Nonetheless, individual pagans and individual Islamic antagonists are represented as similar or, as in the case of the mothers-in-law, virtually interchangeable in the tale.

11. Schibanoff, "World's Apart," 63.

12. Schibanoff, "World's Apart," 79.

13. In a response to my essay, my student, Wahid Omar, suggested that the description of Islam as sweet only reinforces its orientalist representation; here the religion of Islam is presented as another spice.

14. J. R. R. Tolkien, ed., *The Ancrene Wisse: Corpus Christi College Cambridge 402* (Oxford, 1962), 43.

15. Sheila Delany, "Womanliness in the Man of Law's Tale," in her *Writing Woman* (New York, 1983), 36–46.

16. A. S. G. Edwards, "Critical Approaches to the 'Man of Law's Tale,'" in *Chaucer's Religious Tales*, ed. Elizabeth Robertson and C. David Benson (Cambridge, 1990), 85–94.

17. V. A. Kolve, *Chaucer and the Imagery of Narrative: The First Five Canterbury Tales* (Stanford, CA, 1984), 297–358; Eugene Clasby, "Chaucer's Constance: Womanly Virtue and the Heroic Life," *Chaucer Review* 13 (1979): 221–33; C. David Benson, Introduction to *Chaucer's Religious Tales*, ed. Robertson and Benson.

18. I am grateful to David Benson for alerting me to this striking contrast.

19. I am grateful to David Benson for pointing out the feminization of Alla in this tale.

20. Carolyn Dinshaw, "The Law of Man and Its 'Abomynacions,'" in her *Chaucer's Sexual Poetics*, 65–87.

21. Jill Mann, "Suffering Woman, Suffering God," in her *Feminist Approaches to Geoffrey Chaucer* (Atlantic Highlands, NJ, 1991), 128–64.

22. Schibanoff, "World's Apart," 70.

23. This passage is very difficult to interpret since Chaucer is vague about the meaning of British Gospels. Is it a potentially heretical text and why then does the knight swear on it? Does a hand smite him from heaven because he swears falsely or because he swears falsely upon a non-standard translation of the Bible? Is the knight being associated with heresy? We do not know if the book belongs to him or the court. If it is the court's then perhaps Chaucer is making a point here about the power of British, that is English, Bibles.

24. Caroline Walker Bynum, *Holy Feast and Holy Fast: The Religious Significance of Food to Medieval Women* (Berkeley, 1987).

25. Elizabeth Robertson, *Early English Devotional Prose and the Female Audience* (Nashville, TN, 1990).

26. Verena Conley, Review of Hélène Cixous: *Writing the Feminine*, in *Rocky Mountain Review of Feminist Language and Literature* 40, nos. 1–2 (1986): 97.

27. See *Bede's Ecclesiastical History of the English People*, ed. Bertram Colgrave and R. A. B. Mynors (Oxford, 1969), XXV.72–79.

28. For a discussion of Kristeva's theory of the abject see Julia Kristeva, *Powers of Horror: An Essay in Abjection*, trans. Leon S. Roudiez (New York, 1982).

29. Eamon Duffy, *The Stripping of the Altars: Traditional Religion in England 1400–1580* (New Haven, CT, 1992). Margaret Miles, *Image as Insight: Visual Understanding in Western Christianity and Secular Culture* (Boston, 1985).

30. See Kolve, "The Rudderless Ship and the Sea," in his *Chaucer and the Imagery of Narrative*, 297–358.

31. The association of women and fluids permeates Irigaray's work, but see, for example, her *Amante marine de Friedrich Nietzsche* (Paris, 1980).

32. See Edwards's review of the criticism, "Critical Approaches to the 'Man of Law's Tale.'"

33. Julia Kristeva, "Women's Time," in *The Kristeva Reader*, ed. Toril Moi (New York, 1986).

34. I am indebted to Timothy Morton for alerting me to this origin and for general discussions about the range of meanings invoked by the word spice.

35. Chaucer's celebration of imagery here suggests his engagement with Lollard concerns about the dangers of imagery in Christian teaching. For further discussion of the tale's engagement with Lollardy see my longer version of this essay in *Studies in the Age of Chaucer* 23 (2001): 143–80.

CONTRIBUTORS

Daniel Boyarin is Taubman Professor of Talmudic Culture at the University of California, Berkeley. He is the author of *Carnal Israel: Reading Sex in Talmudic Culture; Unheroic Conduct: The Rise of Heterosexuality and the Invention of the Jewish Man;* and *Dying for God: Martyrdom and the Making of Christianity and Judaism.* He is the coauthor of *Powers of Diaspora: Two Essays on the Relevance of Jewish Culture* (Minnesota, 2002) and the coeditor of *Jews and Other Differences: The New Jewish Cultural Studies* (Minnesota, 1997).

Sharon Farmer is professor of history at the University of California, Santa Barbara. She is the author of *Surviving Poverty in Medieval Paris: Gender, Ideology, and the Daily Lives of the Poor* and *Communities of Saint Martin: Legend and Ritual in Medieval Tours,* and the coeditor of *Monks and Nuns, Saints and Outcasts: Religion in Medieval Society.*

Ruth Mazo Karras is professor of history at the University of Minnesota. She is the author of *Slavery and Society in Medieval Scandinavia, Common Women: Prostitution and Sexuality in Medieval England,* and *From Boys to Men: Formations of Masculinity in Late Medieval Europe.* She has written numerous articles on medieval gender and sexuality.

Mathew S. Kuefler is assistant professor of history at San Diego State University. He is the author of *The Manly Eunuch: Masculinity, Gender Ambiguity, and Christian Ideology in Late Antiquity.* He translated "The Life of the Dear Friends Amicus and Amelius" for *Medieval Hagiography: An Anthology* and contributed to *A Handbook of Medieval Sexuality.*

Martha G. Newman is associate professor of history at the University of Texas at Austin. She is the author of *The Boundaries of Charity: Cistercian Culture and Ecclesiastical Reform, 1098–1180* and is currently working on a monograph exploring gender and social status in twelfth- and thirteenth-century monastic miracle stories.

Carol Braun Pasternack is associate professor of English at the University of California, Santa Barbara. She is the author of *The Textuality of Old English Poetry* and the coeditor of *Vox intexta: Orality and Textuality in the Middle Ages.* She is now working on a monograph titled *The Individual, the Family, and the Text in Anglo-Saxon England.*

Kathryn M. Ringrose is a lecturer on Byzantine, late antique, and gender studies at the University of California, San Diego. Her book *Transcendent Lives: Eunuchs and the Construction of Gender in Byzantium* is forthcoming.

Elizabeth Robertson is associate professor of English and director of British studies at the University of Colorado at Boulder. She is the author of *Early English Devotional Prose and the Female Audience* and the coeditor of *Chaucer's Religious Tales* and *Representing Rape in Medieval and Early Modern Literature.* She has written a variety of essays on women and religion in medieval English literature, and (with Jane Burns and Roberta Krueger) she founded *The Medieval Feminist Newsletter.*

Everett K. Rowson is associate professor of Arabic and Islamic studies at the University of Pennsylvania. He is the author of *A Muslim Philosopher on the Soul and Its Fate* and coeditor of *Homoeroticism in Classical Arabic Literature.* He is currently working on a monograph titled *Homosexuality in Traditional Islamic Societies.*

Michael Uebel is assistant professor of English at the University of Kentucky, where he teaches medieval literature and critical theory. He has published on the topics of medieval masculinity, critical historicism, utopic thinking, and masochism. He is the coeditor of *Race and the Subject of Masculinities,* and his book on the inception of utopia in the twelfth century is in progress.

Ulrike Wiethaus is professor of humanities at Wake Forest University. She is the author of *Ecstatic Transformations: Ecstasies and Visions in the Work of Mechthild of Magdeburg and Transpersonal Psychology,* editor of *Maps of Flesh and Light: The Religious Experience of Medieval Women,* coeditor of *Dear Sister: The Correspondence of Medieval Women,* and translator of *Agnes Blannbekin: Life and Revelations of a Viennese Beguine.* She is currently working on a study of alterity in German medieval mystical writing.

MEDIEVAL CULTURES